was very wide. With keen perception and in lucid prose, Mr. Weinstock has given us the definitive picture of a remarkable man who, suffering always under terrifying handicaps, enormously enriched the world's store of memorable melody.

The volume is illustrated and contains a complete list of Tchaikovsky's compositions as well as a bibliography and an index.

Herbert Weinstock is the author of *What Music Is; Donizetti and the World of Opera in Italy, Paris, and Vienna in the First Half of the Nineteenth Century; Handel; Chopin: The Man and His Music;* and—with Wallace Brockway—*The World of Opera* and *Men of Music.*

By Herbert Weinstock

WHAT MUSIC IS *(1966)*

DONIZETTI AND THE WORLD OF OPERA IN ITALY, PARIS, AND VIENNA
IN THE FIRST HALF OF THE NINETEENTH CENTURY *(1963)*

THE WORLD OF OPERA *(with Wallace Brockway)* *(1962)*

HANDEL *(Handel Bicentenary Edition, 1959)*

MEN OF MUSIC *(with Wallace Brockway)* *(revised, enlarged
edition, 1950)*

CHOPIN: *The Man and His Music* *(1949)*

TCHAIKOVSKY *(1943)*

TCHAIKOVSKY

TCHAIKOVSKY
From a portrait by N. D. Kuznetsov (1893)

TCHAIKOVSKY

HERBERT WEINSTOCK

New York   ALFRED A KNOPF   1966

MANUFACTURED IN THE UNITED STATES OF AMERICA

REPRINTED FOUR TIMES
SIXTH PRINTING, OCTOBER 1966

PUBLISHED IN CANADA BY RANDOM HOUSE OF CANADA LIMITED.

*This is a Borzoi Book, published
by Alfred A. Knopf, Inc.*

FOR BEN MEISELMAN

"Music is not illusion, but revelation rather. Its triumphant power resides in the fact that it reveals to us beauties we find nowhere else, and that the apprehension of them is not transitory, but a perpetual reconcilement to life."

TCHAIKOVSKY, *in a letter to Nadezhda Filaretovna von Meck, December 15, 1877.*

ILLUSTRATIONS

Introduction

T CHAIKOVSKY has been dead fifty years. During the five decades since 1893, many of his compositions, both large and small, have won — and maintained — worldwide popularity. Yet no full-length biography of him has been written in English. For the English-speaking world the chief, almost sole source of information about Tchaikovsky's life has been Rosa Newmarch's condensation (first published in 1906) of Paul Juon's German translation of Modest Tchaikovsky's official biography of his brother. From scattered earlier publications of various kinds Mrs. Newmarch had constructed her brief *Tchaikovsky* (1900), an admirable pioneering work. Of its 232 pages, exactly 110 were devoted to biographical material. The only other ponderable book in English was, for a long time, Edwin Evans, Jr.'s *Tchaikovsky*, published in 1906 and sketchily revised in 1935. English and American musicology and biography, which in the interim devoted some fruitful attention to other Russian composers, notably the nationalists, continued to ignore the rich untapped veins of source materials that existed in Russia about the most popular Russian composer of them all.

Beginning early in the 1920's, Soviet cultural authorities set competent editors to work on the vast accumulation of Tchaikovskyana lying unsorted and substantially unread in the archives of the Tchaikovsky Museum at Klin, the Moscow Conservatory, the former St. Petersburg Conservatory, and several other depositories. Under state sponsorship, books dealing with Tchaikovsky began to be published. The surviving correspondence was edited, annotated, and published. Literally thousands of letters that had not appeared earlier, or had been used in bowdlerized versions, were made available. Tchaikovsky's important exchange with Nadezhda Filaretovna von Meck made three huge volumes, and there were in addition his letters to the publisher Jürgenson, to members of his own family, and to a miscellany of friends, business and social acquaintances. Whole areas of his life left unexplored or undescribed by Modest — and therefore by all English writers since Mrs. Newmarch — were laid open to musicology and biography.

Correctly sensing the high-relief dramatic values of Tchaikov-sky's singular relationship with Mme von Meck and of the sensa-tional possibilities in the story of his marriage, Catherine Drinker Bowen and Barbara von Meck in 1937 brought out *"Beloved Friend."* Relying largely on the von Meck correspondence, they produced a fictionized and luridly coloured story of fourteen of Tchaikovsky's fifty-three years. By the accident of its popularity, their book spread a picture of Tchaikovsky that is, in its overem-phasis, as false as Modest's had been in its gentle deceptions and lack of any emphasis whatever. Also, wholly apart from all ques-tions of the dependability of *"Beloved Friend,"* it has now been rendered obsolete within its self-set limits by the publication in Russia of large amounts of further materials. There have been ad-ditional volumes of Tchaikovsky's correspondence, Russian biogra-phies based on fresh information, and one truly magnificent source book — published as part of the centenary celebration of his birth — called *The Days and Years of P. I. Tchaikovsky: Annals of His Life and Work.* This is a diary with an entry for every day in his life on which anything of interest in connection with him occurred or was recorded. It contains extracts from letters, from contempo-rary diaries published and unpublished, from critical reviews of his works, from books dealing with collateral materials, and from his own writings, as well as 114 pages of the most comprehensive indexes and lists I have ever seen.

Once assured that this material was available in the United States and that I could depend on the close, continuous collaboration of Sonia Volochova, to whom the Russian language is native, I em-barked on the present book with the aim of producing, as the first full-length biography of Tchaikovsky written in English, a book that would take full advantage of the vast mass of material that was unknown to Modest, deliberately disregarded by him, omitted by Mrs. Newmarch, or only recently collected and published. I realized beforehand that my chief problems would be those of se-lection and proportion, my intention being as faithful a panorama as I could achieve of Tchaikovsky's life — all of his life — presented against those segments of historical background before which that life was lived.

I have found that there is scarcely one page in Modest's *Life and Letters* without some misstatement of fact, accidental or deliberate, or some purposeful elision. This unreliability extends even to his

quotations from his brother's letters. It has been impossible for me
to point out all of these, or to indicate, except in rare instances, the
points at which modern research remakes the picture of Tchaikovsky. Impossible because otherwise I should have produced a book
containing fifty lines of footnotes to each ten of text. Instead I
have chosen to present a full bibliography, Russian sources included, for those who wish to make further research, and have indicated the few places in my narrative in which I have deserted
fact for surmise with "It may be that . . ." or "It is possible that
. . ." or "It has been said that. . . ." Those rare instances aside,
the facts presented are exactly that, having been drawn from and
checked against reliable sources.

This is a biography, not a critical study of Tchaikovsky's music.
Except where neglect, overemphasis, or misapprehension of a given
composition made me feel that discussion of it was called for, I have
expressed my own judgments of that music only inferentially. It is,
of course, clear that I should not have written this book at all had I
not had a high opinion of at least some of that music.

In the text, all Russian titles of compositions have been translated into English, except where such titles consist of, or include,
proper names, in which cases use has been made of the transliteration that seems to me most closely to approximate the sound of the
spoken Russian. There is no adequate reason for calling Russian
pieces by French names unless the composer himself did so. Thus
I have used *Slavic March* rather than *Marche slave*, *The Queen of
Spades* rather than *Pique Dame*, "Pathetic" Symphony rather than
Symphonie pathétique (and *Yevgeny Onyegin* rather than *Eugène
Oniéguine*). Italian, German, and French titles have been left in
the original languages. With regard to Russian names of people,
I have again tried to approximate as closely as possible to the
spoken sound of the Russian, completely disregarding such Teu-
tonisms as Tschaikowsky and Tschaikowskij and such Gallicisms as
Borodine and Moussorgsky. Exceptions from this sensible rule have
been made only where to follow it would be to fly in the face of
universal usage. I have had, that is, to sacrifice the logical Chaikovsky for the familiar Tchaikovsky, the more nearly accurate
Rakhmaninov for Rachmaninoff, and — with Tolstoy's first name
— Lyov for the inexplicable Lev.

I have been arbitrary about the difference of twelve days obtaining between the Julian and Gregorian calendars during the nine-

teenth century. Rather than give all Russian dates twice, as is often done (May 12/24), rather than explain each date in a footnote, I have simply made all dates Gregorian, not scrupling to change them even in quotations.

My indebtedness to Russian editors and writers is acknowledged above and in the bibliography. I have also relied, to a limited extent and where their statements could be checked, on Modest Tchaikovsky and Rosa Newmarch. For assistance of many kinds I wish to thank Mrs. Andrew Carnegie, Walter Damrosch, Nicolas Slonimsky, the Embassy of the U.S.S.R. (Washington, D. C.), the Consulate General of the U.S.S.R. (New York), the American-Russian Institute, and the invariably helpful staffs of the Music Room of the New York Public Library (Fifth Avenue) and the Music Library (Fifty-eighth Street). For suggesting emendations I wish to thank Edna Weinstock, Grace Robert, Alfred A. Knopf, Wilson Follett, and Horace Gibson. For painstaking and expert assistance in preparing the index my thanks go to Benjamin Meiselman. The size of my gratitude to Sonia Volochova is scarcely to be contained in the literally accurate statement that without the hundreds of pages of careful translation she produced over a period of more than one year, the writing of this book could not have been undertaken.

·   ·   ·

The list of Tchaikovsky's works (page 368) is as inclusive as possible, and is, I believe, the first complete catalogue published in English. The bibliography (page 383) includes important books in Russian and German as well as books in English. There are two indexes — the general index (following page 386) and a special index to the Tchaikovsky works mentioned in the body of the text (page xxvi).

HERBERT WEINSTOCK

TCHAIKOVSKY

I

PIOTR ILYICH TCHAIKOVSKY was born at Votkinsk, in the cisuraline province of Vyatka, on May 7, 1840. The Russia into which he was born was, musically speaking, a country of native amateurs and trained foreigners. A few decades earlier, Russian composers had been extreme rarities, lonely men trained by foreigners, most of them Italians. Foreigners had held all the important official musical posts. Russian secular music, excepting folksongs and folk dances, remained Italianate, with weak infusions, here and there, from France and Germany. Religious music differed from it only because its Byzantine heritage had not been dissipated entirely.

In 1734 the Empress Anne, who loved pageantry, Germans, freaks, and new toys, imported an Italian operatic troupe headed by Francesco Araja. This Neapolitan became her *maestro di cappella,* holding that position through the brief reign of the infant Tsar Ivan VI and most of that of Elisabeth. He composed many operas, of which *Procris and Cephalus* is often credited with having been the first to be sung in Russian.[1] He inaugurated the long reign of the musical Latins by setting in Russia the same taste for Italianate music that already ruled in a large part of western Europe.

Catherine the Great became an intelligent patroness of music. In 1766 she began inviting distinguished Italians to head various imperial musical activities. She sent for Baldassare Galuppi, who was to be followed by Tommaso Traetta, Giovanni Paisiello, and Giuseppe Sarti. Most of these eminent leaders of music in eighteenth-century Italy spent but a few years at the St. Petersburg court. Sarti, however, was particularly favoured by Catherine, and spent the last eighteen years of his life in Russia, first as court conductor, then as director of a music school in the Ukraine, and finally as director of a conservatory in St. Petersburg. One of the

[1] *Procris and Cephalus* had a libretto by the Russian writer Alexander Petrovich Sumarokov.

numerous librettos he set while in Russia is believed to be by the
Tsarina herself.

Shortly after Sarti's arrival, there followed Domenico Cimarosa
and Vicente Martín y Solar, the Italianized Spaniard who was a
rival to Mozart and has been credited with a composition that
initiated the Viennese waltz craze. During the last years of Catherine's reign, throughout that of her melancholy son Paul I, and
well into the fateful one of Alexander I, musical Italians continued
to appear and to hold sway. Muzio Clementi visited Russia during
these years and stopped off in St. Petersburg to give lessons. In
1797 an Italian opera company was making a gleam of light in
Paul I's gloomy capital. Its conductor, Catterino Cavos,[2] enchanted
the Petersburgers so successfully that he settled in their city, composing operas for them in Italian, French, and Russian. He is notable for having made some adaptive use of Russian folk melodies
in his operas. His *Ivan Susanin* (1815), based on the same story
that Glinka set in *A Life for the Tsar,* proved immensely popular.
Cavos lived into the reign of Nicholas I and died in the year of
Tchaikovsky's birth.

From 1803 to 1811 the conductor of Alexander I's imperial opera
was the sprightly composer of *La Dame blanche,* François-Adrien
Boïeldieu, who had fled Paris to escape a shrewish wife. In 1808,
as though further to vary the Italian domination, the widely famous German pianist Daniel Steibelt, who had once contested improvisation laurels with Beethoven, settled in St. Petersburg. He
shortly became *maestro di cappella* to Alexander I, and remained
in Russia until his death in 1823. In St. Petersburg, too, the talented
Irish pianist, composer, teacher, and forerunner of Chopin, John
Field, taught, played, and composed, his pupils including Glinka.

There had, of course, been Russian musicians, though they had,
without exception, been distinguishable from their Italian contemporaries only as imitations are distinguishable from originals. The
earliest native composer of importance was Maxim Sozontovich
Berezovsky (1745–78). Having written the propitiatory pseudo-
Italian opera on a classical theme — his was on Demophon — Berezovsky, who most wanted to compose religious music, applied for
a position in the imperial choir. His application was rejected, perhaps because he was not a foreigner, and he committed suicide at

---

[2] Cavos was the great-great-grandfather of Diaghilev's friend and collaborator, the painter Alexandre Benois.

the age of thirty-three. The slightly younger Dmitri Stepanovich Bortnyansky (1751–1825) was luckier. Having studied with Galuppi in both St. Petersburg and Venice, and having turned out the customary opera (*Quinto Fabio*, Modena, 1778), Bortnyansky became director of the imperial chapel. He was a prolific composer whose pretty and slavishly Italianate religious music was highly regarded. His collected church works were published in 1882, in ten volumes edited by Tchaikovsky, who found them very boring indeed.

During Catherine the Great's last years, and increasingly under Paul I and Alexander I, native Russians turned to opera and song with success. Most of their names are shadowy today — Yevstigney Fomin (1761–1800), the Titov family, of whom the most prominent was Alexey Nikolayevich (1769–1827), and Alexander Nikolayevich Alabyev (1787–1851), the original arranger of that much arranged song *The Nightingale*, one of Tchaikovsky's first musical enthusiasms. The most appreciable talent of the period was Alexey Nikolayevich Verstovsky (1799–1862), a pupil of both Field and Steibelt, who became inspector of the imperial opera in 1824, and general director in 1842. This prolific composer purchased wide popularity with his Singspiel-like opera *Askold's Tomb* (1835), which was performed hundreds of times in Russia.[3] Verstovsky was looked back to by Tchaikovsky's Russian nationalist contemporaries as the most plausible precursor of their school, of which the titular founder was Mikhail Ivanovich Glinka.

Glinka, as a composer, was little different from Verstovsky, except that he always remained something of an amateur, while Verstovsky was a full-fledged, practising professional. Glinka was more lavish in using adapted folk music, and took hesitant steps toward unifying his operas by the already ancient system of attaching label-motives to situations and personages of the plot. Although an artist of wavering taste, Glinka was gifted with melodic and rhythmic originality, and possessed sufficient orchestrating talent to cover up his often feeble harmonic sense. His first opera, *A Life for the Tsar* (1835), presented by the imperial opera in St. Petersburg on December 9, 1836, has a rousing patriotic story, patches of brilliantly used folk melody, and a modicum of sprightly action. It

[3] On December 15, 1869 *Askold's Tomb* was presented at the Théâtre Français in New York, in all probability the first opera in Russian, if not the first complete Russian opera, to be sung in America.

was not looked upon as revolutionary (it was not), and it captured public fancy. The Iron Tsar presented Glinka with a valuable token, and appointed him imperial *maestro di cappella*. At that hour Glinka seemed well situated to rival Verstovsky, who had reaped the same sort of reward from *Askold's Tomb* the previous year.

But Glinka made the mistake of thinking. He experimented, and did not repeat the music of *A Life for the Tsar* to another libretto. Six years to a day after the *première* of that lively, rather commonplace work, he allowed the imperial opera to mount his *Ruslan and Lyudmila*. To its wholly invertebrate libretto he had composed a score that was, in part, of startling originality. *Ruslan and Lyudmila* was therefore a comparative failure with the public. In it Glinka may be said, by some stretching of the terms, to have invented singlehanded the musical dialect that has ever since been recognized by foreigners as "Russian," an idiom of melodic turn, rhythmic device, and harmonic motion as instantly determinable as the "Spanish" style. By making serious use of folk music from several parts of the Empire, he had truly founded the nationalist school. The libretto of *Ruslan and Lyudmila* is even drawn from a fairy tale by Pushkin, whose works were to be mined for decades by Glinka's successors.

Ruslan and Lyudmila was first produced when Tchaikovsky was not yet three years old. He first heard *A Life for the Tsar* before he was ten, and fell intensely and permanently in love with it. Only one other Russian composer of any importance had begun to make his name when Tchaikovsky was a child. Anton Grigoryevich Rubinstein, who later played a curious role in the younger man's life, made his pianistic debut at an open-air concert in Moscow at the age of nine in 1839, and was taken off on his first European tour in 1840, the year of Tchaikovsky's birth.

When Tchaikovsky was born, the facts about the musical scene and the other composers destined to act on that scene during the second half of the century were as follows. Alexander Sergeyevich Dargomizhsky was thirty-seven years old, but had not composed his first opera. Alexander Nikolayevich Serov was twenty, but had not begun to practise either composition or criticism. Alexander Porfiryevich Borodin was six, César Antonovich Cui five, Mily Alexeyevich Balakirev three, and Modest Petrovich Mussorgsky one. Nikolay Andreyevich Rimsky-Korsakov had not yet been born. There was not a first-class music school in the Russian Empire. Opera was popular — largely Italian and French opera. There were no permanent orchestras or ensembles of any sort except military bands. Music by Russians was unknown to foreigners, and all but unknown to Nicholas I's subjects themselves. The nationalist school had been launched, but Russia remained, musically speaking, a century and more behind Italy, Germany, France, and England.

Russian literature, by 1840, had already received major works from three of its pre-eminent figures: Pushkin, three years dead, Lermontov with one year more to live, and Gogol at thirty-one. Not one of the Russian novel's mighty three had yet reached maturity, for Turgenyev had been born in 1818, Dostoyevsky in 1821, and Tolstoy in 1828. The dramatist Ostrovsky was still a youth of eighteen. Aside from Pushkin and three or four lesser dramatist-poets, the educated classes read principally the works of foreigners. Literature, like music, was on the verge of coming into its own at the hands of native artists.

Ballet, the transplanted art that became native, was flourishing in Russia in 1840. It had a long official history by then, a record filled with the names of Italian and other foreign choreographers, composers — mostly of the feeblest sort — and visiting stars. A few natives had reached its summits as dancers, but its Russian heyday lay in the future of Tchaikovsky's development. Secular painting, as usual in Russia, was in a pitiably low state — ikon-makers aside, Russia has not to this day produced a first-rank painter.

Russia in 1840 was as much between clearly defined periods politically as it was artistically. Nicholas I, the Iron Tsar, who had been a child of five when his father, Paul I, was assassinated in 1801, had succeeded his brother Alexander, Napoleon's great antagonist, in 1825. The new reign had opened in popular uncertainty. Alexander's heir presumptive, his brother Constantine, had renounced the throne without notifying his prospective subjects or even his brother Nicholas. When Nicholas learned that Constantine expected him to succeed Alexander, he at first flatly refused, partly because he knew that he was not favoured by the army. Considerable time was lost in the ensuing negotiations, as Nicholas was in St. Petersburg, Constantine in Warsaw. Communications were by post stages. Nicholas finally consented to ascend the throne, and set December 26, 1825 as the day for the oath of loyalty. Secret societies of young officers who had bitterly fought Alexander's repressive policies chose that date for an uprising and won some regiments to their cause on the spurious plea that the well-liked Constantine was the rightful tsar. The rebels took their stand in the square in front of the Senate in St. Petersburg,[4] and before December 26 had passed there was bloodshed. The rebellion collapsed immediately, as did a sympathetic uprising in southern Russia. The most important Decembrist ringleaders were hanged, the less important exiled to Siberia.

Nicholas had always believed in the strict exercise of authority, and the Decembrist revolt helped him harden himself into an unbending tyrant. He was forced, however, to take some steps toward reforming the conditions against which the Decembrists had rebelled: serfdom, the miserable, utterly confused condition of government finances, and the helter-skelter state of the legal code. Some of the reforms he sanctioned were beneficial. But Nicholas bore down on the press with a stringent censorship, had the universities closely watched for signs of liberal unrest, and instituted a system of *agents provocateurs* filtered through all strata of society. He also created the "Third Section," the universally feared secret police. Exile to Siberia became common for the smallest offence against the autocrat's ideas or prerogatives.

Although Russia had not recuperated from the long struggle against Napoleon, Nicholas fought a war against Persia in 1826–8. Then he embarked on another against Turkey and Egypt in 1828–9, saw it carried through to triumph, and signed the Treaty of Unkiar-Skelessi, which purported to guarantee that the Dardanelles and the Bosporus would remain closed to all military ships except Russia's and Turkey's. Next he had to suppress a Polish uprising that resulted not so much from his Polish policy — which had strictly recognized the Polish constitution — as from the Polish leaders' conviction that the territorial expansion they dreamed of would be impossible under Nicholas. They had hoped to annex portions of adjacent Russian and Lithuanian provinces. Instead, Russia took territory from Poland and laid the mines of future dissension. Everywhere, in a confusing series of shifting alliances and concordats, the Tsar threw the considerable weight of Russia behind the principles of legitimacy and the *status quo*, and against the growing demand for the liberalization of government. His policies

---

[4] They are said to have shouted for "Constantine and Constitution" in the belief that the lady was Constantine's wife.

led, in 1840, the year of Tchaikovsky's birth, to the Quadruple Alliance and to the closest ties, for the time being, with England.

The first railroad in Russia, from St. Petersburg to Tsarskoye-Selo, was opened in 1838. At Nicholas's accession there had been neither rail nor telegraphic communication between his nation's two capitals, the former being begun in 1842, the latter established in 1851. At the beginning of his reign there were six universities in a country whose population was estimated at 60,000,-000. There were forty-eight gymnasia, with approximately 5,500 students, and 337 schools, with about 30,000 in attendance. A few private schools swelled this minute total, and Nicholas himself fostered several technical academies, including the St. Petersburg Institute of Technology (1828) and the Moscow Institute (1844). Serfdom had begun to break down under Alexander I. Nicholas, two years after his accession, authorized a law stating that peasants could not be bought unless the purchaser owned enough land to support them. In 1833 he sanctioned another law forbidding the disruption of a family by the purchase or sale of one of its members.

Russia in 1840 was struggling from its own peculiar mixture of feudalism and autocracy into a liberalism too partial and grudging to forestall the assassin and the nihilist, too half-way to render unnecessary the violence of the twentieth-century revolutions. It was struggling, on the intellectual and artistic level, to express itself through its own natives in their own languages, and simultaneously — at times contrarily — to make a cultural contribution the great world outside its still formidable borders would heed. It was this mighty but immature Empire into which, that May 7 of 1840, Piotr Ilyich Tchaikovsky was born.

II

PIOTR ILYICH was the second son [1] of Lieutenant Colonel Ilya Petrovich Tchaikovsky, chief inspector of the Kamsko-Votkinsk mines and metallurgical works. Votkinsk is on the border between the provinces of Vyatka and Perm, and Siberia is only 325 miles away. But the town has long been an important iron centre, and while the province's one railway (Perm-Archangel) missed it, it became an important manufacturing town, supplying knit goods, locomotives for the Siberian railroads, tarantasses, and steamers for the Caspian routes. A majority of its manufactures used iron that was locally mined and processed, and the chief inspector of the mines and works was therefore a prominent citizen. Ilya Petrovich Tchaikovsky was never credited with brilliant achievements or creative originality. His sons regarded him as charming but uncultured and of limited intelligence. He was a highly respected member of the middle official class. For a time he owned ten serfs, largely the family of his cook.

At thirty-eight, having been left a widower with an infant daughter, Ilya Petrovich in 1833 made a notably respectable second marriage. Alexandra Andreyevna Assier, a St. Petersburg girl, while the granddaughter of a Frenchman who had fled to Russia from the Revolution, was the daughter of a state councillor. She was educated in a girls' orphanage. Little is known or even guessed about her background, except that her grandfather had suffered from epilepsy. She herself was a kindly, commonplace woman of sedate, if not morose, disposition. She appears to have been calmly

[1] Ilya Petrovich Tchaikovsky (1795–1880) had eight children. By his first wife, Marya Karlovna Keiser, whom he married in 1827, he had one daughter, Zinaïda Ilyinishna (1829–78), later the wife of Yevgeny Ivanovich Olkhovsky. By his second wife, Alexandra Andreyevna Assier (1813–54), he had, in addition to a daughter who died at birth, five sons — Nikolay Ilyich (1838–1911), Piotr Ilyich (1840–93), Ippolit Ilyich (1843–1927), and the twins, Anatoly Ilyich (1850–1915) and Modest Ilyich (1850–1916) — and one daughter, Alexandra Ilyinishna (1842–91), later the wife of Lyov Vasilyevich Davidov.

ILYA PETROVICH TCHAIKOVSKY
From a photograph (1860)

ALEXANDRA ANDREYEVNA TCHAIKOVSKAYA (1848)
From a daguerreotype

satisfied with her life with Ilya Petrovich, who outlived her by twenty-six years and married for a third time in 1865. Alexandra Andreyevna was tall and handsome. Piotr Ilyich recalled her as having beautiful eyes and large, well-formed hands. Others described her as inclined to fat in her last years. She spoke both French and German, and played the piano and sang in a pleasant, amateurish way, as did one of her uncles. Her sister Yekaterina Andreyevna Schobert was a semiprofessional musician much in demand in St. Petersburg social life.

Piotr Ilyich was always angered by any suggestion that some of his forebears might have been Poles. He wanted to insist on the Tchaikovskys' entire Russianness, for he loved Russia truly. The family had been Russian of the middle official class for some generations.[2] No trace of artistic talent, and little of artistic taste, could be found in the family annals by the composer's beloved and worshipful brother-biographer, unless it was the fact that as a young boy his father had tried unsuccessfully to play the flute. Speaking of a promotion that came to his father in 1837, Modest wrote: "His career cannot have been brilliant, for it took him twenty years to achieve a lieutenant-colonelcy. But that he had become a member of the Science Committee of the Institute of Metallurgical Engineers by the time he was thirty, and that he lectured on mining law and statistics, proves that he was a capable and hard-working member of his profession." He was, in short, the kind of genial, sympathetic man who is loved by his family, liked and admired by his neighbours and numerous friends, and respected by his confreres, but who remains unknown to the larger world unless — as in Ilya Petrovich's case — he happens to sire a genius.

The Tchaikovskys had a generous income and hospitable habits. Their comfortable house was the social centre of Votkinsk. Most of their frequent guests were young couples, like themselves attached to the mines, and therefore in temporary exile from Moscow or St. Petersburg. Modest also remembered "a most intellectual English family." All were no doubt pleased at being on intimate terms with Ilya Petrovich, who, as head of the mines, in reality

---

[2] It is sometimes stated, without the advancing of any proof, that Ilya Petrovich's father, Piotr Fyodorovich, who lived in the province of Kazan, was a nobleman. His father, in turn, is described as Fyodor Afanasyevich, officer in a regiment of Cossacks. Modest spoke vaguely of one of the Tchaikovsky ancestors as an Orthodox Russian from the district of Kremenchug.

ruled the town and environing countryside, having well-defined police and legal powers and command of one hundred Cossacks. Guests must, like the couple's children, have found the father jolly, the mother stately and a little remote, given to moods.

Two years after Piotr Ilyich's birth, Alexandra Andreyevna bore her daughter, Alexandra Ilyinishna, in 1843 her third son, Ippolit Ilyich. On September 9, 1844, in a letter to his wife, who was visiting St. Petersburg, Ilya Petrovich noted that "Sasha" (Alexandra Ilyinishna) and "Petya" (Piotr Ilyich) had concocted a song called "Our Mama in Petersburg." This typically childish feat is the first mention of music in connection with a boy whose life, once he had discovered his vocation, was to be saturated with music in an emotional and subjective way scarcely matched in musical history. There were at least two musical instruments in the Tchaikovsky house: a piano, on which Piotr Ilyich was soon improvising and imitating, and — more important by his own declaration — an orchestrion.

The orchestrion was a large music-box provided with stops enabling it to approximate the sounds of several orchestral instruments. The Tchaikovsky orchestrion had an intelligently chosen repertoire, including *Vedrai carino* and other excerpts from *Don Giovanni,* and numbers from the operas of Rossini, Donizetti, and Bellini. All his life Piotr Ilyich loved Mozart above all other composers, and in 1878 stated that it was because of Mozart that he had devoted his life to music. He always recalled with gratitude the orchestrion that had passed him into Mozart's world of exquisite sound. Rossini, Donizetti, and Bellini influenced him too, helping his enduring taste for Italianate melody, dance rhythms, and ripe harmonies. Sometimes the boy's mother played and sang. Or an amateur musician named Mashovsky visited the family, played Chopin dashingly, heard the tiny boy attempt two mazurkas, and kissed him effusively on both cheeks when he managed to perform them with some style. This praise delighted Piotr Ilyich more than anything that had ever happened to him.

Late in 1844 Piotr Ilyich began non-musical studies with a governess. Fanny Dürbach had been brought by his mother over the three-week journey from St. Petersburg principally to instruct his six-year-old brother Nikolay and his cousin Lydya Vladimirovna Tchaikovskaya, an additional member of this large household. Despite her name, Fanny Dürbach was a Frenchwoman, and despite that a devout Protestant. This lucky choice as a governess was twenty-two when she went to Votkinsk. She remained interested in her pupils all her life and outlived Piotr Ilyich, eventually writing chatty and generally trustworthy reminiscences of her contacts with him. She had scarcely been installed in the family, prepared to teach only the older children, when Piotr Ilyich began pleading to join the lessons. This was finally permitted, and the four years of Fanny's stay were a happy period of swift mental development for the boy. At six he had become fluent in both German and French.

Fanny immediately recognized unusual quality in the youngest of her pupils. He was not pretty, and he was careless about both cleanliness and the condition of his clothing. He would not take the physical exercise Fanny thought essential for a growing boy. But he had charm (she called him a "porcelain child"), a capacity for affection, and an original and wayward individuality that won her heart. She tried to discourage his absorption in music, for which she did not care. She considered his reactions to sounds exaggerated and unhealthful. When he could not get to the piano to improvise, he drummed out tunes with his fingers on a windowpane. Once he cut himself sharply by breaking the glass in complete absorption with what he was hearing mentally. For a brief period thereafter he tried to interest himself in learning to paint, but could not remain away from music.

After playing the piano Piotr Ilyich was often overwrought, nervous, and sleepless. Following an evening party for which the children had been allowed to stay up and at which there had been music, Fanny went to his room. He was sitting up in bed, feverishly and confusedly crying. When she asked what troubled him, he replied: "The music, the music!" The music had long been silent, and she waited for further explanation. "Oh, the music!" he repeated. "Save me from it." He indicated his head. "It's there, in there," he explained. "It won't let me rest."

Mlle Fanny thought that she had discovered literary talent in Piotr Ilyich. Within a few months he had become in every sense her star pupil, far outshining his cousin and older brother. In 1847 he wrote a number of brief poems in French and set out to write a life of Joan of Arc,[3] completing one chapter. These childish ef-

[3] Schiller's *Die Jungfrau von Orleans* was the basis of a libretto to which he composed a four-act opera in 1878–9.

forts to write in an adult manner continued until 1848, when Fanny left the Tchaikovsky employ. Although Piotr Ilyich never became as accomplished a literary artist as Berlioz, Schumann, or Wagner, he was in later years able to express himself fluently and well, and his occasional pieces for periodicals often had point and vigour.

Passionate adoration of Mlle Fanny did not swerve the excitable Piotr Ilyich from music. She noted that the moment his lessons were finished he rushed to the piano. "When left to his own devices, he preferred music and poetry to any other pastimes." About one year after Fanny's arrival at Votkinsk, his parents gave the boy's musical desires some rein by hiring a young woman to give him primary lessons. He always recalled Marya Markovna Palchikova with amused pleasure. Her attainments were narrow, for he was quickly able to match her at sight reading. When he had become a famous composer, she wrote asking him for money. He had some sent to her, but remarked that her knowledge of musical literature must have been signally limited: he could not recall one single piece that she knew. Fanny, by much the more worldly of the teachers, nevertheless regarded Marya Markovna and her influence over the boy's emotions with reasonable misgivings. She understood that he might grow up with the urge to make himself a professional musician, a career she regarded as too difficult for its small rewards.

In the autumn of 1846 Ilya Petrovich and Alexandra Andreyevna made the long journey to St. Petersburg to attend the graduation from the Yekaterinsk Institute of his eldest daughter, Zinaïda, then seventeen years old. The girl returned to Votkinsk with them, adding a new element to the already complex household. Nobody in the family ever spoke or wrote much about Zinaïda. Her character is shadowy, but at seventeen she was naïve and self-centred. She jolted the artificial world Piotr Ilyich had been evolving for his own inner pacification by being, from his point of view, the first adult who did not baby him. He never showed the smallest affection for her, and it is at least probable that he disliked her from the beginning. In his half-sister Piotr Ilyich encountered for the first time that external world, detached from his own ego and intent upon its own desires and interests, that was sometimes to seem to him malign and stifling.

In February 1848 Ilya Petrovich resigned from his position in Votkinsk and was retired from government service with the rank of major general. In September, Fanny Dürbach became governess in another family, and Piotr Ilyich did not see her again for forty-four years. Later that same month the Tchaikovskys completed plans to remove from Votkinsk, and in October travelled to Moscow for a visit. Ilya Petrovich had believed that a favourable appointment awaited him, but arrived to find that a treacherous friend to whom he had confided his good fortune had himself pre-empted the position. Cholera was epidemic in the ancient capital; one of the Tchaikovsky servants contracted it. So in November the family hegira continued to St. Petersburg, where a house was chosen on Vasilyevsky Ostrov.

Piotr Ilyich had, by this stage in his life, moved a long way on the road to neurasthenia. He cried easily, puttered aimlessly at minor occupations, wrote hysterical letters to his beloved, lost Mlle Fanny, grew morose, pallid, and unwell, and moped feverishly about the house. His mother was overworked and preoccupied with family affairs, removals, and resettlings. She left the young children in the half-hearted care of Zinaïda. From being a pampered baby, gazed at admiringly, he found himself transformed into a nuisance shunted about as best suited the practical needs of several apparently unsympathetic people. Worse, he had hardly accustomed himself to the new surroundings of St. Petersburg when, with his brother Nikolay, he was sent to the Shmeling Boarding School and thus projected into a wholly impersonal world of tutors and boys his own age. What might have been ideal education for a normal eight-year-old boy was wrong for him. He could not assimilate the sort of experience the school offered, and began to have frequent alarming attacks of undiagnosable sickness. His mother's letters to Fanny Dürbach were full of phrases like "Petya is a changed boy . . . he is capricious . . . nothing interests him" and "Petya is unrecognizable, he's lazy, does nothing, I don't know what I shall do with him. He often makes me cry."

It is difficult to understand exactly what Alexandra Andreyevna expected her sons to do in addition to their schoolwork. They were away from early morning until five o'clock in the afternoon, and often laboured at homework until midnight. Under that regime an eight-year-old boy could hardly have had leisure or extra energy for other activities. There was, of course, basis for the mother's worry: her son was becoming a full-fledged neurasthenic. But the cures and preventives, if they existed at all, were not in her hands.

In December, Nikolay and Piotr Ilyich both had measles. Nikolay recovered quickly, but when Piotr Ilyich showed no continuing stigmata of the disease, but was still unwell, a physician diagnosed his ailment as "spinal brain disease." That the boy's trouble was psychic rather than physical is more than likely. His life long he suffered from a variety of complaints and ailments, a preponderant majority of which closely resemble the subjective illnesses of a neurasthenic. On this particular occasion the physician prescribed complete rest. The boy did nothing for six months. This vacation improved his apparent health, but badly served his mental state. It cut him off from the one activity he had enjoyed after the defection of Mlle Fanny, piano lessons from a man named Filippov. Despite his parents' efforts to please him by taking him often to the opera, he continued irritable and nervous.

Lessons with Filippov were not renewed. Before Piotr Ilyich's half-year of rest was complete, the Tchaikovskys once more had moved. Ilya Petrovich accepted a position as manager of privately owned factories at Nizhni-Nevyansk and Alapayevsk in the province of Perm, just east of the Urals and on the border of Siberia. He took his family to Alapayevsk in May 1849. Nikolay was left in boarding school preparing for the School of Mines. Separation from his eldest brother multiplied Piotr Ilyich's unhappiness: neither Ippolit, aged six, nor Alexandra, aged seven, could take the place of an eleven-year-old brother with a boy who was himself nine. Zinaïda was the poorest of substitutes for Mlle Fanny, and Piotr Ilyich's studies were lapsing. When letters from St. Petersburg began to retail Nikolay's excellent work in school, thoughtless elders openly compared him to Piotr Ilyich, to the latter's disadvantage. No one now encourgaed or took time to share his interest in music. He found his only anodyne for inner loneliness in writing to Mlle Fanny. He looked back upon her tenure as a grown man, tired by life, may look back upon a lost, impossibly happy childhood. He was not yet ten years old.

Although Ilya Petrovich's private employment was not so highly honoured or so highly paid as his government office had been, the Tchaikovskys still lived in more than comfort. Their Alapayevsk home was large, and their naturally hospitable tendencies soon all but re-established the feeling of the house at Votkinsk. Alexandra Andreyevna was in her sixth pregnancy, and management of the household devolved increasingly on Zinaïda and the servants. By the summer of 1849 Piotr Ilyich seemed sufficiently well to be allowed some activity again. His parents began to make inquiries about a suitable governess.

At this period Piotr Ilyich wrote to Fanny Dürbach: "Only books amuse me. Reread Christmas Eve [4] recently, but now I have nothing to read . . . how can I get . . . Télémaque or The Letters of Mme de Sévigné; . . . I should also very much like The Spirit of Christianity." Then, in a phrase that he was to vary a thousand times, he added: "But I can understand nothing." This statement is not, of course, to be taken literally from a ten-year-old who would reread Gogol and long for Fénelon and Mme de Sévigné.

On December 6, 1849 a new governess, Nastasya Petrovna Petrova, opened a more beneficial era in Piotr Ilyich's life. Only ten days after her advent, Alexandra Andreyevna was able to tell Mlle Fanny: "Petya is becoming more tractable since he began to study with the new governess." True to his emotional make-up, he continued to have hours of depression and nameless impatience. Then he would cry at a word that displeased him. But he began to recover interest in life. By March 1850 he himself was writing Mlle Fanny that he was sad a large part of the time, and was hardly ever away from the piano, "which comforts me a great deal." On May 13 of that year his mother gave birth to her last children, twin boys who were christened Modest Ilyich and Anatoly Ilyich. The day after their birth Piotr Ilyich wrote Mlle Fanny: "I have already seen them several times, and each time they have seemed to me to be angels come to earth." Although he must shortly have ascertained that they were far from seraphim, Piotr Ilyich formed for the twins an attachment that endured until his death. Indeed, he finally became more closely intimate with Modest than with anyone else.

His parents decided to put Piotr Ilyich with his brother Nikolay in the School of Mines,[5] but this plan was soon altered to one for entering him in the School of Jurisprudence. Almost as soon as Alexandra Andreyevna had recovered from her lying-in, she set off with him for St. Petersburg, where they arrived early in September 1850. On or about October 4 he was matriculated at the school in

[4] In 1873–4 Tchaikovsky composed an opera to a libretto based on Gogol's *Christmas Eve*. Known first as *Vakula the Smith*, it was later revised as *Cherevichki*, also called *Oksana's Caprices*.

[5] Ilya Petrovich had been graduated from this school in 1817.

the two-year preparatory course. One week later he had to bid
farewell to his mother, who was returning to Alapayevsk. As the
moment of her departure drew near, Piotr Ilyich excited himself
into a state close to hysterics. Nothing the frantic woman could
say quieted him. Promises to return soon unloosed more tears.
Embrace after embrace only made his forehead hotter, his eyes
redder, his sobs less controllable. When Alexandra Andreyevna at
last stepped into the waiting carriage, the boy had to be forcibly
restrained from going with her. And as it began to get under way,
he broke from those holding him, ran to the carriage, and clung
desperately to one of the turning wheels. Decades later the grown
man remembered that hour as the most terrible of his life and shud-
dered when speaking of it. He turned from the spot where the
carriage had stood to two years of misery, nostalgia, and despair,
lightened on occasion by the arrival of a visitor from Alapayevsk
and by the company of Nikolay.

III

ALEXANDRA ANDREYEVNA had given Piotr Ilyich one dazzling treat before she returned to Alapayevsk. She had taken him to a performance of *A Life for the Tsar*. It was not the first time he had heard Glinka's opera, but his mental state at the time, the nature of the music, and the new effect it had on him combined to make this, for his future, one of the determining events of his childhood. In later years he fully realized and openly acknowledged the influence on himself of Glinka's use of folk music. He also pointed out its more direct influence on the nationalist composers. Of Glinka's orchestral fantasy *Kamarinskaya* he was later to write: "The contemporary Russian school is all in it, just as the whole oak is in the acorn."

Piotr Ilyich had, like Nikolay, been left as a boarder in school. However, Alexandra Andreyevna had arranged with her husband's friend Modest Alexeyevich Vakar to keep in touch with the boy and in general to guard his welfare. In November an epidemic of scarlet fever sped through the School of Jurisprudence. Vakar immediately took Piotr Ilyich to live in his home. The boy did not himself contract the fever, but evidently introduced its germs into the Vakar household, for his hosts' eldest son contracted it and died. This shock cast Piotr Ilyich back into the terrified depression of the days following his mother's departure. He feared that the dead boy's parents, despite common sense and their friendly efforts to show that they did not hold him responsible, must feel that he had been the agent of their tragedy.

The fourteen months following his matriculation in the School of Jurisprudence were otherwise uneventful for the boy. He worked reasonably hard at his lessons, wrote sentimental, complaining letters to Alapayevsk — in one of which he enclosed a poem on prayer that he had just written — and was shifted from one temporary guardian to another. His marks in school were excellent except in Religion and Latin, and later in Mathematics. If he neglected his studies, he was punished by being denied the customary free

19

Sunday to spend with the family of his current guardian. He passed six weeks of the summer of 1851 in the country, and for a time was carefree. His lifelong love of the Russian countryside was already strong.

In September and October, Ilya Petrovich, again on the verge of resigning a position, visited St. Petersburg. He was on easy, congenial terms with his sons, and Piotr Ilyich in particular enjoyed time spent with this man forty-five years his senior. When Ilya Petrovich left St. Petersburg to go to Alapayevsk again, there was no such sentimental crisis as had been caused by Alexandra Andreyevna's departure one year earlier. Piotr Ilyich's love for his father lacked the intensity of that for his mother. Also, he was learning to face inevitabilities with more becoming calm. He evidently used some of the December-January school recess for renewing his acquaintance with music. His first mention in many months [1] of what had formerly been his consuming interest occurred in a letter to his mother early in 1852: "Recently I played the piano at school. I began The Nightingale, and then remembered other times when I played it. Immense sadness overwhelmed me. I recalled how I played it at Alapayevsk while you listened; how I played it four years ago here in Petersburg with my teacher Filippov; how you sang it with me — in a word, I remembered that this was always our favourite piece."

The month of Piotr Ilyich's twelfth birthday was for him a time of great happiness and excitement. Almost on that very day his family arrived from Alapayevsk to take up permanent residence in the northern capital. By the end of the month it was clear that, despite being one of the youngest students, he would pass his examinations and be graduated from the preparatory classes into the School of Jurisprudence proper. The summer of 1852 was a happy one, too, for then the entire family went to Chornaya Ryechka, the country estate of friends. There were gathered Ilya Petrovich, Alexandra Andreyevna, Zinaïda, Nikolay, Alexandra, Ip-

---

[1] Modest stated that thirty-nine letters written during Piotr Ilyich's first two years in school were preserved. Only two of them mentioned music. One noted that he had played a polka for a few of his fellow students, and had been practising a piece learned three years earlier. The other recalled with pleasure the performance of *A Life for the Tsar* he had attended with his mother, and stated that some time he would tell her the plot of *Der Freischütz*.

polit, and the two-year-old twins, Modest and Anatoly, besides
aunts, uncles, and cousins. There was a piano. There was music.
The boy studied out the soprano part in a florid duet from Rossini's
Semiramide and sang it to the willing contralto of one of his aunts;
he took pride in his natural trill. The same aunt went through the
entire score of *Don Giovanni* with him, further exhilarating his
passion for opera and intensifying his devotion to Mozart.

Piotr Ilyich's studies progressed satisfactorily. Each year he
moved to the next class without apparent difficulty. In the one he
entered at about the time of his thirteenth birthday he began to
make friendships of more than passing value. One of the boys with
whom he associated was Alexander Nikolayevich Apukhtin, a literary prodigy at thirteen, and destined to develop into one of Russia's foremost lyric poets. With Apukhtin, Piotr Ilyich discussed
poetry. But his closest friend among the students was Vladimir
Stepanovich Adamov, like himself enthusiastic over music and
enraptured by opera. The sober and scholarly Adamov left school
to work his way up to one of the most responsible posts in the
Ministry of Justice. He was almost the only friend to whom Piotr
Ilyich felt able to disclose the depth and strength of his musical
emotions, and the two boys soon were sincerely attached to each
other.

Piotr Ilyich became something of a leader in school activities.
His cronies were all boys of intellectual bent, mostly members of a
group that edited a magazine for the lower grades. To this he
contributed *A History of Literature in Our Class,* described by
Modest as very cleverly written. Evident in the annals of his school
years and in his friends' recollections of him is the personal charm
he emanated all his life. He inspired affection easily. Whether his
friends failed to notice his morbidities or found them outweighed
by his liveliness of character and mind, he was known chiefly for
his intense personal charm, his sloppiness of appearance, and a
soft, sensitive gentleness that was almost feminine. He slid along
without plans or intentions, a peaceable and lazy little boy. He
kept his black internal struggles for the privacy of his room. Only
much later did he develop the habit of always having one vis-à-vis
or correspondent with whom to share the wide, undependable
fluctuations of his emotional temperature.

The year 1854 began with family festivities, when Zinaïda married Yevgeny Ivanovich Olkhovsky. Piotr Ilyich's fourteenth birth-

day passed. In June his mother was stricken with cholera, the disease of which Russians stood in most terror. Under excellent medical care she rallied briefly. A relapse forced the application of the final known treatment, immersion in hot water. So suddenly as not to have time for any final words, Alexandra Andreyevna died on June 25. Immediately Ilya Petrovich was down with the same disease, and for a time no hope was held out for his recovery. At fifty-nine, however, his vigorous constitution served him well, and he rallied, to live, hale and lively, for twenty-six years more.

The effect of his mother's death on Piotr Ilyich may be gauged by the fact that two and one half years passed before he felt able to write Mlle Fanny a letter informing her that it had occurred. His attachment to Alexandra Andreyevna was not the ordinary love of a boy for his mother. It had the intensity of a lover's passion. One school of psychoanalysts might call it an Œdipus complex, another say that psychically the boy found the world too difficult and had a subconscious desire to leave it by re-entering the womb from which he had issued. Whether Piotr Ilyich's frantic and undiminishing love for his mother was the result of congenital abnormality, or whether abnormality developed out of that love, it is impossible to read his childish letters to her, feel his crushed and despairing reaction to her death, or even look at his remarks about that death decades later, without becoming certain that there was a causal connection between his emotional relationship to Alexandra Andreyevna and his homosexuality.

When Ilya Petrovich had recovered sufficient health, he took his family to Oranienbaum, on the Gulf of Finland opposite Kronstadt, for the summer. There Piotr Ilyich turned fiercely to music as all that could assuage the unbroken misery of never again being with his mother. He composed and noted down a waltz, which he dedicated to his former governess Nastasya Petrovna Petrova. This, probably the first complete original composition Piotr Ilyich ever wrote out, does not survive. He considered composing a comic opera to a libretto called *Hyperbole,* but dropped the project because the text consisted largely of recitatives and arias: he wanted more duets, trios, and other concerted numbers. Back in St. Petersburg in the autumn, he included in his courses at the School of Jurisprudence singing lessons from Gavril Akimovich Lomakin, a distinguished choral conductor and teacher at the Free School of

Music. That the boy's voice had begun to deepen is proved by Lomakin's having assigned him the alto part in a trio.

Classes and study at the School of Jurisprudence pursued their accustomed way, but music was becoming an important component of Piotr Ilyich's days. He began to go to operas, concerts, and plays. At home his family was breaking up in the wake of Zinaïda's marriage and his mother's death. The Crimean War was dragging out its futile course, and Ippolit had entered the navy in 1854. There he prospered, eventually becoming an admiral. Alexandra started attending classes at the Smolny Institute. Insensibly Piotr Ilyich began to look upon the four-year-old Modest and Anatoly as his responsibility and to give them the brightest substitute he could imagine for a mother's or a sister's care. To the end of his life he liked small children, and they him. Both Anatoly and Modest later testified to the excellence of his care when they were young. He was almost equally fond of Alexandra.

The Crimean War was strewing the roads of the south with Russian soldiers dead of disease, and the siege of Sevastopol was half through its terrible year when, on March 2, 1855, Nicholas I died. There succeeded to the throne his thirty-six-year-old son, the brilliantly educated, well-intentioned, and ill-starred Alexander II. His accession did nothing to divert the course of the war, which ended in the Treaty of Paris in March 1856, a diplomatic defeat for Russia. The fact that this defeat ended for a time Russia's interference in the affairs of western Europe — which had been the deliberate policy of Nicholas I — turned the new Tsar's attention to internal affairs and helped inaugurate a brief period of reforms. Had partial measures been able to cure the economic and social ills from which his Empire was suffering, the liberal and enlightened intentions of Alexander II might have cured them. What his stopgap reforms did accomplish was the lifting of the intellectual and moral winter that Nicholas's iron will had clamped down across all his vast domain. Censorship became less stringent, for some years there was less fear of the secret police, and increasingly large numbers of the middle class — even to some extent the peasants and proletariat — breathed more easily for a time. It was the Russia of Alexander II in which Piotr Ilyich was to reach maturity and accomplish a large part of his life's work.

While Sevastopol was standing siege, Piotr Ilyich was desultorily studying the piano under the School of Jurisprudence's teacher, Bekker. At about the time of Alexander II's accession, however, Ilya Petrovich granted the boy's wish, and hired a private instructor for him. This was Rudolf Vasilyevich Kündinger, a pedagogue of prominence. After some months of these lessons Ilya Petrovich, evidently at his son's insistence, asked Kündinger whether it would be wise for Piotr Ilyich to devote himself exclusively to music. Kündinger replied that the life of a musician in Russia was an extremely arduous one, and that, besides, he could detect no spark of genius in Piotr Ilyich, though the boy did have unusual powers of improvisation and some harmonic sense. There can be no question of criticizing Kündinger for blindness in this matter. Piotr Ilyich developed slowly in music, and until long afterwards produced nothing that could be allied to genius. Kündinger's advice settled the matter: Piotr Ilyich was told to finish his course in the School of Jurisprudence, and then hope for a minor post in the Ministry of Justice.[2]

All of Piotr Ilyich's time except one morning and two evenings each week was taken up by advanced schoolwork. He would have liked to hear symphony concerts, but they were rare in St. Petersburg. As the only place where he could hear a good orchestra, competent conducting, and eminent soloists, he therefore frequented the Italian opera. Such international songbirds as Enrico Tamberlik and Angiolina Bosio visited St. Petersburg often during these years. Piotr Ilyich was particularly impressed by a soprano named Lagrua, especially in her highly dramatic rendition of the name role in *Norma*. His only method of becoming acquainted with music for orchestra was by studying scores in piano transcriptions. These too were rare — and expensive. Modest states that up to the time when he was twenty-one, Piotr Ilyich did not know how many symphonies Beethoven had composed, and had no acquaintance whatever with Schumann.

In 1855 Ilya Petrovich removed, with his younger children, to a house occupied by his elder brother, Piotr Petrovich. This sternly religious ex-soldier of seventy had become a recluse in his home, where he spent his time writing unending tracts on mystical subjects. His wife continued to encourage normal gaiety in her own

[2] Years later, Kündinger recalled him as a boy with a remarkable memory, an acute ear, and a certain talent for harmony, who had made small progress in three years.

children, and her personality was remembered with pleasure by her nephews. Relations named Schobert likewise joined this household, and through them Piotr Ilyich met a very odd character indeed. This was a Neapolitan singing teacher named Piccioli. He was a decayed dandy, dyed his hair jet black, though reputed to be between sixty and seventy, and painted his cheeks the colour of youth. The Tchaikovsky children were told that he wore a device at the back of his head to smooth out his wrinkles, and Modest remembered staring at Piccioli's head in the hope of learning how the device worked.

Piccioli would not grant the name of music to anything but the operas of Rossini, Bellini, Donizetti, and the young Verdi. He was known to feel sorry for Mozart and Beethoven. Piotr Ilyich had learned to enjoy Meyerbeer and Verdi in addition to his original favourites, Mozart and Glinka. But he did not argue with the voluble Italian. Instead, he listened, absorbing the lore of opera, the technique of singing, and a wide smattering of other information. For a time he and Piccioli were real friends despite the wide disparity in their ages. He even tried his unpractised hand at the composition of a song to an Italian translation of a poem by Fet. This *Mezza notte*, which Piotr Ilyich had printed at his own expense, was stigmatized by the usually respectful Modest as "a mere empty amateur effusion."

In the spring of 1858 the large and miscellaneous group of Tchaikovskys and Schoberts living under Piotr Petrovich's ample roof was jolted by the news that Ilya Petrovich had lost his money. He had always been gullible, but this time misplaced confidence had especially unhappy results. He was sixty-three, and had again to seek employment. Fortunately, he had not to look long: he was appointed director of the St. Petersburg Technological Institute. Again life continued its even tenor.

On May 13, 1859, six days after his nineteenth birthday, Piotr Ilyich was graduated from the School of Jurisprudence, thirteenth in his class, and was handed a diploma entitling him to the rank of government clerk. At his own request, he was attached to the Ministry of Justice. Seven months later he was promoted to be junior assistant to the chief clerk, and in February 1860 he became senior assistant. Although he once mutilated an important document by tearing piece after piece from it and then chewing the pieces to pulp while he talked to someone, his career in the Ministry seems to have been honourable, if without distinction. During this period he became something of a fop, careful to be in tune with the latest fashions. He frittered away his time out of the Ministry in the most frivolous pursuits. He frequented theatres, especially for opera, ballet, and French plays. He tried hard to be a dashing young blade, and was in some demand at parties because he was always willing to improvise waltzes and polkas at the piano. He was, that is, undistinguishable from a dozen or a hundred other young government clerks of good family in St. Petersburg.

On November 18, 1860 another break was made in the Tchaikovsky family: Alexandra Ilyinishna married Lyov Vasilyevich Davidov, son of a prominent Decembrist. The young couple left immediately for the Davidov properties at Kamenka, in the province of Kiev. Piotr Ilyich had always been fond of his sister. Separated from her, he began to make her his confidante by letter. Their friendship improved and lasted. Later her children became his special delight, Kamenka in the Ukraine his choice place of refuge. Her son Vladimir Lvovich became, with Modest, the most intimate friend of his last years and the dedicatee of the "Pathetic" Symphony.

Two forces were pulling the twenty-year-old Piotr Ilyich back and forth between them. One part of him was a young and physically healthy animal, gregarious, wanting gaiety, liking to be frivolous, and conscious of sexual desire. There is naturally no record of his earliest sexual experiences. But phrases used by Modest about this period strongly suggest that it was then that Piotr Ilyich — whose inmost secrets Modest eventually came to share — first gave reign to his homosexual yearnings. Modest writes of "this slough of a petty, useless, and vicious existence . . . this feverish pursuit of pleasure . . . moments of agonizing despair . . . some unknown [3] event in his life." Homosexuality was far from uncommon in Russia, particularly among the upper and military classes.

[3] It may be assumed that Modest in truth knew what the event was. But he literally adored Piotr Ilyich and, when he came to write his brother's biography, would reveal nothing that might be taken as a reflection on the dead composer. Also, he was himself homosexual, and still felt the need — which had always been in Piotr Ilyich's mind and his own — of concealing what the world regarded as shameful. He doubtless knew that gossip had already spoken the truth, but he refused to give gossip the backing of official statement.

Yet, even when writing to each other as grown men, Piotr Ilyich and Modest took the precaution of referring to it as *This*. Their secret lay like a blighting shadow across much of Piotr Ilyich's life and was the direct or indirect immediate cause of much of his tragedy.

Against the pull that took the young government clerk night after night into ballrooms and perhaps less respectable centres of pleasure was the unending compulsion, sometimes in abeyance but never wholly ignored, to devote his life and energy to music. This omnipresent desire to become a composer he connected with the "better side" of his nature. He nurtured it intermittently by taking more part in his home life, by hard work, by not being frivolous or foppish or incontinent. Writing of his periodic fluctuations between *boulevardier* and serious young musician, Modest says: "The psychological side of this change, the pathetic side of the struggle he went through for more than two years, must always remain undisclosed. Not that his correspondence from this period is scanty, but because Piotr Ilyich jealously hid the secrets of his inner, spiritual life. No outsider was ever allowed to meddle with them. He chose to pass through dark hours alone. To the outside world he remained the same serene and cheerful young man."

It was Ilya Petrovich who, in March 1861, reopened to his son the prospect of an artist's life. At the dinner table one night, talk turned on Piotr Ilyich's talent. His father said that it was still not too late for him to choose a musical career. With his usual pessimism Piotr Ilyich himself thought it too late. "They have made an official of me," he wrote Alexandra, "though a poor one . . . and at the same time I am to be studying thoroughbass!" He toyed with the attractive prospect of abandoning the Ministry of Justice in order to devote himself wholly to music. What deterred him was that he had no implement but a great love of music. No convincing proof of his talent existed. He was by no means in a financial condition that would allow him to launch his career as a dilettante. He stayed on at the Ministry.

After several years of study, conference, and preparation in local, regional, and national committees, the pet project of Alexander II, the manifesto abolishing serfdom in Russia, was signed by the Tsar on the sixth anniversary of his accession to the throne, March 3, 1861. Piotr Ilyich, always emotionally involved in the affairs of his country, and curious to see the reaction of the people to this news, attended a church meeting when the emancipation manifesto was read. His father had been a serf-owner, and Piotr Ilyich had lived enough in towns and villages to know something of the evils of serfdom as an institution. Like many other young Russians he must have felt that the manifesto promised a new era.

Piotr Ilyich's friendship with Alexander Nikolayevich Apukhtin had ripened into an intimacy so close that for a time the two young men saw each other every day. They discussed and read poetry together. Otherwise Piotr Ilyich continued to fritter away his time out of the Ministry. He often visited a family named Yesipov, and took part in amateur theatricals with them. He met a Mme Herngross, and stated that he was a little in love with her daughter Sophie. A key to his reaction to the several girls to whom he paid passing attention at this time is to be seen in a letter he wrote to Alexandra Davidova. Someone had told him that two young ladies were in love with him, and he remarked: "This story flatters my vanity." There is never one word about his own feeling for the young ladies under discussion.

In the early summer of 1861 a friend of Ilya Petrovich's, V. V. Pisarev, suggested that Piotr Ilyich go to western Europe on a business trip with him, acting as interpreter. In June the young man wrote his sister of this "alluring, unrealizable dream," but in July it became a reality. Shortly he found himself in Berlin. Foreign travel was a novelty to Russians, for not many years had elapsed since it had been forbidden except under rare special circumstances. Berlin did not please Piotr Ilyich. He visited a large *café dansant* and attended a showing of Offenbach's *Orphée aux Enfers*. Then he calmly wrote home: "Now we are thoroughly acquainted with Berlin, and have had enough of it." The travellers moved on to Hamburg, which pleased him little more. Of Antwerp, Brussels, and Ostend he had almost nothing to say, though at the last place he delighted in watching a stormy sea and hearing it roar.

Piotr Ilyich's first sea voyage took him to England, whence he could scarcely wait to get to Paris, as letters from Russia were promised there. He granted London some degree of passing interest, but found it gloomy because of constant rain and lack of sunshine. Early in August he attended a concert by the twenty-seven-year-old Adelina Patti, who had made a sensational London debut in *La Sonnambula* only three months earlier, and wrote Ilya Petrovich that the singer failed to impress him.

Having remained loyal to Russia through Germany, Belgium, and England, Piotr Ilyich capitulated to the immemorial charm of Paris. Like most Russian visitors of the period, he found the French metropolis echoing with siren voices. Six excited and happy weeks there were what he enjoyed most of the whole journey. Some time after the middle of August he attended performances of *Il Trovatore*, and *Les Huguenots*. Not awed by the Salle Le Peletier, in which the Opéra was then housed,[4] he wrote his father that, though the staging was generally excellent, the theatre — and all Paris theatres — and the performances were "of course inferior to those in St. Petersburg." In no letter did he fail to add words of encouragement or advice for "Tolya" and "Modya," his beloved eleven-year-old brothers.

Toward the end of his stay in Paris, Piotr Ilyich had a quarrel with his employer and travelling companion, experiencing what Modest referred to as "complete disenchantment with him." Scenes of unpleasant character followed, and Piotr Ilyich made the return trip to St. Petersburg alone. By early October he was at home, and no doubt smothering Anatoly and Modest with effusive, well-meant attention. While his first foray abroad must have had some small maturing effect on him, he learned little from it. That he had indulged in a few wild escapades was proved on his return by his determination (one of a series of determinations) to reform, to become more serious, to devote himself to better things. He referred to the trip as "a colossal piece of folly," adding for Alexandra Davidova's benefit: "You know I am weak: as soon as I have money I throw it away on pleasure. This is vulgar, foolish — I know that, but it seems to be in me. Where will it take me? What can I hope for? It is awful to contemplate. I know that a time will come when I shall no longer possess the strength to battle life's obstacles. Until then I'll do all I can to enjoy it. For two weeks everything has gone badly. My work has been very poor. Money disappears like smoke. In love — no success. But a better time will come soon. PS. — I am studying thoroughbass, and am getting on well. Who knows? It may be that in three years you'll be listening to an opera by me and singing my arias."

Piotr Ilyich's lessons in thoroughbass (he was also studying Italian) were being taken in public classes held by the Imperial

[4] The present Opéra, begun the year of Piotr Ilyich's visit, was delayed by the Franco-Prussian War and did not open until January 5, 1875.

Russian Musical Society at the Mikhailovsky Palace. His teacher
was Nikolay Ivanovich Zaremba. Zaremba, then forty, had learned
harmony from one of the renowned German pundits of the day,
Adolph Bernhard Marx, and it was theory according to Marx that
he taught. It would seem to have been in Zaremba's class that Piotr
Ilyich made the acquaintance of Vladimir Vasilyevich Bessel, a
violinist who later became a publisher both of music and of two
successive musical magazines. Bessel, who was Piotr Ilyich's junior
by three years, outlived him, and wrote a book of reminiscences
that contributed much to the bringing of the composer's shadowy
figure into three-dimensional life. By the middle of December 1861
Piotr Ilyich's letters to Alexandra Davidova again had taken on
more serious colouring: "I think I told you before that I have
started the study of theory with success. You will agree that with
my somewhat unusual talent (I trust you won't take this for brag-
ging) it seems silly not to try my luck in this line. I dread only my
own lethargic nature. In the end my laziness will win; but if it
doesn't, I promise you that I'll do something. Luckily it still is not
too late." He had changed his mind about time.

At the Tchaikovsky home there were only Ilya Petrovich, Piotr
Ilyich, and the twins. Nikolay had received a government position
in the provinces, and Piotr Ilyich more than ever supervised Anatoly and Modest. "I recollect having made two discoveries that
astonished me," Modest wrote of this period. "The first was that the
two concepts 'brother Piotr' and 'work' were not necessarily opposed; the second was that there existed, in addition to pleasant
and interesting music, another kind, exceedingly unpleasant and
boring, that seemed nevertheless to be the more important of the
two." Piotr Ilyich, that is to say, was working at his lessons and was
writing exercises. He was also acquainting himself further with the
classical and contemporary musical repertoire by poring for hours
over any score he could buy or borrow. Music was absorbing so
much of his free time that he could only with difficulty find hours
for dancing, drinking, and the other pleasures he had formerly cultivated with determination. He narrowed his circle of friends to
only Adamov and Apukhtin. Evenings he sometimes accompanied
his father to the theatre or stayed at home to play cards with him.

During 1862 Piotr Ilyich learned that there would soon be vacant in the Ministry of Justice a higher position, one to which his
background and experience excellently fitted him. He therefore ex-

erted every effort to present the best possible face to his superiors,
applying himself diligently to tasks that bored him almost to tears,
working more assiduously than anyone had seen him work before
except at music and the pursuit of sensation. He had completed the
harmony and thoroughbass course under Zaremba in December of
the previous year, and for a while music fell slightly into the background. But word got around that the Russian Musical Society was
about to open its own school. At the beginning of September, Piotr
Ilyich applied for admission, and was accepted.

   The St. Petersburg Conservatory of Music (not its official name,
but the one by which it came to be known) was the creation of two
people of enormous energy and wide vision. The less important of
them was the most remarkable woman of her time in Russia, Grand
Duchess Yelena Pavlovna. This German woman (she was born a
princess of Württemberg) had married Grand Duke Mikhail Pavlovich, youngest son of Paul I, and was therefore sister-in-law to
Nicholas I and aunt to Alexander II. She was vigorously intelligent,
liberally sympathetic, and very musical. In 1849, at the age of
forty-two, she was the widowed mother of two girls. When life at
last permitted her time to devote to things she loved most, Yelena
Pavlovna became the patroness and intimate friend of the young
man who was the more important founder of the St. Petersburg
Conservatory. This was Anton Grigoryevich Rubinstein.

   When he met Yelena Pavlovna, Rubinstein was twenty-two, and
a pianist renowned throughout Europe. He had already composed
one opera, *Dmitri Donskoy*, that had achieved performance in St.
Petersburg. In a short time he and the Grand Duchess were close
friends, and the young Jew had become music master in her villa
on Kamenoi Ostrov, the island in the Neva after which he was to
name his popular salon piece. Soon he was travelling about Europe
with her, and their names were being tossed together by gossips,
whether with or without reason no one knows. In about 1856 the
project for a musical society that would both give concerts and
provide professional training to Russian musicians, and thus raise
their pitiable status, was under discussion between them. They
invited other enthusiasts to consult with them, and very early in
1859 the Russian Musical Society held its preliminary meeting.
Yelena Pavlovna persuaded Alexander II to give the Society his
imperial sanction despite his nervous distrust of all organizations.
In November its first public concert was presented, with the great

Rubinstein himself playing his own Piano Concerto in G, opus 45. Yelena Pavlovna arranged to have the Society's classes held in her home, the Mikhailovsky Palace. It was there that Piotr Ilyich had gone to study with Zaremba.

The Society was a success from the beginning. Its classes grew, its concerts prospered. Soon it needed its own building. Yelena Pavlovna appealed to the Tsar, who had learned to admire and trust her, and won from him the promise of both sanction and subsidy. Early in the winter of 1861–2 the St. Petersburg Conservatory, Anton Rubinstein director, opened its doors in a luxurious former private home on the Neva. Its youthful teaching staff included, besides the great pianist, then thirty-two, the Polish violinist Henri Wieniawski (twenty-seven), the Polish pianist and teacher Theodor Leschetizky (thirty-two), the Russian cellist and composer Karl U. Davidov (twenty-four), previously first cellist of the Leipzig Gewandhaus, Lomakin, and Zaremba. In every department it was a staff worthy of imperial largess. Classes opened on September 20, 1862, and among the earliest to matriculate was Piotr Ilyich Tchaikovsky.

At first Piotr Ilyich studied only with Zaremba — a stiff course in strict counterpoint and the church modes, using the ironclad text of Johann Gottfried Heinrich Bellermann, then Prussian Royal Music Director. Later he likewise studied piano and flute and had a few organ lessons. Two days after the Conservatory opened, he wrote Alexandra Davidova: "Sooner or later I shall abandon my present job for music. Don't think that I'm dreaming of becoming a great artist. . . . Whether I become a famous composer or only a struggling teacher doesn't matter. My conscience will be at rest, and I shall no longer have the unhappy right to grumble at my lot. Of course, I shan't resign from my present job until I'm certain that I'm no longer a clerk, but a musician." He began to alter visibly. The fop of a few years earlier became a grubby and sallow student. He indulged in social pleasure less and less, and at last not at all. He worked numbly through his long hours at the Ministry of Justice, and then rushed off to music, either classes at the Conservatory or practice and study at home. His more flippant friends, puzzled at first, then irritated, finally dropped him.

One new friend, however, made up for any number lost. This was an intense seventeen-year-old youth, Herman Avgustovich Laroche, who eventually developed into an interesting, if wayward,

TCHAIKOVSKY IN 1863
From a photograph

music critic and one of the most ardent champions of the music of Tchaikovsky. He was musically far more accomplished and sophisticated than his five-year-older friend. He had composed a march and an overture before his tenth birthday. He was well read, an able linguist, and poised far beyond his years. Witty and vivacious, he charmed Piotr Ilyich from the hour they met in a piano class, and he quickly supplanted all other non-family relationships. Laroche seems to have been absolutely sure of Piotr Ilyich's talent at once. Unquestionably this bolstering of his self-esteem helped Piotr Ilyich toward the fateful decision to resign from the Ministry of Justice and leap, all but unsupported, into a purely musical life.

Nikolay Tchaikovsky, now a provincial official on his way up in the world, was shocked at the prospect of his brother's throwing away a solid future in the bureaucracy. Knowing Piotr Ilyich's great admiration of *A Life for the Tsar*, Nikolay stated mildly that he could see no reason for believing that his brother would turn into another Glinka. "I may never be another Glinka," Piotr Ilyich replied, "but the day will come when you'll be proud of me." Both parts of this prediction eventually came to be certainties. Whatever he became, Piotr Ilyich was never another Glinka, and his entire family did become proud of him — even Provincial Official Nikolay and Naval Officer Ippolit.

Another influence edging Piotr Ilyich toward his daring move came from within the Conservatory. One day after class one of his teachers called the pupil aside and remarked that he was not being diligent at his work. He then made it clear that he regarded this as particularly shameful because Piotr Ilyich was talented. The youth was deeply touched and strongly fortified by this critical praise. Laroche says that the teacher was Zaremba, and that from this moment on, Piotr Ilyich started to apply himself with zeal that remained steady during his terms at the Conservatory. Nikolay Dmitryevich Kashkin, another of Piotr Ilyich's contemporaries who became a critic and teacher, contradicted Laroche on details of this story, saying that it was not Zaremba, but Rubinstein himself who had encouraged Piotr Ilyich to make the most of his talent. Early in 1863 Rubinstein excused Piotr Ilyich from the ordinarily compulsory class in piano so that he could apply himself entirely to theory and to the director's own class in composition, which he had entered late in 1862. For Rubinstein, Piotr Ilyich conceived a respectful adoration that endured, despite many buffetings, for long years. Praise was scarcely praise to him unless Rubinstein spoke it, and all adverse criticism except Rubinstein's (and his own) could somehow be overcome. In fact, his attitude toward the older musician was very like a worshipper's toward a god made visible. "Tchaikovsky worked in an amazing manner," Rubinstein later told Kashkin. "Once in the composition class I told him to write out contrapuntal variations on a given theme, and mentioned that in this sort of work not only quality but quantity was important. I thought that he might write about twelve variations. Not at all. At the next class he gave me over two hundred."

Piotr Ilyich was much sought out as an accompanist, partly because of his facility at transposing and improvising. During the early spring of 1863 he twice accompanied at public concerts, one each at the Bolshoi and Marinsky, and took part in a musicale at Yelena Pavlovna's palace. He told Alexandra Davidova that he was worn out by the activity of the Lenten season. He also informed her that he had finally and irrevocably decided to give his life entirely to music. He had not received the appointment he had worked for in the Ministry and was using that slight as a pretext for resigning. Perhaps he would obtain a teaching post in the Conservatory. "I'm certain only of one thing, that I shall be a good musician. . . . All my teachers are satisfied with my work, and tell me that if I'm diligent I have a great future." A short time after leaving the Ministry he could not recall exactly what his work there had been.

On the practical side, life must have appeared exceedingly uncertain to the dedicated artist of twenty-three. Ilya Petrovich's finances were in poor condition: at sixty-eight he had found his directorship of the Technological Institute too demanding and had resigned. Modest and Anatoly, at thirteen, had to be supported, and there was little money left over for a grown son, even one whose decision to abandon an assured livelihood for the sake of music had been met, not with opposition, but with every attempt at comprehension. Piotr Ilyich went off to spend the summer with Apukhtin. When he returned to St. Petersburg in the autumn, he had been metamorphosed into the very mould of a Bohemian. He still owned a fashionable coat, but it had become frayed. He had permitted his once neatly plastered hair to become long, perhaps in emulation of Anton Rubinstein, whose bobbed locks were renowned. He returned, not to the teeming near-luxury to which his childhood had accustomed him, but to a barely comfortable house containing only Ilya Petrovich and the twins. His father gave him a room and some meals, but could not afford an additional allowance. Anton Rubinstein, however, produced a few private pupils for him, and he was content. Modest could remember no period of his brother's life during which he remained so cheerful. "In a small room," he says, "holding only a bed and a writing table, he set out bravely on his new, laborious life, and there he spent many nights in arduous work." Piotr Ilyich was twenty-three. For him childhood and youth were over. He was about to become a composer and a grown man.

IV

No longer a civil servant, Piotr Ilyich laboured tenaciously at the task of becoming a good musician. Several of his classroom compositions and exercises survive from 1863, 1864, and 1865. They lack musical interest. In attempt after attempt to please Zaremba and Anton Rubinstein the novice was restricting himself. Perhaps this was good training. But Zaremba admitted no music later than Beethoven and Mendelssohn, while Rubinstein was consciously old-fashioned and in particular set his whole strength as a pedagogue against the expanded orchestra of Meyerbeer, Liszt, and Wagner. That enriched instrument was to be Piotr Ilyich's own voice in the best of his mature compositions. There was already artistic tension between master and pupil, brought to the surface especially at those moments when Piotr Ilyich's partiality for splashes of brilliant instrumental colour would appear in pieces submitted to Rubinstein. So Piotr Ilyich, to whom the master's tacit approval was better than praise from others, tried conscientiously to hold himself in check and composed lifeless music. Those of his student compositions that were not destroyed or left in unpublished form may still occasionally be found in libraries and old-music stores. They sound remarkably like the works of Anton Rubinstein. They are melodious enough, correct enough, but watery and unflavoured.

However, the best and most Tchaikovskyan of these early pieces was also composed for Rubinstein's course. It carries the high opus number 76, for it was published posthumously. Piotr Ilyich was greatly moved by the plays of Alexander Nikolayevich Ostrovsky, of which *The Storm* was one of the best. In 1864, on staff paper that he was using for an orchestration of some of Schumann's *Études symphoniques*, he began to sketch an overture to *The Storm*. During the summer, which he spent as a guest of Prince Alexey V. Golitsin at Trostinets in the province of Kharkov, he completed its orchestration. Far enough from St. Petersburg to feel safe, he used divided violins, violins tremolo, harp, tuba, and

English horn, none of which was permitted by Rubinstein. Falling sick just as he prepared to return to St. Petersburg, he sent the score to Laroche, asking him to pass it on to Rubinstein for criticism. Poor Laroche was forced to weather one of the master's vitriolic outbursts, directed against him as though he, and not Piotr Ilyich, had composed the offensive music.

Part of Piotr Ilyich's difficulties with Rubinstein grew out of differences between their musical backgrounds and temperaments. The most advanced music — advanced, that is, in orchestration and in deviation from the supposed norms established by Beethoven — that Rubinstein would allow his students to emulate was in the works of Mendelssohn and Schumann, though his own windy compositions scarcely stopped there. Piotr Ilyich, on the other hand, had begun by admiring Glinka, and was becoming familiar with the operas of Meyerbeer. At concerts of the Russian Musical Society he had been imbibing the more heretical idioms of Liszt, Berlioz, and Wagner as conducted persuasively by Rubinstein himself. In 1862 Wagner visited St. Petersburg, conducting excerpts both from his early operas and from the completed portions of *Der Ring des Nibelungen*. Piotr Ilyich was bewitched by Wagner's instrumentation, though the music itself signified little to him. He took the German's monstrous orchestra for what it was, a new and marvellous instrument, and could never understand Rubinstein's objection to it. He loved the classics as much as Rubinstein did, but never made the withering error of confining himself to the musical tools of their era.

Piotr Ilyich continued to have pleasant social contacts with proper young ladies of his own age. In the autumn of 1863 Alexandra Davidova's mother-in-law settled in St. Petersburg with four of her daughters and a young son. Both Alexandra Ivanovna Davidova and her elderly unmarried daughter Yelizaveta interested Piotr Ilyich because of their memories of the reign of Alexander I and of the Decembrist revolt. Both had known Pushkin, and Yelizaveta could tell him personal anecdotes about Gogol. One of the other daughters, Vera, was attracted by Piotr Ilyich, by his musical attainments most, perhaps, but it may be also by his black hair and blue eyes, his dishevelled appearance and pensive expression. He grew to like her and eventually dedicated to her the earliest of his compositions that became world-famous. But when his sister hinted that the girl was falling in love with him, he replied: "If this were true, I should be greatly displeased." Never did his response to the girls who found him an attractive companion show the intensity of infatuation, much less that of physical passion. Nor are there any hints that he was giving in to the urgings of the hidden side of his nature in any overt way. He was passing through a period of work that allowed him no time for erotic stimulation, he was successfully downing temptation, or he was adept at covering up sorties. What matters is that he enjoyed the superficial activities of normal life and presented an acceptable face to those about him. It has, of course, been suggested that his relationship with Laroche was in part erotic, but nothing recorded of Laroche gives this rumour the appearance of truth.

Private piano lessons brought Piotr Ilyich a tiny income. He went with Laroche to as many concerts as possible. At one of the Russian Musical Society's evenings the Overture to Glinka's *Ruslan and Lyudmila* inflamed them both with bright enthusiasm. Of the night when Piotr Ilyich met Alexander Nikolayevich Serov, the violently pro-Wagnerian and anti-nationalist critic whose *Judith* had been the most successful opera of the preceding season, Laroche said: "I remember that on that particular night Dostoyevsky talked at length — and very foolishly — about music, as literary men do who do not understand it at all." It would be interesting to know what foolish things Dostoyevsky said.

For some years Ilya Petrovich Tchaikovsky had been spending considerable time with a widow named Yelizaveta Mikhailovna Alexandrova (*née* Lipport). Piotr Ilyich, too, found her sympathetic and had fallen into a habit of discussing his problems and plans with her. It was no shock to him when in 1865, at the age of seventy, his father married her as his third wife and introduced her into his household. She was able to add a needed touch to his own care of Anatoly and Modest, now fifteen. Piotr Ilyich spent part of that summer at the Davidov estate at Kamenka. The estate belonged to Lyov Vasilyevich's elder brother, Nikolay. This intelligent and studious man was a political reactionary, and Modest always believed that his influence won Piotr Ilyich from a vague youthful liberalism to a more conservative political view.

Again Piotr Ilyich tried his hand at a composition for orchestra, this time with encouraging results. It was a set of character dances known as *Dances of the Serving Maids*. Early in September 1865 these were performed at an outdoor concert held in Petropavlovsky

Park. They were conducted by Johann Strauss, Jr., the internationally renowned waltz king, entirely to their composer's satisfaction. The first real public performance he had ever received, coming under such glamorous auspices and turning out so well, mightily cheered Piotr Ilyich at an hour when cheer was not plentiful. He was finding the financial side of life difficult and depressing. Also, he had been forcing himself to translate into Russian, at Anton Rubinstein's request, Gevaert's *Traité général d'instrumentation*, and his eyes had begun to tire and worry him. Here, at Petropavlovsky Park, was a sign, however transitory, that something besides obscurity and penury might be his future.

Almost simultaneously with the performance of the *Dances*, Piotr Ilyich received other encouragement. Nikolay Grigoryevich Rubinstein invited him to teach theory at the newly formed Moscow Conservatory of Music. Behind this invitation lay a curious story. In 1860, with his brother Anton's approval and assistance, Nikolay had founded the Moscow branch of the Russian Musical Society. It flourished, and Moscow flocked to take lessons of its own Rubinstein and to hear the concerts he arranged. Shortly Nikolay had income enough (in excess of six hundred rubles — about three hundred dollars — per month) to move from his crowded apartment to a large house. In 1866 his school was granted an imperial charter. Its faculty was not so brilliant as the one Yelena Pavlovna and Anton had gathered in the northern capital, but Nikolay had originally intended to have one first-rank star besides himself in the cast and had invited Serov to become his harmony instructor. That difficult man accepted. Then, on November 6, 1865 (Piotr Ilyich was again in the audience), Serov's second opera, *Rognyeda,* had a tempestuously successful *première* at the Marinsky in St. Petersburg. Moscow, on the other hand, did not entirely share this enthusiasm. Serov was becoming a great figure in St. Petersburg. He notified Nikolay Rubinstein that he had changed his mind and would not proceed to Moscow to teach.

Nikolay, for once, was at a loss. He wrote to Anton, asking him to recommend someone to teach the theory of composition in not too academic a way, someone who would work hard. Anton replied that he was certain he had exactly the man, young Piotr Ilyich Tchaikovsky. Nikolay at once dispatched an invitation to the young man, who was only five years his junior. Either immediately or in a very short time Piotr Ilyich accepted the position at a monthly stipend of fifty rubles (twenty-five dollars), a smaller sum than he had been earning in St. Petersburg.

The school term that would complete Piotr Ilyich's formal musical education was not quite over. While still in St. Petersburg, he was very actively composing. From August to October 1865 he composed a String Quartet in B major, and put into shape an Overture in F major. The quartet incorporated the theme of a Little Russian song he had heard at Kamenka and had already arranged for singing.[1] It was played on November 11 by a student quartet at the Conservatory, the violist being Bessel. On November 26 Piotr Ilyich, despite appalling stage fright, made his debut as a conductor with the Overture. From October to December he worked on his graduation thesis, a cantata setting of the Schiller *Ode to Joy* that had supplied the text for the choral movement of Beethoven's Ninth Symphony. All this time he continued to be annoyed by fatigue and eye strain. Further, he began to doubt the wisdom of his choice to become a musician rather than remain a government clerk. One of his friends thereupon suggested that he return to government service as an inspector of meat. Piotr Ilyich decided to stick to music.

In September 1865, as though to convince himself, Piotr Ilyich wrote Alexandra Davidova that he was continually more certain that music was the only road for him. Shortly after that, his extremely strait financial condition made his assurance waver. He looked less and less healthy. He toyed again with the idea of trying to re-enter government service. But he kept at work. At last, on January 10, 1866, the day of the examination arrived. Piotr Ilyich was too terrified by the prospect of submitting to a viva-voce catechism in public to be present. This enraged Anton Rubinstein, who threatened to hold up the awarding of his diploma until he hewed to the line. The performance of the *Ode to Joy* cantata, however, was allowed to proceed. Two days after that, the young man was awarded his diploma *in absentia* and was given a silver medal.[2]

Individual reactions to the cantata were characteristic. Anton

---

[1] The theme turned up again in the *Scherzo in Russian Style* for piano which, with an *Impromptu*, make Tchaikovsky's opus 1.

[2] The citation listed his grades: "Theory of composition — excellent. Instrumentation — excellent. Orchestration — good. Pianoforte — very good. Conducting — satisfactory."

Rubinstein, rejecting Piotr Ilyich's request that it be performed by the Russian Musical Society, said that important changes would have to be made in it before it would be worthy to appear on programs with the works of Piotr Petrovich Sokolsky, Kristianovich, Balakirev, and Rimsky-Korsakov. Serov did not like it at all. The young nationalist admirers of Glinka and followers of Dargomizhsky — Balakirev, Rimsky-Korsakov, and Cui — liked it even less. Cui was more denunciatory than usual, continuing to hurl abuse at the cantata three months after its unique performance. "In short," he summed up, "I shall state only that composers like Reinthaler and Volkmann will perhaps rejoice over Mr. Tchaikovsky's Cantata, and shout: 'Our number is increased.'"

Laroche felt otherwise. Piotr Ilyich had left for Moscow. Writing to him there, his friend said: "I consider yours the greatest musical talent of Russia's future, stronger and more original than Balakirev's, loftier and more creative than Serov's, much more refined than Rimsky-Korsakov's. . . . Your own original creations probably will not appear for another five years. But those ripe and classic works will surpass anything we have heard since Glinka. To conclude: I do not honour you so much for what you have accomplished as for what the strengthened vitality of your genius one day *will* accomplish. The proofs you have given up to now are but solemn pledges to outdo all your contemporaries."

Little information survives about the composition of a Sonata in C sharp minor for piano that Piotr Ilyich completed before leaving St. Petersburg for Moscow. The manuscript bore the date of its completion, 1865. After his death — in 1900 — it was published by Jürgenson. At once it lapsed back into obscurity, a state from which no pianists see fit to lift it. Yet it is, for a youthful work of obviously imitative quality, of real interest. It is on a big scale: its four orthodox movements occupy forty-eight pages. It is eminently pianistic: Piotr Ilyich's ideas had not yet evolved to the stage in which they would fit the keyboard badly or not at all. It shows the effects of studying Schumann, by no means a good teacher for an aspiring composer of sonatas. Here and there in it, separated by pages of earnest mechanical development, are passages out of which the mature Piotr Ilyich could grow, curves of speechlike melody shored up on richly harmonized structures. Curiously, the sonata begins in C sharp minor and ends in D flat major.

It was with a painful wrench that Piotr Ilyich tore himself away

from St. Petersburg. Despite its dampness, its iron cold, its un-
healthfulness, it contained his father and stepmother and Anton
Rubinstein. He had enjoyed his first small successes there. There,
too, were Laroche, his best friend, and his beloved twin brothers,
of whom Modest in particular was now becoming an intimate and
confidant rather than a younger charge. Modest was developing
a character and interests much closer to his own than those of
anyone else in the family. But Moscow meant opportunity and
position. Piotr Ilyich arrived there on January 18, 1866, by train,
and was met at the station by Nikolay Rubinstein. As Piotr Ilyich
had grown a full clipped beard some time after 1863, while Rubinstein, who was short and stocky, wore only a moustache and small
whiskers under his lower lip, the two young men must have appeared to be exact contemporaries.

The day after his arrival in Moscow, Piotr Ilyich was installed in
a room at the Conservatory. Rubinstein gave him plenty to eat and
— probably, as he was Nikolay and not Anton — plenty to drink,
and improved his general appearance by presenting him with a
reasonably new frock coat that Wieniawski had left behind when
departing after a visit. During the week before his classes started,
Piotr Ilyich explored Moscow and met his colleagues. He went to
the Bolshoi and Maly Theatres, was introduced to Nikolay Dmitryevich Kashkin, and accustomed himself a little to Nikolay Rubinstein's tempestuous and convivial ways. Also he elaborated
sketches for an Overture in C minor and then orchestrated it. He
submitted it to Nikolay Rubinstein, who found it unsuitable for
performance by the Russian Musical Society. Piotr Ilyich thereupon sent it to Laroche, instructing him to ask Anton to perform it
in St. Petersburg. Neither Anton nor Anatoly Konstantinovich Lyadov, conductor of the opera concerts, would touch it. Years later
Piotr Ilyich came upon this unplayed and unpublished manuscript
and scrawled across its cover the words "terrible rubbish." [3]

Piotr Ilyich's co-workers at the Conservatory varied widely in
character and in attitude toward him. Nikolay Rubinstein had
married in 1855. His wife and her family proved unsympathetic
toward his music, and in particular toward his giving piano recitals,
and resented his lack of attention to her. The divorce had come in
1857. At the time of Piotr Ilyich's arrival in Moscow, Nikolay was

[3] The Overture in C minor was played for the first time at Voronezh in 1931,
during a concert conducted by K. S. Saradzhev.

in full sail on his stormy course of many hours of devoted work during the day, followed by long night hours of card-playing, drinking, and affairs with easy women. He demanded that those of his teachers whom he liked should be his boon companions after hours. He liked the retiring and awkward Piotr Ilyich and joyfully believed that he had found in him talent for conviviality, marked by a capacity for alcohol almost equal to his own. Friendship, however, did not swerve his musical standards, and for a long time his reaction to Piotr Ilyich as a composer was dubious and unhelpful. Piotr Ilyich, on his part, at first regarded Nikolay the musician as inferior to his brother Anton, an opinion he later modified.

Nikolay Dmitryevich Kashkin, one year Piotr Ilyich's senior, was happily married. He and his wife charmed the newcomer, who gladly spent hours of carefree time with them. Kashkin was a talented pianist and had already some reputation as a critic. Nikolay Rubinstein sometimes bowed to his opinions, and it is probable that Piotr Ilyich sought his advice. Also at the Conservatory was Konstantin Karlovich Albrecht, an able cellist and choral conductor, son of a German immigrant who had conducted at the St. Petersburg imperial opera.

The tuition fee for students in Piotr Ilyich's class was set at three rubles (equivalent to a dollar and a half) per month. On January 25, 1866 he gave his first lecture, during all of which he stood in a clammy sweat of stage fright. The lessons soon went well, however, and it was evident to all that he was an adequate, if not inspired teacher. He began to feel more at home in Moscow, though he wrote to Alexandra Davidova that it would be a long time before he could contemplate "without horror" the idea of staying in that strange city "for years — perhaps for ever." He was enjoying *Pickwick Papers* (in Russian). He told Modest and Anatoly that Dickens had much in common with Gogol, but lacked the Russian's profundity. He was working at a new composition for orchestra and a manual of instructions for the Conservatory teachers, and was nibbling at the idea of composing an opera, rejecting one after the other suggestions about librettos made by Nikolay Rubinstein.

Piotr Ilyich paid several visits to a family named Tarnovsky, a group that included "two lovely nieces." One of these girls he described to Modest as "the loveliest I ever saw in my life. I am very much taken with her," he added, "which causes Rubinstein to be a perfect nuisance. The moment we arrive at her home, the rest begin to tease me, and leave me alone with her. She is nicknamed 'Mufka,' and I am wondering whether I dare to call her that too. I only need to know her a little better. Rubinstein has also been in love with her, but his sentiments have now cooled." Shortly afterwards this young lady married an army officer.

During February, at Nikolay Rubinstein's request, Piotr Ilyich reworked his Overture in F major, originally scored for the small St. Petersburg Conservatory orchestra, turning it into a work for full symphony orchestra. On March 16 Nikolay Rubinstein conducted it, and Piotr Ilyich was greeted with loud applause. After the concert Rubinstein gave a supper at which the happy, flustered composer had to face a prolonged ovation. For the moment Moscow was turning toward him the pleasantest of its many faces. With that encouragement he began to put down some preliminary ideas for the symphony he had been considering. It was to be called *Zymniye Gryozi* (*Winter Reveries*). On April 5, in a café, he picked up a copy of the *Sankt-Peterburgskiye Vyedomosti* and read his first press notice, César Cui's vehemently nasty review of his *Ode to Joy* cantata ("the composer Tchaikovsky is altogether weak").

"When I read this terrible judgment, I hardly know what happened to me," he told A. I. Brullova.[4] "Everything went black before my eyes, my head began to spin, and I ran out of the café like a madman. I was unaware of what I was doing, where I was going. The whole day long I aimlessly wandered the streets, repeating to myself: 'I'm sterile, insignificant, I shall never amount to anything, I have no talent.' And the thought of going home, where Father would begin to prove how right he was in opposing my musical career, oppressed and tortured me."

The golden age that many liberals had hoped would follow in the wake of Alexander II's reforms had not come. Public opinion had begun to make its weight felt more than the Tsar conceived to be fitting, and he veered back to the repressive, tyrannous methods of his father. As a result, revolutionary movements began to move silently in dark places. On April 16, 1866 a terrorist named Karakozov fired a revolver at the Tsar, but failed to assassinate him. Rumour instantly made Karakozov a Pole. Feeling blazed up

---

[4] Quoted from the unpublished recollections of A. I. Brullova.

against his supposed countrymen. The following day Piotr Ilyich went to the Bolshoi Theatre to hear a performance of *A Life for the Tsar,* in which Poles play a villainous role. He immersed himself in a copy of the score as the opera unrolled, and utterly failed to hear or see the audience's unrest, which was turning the performance into an anti-Polish demonstration. Even when his neighbours began to mutter against him, disliking this silent man interested in the music and not in shouting against Poland, he kept his mind and eyes on the score. Finally his ejection from the theatre was angrily and vociferously demanded. He looked up, found himself the centre of unfriendly attention, did not know why, and rushed from the theatre as the Tsar's portrait was being brought onto the stage.

Piotr Ilyich became further involved in imperial affairs because of the approaching marriage of the Tsarevich (Alexander III) to Princess Dagmar of Denmark. Rubinstein suggested that he compose, for performance during the couple's visit to Moscow, an overture incorporating the Danish national hymn. This commission, added to his classwork, labour on other compositions, and the hours necessarily devoted to Rubinstein's after-work gaiety and his own social life, began to tell on Piotr Ilyich's health. He suffered from insomnia, extreme nervousness, and throbbing pains in the head. He referred to these last as "apoplectic symptoms" and as "strokes," but there is no sign that they were anything more alarming than any pain in the head. Yet he wrote Anatoly that he was convinced that he would die and leave his symphony unfinished.

The young instructor was widening his acquaintance. One of his new friends was the much admired dramatist Ostrovsky. More important to his personal life was a man named K. N. de-Lazari, who introduced him into the country home of Vladimir Petrovich Begichev, intendant of the Moscow imperial opera. This handsome elderly rake was married to an ex-singer whose past was almost as crowded with romantic episode as his own. She had been married before, and her two young sons, Konstantin and Vladimir Shilovsky, were attractive boys (Vladimir, the younger, was fourteen) and already amateurs of music and literature. Piotr Ilyich formed a strong attachment to the members of this curious household. Vladimir Shilovsky later became for a time his favourite pupil and chosen travelling companion, and Konstantin assisted him in evolving a libretto from Pushkin's *Yevgeny Onyegin.*

On May 13 Anton Rubinstein conducted Piotr Ilyich's reorchestrated Overture in F major at a public concert at the Mikhailovsky Palace in St. Petersburg. Apukhtin wrote his friend that the piece had been well received and had pleased him personally very much. Performance in Moscow, and to applause, had been happiness for Piotr Ilyich, but performance under the baton of Anton Rubinstein was another thing. It meant the success he valued most. Shortly after he had received this news, he wrote Alexandra Davidova that his health had improved. For a while it had been perfect, and he had been kept awake by insomnia only one night. Later his "strokes" began to recur. He had begun, that is, the orchestration of his *Winter Reveries* Symphony, the composition that caused him more anguish than any other he ever wrote.

Piotr Ilyich had remained in Moscow steadily since his arrival there on January 18, except for one visit of a few days to St. Petersburg in early April and very brief excursions into the country. He had been planning to spend the summer at Kamenka with the Davidovs, taking the twins with him. But the condition of the highroads would not permit the journey by diligence, and his pocketbook would not allow for a private post chaise. So Anatoly was sent directly from St. Petersburg to Kamenka, while Modest accompanied Piotr Ilyich on a visit to Lyov Davidov's mother in the country near Peterhof not far from the northern capital. It was good to be again with Yelizaveta and Vera Davidova, even better to be able, once in a while, to visit his father, who was staying near by. There was a piano at the Davidovs', and Piotr Ilyich sat at it constantly, playing over Schumann's First and Fourth symphonies and *Das Paradies und die Peri,* as well as Mendelssohn's "Italian" Symphony, some of them as duets with the Davidovs. The surrounding scenery was attractive. They made a trip to the romantically beautiful shores of Lake Ladoga. Next to having gone to Kamenka, it was the best sort of vacation. Happy at first, Piotr Ilyich began to work steadily at the *Winter Reveries* Symphony, and all pleasure was dispelled.

In the summer of 1866 Piotr Ilyich Tchaikovsky was a composer of narrow experience. He was inadequately prepared for the composition of a full-fledged symphony. He had to labour at it in the most nerve-racking way. Soon his days and nights were full of nothing but musical materials that would not behave as he ordered, ideas that would not mature, melodic turns and harmonic progressions and formal developments in rebellion against his brain and his hand. All his nervous symptoms returned intensified. Near the end of July he was prostrated by a breakdown of his nervous system. He suffered from terrifying hallucinations — nightmares while he slept and a dragging sensation of dread when he awoke. A physician was able to quiet him somewhat. This man told anxious friends and relatives that Piotr Ilyich had been on the edge of losing his mind and was still in a grave condition. Complete rest was mandatory, and there was to be no more composing for the time being. Piotr Ilyich was so frightened by what had happened that he abandoned night composing for ever.

For an overworked, hypersensitive, and neurasthenic young man of twenty-six to have a nervous breakdown is not extraordinary. In the case of Piotr Ilyich, however, it requires, not an explanation, for that is impossible, but the putting forward of possible causes. No record survives of his having had a serious illness except the quite unbelievable diagnosis that the after effect of his early measles had been spinal meningitis. He appeared to be of vigorous physique, and was able to drink exceptionally large amounts of alcohol without noticeable harm. Yet he suffered intermittently from what he called his "apoplectic strokes" (they were not) and "heart cramps." He was terrorized by hallucinations and phobias more awful to him than any reality. He was clearly neurasthenic. It is established that he was homosexual and unhappy about it. The facts and hints make it very difficult not to guess that the chief cause of his mental tempests and nervous disorders lay in a combination of difficult sexual repression, fruitless attempts to fall normally in love, and omnipresent fear that an unfriendly and unsympathetic society would discover his secret nature and true erotic tendencies.

No records survive from this epoch to prove that Piotr Ilyich at times overcame his repression, sense of guilt, and fear and followed his homosexual yearnings to their natural expression. The names of his lovers are, of course, lacking. It is likely that Vladimir Shilovsky became one of his young manhood and his nephew Vladimir Lvovich Davidov one of his old age. It is also possible that, like many homosexuals, he found numerous fleeting partners for his passion. Gossip connected him with boys studying at the Conservatory. Conceivably, it would be interesting to have their names. But their names would not alter the important fact: that his erotic nature and his struggle with it deeply dyed his whole mature life, helping to lend his personality and some of his music a sombre, sensual, introspective, and self-pitying hue that at times marks him off sharply from his countrymen.

For it is a provable fact that Russian music is not predominantly sombre, sensual, introspective, or self-pitying. It is, in truth, the most objective music imaginable. It is vigorous — bumptious almost, full of gay dance rhythms, illustrated with sharply coloured pictures. Mussorgsky was at his greatest when depicting individuals and groups as realistically, inclusively, and objectively as music can depict them. What sadness there is in his music is awareness of the inherent sadness of man's fate. Rimsky-Korsakov is all picture-book glitter — perhaps escape from a painful life, but no direct projection of it. Borodin and Balakirev portray the characters of varied Russian peoples as Mussorgsky did, though with less power, or make absolute music of the least self-expressive sort. Neither Stravinsky nor Prokofiev nor Shostakovich beats his breast or cries out his pain. Tchaikovsky himself in an overwhelming majority of his compositions is joyous, recklessly splashed with brilliant colour, on the verge of the dance. It would be possible to arrange many concerts of his music in which the morbid, wound-probing note that uninformed critics have taken to be his signature would not be sounded a single time.

Foolishly and falsely we have been taught to expect Russian art to be sad and sombre. Long acquaintance with it at first weakens and then overturns the results of such blind teaching. Unless we are automatically to find bereavement and misery in every minor chord or church mode, we shall find Russian music, far from being introspective, largely concerned with the evocation and description of events and things and people outside the composers' own minds and psyches. It is true that much Russian music of the past seventy-five years has had a note of melancholy, particularly in the works of minor men like Arensky, Glazunov and Rachmaninoff. But that note is precisely the heritage of Piotr Ilyich Tchaikovsky at his most personal, at those moments when he seemed able to translate his hopelessness and tragedy directly into the language of music, without the need of intervening thought.

Piotr Ilyich was unable to finish the *Winter Reveries* Symphony during the summer of 1866. He decided to submit it unfinished to the two masters of his student days, Anton Rubinstein and Zaremba. They could, if it pleased them, see that it was performed by the St. Petersburg Russian Musical Society. But they condemned it without mercy, selecting for bitterest disapproval the exact features of the composition Piotr Ilyich most valued. They demanded numerous revisions, which he reluctantly undertook in November. It was the old gap between generations, with defenders of the musical manners of their own youth on one side and a proponent of new manners on the other. Piotr Ilyich's First Symphony, which today sounds inordinately tame, tentative, and faded, was too modern for Anton Rubinstein and Zaremba.

Piotr Ilyich began to feel that he was received with more sympathetic understanding in Moscow than in St. Petersburg. His homesickness for the northern capital began to leave him. He started to think of Moscow as home, despite the presence in St. Petersburg of the twins, who were again living with their father. He had a helpful, if trying friend in Nikolay Rubinstein, stimulating colleagues in Kashkin and Albrecht, intimate friends in the Tarnovskys and the Begichevs. He returned to Moscow eagerly and found it good. His salary now amounted to the equivalent of six hundred dollars per year. On September 13, 1866 the Conservatory reopened in larger quarters. The fashionable Muscovites turned out en masse for its dedication. There was a banquet. Piotr Ilyich, conquering his shyness, made an eloquent toast to Anton Rubinstein and the St. Petersburg Conservatory and then thoroughly enjoyed the abundant food and drink. He wanted Glinka's to be the first music played in the new building, and so began the impromptu after-dinner concert by himself playing from memory the Overture to *Ruslan and Lyudmila*.

On the 9th of November 1866 the Tsarevich was married to Dagmar of Denmark, sister to the future Queen Alexandra of England. Piotr Ilyich had completed his *Festival Overture on the Danish National Hymn* within the designated time and had dedicated it to the Tsarevich. During the imperial couple's ceremonial visit to Moscow it was performed in their presence. Pleased by this well-turned compliment to his wife, the Tsarevich presented the composer with a set of gold and turquoise studs. Finding these far above his customary style of dress, Piotr Ilyich at once sold them to one of his colleagues. The *Festival Overture* is an excelling piece of musical joinery, for which reason its composer continued to admire it beyond its deserts. It could be played today, should a suitably Danish occasion arise. No other reason would suffice for reviving it.

The *Winter Reveries* Symphony, unperformed, continued to fret Piotr Ilyich. It was still St. Petersburg's rather than Moscow's approval that he craved. Possibly Nikolay Rubinstein could have been wheedled into putting it on a Musical Society program, but Piotr Ilyich allowed only the third movement to be heard in Moscow, on December 22, 1866. This alternately skittish and banal section is of interest because it contains, as its trio, the first of those orchestral waltzes of which he wrote so many, and so many better than this. Piotr Ilyich reworked and completed the four movements and again tried to persuade someone in St. Petersburg to play the entire symphony. Again Anton Rubinstein rejected it curtly, despite the revisions that had been made along lines suggested by Zaremba and himself. Finally Nikolay Rubinstein conducted the two middle movements in St. Petersburg in February 1867. There was brief handclapping that could hardly be called applause. Curiously, the beautiful second movement, an evocative "adagio cantabile" headed: "Desolate country, country of mists," did not instantly arouse enthusiasm. It is scored for only muted strings, woodwinds, and horns, and in it there is a faint tincture of unmistakable Tchaikovsky, diluted with contemporary clichés, but recognizable and individual to this day. It is adept musical painting, suffused with the calm melancholy of many heavily shadowed landscapes. At last, on February 15, 1868, in Moscow, the Russian Musical Society, conducted by Nikolay Rubinstein, performed the whole symphony. It was an undeniable success. The audience shouted for its composer, who, in a spasm of embarrassment, appeared on the platform in unpressed clothes, squeezing his hat in his hands. This time the songlike second movement had made its effect: writing to Modest and Anatoly, Piotr Ilyich said that it had pleased most.

Despite its reception, the First Symphony was not played in Moscow again for sixteen years. It has never been popular anywhere. James Gibbons Huneker, in 1899, still found the instrumentation modern, but discovered Mendelssohn's "saccharine volubility . . . saccharine cantabile . . . damnable fluency" in it. The finale, for him, "smacked of the Calmuck," but the symphony as a whole was "monotonously in the key of G minor." Of the opening movement — *Winter Reverie on a Journey* — he added that the slush must have been ankle-deep. Ernest Newman was more apposite when, in 1901, he described the First Symphony as "one desperate attempt . . . to look at music and life through the eyes of a formalist." The cause of the symphony's failure was the cause of the unnerving struggle its composition had been to Piotr Ilyich: he could not write a symphony that would simultaneously stay within the formal bounds of earlier symphonies — thus pleasing Anton Rubinstein — and contain music he felt inside himself and had to get out.

On November 20, 1866, writing to Anatoly that he was about to make the suggested revisions in the First Symphony, Piotr Ilyich added: "Then perhaps an opera. There is a possibility that Ostrovsky himself will write a libretto for The Voivode." Ostrovsky had been a law student and a government clerk. His experience in law courts, however, had spurred him to write the first of the satiric social plays that made him famous. During the repressive reign of Nicholas I he had been dismissed from government service because of the liberal attitude implicit in his writings, and had been under surveillance by the secret police, though the Tsar had said of one of his plays: "This is not a drama, but a lesson." Alexander II's regime found a more useful place for Ostrovsky, sending him into the territories around the upper Volga to compile a report on conditions there. In 1866, at the age of forty-three, he was a man of national fame, and Piotr Ilyich rightly felt that a libretto drawn by him from one of his plays would be good fortune.

Ostrovsky agreed to cut down the play's prologue and five acts to usable operatic length. By March 17, 1867 the text for the first act was in Piotr Ilyich's hands. Three days later the composition of the music was begun. It was interrupted immediately by work on a piano piece. Originally called *Caprice,* this became the *Scherzo in Russian Style* of opus 1. It was played by Nikolay Rubinstein on April 12 at an extraordinary session of the Russian Musical Society. His superb technique made light of its very unpianistic difficulties, wide skips and blocks of octave-width chords. When this piece was complete, Piotr Ilyich turned back to work on Act I of *The Voivode.* To his anguished fury, he could not find the Ostrovsky text. For weeks he intermittently kept searching for the lost sheaf of papers, but never found them.

Early in June, Piotr Ilyich bravely set out to spend the summer in Finland, taking Anatoly with him. He had innocently believed that the few rubles (equivalent to about fifty dollars) he had in his pockets would carry the two of them through the summer. They reached Vyborg, where they soon found themselves with funds for only a few days. It would be easy, they thought, to borrow money from their father, so they took the first boat to St. Petersburg. Ilya Petrovich had left for the Urals and his own summer holiday. With almost the last kopecks they had, they bought steamer tickets to Hapsal, on the Baltic coast in Estonia. They had to take low-class passage, and nearly froze during the night, but were buoyed up by assurance that Mme Davidova and her daughters would be at Hapsal to welcome them. This proved to be justified, and they settled down happily for the rest of the summer.

Ostrovsky began to rewrite the libretto of *The Voivode* from memory. Parts of it reached Piotr Ilyich in Hapsal, and he rushed eagerly to work on his first opera. He was soon pestering the dramatist by mail with requests and suggestions for alterations in the plot, the characters, and the order of scenes, the result of which was that Ostrovsky abandoned the project after completing one act. Other activities interrupted Piotr Ilyich's work on the opera. He conceived the idea of memorializing his visit to Hapsal in a piano composition to be dedicated to Vera Vasilyevna Davidova. This *Souvenir of Hapsal*, published as opus 2, was divided into three sections. The first, *Ruins of a Château*, is sombre, a little like a fragment of Mussorgsky's *Pictures at an Exhibition*. The second, a revised composition of Piotr Ilyich's student period, is a commonplace Scherzo. The third, however, covering only three pages of engraved score, was to make the name of Piotr Ilyich Tchaikovsky internationally known before any of his best works had been heard outside Moscow and St. Petersburg. It was the F-major *Song without Words*, destined, like Anton Rubinstein's *Melody* in the same key, to become an unmitigatedly popular salon piece.

Although Piotr Ilyich wrote Alexandra Davidova that many events of his stay at Hapsal had convinced him that he was nurturing the seeds of "a disease called misanthropy," and that he was often overwhelmed by spells of intense hatred for people, he admitted that *The Voivode* was growing satisfactorily. He reorchestrated his *Dances of the Serving Maids*, turning them into a second-act ballet for the opera. On August 26 he left Hapsal, feeling that his vacation had been mostly well used. He spent one week in St. Petersburg, leaving Anatoly there, and went back to Moscow, which he had begun to consider his home. His friend Laroche was there, having accepted Nikolay Rubinstein's bid to the Conservatory. St. Petersburg was constantly becoming less attractive to Piotr Ilyich. He had suffered Anton Rubinstein's disdain too often and had almost completely revised his opinion of the comparative worth of the two famous brothers. Also, the nationalist followers of Glinka and Dargomizhsky — Cui, Borodin, Balakirev, Mussorgsky, and Rimsky-Korsakov — supported by the powerful critical pen of Vladimir Vasilyevich Stasov, had begun to bear great weight in the musical affairs of the northern capital. Piotr Ilyich was separated from them, not so much by their expressed aims as by their constant attacks on the Rubinsteins and their musical styles and techniques, attacks he necessarily felt to include his own works. In June, furthermore, Anton Rubinstein, tired of routine and at loggerheads with some of his staff on the matter of graduating students he thought unworthy, resigned as director of the St. Petersburg Conservatory and of its concerts. Zaremba then headed the school, but the concerts were taken over by the nationalist leader, agitator of the Five, Mily Alexeyevich Balakirev. His family aside, there was now nothing to draw Piotr Ilyich back to St. Petersburg.

Early in October, Piotr Ilyich was still urging Ostrovsky to complete the libretto of *The Voivode*. When it became evident that the busy dramatist would be interminably delayed in this work, Piotr Ilyich completed the libretto himself. Between text and music he was constantly at work on it, and everything he remembered and heard that could be tortured to fit it was metamorphosed into a number for the opera. He passed a day with Laroche in suburban Kuntsevo, heard a peasant girl singing, noted down the song, and incorporated it into *The Voivode* when he reached home.[5] By early December, he had finished the third act. On December 14 Nikolay Rubinstein conducted the dances from the opera. They were received with enthusiasm and were twice repeated in Moscow that winter.

The date of Piotr Ilyich's meeting with Piotr Ivanovich Jürgenson is unknown. This far-sighted man, four years the composer's senior, had established a music-publishing business in Moscow in

---

[5] This folksong, known as *The Nightingale* (not the melody used by Alabyev), was later transferred by Tchaikovsky to another opera, *The Oprichnik*.

1861, starting out with much needed inexpensive editions of the classics. In the days when Piotr Ilyich was all but unknown, Jürgenson began to publish his compositions. Later, influenced by the same justified assurance in victory for his own tastes, he performed the same office for the Five. He helped found the Moscow Conservatory. He became a member of the directorate of the Russian Musical Society. He was a genial, liberal, and broadly intelligent man, and his house prospered. When he died in 1904, leaving the firm of P. Jürgenson to his sons, he had published all but a little of the best music composed in Russia for forty years, including practically all of Tchaikovsky. Writing about 1900, Modest stated that the Jürgenson fireproof vaults contained some 200,000 engraving plates, more than 70,000 of them devoted to Piotr Ilyich. Jürgenson's friendship, advice, and highly honourable, but not inflexible financial dealings were of major help to the composer all during the last part of his life.

The even tenor of Moscow days was ruffled late in December 1867 by the arrival from St. Petersburg of one of the recognized great among composers, Hector Berlioz. This aging and embittered man had been invited to Russia by Dargomizhsky and Balakirev, who regarded him as a god. Twenty years earlier, in the incandescent splendour of his maturity, Berlioz had visited Russia through the influence of Glinka and had been received with acclaim by the aristocratic musical public headed by Prince Vladimir Odoevsky. On that earlier visit he had earned large sums by giving concerts. Now he was, Piotr Ilyich wrote, "an aged and broken man, persecuted both by destiny and by his fellows." The magic of his name and his conducting still wove a spell, though his famous red hair had turned grey. His concerts all but repeated the successes of 1847. Piotr Ilyich intensely admired Berlioz as "the personification of selfless work and burning love for art," and called him "a noble and energetic fighter against ignorance, stupidity, vulgarity, and routine."

Piotr Ilyich was shy of approaching Berlioz because of the sponsorship of Dargomizhsky and Balakirev. Nevertheless, when Moscow musicians honoured the visitor at a banquet, Piotr Ilyich agreed to perform what was for him a terrifying duty, a true act of homage. He would make a speech. Rising at the banquet table, he spoke in French, describing with honest enthusiasm those of Berlioz's accomplishments that seemed to him most honourable.

It was a good and well-received flight of oratory. Shortly thereafter Berlioz returned to Paris. Little more than one year later, on March 8, 1869, he died.

During Berlioz's visit to Moscow, Stasov, the brilliant critical apologist for Dargomizhsky and the Five, was there. Piotr Ilyich met him. In January 1868 Balakirev also visited Moscow. Piotr Ilyich met him too. From these two men he gathered the impression that the St. Petersburgers were not necessarily his enemies, but were truly and deeply interested in him and in his music. Although he resented their efforts to convert him to the nationalist creed, he began to establish friendlier relations with them. By February 2 he had relaxed his antipathy to them sufficiently to send the dances from *The Voivode* to Balakirev with the request that he conduct them in St. Petersburg.

During February, Piotr Ilyich embarked on the orchestration of the third act of *The Voivode*. He was impatient to be done with it, as he already was seriously considering a second opera. The successful first complete performance of his *Winter Reveries* Symphony at this time was balm to an old wound, especially as he had deleted from it the changes made at the suggestion of Anton Rubinstein and Zaremba.[6] He was in high spirits and therefore permitted himself a rash step: he agreed to conduct a public performance of the *Voivode* dances at a benefit concert for the relief of victims of a terrible winter famine. Kashkin thus describes that occasion, Piotr Ilyich's debut as a professional conductor:

When I went backstage to discover how the debutant was feeling, he informed me that, to his own great surprise, he was not at all nervous. I returned to my seat before his turn came. When Tchaikovsky actually came out on the platform, I saw that he was quite *distrait*. He emerged timidly, as though he would have liked to hide or run away. When he mounted the podium, he looked like a man in desperate anguish. He forgot his composition entirely: he did not see the score

[6] The First Symphony was published exactly as Tchaikovsky originally composed it except for part of the first movement. Zaremba had strongly objected to the second theme, and Tchaikovsky had substituted another for it. When he decided to return the music to its original condition, he had completely forgotten the theme he had taken out and was never able to reconstruct it. The present second theme is therefore the one he inserted to please Zaremba.

before him, and gave all the indications at the wrong times. Fortunately, the musicians knew the music so thoroughly that they paid no attention to his wrong indications and got through the dances quite satisfactorily in spite of him. After the concert Piotr Ilyich told me that in his fright he had had the sensation that his head was going to fall off his shoulders unless he held it tightly in place.

Kashkin's last sentence is meant literally. Piotr Ilyich had been so completely convinced that his head was about to fall off that he had reached up with one hand and held onto his beard. It is little wonder that he could not conduct. It is even less wonder that he was so thoroughly scared by his podium debut that ten years had to pass before he could be coaxed to conduct again. There was nothing rational to cause his fear: he eventually became a more than passable conductor. It was the unreasoning panic of a man with a deeply rooted fear of his fellows and a gnawing, continuous doubt of his own talents and abilities.

The concert of March 2, 1868 was important to Piotr Ilyich for another reason. Among the compositions associated with his dances on the program was a *Fantasia on Serbian Themes* by Rimsky-Korsakov. Six days later, in a periodical called *Entr'acte,* a critic who signed himself "Stranger" spoke of Piotr Ilyich's dances as having "loftiness of aim . . . masterly conception and handling of the themes, great taste in the orchestration and use of folk colour." Continuing, the reviewer thrust aside Rimsky-Korsakov's *Fantasia* with the adjectives "colourless and inanimate." Piotr Ilyich was pleased by the praise of his own work, but enraged by the undeserved dispraise of Rimsky-Korsakov's. He had learned to admire the *Fantasia* during rehearsals and had conceived a feeling of respect for its composer. He wrote a lengthy criticism of the *Fantasia,* an article full of understanding praise, and sent it to a periodical called *Sovremennaya Lyetopis,* in which it appeared in March. Piotr Ilyich's debut as a critic caused a small sensation in Moscow; in St. Petersburg it was hailed with joy. Had a heathen been converted to nationalism, perhaps even to the Pan-Slavic movement of which the *Fantasia* was a result? At any rate, a member of the Rubinstein clique had raised a clear voice in support of a member of the Five. Every nuance of Piotr Ilyich's critique was discussed with grave seriousness in the Dargomizhsky-Balakirev circle, while "Stranger" answered it in vain.

Before Piotr Ilyich's article had been published, Balakirev had

written him that the dances from *The Voivode* would be performed that season.[7] Everything at once increased his feeling of
friendly curiosity about the St. Petersburg group. He spent his
Easter vacation in St. Petersburg with his father. While there, he
was taken several times to the inmost temple of the nationalists,
the house in which the bedridden Dargomizhsky[8] was working
against time and death to complete *The Stone Guest*. With an attitude like that of some young German composers toward the
music of Liszt and Wagner, the members of the Five looked to
this work to be the revealed scripture of their religion, the Russian *Zukunftsmusik*. Piotr Ilyich became friendly with Balakirev,
Cui, Stasov, and Rimsky-Korsakov, but never had more than superficial contacts with Borodin and Mussorgsky. He learned to appreciate some of the compositions of the Five, but could never accept
them as a school or subscribe to their rules, tenets, and regulations.
They, on their side, treated him with respect, keeping their well-
deserved right to appraise him differently from composition to
composition.

Piotr Ilyich never had sympathy for music (least of all, his own)
that was not technically smooth, and was consequently always being exasperated by roughnesses, particularly in Mussorgsky. Except for the mature Rimsky-Korsakov, the Five were equally out
of sympathy with contemporary music that was technically smooth
but neither overtly Russian nor overtly of some other national
school, and were consequently irritated by the numerous minor
compositions in which Piotr Ilyich's fluency worked by itself.
For each other's most valuable attributes, whether implied or cre-
atively expressed, all concerned had intelligent and sympathetic
understanding. The nationalists played Tchaikovsky in St. Petersburg; he became their unofficial ambassador to the Moscow branch
of the Russian Musical Society.

On April 28, writing from Moscow to Alexandra Davidova, Piotr
Ilyich had something more personal than the Five to discuss. "I
spent the time in St. Petersburg very pleasantly. I am troubled by
only one thing — Vera [Vera Vasilyevna Davidova]. . . . I quite
see how all this ought to end. But what can I do if I sense that my

[7] The dances do not seem to have been performed in St. Petersburg before
February 6, 1869, and then in a concert conducted by Nikolay Rubinstein.
[8] This was not the first meeting of Dargomizhsky and Tchaikovsky. Begichev
had introduced them in his Moscow home some time earlier.

feeling for her would turn to hatred if the question of marriage between us ever became serious?" He was fond of his Vera, but did not want her too near. Marriage, when Piotr Ilyich considered it thoughtfully, must have seemed a prison equipped with torture chambers and cells for the starving of his inmost nature on unimaginable diets less nourishing and less savoury than bread and water.

Early in June, Piotr Ilyich travelled to western Europe with K. N. de-Lazari, Vladimir Shilovsky, and the boy's stepfather and guardian, Vladimir Begichev. He was to continue giving Vladimir Shilovsky music lessons. They visited Berlin. The party intended to make a grand tour of the beauty spots of central Europe. But Shilovsky, always delicate, showed unmistakable symptoms of tuberculosis, and they rushed him off to a renowned specialist in Paris. During this visit of two weeks Piotr Ilyich went often to both plays and operas. What impressed him about the French stage was "the skill by which effects are arrived at by the simplest means." Of the operas he wrote Alexandra Davidova: "I remarked no singer with an exceptional voice, and yet what fine performances! How carefully every detail is studied and thought out! What earnest care is given to each item, no matter how insignificant, that goes toward creating the overall effect! We have no concept of such performances." In August, Piotr Ilyich stopped to visit the Davidovs, Anatoly, and Modest at Sillamegi, near Narva. By the beginning of September he was again in Moscow. There he learned that his salary at the Conservatory had been increased to the equivalent of about seven hundred dollars per annum. He faced the season of 1868–9 with a refreshed mind.

V

WHEN Piotr Ilyich found himself facing the unfamiliar members of his first Conservatory class of the season, he was acutely embarrassed. He had forgotten the protective poise necessary for his teaching. His discomfort became so acute that he had to leave the classroom for ten minutes from fear that he would faint. It took him several days to become reaccustomed to routine. Stepan Alexandrovich Gedeonov, director of the imperial theatres, was in Moscow and had ordered the immediate institution of rehearsals of *The Voivode* for a *première* at the Bolshoi late in October. The first two rehearsals had been held before Piotr Ilyich was made aware that they were to start. Others were held intermittently up to the *première*, which occurred on February 11, 1869. Piotr Ilyich himself played the accompaniments on the piano at several of the early rehearsals.

On September 21 Piotr Ilyich went to the Bolshoi to the first performance given by a visiting Italian opera company headed by an impresario named Merelli.[1] The company had been in Moscow since the preceding spring, but only now did they get around to opening with a performance of Rossini's *Otello*. A young tenor named Roberto Stagno made an auspicious debut in the role of the Moor, initiating a career that was to carry him all over the world. The greatest applause, however, went to the Desdemona, Désirée Artôt. She was the granddaughter of a renowned French bandmaster, horn-player, guitarist, violinist, and singing teacher who had settled in Brussels. Her father had been an equally renowned horn-player and professor at the Brussels Conservatoire. Both Maurice and Jean Désiré had added Artôt to their true family name, Montagney. Born in Paris in 1835, Mlle Artôt had studied with Pauline Viardot-García, and had made her Opéra debut at twenty-three. As Desdemona she delighted Moscow, promised success to Merelli's company, and enchanted Piotr Ilyich Tchaikovsky.

[1] Probably the same Merelli who, at Milan in 1839, had staged *Oberto, Conte di Bonifacio*, the first opera of young Giuseppe Verdi.

Sixteen days after the performance of *Otello*, Piotr Ilyich was writing that Artôt had a magnificent personality, and that he had won her friendship. He was working on a symphonic poem to be called *Fate*, but his letters spoke more of Artôt than of it. The rehearsals of *The Voivode* were temporarily discontinued because Piotr Ilyich sensed that the presence of the Merelli troupe distracted the attention of the chorus and orchestra — and perhaps himself — too much. They would begin again when Merelli took his players away. Prince Vladimir Odoevsky noted in his diary: "Tchaikovsky seems to court Désirée Artôt a great deal."

During October, Piotr Ilyich composed for piano his opus 4, a *Waltz Caprice* dedicated to the pianist Anton Door. This is a lengthy, vacuous salon piece. But his opus 5, composed in November, also for piano, was the *Romance* in F minor dedicated to Artôt. This melodious trifle, long a favourite recital ornament with Nikolay Rubinstein, was to become as familiarly commonplace as the *Song without Words*. Rubinstein first played it at a benefit concert for poor students of the University of Moscow on December 20. On the same program the dances from *The Voivode* were played to clamorous applause.

Piotr Ilyich's feeling toward Désirée Artôt was infatuation. Laroche describes her as not good-looking. He adds, however, that "her charm was so great that she conquered all hearts and turned all heads as though she were the most beautiful of women." She was a dramatic soprano with enough low notes to sing mezzo roles, and with sufficient agility to sing roles starred with *colorature*. Laroche describes her voice as sounding more like an oboe than a flute, and adds that "everyone who heard it was fascinated and carried away." Many who knew her testify to her sparkling and probing intelligence, and Laroche confirmed the usual judgment when he wrote: "It is not too much to say that in the entire realm of music, through the entire gamut of lyric emotion, there was no idea or form of which this admirable artist was unable to give a poetic account. She was equally at home in tragic, comic, and farce roles."

It was this many-talented artist with whom Piotr Ilyich was infatuated. By January 1, 1869 he believed that she had agreed to marry him. Writing to his father on the 7th, he said:

As rumours of my engagement must have reached you, and you may feel hurt at my silence on the subject, I shall tell you the whole story. I made Artôt's acquaintance in the spring, but called on her only once, when I attended a supper given after her benefit. When she returned here in the autumn I did not call on her for an entire month. Then we met accidentally at a musical soirée. She expressed surprise that I had not called, and I promised to do so, a promise I should never have kept (because of my shyness with new friends) if Anton Rubinstein, stopping briefly in Moscow, had not dragged me to see her. After that I constantly received invitations, and fell into the habit of going to her house every day. Soon we began to feel a mutual glow of affection, and an understanding resulted immediately. Naturally, the question of marriage, which both of us desire, arose at once, and if nothing prevents it, our wedding will take place this summer. But the trouble is that there are several obstacles. First, there is her mother, who always stays with her and has a lot of influence over her daughter. She does not favour the marriage, considering me too young and probably fearing that I should expect her daughter to remain in Russia permanently. Secondly, my friends — Nikolay Rubinstein in particular — are trying everything to prevent my marriage. They insist that if I marry a famous singer I shall play the pitiful role of " his wife's husband"; that I shall live at her expense and follow her about Europe; and finally that I shall lose all chances for work, so that when my first love has cooled I shall have nothing but disillusionment and depression. The risk of such a catastrophe might perhaps be avoided if she would agree to abandon the stage and live in Russia. But she declares that despite all her love for me, she cannot make up her mind to abandon the profession that earns her such large sums and to which she has grown so accustomed . . . we have agreed that I am to visit her this summer at her country place (outside Paris), when our fate will be decided. If she will not consent to give up the stage, I, for my part, am not in a hurry to sacrifice my future; for I can see clearly that I shall give up the opportunity of making my own way if I blindly follow her around. You see, Papa, my situation is extremely difficult. On the one hand, I love her, heart and soul, feel that I cannot exist without her any longer; on the other hand, cool common sense tells me to weigh more carefully the misfortunes with which my friends threaten me. I shall await, dear one, your opinions on this matter.

Ilya Petrovich replied on January 10 with a sympathetic and comprehending letter full of the best advice: Piotr Ilyich should examine his feelings carefully, think things out, make up his mind, act decisively. A young man passionately in love would surely have taken it as a benediction of his desires. Piotr Ilyich, it may be assumed, was in love, but with the dazzling artist Désirée Artôt rather than with the woman herself. When the spell of her artistry was not spurring his passion, he wavered. Writing to Anatoly, he said: "As regards the love interlude in my life, which you know about . . . I am now very doubtful that I shall ever tie the hymeneal knot. Things have begun to go a little wrong. Later I shall tell you more about this, but now I haven't time."

He lacked time because his native passion was claiming him again: with the departure of Merelli's company, daily rehearsals of The Voivode had begun. He was also at work on sketches for a new opera. He had become interested in a collection of Russian folksongs edited by Balakirev, and had received permission to transpose twenty-five of them for piano duet. Early in February, Nikolay Rubinstein, conducting a concert of the St. Petersburg Russian Musical Society, included the dances from The Voivode on the program. He was beginning to realize that Piotr Ilyich Tchaikovsky, composer, might become one of the brightest stars in his cast at the Moscow Conservatory, outshining the lost Serov. Piotr Ilyich told Anatoly that though rehearsals of the opera were going badly,[2] everyone concerned was working hard and giving him reason to hope for satisfactory results. At one of these rehearsals Nikolay Rubinstein came up to him to gloat: news had come that while appearing in Warsaw Désirée Artôt had married a Spanish baritone named Mariano Padilla y Ramos. Piotr Ilyich turned pale. "Well," Rubinstein added, "wasn't I right when I told you she didn't need you as a husband? He's the right mate for her. But you — understand — you are needed by us, by Russia, and not as the servant of a famous foreigner." Piotr Ilyich turned away without answering and left the theatre.

A man of thirty wholly in love for the first time, and particularly a man of Piotr Ilyich's stormily emotional temperament, would hardly recover in a day or two from such brutal treatment by his beloved. The blow to his pride he might be able to overcome so rapidly, even to the point of smiling at his own discomfiture. But passion unsatisfied and love rejected die away less easily. Yet the

---

[2] An opera by a Russian composer was given only the small orchestra used for ballet, though the Italian operas had a full quota in the pit. Old sets and costumes were also deemed sufficient for the works of native composers. The finale of one act of The Voivode had to be curtailed in rehearsal because two of the singers could not master a passage in which two notes of equal length in one voice were to be sung against triplets in the other.

fact is that in a very few days Piotr Ilyich was back at the rehearsals, calm, completely absorbed in his work, apparently quite content. Once only he threshed out against what Artôt had done: he told Modest that it was necessary to know all the details of his relations with Artôt in order to realize fully how absurd her marriage was. But he had not even lost a friend, for he was to meet Désirée Artôt more than once in future years on the most pleasant terms. That Artôt still had the power to move him is proved by the fact that when she reappeared at the Bolshoi the following December to sing Marguerite in *Faust*, he sat rigid in his seat throughout the performance, opera glasses to his eyes, tears running down his cheeks. He thought then that she sang better than ever before.

No proof exists that Désirée Artôt had ever intended to marry Piotr Ilyich. That she liked him, felt affection for him, and enjoyed his companionship is certain. She had an almost instant appreciation of his talent. But she was far too worldly not to have realized that he would not do as a husband. While she remained in Moscow, she perhaps enjoyed playing the game of engagement with him, and that was all. It is idle to speculate what effect sincerity on her part, or a determination to marry her young Russian admirer, might have had on his career. Perhaps, and only perhaps, a woman of her intelligence and artistic sensibility could have metamorphosed him into a satisfactory and contented husband.[3] For him, however, fate had another sort of marriage in store.

February 1869 was memorable for Piotr Ilyich because of more than Artôt's defection. On the 11th of that month, at Moscow's Bolshoi Theatre, the *première* of *The Voivode* was well received. On the 27th his first large composition for orchestra after the *Winter Reveries* Symphony, the symphonic poem *Fate*, was conducted at a Russian Musical Society concert in Moscow by Nikolay Rubinstein.

Piotr Ilyich may well have considered *The Voivode* a brilliant success. The audience gave every sign of enthusiasm. Fifteen times they called the composer out on the stage, once to accept a floral wreath. The opera was repeated five days later. On the 18th Prince Vladimir Odoevsky, who had been unnerved by the odd sounds

---

[3] Désirée Artôt's marriage to Padilla y Ramos turned out well. He died in 1906, she in 1907. Their daughter, known as Lola Artôt de Padilla, achieved some fame as a singer. It is possible to hear her voice on old phonograph records.

produced by the Bolshoi's cymbals — they were dented — sent Piotr Ilyich a set in gratitude for "the masterly composition Voivode." By March 14 the opera had achieved five performances. Yet *The Voivode* was not a success. On February 21 in *Sovremennaya Lyetopis* Laroche attacked it savagely. He wrote that it wavered uncertainly between the Italian and German manners and wholly lacked the stamp of Russian style. He granted several separate numbers musical beauty, but asserted that the totality revealed the composer's small ability to solve problems of text and situation.

Piotr Ilyich was sharply offended by Laroche's review. Ivan Alexandrovich Klimenko, an architect and devoted musical amateur who admired the composer inordinately, wrote that the two men met the day after its appearance. "Did you receive my review, Piotr Ilyich?" Laroche inquired. "Yes," the enraged man replied, "I did receive it. I tore it up and threw it into the furnace as it deserved." He broke with Laroche on the spot and did not meet him on friendly terms again until two years had passed. It may be that the reviews kept the public away from *The Voivode*. More likely the opera itself had not succeeded and the first-night applause had been for Menshikova, or merely polite and unthinking. When the fifth performance proved to be the last demanded, Piotr Ilyich destroyed the score. All that survives of it is the Overture, one chorus, an entr'acte, and the dances.

Fate began with as much promise and fared little better. Nikolay Rubinstein conducted it at a Moscow Russian Musical Society concert on February 27. Piotr Ilyich himself said that the public seemed to like it. He was inclined, for the hour, to regard it as the best work he had accomplished, and added that this opinion was shared by others. He sent the score to St. Petersburg with the request that Balakirev conduct it there, adding: "I want to dedicate this work to you, but before doing so I should like to know that you do not find it utterly distasteful." Balakirev performed it on March 29. In the interval, however, Laroche's review of the Moscow performance had appeared. It continued the bitter, seemingly personal tone of his criticism of *The Voivode*, stating that "instead of a gloomy monologue of disillusionment, it resembles a battle, an uprising, or a cataclysm of the elements." On April 13 Cui's criticism of the St. Petersburg performance was scarcely more welcome, despite its modicum of praise. "Written in a completely free form," he decided, "and a stranger to hackneyed mannerisms, it arouses great interest from beginning to end." He was more acute in his summary: "As a whole, however, *Fate* creates a curious impression because the gloom of the first part, the beauty of the Andante, and the comic caricature of the Allegro cannot be reconciled, and mystify us as to Tchaikovsky's intention."

Most interesting of the reactions to *Fate* was Balakirev's. His letter at once reveals much of the Five's official attitude toward music, shows that Balakirev was inclined to take Piotr Ilyich's talent as proved, and displays his own curiously didactic and mandatory mind:

Your Fate has been played, and I venture to hope that the performance was not bad — at least, everyone appeared to be satisfied with it. There was little applause, because, I think, of the hideous crash at the close. The composition itself does not please me; it is insufficiently thought out, and shows signs of having been composed in a hurry. The seams and basting threads are everywhere apparent, the form is completely unsuccessful. Laroche says that this is because you do not study the classics enough. I put it down to a different cause: you know too little of modern music. You will never acquire freedom of form from the classics. Nothing new is to be found there. They can give you only what you learned when you sat on the student benches and listened respectfully to Zaremba's profound lectures on " The Connection between Rondo Form and Man's First Fall."

. . . I am writing to you with entire frankness, and feel certain that you will not give up your intention of dedicating Fate to me because of what I say. The dedication is very precious to me as showing your regard. On my part, I reciprocate that regard.

Piotr Ilyich's vanity was ruffled by Balakirev's tone, but he took no offence at the specific criticisms, and carried out his intention of dedicating the piece to him. However, he did not publish *Fate*. A few years later he destroyed the score, and in 1876 referred to the piece as "no longer in existence." After his death, however, orchestral parts were located, and a score re-created from them was issued posthumously as his opus 77.

Early in 1869 Piotr Ilyich had written Anatoly that he was already at work on a new opera, but would not reveal its subject for a while. On February 27, he added that work on it was delighting him, and that he felt satisfied with what he had done. During the early spring, he turned out sketches for it as rapidly as possible, wanting to have it finished so that he could pass his summer vacation in orchestrating it. Sight unseen, Gedeonov had promised to stage it in November. The libretto, by Vladimir Alexandrovich Sollogub,[4] was based on Piotr Ilyich's favourite poem, Zhukovsky's *Undine,* which appealed to the composer as opera material for the singular reason that it did not require scenes laid in Russia.

The history of Piotr Ilyich's *Undine* was even less happy than that of *The Voivode.* He completed the orchestration during the summer of 1869; in August he sent score and libretto to the director of repertoire in the St. Petersburg theatres, who turned it over to the Marinsky's inspector of music. In October, Piotr Ilyich addressed Gedeonov, asking whether *Undine* had been incorporated into the repertoire. About one month later he received word that it would not be staged until the following season. Excerpts containing an important piano part were played in Moscow in March 1870, when Nikolay Rubinstein took the solo instrument. They met with little approval. In 1873 Piotr Ilyich recovered the score, which had been mislaid in St. Petersburg, and burned it, saving three numbers — a wedding march that became the second movement of his Second Symphony, an aria later incorporated into incidental music for Ostrovsky's *Snyegurochka,* and an Adagio he made use of in *Swan Lake.*

By the spring of 1869 Grand Duchess Yelena Pavlovna had become acutely dissatisfied with Balakirev's handling of the St. Petersburg Russian Musical Society concerts. She was not sympathetic toward the music of the Five, and though Balakirev often strained his tolerance to conduct compositions of the sort she required, she took steps to have him removed. When Piotr Ilyich heard of Balakirev's resignation, he contributed to *Sovremennaya Lyetopis* an article defending Balakirev and attacking the Grand Duchess's interference in questions of taste and style. This further increased the nationalists' feeling of friendliness for him. Rimsky-Korsakov said that the article "impressed everyone very favourably by its warmth and forcefulness." In numerous critical pieces

---

[4] Not to be confused with the noted poet Fyodor Sollogub (pseudonym of Fyodor Kuzmich Teternikov), who was only six years old when Tchaikovsky composed *Undine.* Count Vladimir Alexandrovich Sollogub belonged to a far earlier generation, having been born in 1814. His *Undine* libretto had been written in 1848 for Alexey Fyodorovich Lvov, composer of the national anthem, *God Save the Tsar.*

written during the succeeding few years Piotr Ilyich wrote appreciatively of both Balakirev and Rimsky-Korsakov.

Family matters during the spring and early summer of 1869 occupied whatever of Piotr Ilyich's time was not absorbed by teaching and work on *Undine*. In May, Anatoly was graduated from the School of Jurisprudence and was assigned to a criminal court at Kiev. In June, Ippolit married Sofya Petrovna Nikonova, and Piotr Ilyich attended the wedding. He spent his summer vacation with the Davidovs at Kamenka. All the immediate family was there but for Nikolay, and Piotr Ilyich thoroughly enjoyed himself. It was during this visit that he heard a baker singing a song, the words of which began: "Vanya sat on the divan and smoked a pipe of tobacco." He noted down its melody, which was to become that of the most popular string-quartet movement ever composed, the *Andante Cantabile* of his First Quartet. Early in August he returned to Moscow.

Balakirev was temporarily living in Moscow, and he earnestly developed Piotr Ilyich's friendship. During the late summer the two of them went to visit the poet A. N. Pleshcheyev at Tsaritsyn. A little later, after Piotr Ilyich had moved — still with Nikolay Rubinstein — to new and larger quarters, he entertained, his guests including Balakirev, Borodin, Klimenko, Kashkin, the critic Yury Karlovich Arnold, and Pleshcheyev. He did not always find Balakirev agreeable, confiding to Anatoly by letter that "he is a very fine man, and well disposed toward me, but I can't get soul to soul with him. I don't quite like the narrowness of his musical opinions or the sharpness of his tone." Nevertheless, when Balakirev left Moscow, Piotr Ilyich added that the farewell had been touching.

With *Undine* completed, Piotr Ilyich did no composing for several months. As late as October 16 he complained that not one half-passable musical idea entered his head. Bessel had commissioned from him a piano-duet arrangement of the Overture to Anton Rubinstein's opera *Ivan the Terrible*, but it was only toward the end of October that he once more initiated an original composition. In the meantime he read compositions he did not know, and attended the season of opera at the Bolshoi. He studied Schumann's *Faust* and several new German overtures. Of a Gounod symphony he told Balakirev: "This is the charming lisping of a classically attuned child. . . . I had the patience to examine it carefully from beginning to end, and confess I had not expected to meet there the venerable Haydn — who has, by the way, drawn his last breath." Of Rossini's *Semiramide*, as performed at the Bolshoi, he remarked that "despite its stilted style, its discordant notes, and its incredible dullness, it shows flashes of talent." He was less kind to Gounod's *Sapho*, describing it succinctly as "the trashiest of all extant operas." He was happier spending days in what he referred to as "the delightful task of reading Cui's opera *William Ratcliffe*," telling Balakirev that he had not expected it to be "so remarkably good." His own list of compositions he did nothing to lengthen. Instead he fretted, writing Anatoly that he was beginning to find the Conservatory loathsome, and that teaching had already, so early in the season, begun to weary him as it had the year before.

But the mental and creative activity that lifted Piotr Ilyich out of this slough had been begun while Balakirev was in Moscow. Balakirev had composed an Overture to *King Lear*, and now suggested that Piotr Ilyich try his hand at one to *Romeo and Juliet*. The idea struck fire, and in the midst of transcribing the Rubinstein Overture, proofreading his transcriptions of folksongs, and preparing lectures for his new class in musical form, Piotr Ilyich began to sketch it out. On November 9 he wrote Balakirev that it was growing quickly. From that moment on, Balakirev regarded its composition as his own task at least as much as it was Piotr Ilyich's.

Balakirev's intervention in the *cause célèbre* of *Romeo and Juliet* began with a long letter. This detailed the method and plan by which he had composed *King Lear*. After some introduction he continued: "You must understand that up to this point I had no definite musical ideas. These came later, and took their place in my outline. I am certain you will feel the same once your project inspires you." He knew exactly how Piotr Ilyich should induce the frame of mind conducive to creation: "Arm yourself with overshoes and a cane and take a constitutional on the boulevards, starting with the Nikitsky. Allow yourself to be steeped in your plan, and I am certain that by the time you reach Sretensky Boulevard some melody or episode will have come to you." Even this did not content Balakirev. He wanted to compose some part of *Romeo and Juliet* himself: "Just now I was thinking of your overture, and an idea came to me involuntarily. I seem to feel that it

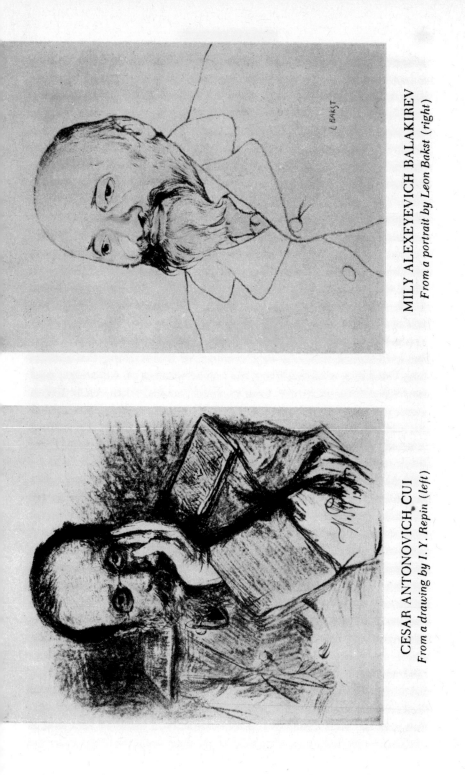

MILY ALEXEYEVICH BALAKIREV
From a portrait by Leon Bakst (right)

CESAR ANTONOVICH CUI
From a drawing by I. Y. Repin (left)

should open with a fierce allegro representing the clash of swords, something like this:

I should begin in that style." Balakirev closed this wholly insensitive letter with a lighter touch. Saying that Piotr Ilyich's letters always did him good, he added: "Your last one, for example, made me so uncharacteristically lighthearted that I rushed out on the Nevsky Prospekt. I didn't walk — I danced along, and composed part of my Tamara as I went."

By November 29 Piotr Ilyich was writing Balakirev that the Overture to *Romeo and Juliet* was complete and was being copied for performance. He enclosed the principal themes, for which his worrisome friend had asked. In response Balakirev criticized them unmercifully, saying that the first sounded like something from a Haydn quartet, whereas it should sound something more like one of Liszt's chorales. He appreciated the melody representing the lovers, but noted that it lacked spirituality, and could well have resembled the second theme of Schumann's *Die Braut von Messina*. Thanking Piotr Ilyich for intending to dedicate *Romeo and Juliet* to him, Balakirev called it "the first of your compositions that contains so many beautiful things that I do not hesitate to pronounce it good as a whole."

Although Piotr Ilyich, after completing *Romeo and Juliet*, had told Anatoly that he thought the composition "rather successful," he followed part of Balakirev's advice. On March 16, 1870 Nikolay Rubinstein conducted *Romeo and Juliet* at a Moscow Russian Musical Society concert. Both Kashkin and Klimenko later testified that it was wholly unsuccessful and went unnoticed. One cause was that Rubinstein's admirers were intent upon demonstrating their loyalty to him — he had been involved in a lawsuit, the decision in which had been made public the previous day. Another cause, however, was the public's continuing indifference to Russian music. Only a very few times was Piotr Ilyich to win enthusiastic response from a Russian audience hearing one of his works for the first time.

Nikolay Rubinstein, however, had begun to appreciate Piotr Ilyich as a composer and was impressed by *Romeo and Juliet*. Passing through Berlin in May, he persuaded the renowned publishing house of Bote und Bock to bring out this composition by his friend and co-worker, who was all but completely unknown in Germany. During the summer and well into the autumn Piotr Ilyich revised it, partly along lines suggested by Balakirev, partly to amend faults he had himself found. In October he wrote his critical friend that he had been unable to make the introduction sound like Liszt, as he had wanted it to express the thoughts of a lonely man (Friar Laurence) aspiring heavenward. In May 1871 Böte und Bock brought out the revised composition, thus much disturbing Balakirev. "It is a pity that you, or rather Rubinstein, should have rushed the publication of the Overture," he wrote. "Although the new introduction is a decided improvement, there were other changes I had wanted you to make. I had hoped that for the sake of your future compositions, this one would remain in your own hands somewhat longer." He concluded with hope that Jürgenson, at some future date, could be persuaded to bring out a "revised and improved version of the Overture."

Romeo and Juliet had been no more successful than the *Winter Reveries* Symphony. Nor was it only Russia that did not take to it. As late as 1878 Piotr Ilyich stated that it had failed in almost every European capital. Vienna, Paris, and Dresden had hissed it, while London and Hamburg had accepted it calmly. To today's audiences, of course, it is an ever welcome fixture of the standard repertoire. Indeed, the love melody, translated into popular song, is known to millions. But European music-lovers of the 1870's were unready for it. It was, in the first place, by a Russian; Russian composers were looked upon by critics and most audiences as barbarians. Not even its being cast, in its final version, in pure sonata form could edge it past the watchdogs of Teutonic music. It made its way very slowly, winning listeners by its lush melodiousness, sincerity, and resplendent orchestration. Piotr Ilyich lived to see it triumph, for the day came when Russian music was *de rigueur*. Then he could go nowhere to conduct without having to include on one program the Fantasy Overture to *Romeo and Juliet*.

Early in December 1869, with the first version of *Romeo and Juliet* complete, Piotr Ilyich had finished the first group of songs he was to publish. Of the half-dozen in opus 6, two are to poems by Alexey Konstantinovich Tolstoy, while two are settings of translated German poems, Heine's *Warum* and Goethe's *"Nur wer die Sehnsucht kennt."* The latter is one of the most famous of songs, a transliteration of Goethe's nostalgic lines into sensuous and unforgettable melody. Piotr Ilyich was seldom at his best in songs: they allowed him too little room for expansion, for the variation and development by which he built his stirring and mighty climaxes. When he produced a good song, it was rarely because he had achieved characterization or drama within its comparatively narrow limits. It was because he had married a sensuous and persuasive melody to words, often inappropriately. If "None but the Lonely Heart" is the best song he composed — a proposition not to be taken for granted — that is because in it the sinuous, melancholy contour of the melody seems the inevitable voice of the words themselves.

The business of everyday life grew more complex and less pleasant. Piotr Ilyich had never found boarding with Nikolay Rubinstein conducive to either calm living or steady work. Rubinstein's appetite for conviviality was Gargantuan, and his drinking, card-playing, and argumentation often filled his quarters with a clamour that distracted Piotr Ilyich. At times, indeed, the disorder drove him to a near-by inn to work: a public house was a place of Lethean quiet compared with Nikolay Rubinstein's rooms. On December 18, 1869 Nikolay's saint's day, an interminable celebration so exhausted Piotr Ilyich that he wrote complainingly about it. He longed to compose another opera, but could not concentrate long enough to seek out a suitable subject. Vera Davidova visited Moscow and made him uncomfortable by showing that she was unwilling to let their relationship continue on its former casual basis.

A professor of botany — Sergey Rachinsky — had, late in 1869, offered Piotr Ilyich a fantastic libretto called *Mandragora*. It had appealed to the hungry composer, and by January 8, 1870 he had completed one number of its score, the "Insect Chorus." He played this over to Kashkin, who praised it highly, but denounced the libretto as unworkable for opera, though he thought that it might serve for ballet. Piotr Ilyich staunchly defended his intention to set it, and the discussion developed into a violent quarrel. At last the weary and unsettled composer, with tears in his eyes, gave in to Kashkin's point of view. Although the "Insect Chorus," in which Laroche detected the influence of Berlioz, was to be played often, no more of *Mandragora* was composed.

"One thing troubles me," Piotr Ilyich wrote to his sister on February 17. "There is nobody in Moscow with whom I can enter into really intimate, familiar, and everyday relations. I often think how contented I could be if you, or someone like you, lived here. I have a deep yearning for the sound of children's voices and for some share in all the small matters of a home — in a word, for family life." Despite the presence of many who were his friends, and of worthy associates who had begun to appreciate his talent, he was lonely. He wanted, and if possible concentrated in one attractive person, a mother, a sister, a lover, and a housekeeper. Despite all its disadvantages and frightening difficulties for him, he had undoubtedly been considering marriage again. This natural longing was to persist in the unnatural setting of his mind until it persuaded him straight into tragedy.

The letter to Alexandra Davidova ended with news that he was about to begin his third opera, on a subject taken from Lazhechnikov's drama *The Oprichnik*. The rest of the school year was a scarcely mitigated torment to Piotr Ilyich. Early in March, when he informed Balakirev that he had begun *The Oprichnik*, he added: "I have become an unbearable hypochondriac as the result of serious nervous disorders. I don't know why, but I am oppressed by incommunicable melancholy yearnings. I should like to go away somewhere and hide myself in an impenetrable, God-forsaken spot."

On May 13, Piotr Ilyich summed up for Klimenko all the causes of his malaise except the most important one, which he could neither discover nor name: "1. Illness — I am getting much too fat, and my nerves have all gone to pieces. 2. My finances are in a bad state. 3. The Conservatory bores me to the point of nausea.[5] I am

---

[5] The treatment of this phrase presents an amusing example of the bowdlerization of Tchaikovsky by admiring editors. Modest, in his official biography, paraphrased it into something much less graphic, and Rosa Newmarch — translating the original with the help of Paul Juon's German translation — rendered it "oppresses me to extinction," a more genteel phrase, but scarcely what Tchaikovsky wrote.

more and more convinced that I lack talent for teaching theory. 4. I am very doubtful that Undine will ever be performed." Later in the same letter he added: "As regards ambition, I must tell you that I certainly have not been flattered recently. My songs won praise from Laroche, but Cui has denounced them, and Balakirev thought them so bad that he dissuaded Khvostova — who wanted to sing the one I had dedicated to her ["None but the Lonely Heart"] — from ruining with its presence a program graced by the names of Mussorgsky & Co." As to work in hand he concluded: "I don't know but what the slow progress of my opera, *The Oprichnik,* is due to no one's taking any interest in what I compose. I doubt that I shall be able to complete it in less than two years."

What Piotr Ilyich needed was a vacation. He had been hoping to spend time at Kamenka with the Davidovs, and possibly with Anatoly and Modest, the latter having been graduated from the School of Jurisprudence during the spring. Word came, however, that Vladimir Shilovsky was desperately, perhaps fatally, ill in Paris, and wanted to see him. He loved the boy, and abandoned his summer plans in order to rush off to France, stopping in St. Petersburg on the way only long enough to learn that the inspectors of the imperial opera, headed by Lyadov, had decided that his *Undine* was not worthy of presentation. He was terrified that he might arrive in Paris to find Vladimir dead. Things were not so bad as that, and during three days in Paris he had time to attend three plays. After two weeks Vladimir had regained enough strength to be taken to a health resort. So, with the boy's new guardian, they proceeded to Soden, near Frankfurt am Main.

Soden was a resort for consumptives. It must have been a depressing environment at best, and Piotr Ilyich wrote Anatoly that he was so overcome by melancholy that he could barely restrain himself from hysterics. In June, however, he heard a Prussian military orchestra that had won first prize in a Paris competition, and was engaged by its faultless playing. He persuaded its conductor to perform Glinka's *Kamarinskaya,* himself attending the performance. One day he would write Modest that his melancholy was subsiding. The next his message would be that his health was excellent, but that he and his companions were dreadfully bored. He went for two days to Mannheim for the Beethoven Centenary, and was powerfully moved by the *Missa Solemnis,* which he described as "one of the most inspired of musical crea-

tions." Another time he went to near-by Wiesbaden to visit Nikolay Rubinstein, and found him "in the act of losing his last ruble at
roulette. . . . He is quite convinced that he will break the bank
before he leaves Wiesbaden."

No one in the little group at Soden had the smallest inkling of
what was fermenting in the chancelleries of Berlin and Paris when,
in July, the Franco-Prussian War broke out. Then they had suddenly to flee — somehow, anyhow, in bulging railway carriages —
to neutral Switzerland. They arrived at Interlaken on July 22.
There they stayed six weeks, while Vladimir's health improved and
Piotr Ilyich dawdled over further revisions in *Romeo and Juliet.*
Before proceeding to Vienna, he was able, despite the war, to
pass a day in Munich with his old friend Prince Golitsin. The
Austrian capital on this visit, he wrote Anatoly, pleased him "almost more than any other city in the world." Thence he took the
long train ride to St. Petersburg, and was back in Moscow by the
middle of September. He was no sooner at home than he began
again to complain of bad health.

The Oprichnik was still not growing satisfactorily. Piotr Ilyich
toyed for a few days with the idea of abandoning it for a four-act
ballet on the Cinderella story,[6] but gave that up quickly. Anton
Rubinstein was in Moscow, and though Piotr Ilyich was covertly
angry at his old master, he was eternally fascinated by his personality and prowess. When Rubinstein's "portrait for orchestra,"
Don Quixote, was rehearsed, Piotr Ilyich was on hand to label it
"very interesting, and in sections superb." When Rubinstein played
at the Russian Musical Society, Piotr Ilyich thought that he did
the Schumann Concerto badly, but called his performance of three
Chopin Études and Mendelssohn's *Variations sérieuses* superb. A
new trio by Rubinstein, however, he could find nothing but bad.
He was disturbed by the disparity between Rubinstein's prolifical-
ness and the small number of his own compositions. All that he
had to show, aside from work on *Romeo and Juliet,* was one new
song to words by Apukhtin (*So Soon Forgotten,* no opus number),
and three trivial piano pieces (opus 9 — *Reverie, Salon Polka,* and
Salon Mazurka).

Piotr Ilyich was also worried over Modest's career. The recent
graduate had been assigned to a position in Simbirsk, and there
his naïveté had led him to make some pardonable errors and

---

[6] He actually signed a contract to deliver this score within two months.

blunders. They were apparently just what might have been expected of any novice, but Piotr Ilyich trembled to hear of them,
and further increased Modest's embarrassment by exaggerating
their importance. He was being so swept up into all sorts of activities that both his sister and his father complained of the long
intervals between his letters. Modest, in his life of Piotr Ilyich,
surmises that some of his letters from the school year of 1870–1
may have been lost, but asserts that early in 1871 Piotr Ilyich began
to thin out his formerly stupendous correspondence. How stupendous it was may be measured by the fact that Laroche alone at one
time possessed more than four thousand of Piotr Ilyich's letters.

VI

Piotr Ilyich found himself in January 1871 nearly as short of funds as Nikolay Rubinstein — who had indeed lost all his money at roulette the preceding summer. His remuneration at the Conservatory had been increased, but remained insufficient for his generosity. He was always unable to resist any request for financial help, and was all his life in the habit of spending and giving away more than he could afford. At this point, however, his pocketbook was slimmer than usual, and he grasped Nikolay Rubinstein's suggestion that he give an entire concert of his own compositions. He planned to use a small hall at the Russian Society of Nobles, but could not depend on filling even that. This precluded his employing an orchestra. He therefore decided to headline the concert with a string quartet that he would compose for the purpose. The month of February was almost entirely used up in its composition.

Now fewer distractions interrupted his working hours. Adamov, friend of his early school days, visited Moscow for a day, and Piotr Ilyich accompanied him on a round of theatre, restaurant, and tavern. Word came from St. Petersburg that his uncle, Piotr Petrovich Tchaikovsky, had died at the age of eighty-five, and he had to write a carefully considered letter of consolation to Ilya Petrovich, his brother's junior by a decade. But whatever else demanded some of his attention, Piotr Ilyich turned back gratefully and at once to the string quartet, which he was dedicating to his botanical friend, Professor Sergey Rachinsky.

The first all-Tchaikovsky concert was scheduled for March 28, 1871. Piotr Ilyich understood that his name alone would not draw an audience, and therefore sought the collaboration of well-known performers. Yelizaveta A. Lavrovskaya, a popular singer, consented to assist, as did Nikolay Rubinstein and the Russian Musical Society Quartet, made up of the Czech violinist Ferdinand Laub,[1]

[1] The *Musical Catechism* that Tchaikovsky translated from German into Russian at about this time was not, as has been stated erroneously, the work of Ferdinand Laub. It was the *Katechismus der Musik* of Johann Christian Lobe (1797–1881), editor of the *Allgemeine Musik Zeitung*.

the future prolific ballet-composer Aloysius Fyodorovich Minkus, the German cellist Wilhelm Karl Friedrich Fitzenhagen, and a Russian named Pryanishnikov. The program read:

String Quartet, D major	MUSICAL SOCIETY QUARTET
"None but the Lonely Heart"	E. A. LAVROVSKAYA
"Only the moon will rise" — from *The*	
Voivode	A. D. ALEKSANDROVA AND
	V. V. BAIKOVA
Reverie and *Salon Mazurka,* opus 9 . .	NIKOLAY RUBINSTEIN
"Both Painful and Sweet," and "So Soon	
Forgotten"	A. D. ALEKSANDROVA
Violin solo	FERDINAND LAUB
Nature and Love	STUDENTS OF MME B. O.
	VALTSEK [2]

Too late to hear the quartet, but early enough to cause a stir among the audience, there entered the hall one of Russia's most famous men, Ivan Sergeyevich Turgenyev. The great novelist mostly lived abroad, but on a brief visit to Russia had considered it worth his while to attend a concert entirely of Piotr Ilyich Tchaikovsky's compositions. When it was whispered about that he had learned of Piotyr Ilyich in western Europe, his appearance at the concert became still more impressive. Modest said: "This attention on the part of the great writer did not go by unremarked, and was of decided assistance to the composer."

The concert was an unquestionable success. What must have warmed Piotr Ilyich's heart most was Laroche's review of it, which once more revealed strong confidence in him: the String Quartet he described as "distinguished by the same delightfully succulent melodies, beautifully and interestingly harmonized, the same nobility of tone — so foreign to the commonplace — the same slightly feminine softness, to which we have become accustomed in this gifted composer. . . . The rest of Tchaikovsky's compositions performed that evening . . . revealed a rich and sympathetic talent."

Today the String Quartet in D major is seldom played. It would

---

[2] This trio for two sopranos and alto was a setting of words by Tchaikovsky himself. He composed it for Mme Valtsek's pupils and dedicated it to her. It was published posthumously.

rest on the shelves altogether, with many others of Piotr Ilyich's compositions, were it not for the second movement, known across the world as "the" *Andante Cantabile*. In structure, in development, in exploration of instrumental resource, it is not so interesting as the opening movement or more interesting than the last. But the treatment of the folksong "Vanya Sat on the Divan" would, by itself, keep a composer's name green for decades. In it Piotr Ilyich hit upon the perfect half-lighted setting for a melody of moving, impersonal melancholy. The melody as he harmonized it survives resetting for any ensemble down to, and including, a swing orchestra, but its popularity does not controvert its evocative beauty on the four instruments for which Piotr Ilyich originally scored it.

The concert past, and a success, Piotr Ilyich turned for a time with rediscovered energy and concentration to *The Oprichnik*. But early in June, happy again to be free of the Conservatory, he set out on his summer vacation. First he visited his brother Nikolay at Konotop. Then he went to Kiev to pick up Anatoly and take him to Kamenka. Alexandra Davidova's children delighted him as much as he delighted them, and during this visit he composed a little ballet for them to perform. This excursion into amateur choreography was called *Swan Lake*. Out of it, three years later, was to grow the first of Piotr Ilyich's full-length ballets. Now, too, he wrote his only full-length book, *A Guide to the Practical Study of Harmony*, completing the introduction last, on August 14. The book is competent, compact, and unoriginal. It was this text that Rimsky-Korsakov — who had become a composer largely by intuition — seized upon three or four years later and used to start his transformation into a theorist and academician.

Before returning to Moscow, Piotr Ilyich made two brief visits to friends. He went first to see Nikolay D. Kondratyev, a wealthy dilettante who owned large properties in the province of Kharkhov, including the village of Nizi. Kamenka had been hot and parched, but here on the banks of the Psyol River it was cool and green. Piotr Ilyich would have been content at Kondratyev's except that his friend filled the days with parties, fêtes, and the entertainment of numerous guests, making the country as much like the city as possible. One guest was glad to move on to Usovo, in Tambovskaya Province, to visit Vladimir Shilovsky. There, he told Anatoly, he was surrounded "by tender care," and entirely at peace. His satisfaction with Usovo was to bring him back to it during future summers.

Piotr Ilyich returned to the Conservatory with more than his usual lack of enthusiasm. What he most wanted was to give up teaching and devote himself entirely to composition. That was not possible, for his income from the sale and performance of his compositions did not exceed the equivalent of $250 per annum, and he could not dispense with the salary of three times that amount paid him by the Conservatory. More immediately, he wanted to escape from Nikolay Rubinstein's thumb and roof, to have for the first time in his life entirely private quarters of his own. He found to take his place as Rubinstein's housemate and boon companion Nikolay Albertovich Hubert, a comrade of his own St. Petersburg Conservatory days who had become a teacher at the Moscow Conservatory and would at last succeed Nikolay Rubinstein as its director. In excited delight, Piotr Ilyich rented a flat of three small rooms.

Modest listed the original furnishing of Piotr Ilyich's flat as: a portrait of Anton Rubinstein, a picture of Louis XVII, a large sofa, and a few cheap chairs. To take care of these and himself, Piotr Ilyich hired a former manservant of Ferdinand Laub's, Mikhail Ivanovich Sofronov. This man was eventually succeeded by his brother, Alexey Ivanovich, who was the mainstay of the whole last part of Piotr Ilyich's life. By the middle of September, Piotr Ilyich was comfortably established in his own rooms. He once again set to work on *The Oprichnik*. Early in October he wrote his brother Nikolay that he had to finish it by the end of the year.

During 1871 Laroche had accepted a position in the St. Petersburg Conservatory. On leaving Moscow, he turned his critical post on *Sovremennaya Lyetopis* over to Hubert, who was both lazy and unwell, and consequently neglected his assignments. Moscow musicians began to fear that the paper's editor might replace him with an amateur, and persuaded Kashkin and Piotr Ilyich jointly to substitute for him. The latter's first review was of the season's opening Russian Musical Society program, November 17. The program and some of his remarks on it were as follows:

Prelude to *Lohengrin* . . . .   RICHARD WAGNER
   "perhaps the most successful, most inspired
   creation of the celebrated German composer"

Concerto for piano and orchestra, E flat major   FRANZ LISZT
    "brilliant"

La Fée d'amour, fantasy for violin and or-
    chestra . . . .   JOSEPH JOACHIM RAFF
    "most interesting"

Symphony No. 8, F major . . . . . .   LUDWIG VAN BEETHOVEN
    "belongs among his unsurpassable creations"

Piotr Ilyich wrote slowly and with difficulty and disliked being a critic. Nevertheless, finding the pay a welcome supplement to his small income, he continued to contribute occasionally to *Sovremennaya Lyetopis* until it suspended publication late in the year. Thereafter he contributed for several years to *Russkiye Vyedomosti*, writing intermittently until 1876, when he stopped writing reviews altogether.

A few of Piotr Ilyich's opinions as expressed during his first season as a critic are of continuing interest. Adelina Patti, who had failed to impress him in London years before, sang Rosina in *Il Barbiere di Siviglia* at the Bolshoi on November 18, and he wrote: "There is something superhuman in the seductive loveliness of her voice, the nightingale purity of her trills, and the fabulous lightness of her coloratura." Reviewing a December concert of the Russian Musical Society, he called Schumann's Fourth Symphony "his last in number and also in quality," and deprecated the colourlessness of its orchestration. In this review he likewise called Chopin's E minor Concerto "unbearably long, senseless, and hackneyed."

On December 14, 1871 Alexandra Davidova gave birth to a son, who was named Vladimir. This child, who became a favourite with Piotr Ilyich as soon as he was able to walk and talk, was to develop into the beloved "Bobyk" of the composer's later years. His life was disordered, unhappy, and finally tragic. He committed suicide at the age of thirty-five, in 1906.

Affairs at the Moscow Conservatory were muddled and threatening in the winter of 1871. Its finances had become so straitened that there were rumours of its dissolution. Writing to Anatoly, Piotr Ilyich said: "I know only one thing: from a practical point of view I shall be sorry and incensed if it falls apart. But for myself I shall be happy. My work has become so distasteful to me, makes me so weak and nervous, that I should welcome any change." His determination to complete *The Oprichnik* by January 1 was weakening: "My opera is progressing very slowly; I hardly believe it will be finished even by Lent."

It did not take long wheedling by Vladimir Shilovsky to persuade Piotr Ilyich to go on a month's trip to Berlin, Paris, and Nice. Before he set out, however, he accepted a commission to compose a festival cantata. The two-hundredth anniversary of the birth of Peter the Great was to be celebrated by a Polytechnic Exposition in Moscow. Nikolay Rubinstein accepted the chairmanship of its musical committee, but when the scheme he proposed proved far too costly, his post was given to the cellist Karl U. Davidov. The other members of the committee included Laroche, Balakirev, Leschetizky, and Mikhail Pavlovich Azanchevsky, the new director of both the St. Petersburg Russian Musical Society and the St. Petersburg Conservatory. They commissioned Piotr Ilyich to compose a cantata to a special text being written by the poet Yakov Petrovich Polonsky, and he agreed. Although the cantata was to be sung in May at the opening of the exhibition, the text was not ready when he left for Germany toward the end of December.

It seemed necessary to Piotr Ilyich that only a very few people should know that he was travelling abroad with Vladimir Shilovsky. He wrote Anatoly that no one but Nikolay Rubinstein was to be told the truth — other people were to believe that he had gone to visit Alexandra Davidova. There were people in Moscow who would have raised their eyebrows and talked knowingly had they realized that he had gone off in mid-year on a pleasure trip with a nineteen-year-old boy. From Nice, on January 13, 1872, he addressed Anatoly characteristically: "I have been in Nice a week. It is very strange to come right from the depths of a Russian winter to a climate that allows one to stroll out without an overcoat, where orange trees, roses, and syringas are blooming, and where the trees have leaves. Nice is lovely. But this gay life is killing. . . . Yet I do have many pleasant hours — those, for instance, when I sit alone on the beach in the glowing (but not scorching) sunshine. But even those moments have a tinge of sadness. What comes of it all? I am old [Piotr Ilyich was not yet thirty-two], and can no longer enjoy anything. I live only on memories and hopes. But what is there to hope for? Yet without hope for the future, life would be impossible. So I dream of coming to Kiev at Easter time and of passing some of the summer with you in Kamenka."

From Nice the two friends went on to Genoa, Venice, and Vienna. Fruits of Mediterranean days were two piano pieces, the *Nocturne* in F major and the *Humoresque* in G major. The *Nocturne* is a trivial and banal salon effusion, but the *Humoresque* is something better than that. It is sprightly, witty, and unmistakably Russian, despite the fact that its middle section is based on a street song Piotr Ilyich heard in Nice. It is unimportant, but its deft high spirits are real. The two pieces were published as opus 10, and carry the dedication "To my friend Vladimir Shilovsky." The popularity of the *Humoresque* has not rivalled that of Dvořák's more sentimental one, but it endures. Like all small piano pieces of its wide general class, it is now better known to radio listeners and record-buyers in many quite insensitive transcriptions than on the piano, which it fits perfectly.

Piotr Ilyich returned to Moscow on February 10, 1872, to find Polonsky's text for the *Festival Cantata* awaiting him. Laroche had looked at it and described it as being "as unmusical as possible." The composer took the work in hand at once, for he was to be paid 750 rubles on its completion, and the performance was only four months off. On February 17 Napravnik finally conducted the first St. Petersburg performance of *Romeo and Juliet* at a concert of the Russian Musical Society, and Cui was enthusiastic: "The composition is a most talented one. Its special merit lies in the excellence of its themes." Touched by this unwonted gentleness on the part of Cui, Piotr Ilyich wrote to Balakirev, asking him to thank the critic.

Now Piotr Ilyich settled down to uninterrupted work. He had agreed to edit for Jürgenson a local music teacher's compilation of children's songs. He was rushing ahead with *The Oprichnik*. And the *Festival Cantata* had to be got through somehow. His correspondents outside Moscow heard little from him between the beginning of February and the middle of May. On May 17, he sent a completed score of *The Oprichnik* to Napravnik in St. Petersburg.[3] About eleven days later he delivered the children's songs to Jürgenson. On June 12 the *Festival Cantata* was conducted by Karl U. Davidov at the opening of the Polytechnic Exposition. On that same day a very weary composer left for Kamenka and the beginning of his summer vacation. Nothing had turned out well. The *Festival Cantata* had been received as such compositions are.

[3] *The Oprichnik* did not reach its *première* for almost two years.

His career as a composer seemed, despite some small success for *Romeo and Juliet* and a handful of minor pieces, to have reached complete stasis.

In the friendly and well-loved surroundings of Kamenka, Piotr Ilyich began to compose his Second Symphony. This now relatively neglected work, one of his most original and best-constructed compositions for large orchestra, was destined both for gratefully accepted success and for years of revision. During the summer of 1872, however, Piotr Ilyich was not ready to settle down to a desk and complete any work. He was more in need of relaxation and gaiety than of the satisfying sense of work accomplished. On July 14, with Modest, he went from Kamenka to Kiev, where they spent several days in the company of a composer named S. I. Donaurov. From Kiev the three of them went for a ten-day visit to Kondratyev at Nizi. On July 28 the brothers set out once more, Piotr Ilyich for Usovo and Modest for Kiev.

They were to travel together by diligence from Nizi to Vorozhba, where their routes branched apart. At a post-house a stop was made for luncheon and a change of horses. In high spirits they ordered a luxurious meal, including wines and liqueurs. In the midst of their gaiety they were informed that fresh horses were not available. Piotr Ilyich, the usually timid Piotr Ilyich, addressed himself loftily to the overseer: "Do you know whom you are addressing?" The man neither quailed nor showed any sign of action. Piotr Ilyich demanded the book in which travellers were supposed to write complaints and other reports of their journeys. Realizing that the name Tchaikovsky would mean nothing to the overseer, he signed his bitter complaint "Prince Volkonsky, Page-in-Waiting." "In less than fifteen minutes," Modest records, "the horses were harnessed, and the head ostler had been sharply dressed down for not having told the overseer that a pair had unexpectedly arrived back from a journey."

Pleased with the success of Piotr Ilyich's ruse, the brothers rode comfortably as far as Vorozhba. They hurried to the railroad ticket office, where Piotr Ilyich reached for his wallet. Horrified, he realized that he had left it behind in the post-house. His money and his papers were in it — and the papers were made out, not to "Prince Volkonsky," but to Piotr Ilyich Tchaikovsky. He and Modest sat down gloomily to think things over. Then the train that was to take Modest to Kiev steamed in, and he had to jump aboard, thrusting what money he had (five or six rubles) into his brother's hands. Piotr Ilyich induced the post-driver to pick up the wallet that night and bring it to him the next morning, and took a room at the Vorozhba inn. According to Modest, he spent a terrible night. "Mice and rats — of which he stood in mortal fear — left him no peace. He waged war all night with these pests, which ran over the bed and made a hideous sound."

In the morning, Piotr Ilyich eagerly awaited the return of the post. It came — but did not bring his wallet. The overseer of the post-house had refused to surrender it to anyone but "Prince Volkonsky" himself. Back to the post-house Piotr Ilyich had to go. Believing that the overseer must have looked into the wallet and discovered the deception, Piotr Ilyich perspired in embarrassment. A glance at the wallet, however, assured him that the respectful man had not opened it. Once more able to act the grandee, he commended the man and asked for his name. "Tchaikovsky," the overseer replied. At that moment Piotr Ilyich was inclined to believe that, after all, the man was aware of his true identity. Later, however, Kondratyev told him that Tchaikovsky was in fact the overseer's name.

At Usovo, where he remained one month, Piotr Ilyich revelled in the quiet, the beauty of the landscape, and the warm friendship of Vladimir Shilovsky. He worked long hours at the Second Symphony. He regained relaxed nerves, peace of mind, and soundness of body. On August 26, entirely refreshed, he set out for Moscow, arriving there the following day. Within two weeks he had removed to new rooms in Kudrinskaya Square and settled down to the season's work.

During September and October, Piotr Ilyich's journalistic duties took him often to the Bolshoi. Among other operas, he heard Serov's *Rognyeda*, a revival of *A Life for the Tsar*, *Ruslan and Lyudmila*, *L'Africaine* ("Meyerbeer's esteem for this altogether unsuccessful opera will for ever remain a mystery to the entire musical world"), *Il Trovatore* ("which has long since set everyone's teeth on edge"), Patti in *La Traviata* ("it is impossible to imagine anything more perfect than the singing of this truly astonishing singer"), and *Fra Diavolo*. He found *Fra Diavolo* "a consolation among the inflated compositions that constitute the repertoire of the Italian opera," while *Aïda*, which he read in score, and in which he thought he detected the influence of Wagner, pleased him by "the beauty of its harmonic combinations, the perfect rounding-out of its original form, and its exquisitely developed melodic designs."

Piotr Ilyich went to St. Petersburg early in November to attend the meeting at which the music committee of the directorate of the imperial theatres was to pass on *The Oprichnik*. On November 4 the committee voted almost unanimously that it was worthy of production. It would have been pleasant to linger in the once-more attractive atmosphere of the northern capital, but he was breathlessly eager to get on with the new composition which, he wrote Modest, "has so engrossed me that I am unable to attempt any other chore." He resented time stolen from it to hear Bolshoi performances of *Linda di Chamounix* and *La Sonnambula*, even though Patti continued to dazzle him. On November 27 he wrote Klimenko that he had completed the Second Symphony, had begun its orchestration — some of which was already in the copyists' hands — and was working furiously to finish that too. He added that he had begun to worry about *The Oprichnik*, to fear that it might be delivered to oblivion as *Undine* had been. "On my honour," he swore, "I shall never again touch a pen if my opera is not performed."

Suddenly Piotr Ilyich's wish to marry turns up again in a letter to his father dated December 4, 1872. Its suddenness must be only apparent, as the prospect was one with which he toyed intermittently for years. He was unquestionably lonely. He was looking for a way to free himself from the oppressive domination of Nikolay Rubinstein, and perhaps thought that as a married man he would more forcibly be able to assert his own views. He was earning almost enough to support a wife, he said — the equivalent of $1,500 a year. Also, his marriage would tend to quiet, if not quiet altogether, the rumours about his personal life that he knew Moscow sometimes discussed. "I confess that at times the thought enters my head of installing a good woman in my house," he told Ilya Petrovich, "a good, plump little woman on the order of your tasty little cream puff. But I'm afraid I'll regret it afterwards." His jocular reference to his stepmother is of real interest because it cannot be doubted that the companion he sought was one who could, to some degree, replace the mother he had long ago lost and never ceased to mourn. He would not have been consistent, when he considered a possible wife, had he not in reality wanted a woman his own age or older who would combine the attributes of mother, housekeeper, and hostess with indifference to marital rights and pleasures.

More and more Piotr Ilyich had to attend operas at the Bolshoi. In December he heard Christine Nilsson in both *Faust* and *Hamlet*, and wrote of her as "a superior artist, whose appearance on the stage of the Bolshoi Theatre marks an epoch in our theatrical annals." He had begun to fret himself about his health, telling his father that he was tiring from overwork and that his eyes had begun to weaken. He had nervous attacks. On December 22 Piotr Ilyich wrote Modest: "At this moment, I have abandoned myself to idleness caused by the absence of the smallest inspiration or urge to creative activity. I have tried to compose some small songs, but everything turns out badly. I can't even find lyrics that please me. How about your undertaking this job and sending me a list of suitable poems?"

One thing was turning out well. On December 21 he wrote Ilya Petrovich that he was practically assured that *The Oprichnik* would reach the stage the following season, having passed both the theatre and the drama committees. Right after January 1, 1873 he was called to St. Petersburg to shepherd it through the final committee — that on music.[4] A favourable decision would mean performance at the Marinsky Theatre. He endured the subtle, prolonged torture of playing it through before the committee. All went well and *The Oprichnik* was unanimously approved. On January 7, at a party, Piotr Ilyich played the last movement of his Second Symphony at Rimsky-Korsakov's house. He told Modest that those present fell into such raptures over it that they almost tore him to pieces. Rimsky-Korsakov's wife, who admired him intensely and had already published a piano-duet transcription of *Romeo and Juliet,* begged him with tears in her eyes to arrange this finale for four hands. Also present was Stasov, who engaged him in extended discussion of his future as a composer. The clock had gone full circle. Piotr Ilyich must have begun to feel that he was more appreciated in St. Petersburg by his former enemies than in Moscow by his friends.

[4] This committee was made up of six imperial directors — those of Russian opera (Napravnik), Italian opera, Russian plays, French plays, German plays, and ballet.

Scarcely was Piotr Ilyich at home again when a long letter from Stasov arrived. The great critic suggested three literary works as points of departure for the composer's next effort — *The Tempest, Ivanhoe,* and *Taras Bulba.* With the last as his theme, Stasov said, Piotr Ilyich would find himself creating music more poetic, passionate, and vital than even the "unexcelled overture *Romeo and Juliet.*" Some two weeks later Piotr Ilyich replied. "I have recalled as much as I can of *Ivanhoe,* and have reread *The Tempest* and *Taras Bulba.* My choice is made — it will be *The Tempest.*" In the impersonally executive manner he shared with Balakirev, Stasov replied six days later with a full outline of the way *The Tempest* should be composed.[5] On February 8 Piotr Ilyich thanked him for his "excellent and, in the highest degree, enticing and inspiring program of *The Tempest,*" but he did not get round to working on the new composition for months, or to completing it until October.

The *première* of the Second Symphony was delayed by news of the death of Grand Duchess Yelena Pavlovna, and was finally scheduled for February 7. Laroche travelled down from St. Petersburg to hear it and review it for *Moskovskiye Vyedomosti.* On the great day Nikolay Rubinstein conducted the orchestra of the Russian Musical Society, to which the symphony was dedicated. The audience was intensely enthusiastic, and the shy composer was summoned to the platform for genuine ovations. The next day he delightedly wrote Stasov that Rubinstein was considering the public demand for its repetition,[6] and that he himself wanted to revise some details of its orchestration.

Laroche's critique completed the healing of the breach between him and Piotr Ilyich. "It is a long time," he wrote, "since I have encountered a work of art with so powerful a thematic development of ideas, such well-motivated and artistically worked-out contrasts." Laroche's enthusiasm, joined to that of the Moscow audiences, probably hastened the St. Petersburg *première* of the symphony, which took place under Napravnik on March 7. There could no longer be any doubt anywhere that Piotr Ilyich Tchaikovsky was to be reckoned as one of the first, and potentially the great-

---

[5] In this letter Stasov criticized the omission from Tchaikovsky's *Romeo and Juliet* of reference to "that inspired Shakespearean creation, Juliet's nurse."

[6] This repetition occurred on April 8. Tchaikovsky was called to the stage after each movement, and was handed a silver goblet and a wreath of laurel.

est, of living Russian composers. The young man who had thrown away a career in the Ministry of Justice had justified his own rashness and Laroche's early confidence.

The Second Symphony as played today has had the benefit of its composer's later thoughts: he revised it in 1879 and 1880. Although such reworkings are frequently ill advised, tending to substitute newly acquired learning for freshness of conception, it is still an exceedingly attractive symphony, light-years in advance of *Winter Reveries* in each department. The first movement is announced and closed by an "andante sostenuto" theme of lyric melancholy, but consists largely of a brilliant and magnificently varied "allegro vivo" based on a folksong, "Down by Mother Volga." The second movement, marked "andante marziale," makes use of the march from *Undine*, which is first presented in an atmosphere of piquant mystery by clarinets and bassoons, while tympani carry the staccato four-four rhythm. The third movement is the least successful, a rushing scherzo full of wayward rhythms lent contrast by a naïve trio that, though charming in itself, is not integrated. But it is the finale — an "allegro assai" ending in a "presto" — that truly crowns the work. Built entirely on two themes — an original melody and *The Crane*, a Little Russian dance-song Piotr Ilyich had heard sung by a butler at Kamenka — it is one perfect answer to the problem of adapting music of folk character to symphonic use. It consists largely of brilliant variations on the folksong, a successful application of modulations in harmony, rhythm, and melodic contour to a melody compelling in itself and adapted to manipulation. No seams show. There is no straining for effect, but only that artfully conceived effect which sounds spontaneous. The Tchaikovsky who became superior to all his contemporaries but Brahms in handling the variation technique here declared his presence.

Nowhere in the Symphony in C minor is there undigested woe, oversubjective probing, or hysteria. Nor is this a symphony of nobility and grandeur. It is, however, a successful work of art, one that sets out to fill the area within clearly defined boundaries, and fill it with living materials well balanced and well contrasted. In later years Piotr Ilyich often set himself more important æsthetic problems than any here solved. Not often after Beethoven, however, did any composer write a true symphony that so effortlessly and well answered every artistic query it asked. Because it is

music-making in the eighteenth-century sense, music made for its
own beauties and not direct personal communication, it lacks the
blackly sombre note that has been called Tchaikovskyan. Other
Russian composers, and Piotr Ilyich himself, have composed symphonies in which there are weightier material, greater isolated
beauties, more originality, and more profundity. None has exceeded this one in achieving exactly the form required by its melodic content.

In February or March, Piotr Ilyich had received from the directorate of the Russian Musical Society the terms of a competition.
The operas submitted were to be settings of a Polonsky libretto
called *Vakula the Smith,* based on Gogol's fantastic story *Christmas Eve.* Behind this competition was a history of fatality. In
1870, while at work on his last opera, *The Power of Evil,* Serov
had dallied with two other projects. One was to compose for Patti
an opera based on George Sand's *Consuelo,* the other to try his
hand at a Russian comic opera. When he told Grand Duchess
Yelena Pavlovna that he had located a suitable subject for the
latter in *Christmas Eve,* she promised to pay Polonsky to write the
libretto. In February 1871 Serov died, with *The Power of Evil* and
Consuelo unfinished and *Vakula the Smith* not begun. In his honour, Yelena Pavlovna decided to offer prizes of one thousand and
five hundred rubles respectively for the best and second-best settings of the libretto. Before her project could be carried out, she
too died, in January 1873. The directors of the Russian Musical Society then decided to proceed with the competition, in her honour
as much as in Serov's.

When Piotr Ilyich received preliminary notice of the prize competition, together with a request for his opinion on it, he answered
in a letter to one of its directors, Prince D. A. Obolensky: "Would
it not be possible for the central directorate to indicate specifically
the sort of music that would be pre-eminently apt to the text —
whether it is necessary to compose separate numbers, or whether,
on the other hand, one ought to follow the most recent trend toward an operatic unity?" He was conscious of Wagner's belief
that the old opera, written as a chain of linked numbers, was out-
worn, and that a continuously unfolding fabric of music would
make the ideal opera. He never approached even the partial realization of this debatable ideal that Wagner achieved in *Tristan
und Isolde* and *Der Ring des Nibelungen,* but eventually found his

own best operatic form in operas that, if they resemble Wagner's at all, are closer to *Lohengrin*.

The Polonsky libretto for *Vakula the Smith* is episodic in the extreme, but bright with local colour and touched here and there with a demented nonsense that is not unattractive. Piotr Ilyich liked it and decided that he would enter the contest if he could be certain in advance that he would win it. He could not risk composing a long opera, having it fail to win the prize, and then having to lay it aside unperformed. So he set about ascertaining whether Rimsky-Korsakov, Balakirev, and Anton Rubinstein — apparently the only three competitors he feared — were going to compose entries. When he had satisfied himself that they were not, he started his own setting of Polonsky's libretto. Because he had misunderstood the closing date of the contest — believing that it was August 13, 1874, whereas it was August 13, 1875 — he hurried more than necessary. He did not realize that he had acted unethically in taking steps that made public the information that none of the entries submitted would be by Balakirev, Anton Rubinstein, or Rimsky-Korsakov, and that one would be a product of Piotr Ilyich Tchaikovsky. Nor did his indiscretions with regard to *Vakula the Smith* end there: as soon as he completed the score, he was to embark on a series of almost Beethovian machinations in its favour.

Piotr Ilyich's increased importance on the Russian musical scene was demonstrated in mid-March 1873 when the commission governing the Moscow imperial theatres invited him to compose incidental music for the performance of Ostrovsky's new play, *Snyegurochka*. He accepted, and was soon receiving the text from the dramatist himself. At one point Ostrovsky suggested that a scene involving blind guzla-players be set as a song with a refrain, "the first verses of each couplet to be sung by one voice, the remaining three by a small chorus." Piotr Ilyich carried out this plan to the letter. On April 6 he informed the commission that the music for *Snyegurochka* was ready, and asked that he be sent the 350 rubles he had been promised for it. The commission agreed to this request despite the fact that Ostrovsky was altering some of the text, thus necessitating revisions in the music. Shortly, however, the play was staged. It was only a moderate success, but the music took hold with the public. It was published as Piotr Ilyich's Opus 12, and parts of it were to be heard on programs until the end of his life. Some of it was based on music originally sketched for

TCHAIKOVSKY IN 1873
From a photograph

Undine. It consists of an Overture, various solos, and a few choruses. Little of it is dramatic, but it includes separate numbers of potent charm. It remained for Rimsky-Korsakov, almost a decade after the *première* of *Snyegurochka,* to turn Ostrovsky's play into a satisfactory opera.

"I have been feverishly busy these last days," Piotr Ilyich wrote his father. "The performance of Ostrovsky's play with my music, the revision of my symphony [the Second] for publication, examinations, and a reception for [Grand Duke] Konstantin Nikolayevich" more than explained the feverishness. He was nervously awaiting his summer vacation. His salary during the school year had risen to 2,302 rubles (approximately $1,150), more than just enough to cover his living-expenses and heedless generosities. When to it had been added his stipend for the *Snyegurochka* music, he elected to spend the summer abroad after brief visits to Kondratyev and to the Davidovs. At last, on June 6, he was free to depart for Nizi.

Beginning with this vacation, Piotr Ilyich sporadically kept a diary or daybook. For long periods he faithfully made entries. Again, he let time slip by without remembering his diary. Only a small portion of the entries he did make has survived. Some of them he destroyed; others were destroyed at his behest by Modest, as his executor. Under date of June 23, he entered: "On the way from Vorozhba to Kiev, after a protracted indifference to music, something suddenly began to play and sing inside me for no reason at all. An embryo theme in B major became enthroned in my head, suddenly enticing me to attempt a symphony. Immediately I decided to discard Stasov's lagging *Tempest* and devote the summer to a symphony that would eclipse all my previous efforts." But though he entered the B-major theme in the book, nothing was ever done with it. He composed no symphony that summer.

At Kamenka, Piotr Ilyich was unwell for several days. He left there on July 8, and was in Breslau three days later. Moving on, "not far from Dresden" he noted down a theme "for the first Allegro," evidently still for the projected symphony. In Dresden, having secured a hotel room, he rushed out to attend a performance of *La Juive,* which he thought "very fine." But his nerves were jumpy, and he left before the final curtain, hurrying to a hotel where he knew that Jürgenson was staying with members of his family. With the Jürgensons he soon set off for Switzerland, visiting Zürich,

Lucerne, Bern, and Vevey. On he went, not enjoying himself, but travelling automatically, to Turin, Milan, Lake Como, and finally Paris. He wrote Bessel, with whom he had signed a contractual arrangement regarding *The Oprichnik,* that he had not composed one note during his foreign journey. Either he had forgotten the themes in his daybook or he had already elected not to write the symphony.

"Amid these majestically lovely scenes and tourist's impressions," he noted at Vevey, "I yearn with my entire soul for Russia, and my heart contracts with a vision of its plains, its meadows, its woods. O dear country of mine, you are a hundredfold lovelier and dearer to me than these beautiful chains of mountains that are essentially nothing but nature's petrified convulsions. Our nature is so beautifully calm!"

By the middle of August, Piotr Ilyich was where he most wanted to be, at Usovo. Vladimir Shilovsky was in Moscow during part of his visit, and Piotr Ilyich spent a blissful two weeks alone. In May 1878, writing to Mme von Meck, he recalled that fortnight: "My spirit was in a state of exaltation and rapture as I spent the days roaming the woods alone, the evenings wandering on the measureless steppe, and the nights at an open window listening to the majestic stillness of the lonely spaces, occasionally disturbed by some undefined sounds of the night." At Usovo he took up work on *The Tempest,* finishing it in rough draft in ten days — "effortlessly," he later said, "as though inspired by some superhuman force." By the middle of September he was again in Moscow.

At once Piotr Ilyich began orchestrating *The Tempest.* He moved again, this time to a flat in the Malaya Nikitskaya. Once more he began what had by this year begun to seem to him a dreary round. There were the usual operas to be reviewed — *I Lombardi,* "abounding in various joyful trepaks," and *Der Freischütz,* which he always loved. There were his boring classes at the Conservatory. There were the familiar struggles to get an opera performed. He wrote Bessel asking him to watch over the fortunes of *The Oprichnik* in St. Petersburg and telling him that there was some chance of its being staged in Moscow the following spring. Bessel was further to inform Stasov that *The Tempest* was ready, but that he would not send it to St. Petersburg until he had heard it performed in Moscow.

Piotr Ilyich had signed a contract with Bessel giving him exclusive rights to the publication of the score and libretto of *The Oprichnik*. In return for these — for which no immediate payment was made — Bessel promised to publish the complete piano score in time for the opera's *première*. For his services in connection with the performance he was to receive one third of the royalties. When, in March 1873, the censor objected to a few of the verses, it was Bessel who smoothed matters and persuaded Piotr Ilyich to substitute inoffensive lines for the condemned text. Whenever the composer became particularly worried over prospects of performance, it was to Bessel that he turned for reassurance and for assistance in prodding the St. Petersburg opera authorities. Bessel gradually became, for the time being, Piotr Ilyich's St. Petersburg publisher and representative.

The Six Piano Pieces published as Piotr Ilyich's Opus 19 were completed on November 8, 1873. The first five are suave salon music of the sort he could turn out wholesale, apparently without thought or effort. The sixth is one of his best piano compositions, the Original Theme and Variations dedicated to Laroche. The resources of harmony, colouring, and rhythm brought to bear on a most malleable melody are to be matched, in piano music after Beethoven, only in the sets of variations Brahms composed on themes by Handel, Haydn, and Paganini. Occasionally a note of tawdriness that Brahms might have rejected creeps into Piotr Ilyich's variations, but in those of lighter mood and in those exploiting rapid tempos the Russian is everywhere the German's superior in spontaneity.

Almost simultaneously with Opus 19 Piotr Ilyich composed six other piano pieces. All dedicated to Anton Rubinstein, they were to make up his Opus 21. Perhaps because they were to be offered to his old master, Piotr Ilyich made one of them a learned Fugue for Four Voices, but not that sort of applied learning could lift any of them from the level of shameless platitude. Only a scant half-dozen of the more than one hundred piano compositions Piotr Ilyich allowed to be published contain anything like the best music he could conceive. The limited dynamic and colour range of the piano did not summon forth his richest conceptions. His position in the world of music would be exactly what it is had he never published a single work for the solo piano.

November 1873 found Piotr Ilyich more restless and worried than usual. The Moscow presentation of *The Oprichnik* seemed to be receding into a blank future. He fretted Bessel over the delays in which the opera was being involved in St. Petersburg. In December, Napravnik, describing himself as "truly concerned over the presentation of *The Oprichnik*, and particularly worried about obtaining the best possible performance of the musical parts," demanded changes in the score, and made new detailed suggestions in regard to casting. He felt that the orchestration overwhelmed the singers. Piotr Ilyich replied that he gladly consented to the conductor's assignments of roles, as well as to the alterations and abridgments, and would come to the northern capital to discuss them. He was displeased with several of the cuts. Agreeing to them had been an unpleasant struggle, though he later recognized their rightness. The visit to St. Petersburg, during which final difficulties with the censor were settled, forced him to spend four whole days on alterations and curtailments of the score.

Personal matters were in no better state than artistic ones. He found his new quarters unsatisfactory and uncomfortable, and moved, again on the Malaya Nikitskaya, to rooms that were "more cramped, but also more comfortable." On December 10 he wrote Modest: "I dine at Shilovsky's quite often, but his society taxes me a great deal. . . . Only this year have I realized that I am quite alone here. I have many friends, but none with whom I can open my soul, as for instance with Kondratyev." Piotr Ilyich never completely recovered the enthusiasm he had once felt for the friendship of Vladimir Shilovsky. Only his financial state was favourable, he said: "Next week the Musical Society will perform The Tempest, and then I shall receive the customary 300 rubles."

On December 19 Nikolay Rubinstein conducted that first performance at the Moscow Russian Musical Society's 168th concert. It was received with so much enthusiasm and such prolonged applause that, like the Second Symphony, it was repeated later the same season. This symphonic fantasy, dedicated properly to Stasov, became one of the staples of Piotr Ilyich's repertoire in those later years when he travelled about conducting his own compositions. Its popularity was real for several decades. Although Piotr Ilyich, while composing it, had told Rimsky-Korsakov that he intended to use the Prelude to *Das Rheingold* and its construction on a single triad as his model for depicting the sea, his fellow composer was right in stating — despite the Wagnerian atmosphere of parts of

The Tempest — that he could discern no perceptible resemblance between Tchaikovsky's ocean and Wagner's river.

The printed score of *The Tempest* carries a programmatic outline of the music: "The sea. Ariel, spirit of the air, obeying the will of the magician Prospero, raises a tempest. Wreck of the ship bearing Ferdinand. The enchanted island. First timid beginnings of love between Miranda and Ferdinand. Ariel. Caliban. The amorous pair free themselves to the triumphant spell of passion. Prospero strips himself of his power of enchantment and leaves the island. The sea." With the appearance of uncluttered spontaneity that Piotr Ilyich's best music always displays when he is not chained by determined adherence to classic development and recapitulation, he has clearly followed the program section by section. More important, he has composed music charged with its own enchantments, music entirely able to dispense with the program. Themes beautiful and strong in themselves are masterfully clothed in appropriate harmonic, rhythmic, and agogic dress. The one portraying Prospero's renunciation of his magician's powers cannot be overpraised: it is worthy of one of Shakespeare's most magical scenes. The present neglect of *The Tempest* by conductors is beyond explanation. It deserves performance as often as *Romeo and Juliet* and *Francesca da Rimini,* far more often than the *Italian Caprice* and *1812.*

Early in 1874 Piotr Ilyich wrote his Second String Quartet, in F major, opus 22. On February 7 he told Anatoly that it was complete and would be played at a soirée at Nikolay Rubinstein's. Shortly thereafter Anton Rubinstein was at hand, and though his brother was away, the private *première* of the quartet took place as planned. Anton, still unable to see in Piotr Ilyich more than a talented pupil, listened to it with what Kashkin describes as "a lowering and fretful look," and then attacked it harshly, saying that it was not in chamber-music style and that he could not understand it. Although the others present, including the players, had been vocally enthusiastic about it, Piotr Ilyich took Anton's criticisms to heart and spent some days in reworking the parts. He then dedicated it to Grand Duke Konstantin Nikolayevich and allowed its first public performance on March 22. This euphonious quartet has stood up well to passing time. It is more notable for the beauty of its melodies and the subtlety of their harmonization

than for either formal justice or brilliant exploitation of string
timbres. But only the Teutonic predisposition that has so long
infected musical circles — and chamber-music circles in particular
— can explain why this richly winning music is neglected in favour
of secondary quartets by major German and Austrian masters and
the best quartets by third-rate ones.

Suddenly, among the many operas and concerts Piotr Ilyich
attended, an artist appeared who was to be of first importance in
spreading his compositions. On March 25 he attended at the Bolshoi a piano recital by Hans von Bülow. The renowned German
musician, whose name was known across Europe because he had
married Liszt's daughter and she had run away with Wagner, was
a revelation to Russian audiences, as he was later to be to those in
the United States. He played the music of the great German composers from Bach on. Piotr Ilyich wrote: "Everything was played
with equal mastery, taste, and amazing ability to transmit the spirit
and mood of the composition objectively." Bülow as a pianist was
at the opposite pole from the flaming virtuoso type established by
Liszt and continued by Anton Rubinstein. He played nothing — or
almost nothing — to display his technical prestidigitation, but chose
his programs with serious and lofty judgment and intent. He
played everything with profound attention to detail. While in
Russia, he heard some of Piotr Ilyich's compositions, and was
shortly returning the high opinion the Russian held of him. Writing to a friend from Kharkov on March 28, Bülow said: "Tchaikovsky is a great talent. I am studying his Variations [opus 19],
which I shall play at a public concert two weeks from today."
Bülow's high opinion of his music was to prove of great value to
the praise-hungry Piotr Ilyich: of an article by Bülow published in
an Augsburg newspaper he later said, "This letter contains an appreciation of me that made me happier than any other laudatory
comment has ever made me." For the first time a western-Euro-
pean musician of international fame had ranked him above the
casual rut of Russian composers.

Early in March, Piotr Ilyich had written Napravnik to inquire if
it was necessary for him to attend rehearsals of *The Oprichnik*.
The conductor's reply was affirmative, for about April 1 the composer went to St. Petersburg and took up temporary residence
with his father. His first interviews with Napravnik were blows to
his artistic pride. The conductor insisted on numerous additional

cuts in the long score. Piotr Ilyich began to have gloomy forebod-
ings about the opera on which he had worked so long. On April 6
he wrote Albrecht that he would be happy to obtain tickets for
those of his Moscow friends who wished to come to St. Petersburg
for its *première*, scheduled for the Friday of Easter week.
"Frankly," he added, "I'd rather none of you did come. There is
nothing really first rate in the opera." To his young pupil Sergey
Ivanovich Taneyev he wrote still more gloomily: "Seryozha, if
you're actually considering coming here just to hear my opera, I
beg you to give up the project, for to tell you the truth there's
nothing exceptional in it, and I shouldn't want you to rush up to St.
Petersburg for its sake."

Alone, news from Moscow was bright. Nikolay Rubinstein conducted the repeat performance of *The Tempest* there on April 19,
and again it was exceedingly well liked. With each new rehearsal
of *The Oprichnik*, however, Piotr Ilyich became more depressed
and irritable. Against his wish, Nikolay Rubinstein was bringing
most of the Moscow Conservatory staff to the *première*, and everything seemed — to Piotr Ilyich, though not to others — to be going
wrong. *Russkiye Vyedomosti* approached him with the suggestion
that he leave for Italy a day or so after the first performance to
review for its columns the initial Italian staging of *A Life for the
Tsar*, scheduled for the Teatro dal Verme, Milan. Eager to get
away from everyone and everything, he agreed.

On the night of April 24 *The Oprichnik* was presented at the
Marinsky Theatre, having been selected by Napravnik for his
annual benefit. Several members of Piotr Ilyich's family, including seventy-nine-year-old Ilya Petrovich, occupied a box. Among
others present were Nikolay Rubinstein, Laroche, Cui, and Azanchevsky. There was no outstandingly fine singer in the cast, but the
ensembles had been rehearsed into smoothness. Orchestra and
chorus performed well. The scenery and costumes were shabby:
the management had taken the precaution of not investing heavily
in an opera whose success was not assured in advance. The reaction of the audience was unmistakably enthusiastic. At the end of
the second act there was a practically unanimous shout for the
composer, who had to drag himself before the curtain. Nobody,
unless it was Piotr Ilyich himself, doubted that *The Oprichnik* was
well launched on a long career.

From the Marinsky, Piotr Ilyich had to go to a gala supper being given to honour him by the combined St. Petersburg and Moscow sections of the Russian Musical Society. Azanchevsky, as director of the St. Petersburg Conservatory, made a speech fruity with praise, leading up to the unexpected news that it had been decided to award Piotr Ilyich the M. A. Kondratyev prize of 300 rubles for Russian composers. A tired, flustered, and unsettled Piotr Ilyich went to his father's house that night wondering how the critics, and in particular Laroche and Cui, would deal with *The Oprichnik*. He was not to find out for some time, as he left St. Petersburg two days later for Italy. On the evening of his departure the second performance of the opera duplicated the apparent success of the *première:* there were calls for the absent composer at the end of the second act, and the choral finale of the third act had to be repeated.

Laroche's critique of *The Oprichnik* appeared in *Golos* on April 29. It was predominantly praise, and included one sentence the Five and their friends must have taken as a direct attack on them and their late mentor, Dargomizhsky: "In its musical aspects, *The Oprichnik* offers the consolation of a blooming oasis after the dramatic-declamatory desert with which Russian composers have been boring us for the last several years." On May 23, in *Musikal-niy Listok,* Laroche again used *The Oprichnik* as a stick with which to belabour the declamatory preoccupation of the nationalists, speaking of Piotr Ilyich as a composer "with a powerful and highly developed talent, who has discerningly chosen the right direction, in opposition to the fashionable theories that have spread across our musical world like a plague."

The opposite side of the argument was Cui's well-loved task: "[*The Oprichnik*] lacks ideas, and is weak almost throughout. It has not one notably outstanding section or felicitous inspiration." It was with the venomous Cui that Piotr Ilyich was by this time inclined to agree. About two weeks after the *première* he had written from Italy: "The Oprichnik constantly torments me. The opera is so wretched that I always ran out on rehearsals (especially of Acts III and IV) so as not to be forced to listen to another note." He saw that it had "no action, no style, no inspiration." But he desperately wanted it to catch on, and a belief that it would not outlast six performances vexed him with the futility of the work he had poured into it. It was to do better than he foresaw, achieving fourteen Marinsky performances in seven years, besides stagings in Kiev, Odessa, and Moscow. But *The Oprichnik* never established itself firmly in the repertoire either in Russia or elsewhere. When Piotr Ilyich finally read Cui's tirade, he wrote Bessel: "In spite of its viciousness, in spite of its monstrous partiality, Cui's criticism is essentially a quite correct evaluation of its merits as a musico-dramatic composition."

VII

Piotr Ilyich had gone directly from St. Petersburg to Venice. On April 29 he wrote his impressions to Modest. He felt ashamed of having gone off to enjoy the south instead of staying at home and paying Modest's and Anatoly's debts. Venice he described as sad, a city of ghosts. "It is a place in which — if I had to stay very long — I'd hang myself out of blank despair on the fifth day." He disliked the "mazes of stinking corridors," and had praise only for the palaces, the paintings of Titian and Tintoretto, and the sculpture of Canova. He had received a telegram stating that the Milan mounting of *A Life for the Tsar* had been postponed until May 12, and he was therefore going south to Rome and Naples.

In Rome, Piotr Ilyich wrote Anatoly on May 1, he continued as a tourist. He had encountered no one he knew, no one friendly in any way. He had visited the Colosseum, the Capitol, the Vatican, the Pantheon, and "the loftiest achievement of human genius," St. Peter's. He could not understand how many Russians could pass their entire lives in Rome. "If distraction is what I wanted, I might just as well have gone to Kiev or the Crimea." Naples was worse, particularly during six days of unexampled bad weather. He managed to visit Pompeii, which impressed him deeply. But every day while in Naples he wept out of homesickness and longing for the beloved ones he had left in Russia. He received word that *A Life for the Tsar* had been postponed again and was being revised to please Italian taste. In utter disgust, he gave up going to Milan.

Home again by the middle of May, Piotr Ilyich still clung to the erroneous belief that his entry in the contest for a setting of the *Vakula the Smith* libretto must be ready by August. As soon as the school term was over, he rushed to N. D. Kondratyev's at Nizi, and by the middle of June was at work on the new opera. He had come to regard *The Oprichnik* as a terrible error that could be corrected only by a new opera that would erase it from his slate. It must be utterly different from the accursed work — a specification that *Vakula the Smith* filled by being comic in nature. Except in those

100

frequent moments of black pessimism during which nothing he had done or could do seemed good to him, Piotr Ilyich never demanded of himself an answer to the cogent question whether his talents were suited to opera or not. Had he faced his critical intelligence with that question, it is possible that he might not have spent so much energy, so many wearying months of composition, rehearsal, and regret, on opera after opera. He might have increased his production of music for orchestra, for which everything in his personal and artistic nature fitted him. He might have deprived the world of the numerous beautiful numbers that lie scattered and (outside the Soviet Union) unperformed in his operas. What he would not have done, had he decided to give *The Voivode, Undine,* the aborted *Mandragora,* and *The Oprichnik* no successor, was deprive the world of a truly first-rate opera. That successful amalgam of suitable text, characterization, cogent music, and theatrical effectiveness was what his subjective, introspective, and vibrantly emotional nature was never able to produce.

Piotr Ilyich was being driven hard by the compulsion to blot out the dismal memory of *The Oprichnik.* In one month he completed *Vakula the Smith.* He moved on from Nizi to Usovo. At once he set to work orchestrating the new opera. On September 2 he completed the orchestration and dispatched the score to the contest committee. A few days later he returned to Moscow, still believing that the judges were about to pass on all the entries and award the prize. Never before or after did he compose an opera so rapidly or with such fierce concentration. Nor did he ever again compose an opera for which he was able to maintain the kind of personal affection he had for *Vakula the Smith,* the affection that was to lead him, in 1885, to try improving it by major revisions.

Once more Piotr Ilyich took new rooms — again on the Malaya Nikitskaya. His old friend, the now prominent poet Apukhtin, came to spend two pleasant days with him early in October. Then the blow fell. Piotr Ilyich learned that the closing date of the *Vakula the Smith* contest was not past, but almost a year in the future, August 13, 1875. He was burning with desire to erase *The Oprichnik* from his own and the public's consciousness. He had composed what he fully believed to be a great opera, his best work. He could not bear to wait ten months or more for its staging. So he did a very foolish thing. He wrote to Napravnik and G. P. Kondratyev, chief régisseur of the Marinsky, asking them to find

out if it would be possible to have *Vakula the Smith* performed
at once, independently of the prize contest.

Piotr Ilyich failed to realize that what he had requested would
be unethical. He had earlier let it be known that he was entering
the contest. Now he was informing the judges that the score already in their hands — probably, at so early a date, the only one —
was his own. He was asking them to jeopardize the chances of
anyone else who might be at work on an entry. He was forgetting
that he had not obtained rights to the Polonsky libretto. Naïvely
he sat in Moscow and awaited a favourable reply. The reply was
that Grand Duke Konstantin Nikolayevich and Napravnik were
displeased with him, and that his ill-advised and unethical request
could not be granted. By its open naïveté and unmistakable honesty his reply, dated October 31, 1874, to a letter from Napravnik
fully exculpates him from any suspicion of deliberate underhand-
edness:

> I learned today that you and the Grand Duke are very angry at my
> efforts to get my opera staged independently of the committee's deci-
> sion. I very much regret that my strictly private letter to you and [G. P.]
> Kondratyev should have been brought to the attention of the Grand
> Duke, who perhaps now believes that I refuse to submit to the terms of
> the contest. The situation can be explained very simply. I had mis-
> takenly believed that August 13, 1874, was the final date on which
> compositions might be sent to the committee, and I rushed my work
> to completion. Only on coming back to Moscow did I learn my error,
> and that I must wait more than a year for the judges' decision. In my
> impatience for performance (which means more to me than money), I
> inquired in reply to a letter of Kondratyev's whether it would be pos-
> sible to get my work put on independently of the prize contest. I asked
> him to discuss it with you and let me know. Now I understand that I
> have made a stupid blunder, as I hold no rights in the opera's libretto.
> You need only have told Kondratyev to write and tell me that I was a
> fool, instead of imputing to me ulterior motives I never had. I beseech
> you to discard all suspicions, and to reassure the Grand Duke, who,
> Rubinstein tells me, is exceedingly annoyed at me.

The members of the committee accepted Piotr Ilyich's explanation.

Opera by Russian composers was still supported only halfheartedly in the state theatres. Piotr Ilyich, though far from a nationalist, resented the authorities' sumptuously expressed preference for

the Italian companies, particularly as its results cheapened the productions of his own operas. He went to a farewell concert organized by a departing Italian troupe at the Bolshoi and was happy to note that it was a failure. He hoped to read in this failure accurate news that the cult of Italian-worship was weakening. In mid-November he made a thorough study of Mussorgsky's *Boris Godunov* and Anton Rubinstein's *The Demon*. He wanted to find good in them. He was eager for Russian opera, and not merely his own contributions to it, to be good.

In Rubinstein's most successful opera he accurately found "many lovely things . . . but a great deal of ballast as well." Mussorgsky he could neither comprehend nor tolerate. He regarded that tormented and often incoherent genius as a bungler, an opinion that should be held against him less in view of Rimsky-Korsakov's position. As a member of the Five and a believer in many of Mussorgsky's theories, Rimsky-Korsakov might have been expected to appreciate *Boris Godunov* more easily than Piotr Ilyich could. He, however, found it necessary, during the 1890's, to rework his friend's opera, lending it exactly that polish and refinement for lack of which Piotr Ilyich had condemned it. Today, when *Boris Godunov* is almost universally looked upon as the towering masterpiece of Russian opera, scarcely anyone who has heard both one of Mussorgsky's original versions of it and the Rimsky-Korsakov revision can find a good word to say of the latter. It is only in the light of seventy years of changing taste that we are justified in astonishment at Piotr Ilyich's writing Modest: "Mussorgsky's music I wholeheartedly send to the Devil: it is the cheapest, the vilest of parodies on music."

During the autumn and early winter of 1874 Piotr Ilyich seemed to be best appreciated as a chamber composer. On November 1 his String Quartet in D major was successfully performed by the Moscow Russian Musical Society. Four days later Modest wrote his brother from St. Petersburg that the Quartet in F had enraptured everyone there during rehearsals. It was performed in the northern capital that day, as was the D major on November 26. Piotr Ilyich said of the F major that he considered it his best composition. "Not a single one of my works poured out of me so easily and simply. I wrote it practically at one sitting." He expressed surprise that the public had not at first taken to it, "since I supposed that compositions written in that manner had everything in their favour for pleasing the public." He must have been even more astonished when Cui reviewed the St. Petersburg playing and referred to the quartet as "a very good and talented composition."

Chamber music, however, was always incidental to Piotr Ilyich's plans and desires. Opera and orchestral music were the two fields in which he felt most at home and in which he craved success. He could not in the winter of 1874–5 — or for almost two years after that — locate a suitable libretto. Hope brightened for a moment when the editor for whom he had once begun a biography of Beethoven suggested a libretto with scenes laid during the fifteenth-century persecutions of the Hussites and Taborites. When Piotr Ilyich asked him for a definite plan, he found that the man had none: "He merely likes the fact that they sang hymns."[1] That hope dashed, he toyed with the idea of a piano concerto, but for some time after mentioning the idea to Bessel in November did nothing about it. The St. Petersburg *première* of *The Tempest,* conducted by Napravnik, brought him happiness and rage in equal parts. Stasov and Rimsky-Korsakov were rapturous about it. Cui admitted that it was "a fine, ardent, and talented composition, marvellously orchestrated, melodious and beautiful." Laroche, however, while agreeing that it contained exquisite details, damned the work as derivative and over-noisy. "Laroche's criticism infuriates me," Piotr Ilyich wrote Modest. "How tenderly he points out that I imitate Litolf, Schumann, Glinka, Berlioz, and God knows whom else. As if I could do nothing but compile from any old source!"

As ever when his creative work was not developing to his satisfaction, Piotr Ilyich became surgically introspective. He tortured himself with ideas of the falsity of his friends, with his own lack of talent, with the conscious and pointed unfairness of the world. Gloom and irritability characterized all his dealings with everyone around him. He played part of *Vakula the Smith* for

[1] In the letter to Modest that contained this remark, Tchaikovsky complimented his brother on writing letters with "the elegance of a Sévigné," and expressed the wish that he would develop his literary vein. "Then," he explained, "I might finally get a good libretto." At about this period Modest began to take up writing as an avocation. A little later he became a critic of some reputation. In addition to several plays and a competent, though overcautious biography of Piotr Ilyich, he eventually wrote the librettos of his brother's *The Queen of Spades* and *Yolanta,* Arensky's *Nal and Damayanti,* Napravnik's *Dubrovsky,* and Rachmaninoff's *Francesca da Rimini.*

Kashkin and a few others, but was in such poor spirits that he wholly failed to infuse his reading with life. He noticed that his hearers were only lackadaisically interested and thereupon rushed from the piano. With the intensely subjective person's lack of vision, he blamed his friends for what happened, and tried their patience with his bitterness. Time and again during his life when these depressions seized upon him, only his pervasive personal charm, his friends' understanding of his mental states, and their belief in him prevented him from alienating everyone he knew.

On December 4 Nikolay Rubinstein, at a Russian Musical Society concert in Moscow, included the Overture to *Vakula the Smith* on the program. Piotr Ilyich, "wholly immersed in the composition of a piano concerto," or as he also said, "wallowing in the composition of a piano concerto with my whole soul (it is going very badly)," had, strangely, no comment to make on the performance. He went to Kiev, where on December 21 *The Oprichnik* was performed. He wrote to Bessel that it had been at least as good as in St. Petersburg. "The opera had a great success. At least, the audience made a lot of noise. The ovations were most flattering. I never expected anything like it. A huge crowd of students escorted me from the theatre to the hotel. I was completely happy." Returned to Moscow, he worked unceasingly at the concerto. It was completed before January 2, 1875, for by then he had finished the piano transcription of it. Three days later, before going to a party at Albrecht's home, he arranged to play it through in a classroom at the Conservatory for Nikolay Rubinstein and Hubert.

Piotr Ilyich's account of that first hearing of the B-flat minor Concerto was given three years later in a letter from San Remo to Mme von Meck:

I played the first movement. Not a word, not one remark. Have you ever had the awkward and absurd experience of cooking and serving food to a friend only to have him remain silent? Oh, for one word, for friendly denunciation, for *anything* to interrupt the silence! In the name of God, say *something!* But Rubinstein never opened his mouth. He was getting ready to deliver the blow, and Hubert was waiting to see what would happen. I did not want æsthetic criticism of my composition, but only technical comment. Rubinstein's silence was thunderous. "My dear fellow," he seemed to be saying silently, "how can I criticize small points when the entire work is antipathetic?" I found strength to play the concerto right through. More silence. "Well?" I inquired as I got up from the piano. Then a stream poured from Rubinstein's mouth. Suave at first, gathering force as it continued, and finally breaking out with the violence of Jupiter Tonans. My concerto was valueless, wholly unperformable. The passagework was so fragmentary, disconnected, and poorly composed that it could not be ameliorated. The composition itself was bad, trivial, vulgar. Here and there I had filched from others. Perhaps one or two pages were worth saving; the rest must be destroyed or completely recomposed. "For example, *that!!* And what does *this* signify?" (Here he caricatured my work on the piano.) "Or look there! How could anyone . . . ?" And so on and so on and so on. The chief element I cannot reproduce: the tone of voice in which all this was uttered. A disinterested witness of the scene could have concluded only that I was an untalented idiot, a hack with no knowledge of composition who had had the temerity to submit his rubbish to a great man. Hubert was stunned by my silence and was undoubtedly amazed that a man with many works to his credit — and a professor of composition at the Conservatory — would calmly and without contradicting accept such a denunciation, which no one would dare to hurl at a student before having examined his work carefully. Then he began to criticize Rubinstein's remarks, trying a little to soften their harshness, but agreeing with them. I was not only astounded, but intensely embarrassed by the whole business. I need friendly advice and criticism, and shall always be happy for it. But there was not a shred of friendliness in the whole event. It was a diatribe delivered so as to wound me very deeply. Rendered speechless by anger and agitation, I left the room in complete silence and went upstairs. In a moment Rubinstein joined me and, noticing my agitation, asked me into another room. There he reiterated that the concerto was impossible, singled out many points at which it required complete revision, and then said that if I would alter the composition as he demanded, he would perform it at his concert. "I shall not alter one single note!" I answered. "I shall publish the work exactly as it is!"

Piotr Ilyich's fury at this thoughtless brutality was justified. So was his decision to dedicate the concerto, not to Nikolay Rubinstein, as he had intended, but to Hans von Bülow, who had showed understanding appreciation of his music. But anger led him to the foolish position of not accepting a single suggestion from anyone with regard to the concerto. On February 21 he completed the orchestration. By May it had been published, for during that month or very early in June he had Klindworth forward a copy of it to Bülow. In July he received Bülow's acknowledgment of the presentation copy. Piotr Ilyich was ecstatic over the lavishly com-

NIKOLAY GRIGORYEVICH RUBINSTEIN
From a photograph (1880 or 1881)

plimentary tone of the German musician's letter, which in part read: "I am proud to have been honoured by the dedication of this splendid work of art, ravishing in all its aspects." Bülow planned to play the concerto during his forthcoming American tour. So it happened that the world *première* occurred in Boston, in Music Hall, on October 25, 1875, with Bülow at the piano and with an orchestra conducted by Benjamin Johnson Lang. The first New York performance, again with Bülow, but with the Symphony Society conducted by Leopold Damrosch, occurred on November 22, nine days after Piotr Ilyich had at last heard it performed. For he had to wait impatiently until November 13 for its Russian *première*, which — largely because of Nikolay Rubinstein's attitude — he allotted to St. Petersburg.

In January 1875, at Nikolay Rubinstein's house, Piotr Ilyich had made the personal acquaintance of the young violinist and future teacher of violinists Leopold Auer. When Auer asked Piotr Ilyich to compose something especially for him, the result, completed in about six weeks, was the *Melancholy Serenade* for violin and orchestra, later published as Opus 26 with a dedication to Auer. Today violinists and orchestras who worry Piotr Ilyich's only Violin Concerto into unrecognizable shapes never let us hear this wistfully charming, unimportant piece. It seems to have been played first at a Moscow Russian Musical Society concert of January 28, 1876, by Adolf Brodsky, while the earliest record of its performance by Auer is that of a St. Petersburg concert on November 18 of that same year. Even at the beginning it was taken to be a very minor effort and created little interest and no reactions.

All the while, Piotr Ilyich's depressed state of mind was constant. He wrote Modest that at times he was so completely disgusted with life as to be on the verge of suicide. News that Ferdinand Laub had died blackened his spirits the more. He found pleasure only in a few concerts and operas: Patti superb in *Il Barbiere di Siviglia,* a good performance of Beethoven's "splendid" Seventh Symphony, of Mozart's "Jupiter" Symphony, which he called "one of the wonders of symphonic music," and of Litolf's Piano Concerto in D minor, "one of the most brilliant works in piano literature." He had little to say of Brahms's First Piano Concerto, though the solo part was taken by Nikolay Rubinstein's and his own brilliant pupil, Taneyev, on this occasion making his debut. Liszt's *Dante* Symphony, he decided, was not "among the celebrated pianist-composer's best works," though he found its novel departures and subject matter intensely interesting.

After completing the First Piano Concerto, however, Piotr Ilyich himself had not been fruitful. In the nearly four months between the day he had written finis to its orchestration and the day he left for his summer holiday, he had added the finishing touches to the *Melancholy Serenade* and had composed or completed the eighteen songs that make up Opera 25, 27, and 28. The songs — not one of which belongs among his most imaginative or best-conceived works — reflect his black mental state in their preponderant melancholy. None of them can have occupied his full creative force. He was no Schubert, no Wolf. Except in rare cases, that is, the composition of songs meant that Piotr Ilyich was marking time, being in no state of equilibrium or eagerness for large effort.

The corrected and proofread score of *Vakula the Smith* had to be made ready for resubmission to the prize committee. On May 24 Piotr Ilyich wrote Anatoly: "All my thoughts now are devoted to my beloved offspring, my dear Vakula. You can't imagine how much I love it. I think I'll lose my mind if it doesn't succeed. I don't need the prize— on which I'd like to spit — though money is a good thing too. What I need is to have Vakula performed in a theatre." With the score safely en route to St. Petersburg, he was ready to leave for Usovo. Two large compositions were taking shape in his mind. One was to be his Third Symphony, the other the ballet *Swan Lake*, which had been commissioned by the imperial directorate of the Moscow theatres. For the ballet he was to receive the equivalent of $400. He accepted the commission partly because of the money, partly because he had long wanted to try his hand at this type of composition.

At Usovo, from June 17 on, Piotr Ilyich was at work on the Third Symphony. By the time he moved on to Kondratyev's estate at Nizi about July 10, he had completed it and begun its orchestration. He put the final touches on it at Kamenka on August 13. Enjoying the company of Alexandra Davidova and her children, his father, and Anatoly, he recovered physical and mental resilience. Simultaneously with the last work on the symphony, he sketched *Swan Lake*, incorporating into it the music that he had composed for the Davidov children three years earlier. He told Taneyev on August 26 that he was tired of working and had decided to indulge in a real vacation until time to return to Moscow. He wanted not to think of music, but added that he had completed two acts of the ballet in rough form.

Rimsky-Korsakov freely admitted that he knew which of the scores submitted in the prize contest was Piotr Ilyich's. On October 17, in fact, he wrote about it to the composer: "There is a great deal in it that I like, but also a great deal I don't like. . . . But what a marvellous and — what is more important — what an original harmonist you are. . . . I don't for a moment doubt that your opera will win the prize." He somewhat tempered this praise by stating that the other entries indicated the sad state of Russian music. In this letter the once proudly untaught member of the Five enclosed some original fugues, asking Piotr Ilyich "to look them over, and make as many comments, both technical and æsthetic, as possible."

In November, at about the time the faithful Jürgenson was issuing both his Second String Quartet and his Piano Concerto in B flat major, Piotr Ilyich went to St. Petersburg to be present at the latter's Russian *première*. This took place on November 13 at a Russian Musical Society concert conducted by Napravnik. The solo part was played by a friend of Piotr Ilyich's school days, Gustav G. Kross. The composer later wrote Bülow that at this performance the concerto was "hopelessly mutilated, particularly by the conducting of Napravnik, who did everything he could to accompany in a manner that succeeded in producing a horrible cacophony instead of music."

Years after the first performances of the concerto both Nikolay Rubinstein and Piotr Ilyich were to recede somewhat from their first positions with regard to its simon-pure original version. Rubinstein was often to play it magnificently, making it a popular staple of his repertoire. Its composer, with the blinders of rage removed from his eyes, was to see the justice of Rubinstein's specific criticisms, particularly of unpianistic passages, and was to revise the scoring. The revised version is the one now performed more often than any version of any other concerto. Its European popularity began with Nikolay Rubinstein. Its greater popularity in the United States had begun at Boston on that October 25, 1875 when Hans von Bülow had played it to a cheering audience.[2] On

[2] "Imagine what appetites the Americans have," Tchaikovsky wrote Rimsky-Korsakov on November 24, 1875. "After every performance, Bülow had to repeat *the entire finale!* Such a thing could never happen here."

that occasion Bülow had cabled Piotr Ilyich of the great success
of "their" concerto, and had received a cabled reply that had cost
the composer the last few rubles he happened to have on hand.
From New York on November 24 Bülow wrote Klindworth: "The
concerto went much better here under [Leopold] Damrosch than
in Boston. It was a distinct success and is to be repeated next
Saturday. In fact, Tchaikovsky has become popular in the New
World; and if Jürgenson were not such a damned jackass, but
would send over a reasonable quantity of Tchaikovsky's music, he
could do a lot of business. Yesterday a woman actually bought
the score of Tchaikovsky's symphony, opus 23,[3] at Schuberth's
simply because there was nothing else of his to buy."

The largest conceivable body of music-lovers has never had
the slightest doubt of the rich beauty of the B-flat minor Concerto.
The very opening, when the orchestral strings sound one of Piotr
Ilyich's unforgettable melodies against majestic piano chords giving the 3/4 rhythm, was one of the best-known passages in music
before swing arrangers stole it entire to make it the theme song of
dance hall and air wave for more than two years. All-Tchaikovsky
programs, which seldom fail to crowd halls and open-air concerts,
are able, now as always, to assure the absence of vacant seats by
scheduling the concerto. To the general public, it is the best known
of Piotr Ilyich's major works, though frequent concertgoers may
have heard any of his last three symphonies as often.

It has been musicologists, particularly the most opaque Teutonic
musicologists, who have reviled the Piano Concerto in B flat minor.
Unable to denounce it for oversentimentality or pathological
gloom, they have attacked it on formal and technical grounds. It
is by no means in true concerto form, they say, though not one of
them has ever isolated true concerto form in a living specimen.
The second subject of the first movement, they say, is insignificant.
Even as revised, the solo is unpianistic. These but begin the tally
of the concerto's vices. What this sort of criticism overlooks is that
the composer was not playing a game by prearranged rules. When
Piotr Ilyich did that, he was as capable of grinding out unmeaning
passages of connective tissue as anyone. He was trying to compose, for orchestra and a brilliant piano soloist, an extended piece
of the best music he could imagine. When the material his imagi-

[3] Bülow clearly miswrote here. He meant either "Tchaikovsky's concerto,
opus 23" [the B flat minor] or "Tchaikovsky's symphony, opus 13" [no. 1].

nation and memory [4] presented to him could not naturally be developed in the manner approved by schoolmen, he disregarded the manner rather than the material. No idea of revolutionizing techniques had any part in this process. He merely set forth his melodies, cast his harmonies, placed his rhythms, and varied his orchestration in the ways that best created and preserved the musical matter his imagination poured out. The result would confound academicians if anything could, and entirely justifies the method. Without bringing in senseless comparisons with piano concertos by Mozart, Beethoven, Liszt, Brahms, or any other, it may be said that Piotr Ilyich's B flat minor is wholly successful from the listener's point of view. Unless it be the amount of satisfaction given to its creator, no other test matters much or long. Led by a conductor with sensitive feelings for ensemble, played by a pianist of unlimited technique, intellectual grasp, and a taste for grandeur, the concerto is entirely and beautifully what Piotr Ilyich intended it to be.

Returning to Moscow, Piotr Ilyich went directly from the railroad station to a rehearsal [5] of his Third Symphony. On November 24 he wrote Rimsky-Korsakov that this did not contain any especially successful novel ideas, though some of its scoring was inventive. Of the five movements, he said, he preferred the first and the two Scherzos. The *première*, with Nikolay Rubinstein conducting, had occurred while Piotr Ilyich was in St. Petersburg — at the November 19 concert of the Moscow Russian Musical Society. He announced that he was satisfied with the way the orchestra performed the symphony, which had been enthusiastically received at the concert.

Reviews of the Piano Concerto had begun meanwhile to appear in the St. Petersburg periodicals. In *Sankt-Peterburgskiye Vyedo-*

[4] At least two melodies in the concerto are borrowed. The principal theme of the first movement ("allegro con spirito"), occurring after the majestic introduction, is that of a Ukrainian folksong Tchaikovsky heard sung at Kamenka. His treatment of it in broken triplets for the piano transformed his borrowing into re-creation. Somewhere in the second movement Modest Tchaikovsky discovered a chansonette — *"Il faut s'amuser, danser, et rire"* — that he and Anatoly had heard sung by a favourite singer and had long whistled about the house. No exact identification of this melody is possible.
[5] Modern composers and conductors will be interested to know that there were customarily only three rehearsals of a new work of symphonic dimensions, no one of which might run longer than two hours.

mosti Cui described it as "talented, but very light." Laroche in *Golos* awarded it a "very, very secondary place" among Piotr Ilyich's works, adding that as it would prove ungrateful for pianists it would have no future. No word in any of the first reviews could have led a seer to the belief that it would become the most popular piano concerto in the international repertoire. About the only comforting item Piotr Ilyich could have found during the third week of November was in *Moskovskiye Vyedomosti* of November 20. It announced the award, by Grand Duke Konstantin Nikolayevich, of the first prize in the opera contest to Piotr Ilyich's *Vakula the Smith*. This was followed by official announcement that the opera would be staged in the northern capital, at the Marinsky, the next season.

On December 3 the Moscow Russian Musical Society's third orchestral concert of the season was highlighted by the first local performance of the B-flat minor Piano Concerto. Nikolay Rubinstein conducted, and Taneyev was the soloist. The composer admired Taneyev's performance, singling out as its chief virtue the young man's ability to "penetrate into the smallest details of the composer's conceptions and interpret them in exactly the spirit and intention the composer dreamed of." Two days later, in *Musikalny Listok*, the work received its first favourable critique when Alexander Sergeyevich Famintsin reviewed it, writing that "it astounds the listener by its lucidity and joyousness of spirit from beginning to end."

Piotr Ilyich kept up his customary activities. At Klindworth's home he and Rubinstein and a few other local musicians met to study and play a score of *Der Ring des Nibelungen*. Klindworth astonished them by the masterly way in which he read and played this complex and difficult music. At the Italian opera Patti still sang to Piotr Ilyich's satisfaction, but in *Les Huguenots,* though he saw that she played carefully and with great warmth and sincerity, he said that "on the whole she remains an unsatisfactory Valentine." He changed his lodgings again, this time to rooms on Krestovozdvizhensky Street. He hopefully awaited the opportunity to look over a new libretto, this time by Modest on a subject from the Middle Ages.

Now there appeared on the Moscow scene a vivacious and witty Frenchman, the forty-year-old Charles-Camille Saint-Saëns. Already a prolific and successful handler of almost every musical genre, Saint-Saëns had, like Piotr Ilyich, failed in the theatre. For *La Princesse jaune* had been only mildly received at the Opéra-Comique in 1872, and nobody had been daring enough to stage his Biblical opera-oratorio *Samson et Dalila*, completed the same year. His brilliant mind and encyclopædic knowledge of music appealed to Piotr Ilyich immediately, and for the duration of the Frenchman's stay in Moscow the two composers enjoyed a flare of intimate friendship. One day they brought to light their shared passion for ballet. Impromptu, with Nikolay Rubinstein's assistance, but without onlookers, they staged a ballet entitled *Pygmalion and Galatea*. The orchestra consisted of a jovial Rubinstein at the piano. Saint-Saëns posed as the stony maid whom Piotr Ilyich, as Pygmalion, wooed into life. It is unfortunate, as Modest remarked, that no one but the three performers witnessed this entertainment. We do not know what music was used.

At the Bolshoi, mixed in among routine performances of Gounod's inescapable *Faust*, there was suddenly an appearance by Désirée Artôt, in *Les Huguenots*. Seven years had passed since the days when Piotr Ilyich had succumbed uselessly to her personality and talent. Now he found her indecently fat and possessed of substantially no voice. In spite of these appalling handicaps, he stated that her talent "still has its way."

Piotr Ilyich, in whom a depressed state of mind had become chronic, had decided to go abroad again. Before his departure he composed one large work and one piano piece. The large work was a cantata to words by Nekrasov beginning: "To touch the heart of man." It honoured the great basso Ossip Afanasyevich Petrov on the occasion of his golden jubilee on the stage. The piano piece, *By the Hearth*, was composed as the partial fulfilment of a commission. The editor of *Nuvellist*, a musical magazine, conceived the idea of having Piotr Ilyich contribute to his pages each month for one year a piano composition appropriate to the month. Piotr Ilyich thought this an easy and insignificant task. He instructed his manservant to prod his memory on a certain date each month. He would sit down and compose the required piece at one sitting and forward it to the editor. He kept to the letter of the contract, producing ten salon minutiæ. Only for June and November did any but the most hackneyed and commonplace ideas occur to him. For June he composed a *Barcarolle* that achieved enduring salon popularity. For November he hit upon the only one of his later piano pieces that both rivals the early *Song without Words* and *Humoresque* in public favour and is of conceivable interest to a pianist. This is *Troika,* a simple melody saved from banality by tiny touches of harmonic change and varied by a charming middle section resembling a Russian peasant dance. For some reason the twelve pieces, later published as Opus 37*bis,* have come to be called *The Seasons,* though *The Months* would clearly be the correct title.

With the cantata and the first chapter of his musical serial out of the way, Piotr Ilyich was prepared to accompany Modest to Germany, Switzerland, and France. Modest had abandoned government service to tutor a deaf and dumb boy, Nikolay Konradi, always called Kolya by the Tchaikovskys. Now he was headed for Lyon, where there was a renowned school imparting a phonetic method for teaching deaf-mutes and where the boy's parents wanted their tutor to study for a year. The brothers went first to Berlin. While there, Piotr Ilyich did little but attend the dramatized version of *Around the World in Eighty Days.* From the German capital they went to Geneva, where the Davidovs were visiting, and there spent ten days. Thence they proceeded to Paris.

Not quite one year before — on March 3, 1875 — Piotr Ilyich's pupil and intimate Vladimir Shilovsky had been present at the Opéra-Comique on the night when *Carmen* had had its mildly successful *première.* He had been so intensely moved by Bizet's opera that he had purchased a piano score and sent it to Piotr Ilyich in Moscow. This gift started the most burning and enduring enthusiasm Piotr Ilyich ever felt for a composition by one of his contemporaries. He was already studying the opera with bright admiration when he heard that Bizet had died. Modest remarked that this news, "only three months after the production of the work, served merely to intensify his almost unwholesome passion for this opera." Now Galli-Marié, creator of the name role, was playing it at the Opéra-Comique, and the brothers attended at least one performance, that on January 20. Piotr Ilyich could scarcely restrain his excitement, first over the opera as such, and then over Galli-Marié's interpretation, which Modest described as combining unbridled passion and mystic fatalism, a combination of elements not unknown in Piotr Ilyich's own works. On January 22 Piotr Ilyich left for Berlin and St. Petersburg. In his travelling bags he had preliminary sketches for his Third String Quartet.

On February 5 Napravnik conducted the first St. Petersburg hearing of the Third Symphony. The audience was friendly and mildly appreciative. At the end of the fifth movement Piotr Ilyich had to appear on the stage. Two days later he was back in Moscow and no doubt wondering what Cui and Laroche would do to his symphony. Cui's review stated that the symphony must be judged on serious grounds. He found the first three movements the best, the fourth poor in content, and the concluding "tempo di polacca" the poorest of all. "Taken as a unit, the new symphony shows talent," he admitted, justly adding: "but we have the right to expect more from Tchaikovsky." Laroche abandoned himself to dithyrambs in the columns of *Golos*. "In the power and significance of its content, in the rich diversity of its form, in the nobility of its style — which bears the imprint of an original and independent talent — and in its rare technical perfection, Tchaikovsky's symphony is one of the greatest musical phenomena of the past decade, not — it goes without saying — in Russia alone, but in all Europe."

It was Cui, and not Laroche, whose judgment of the Third Symphony time has rendered valid. It is a symphonic grab-bag, full of five sketchy and tenuously related movements — a "tempo di marcia funebre" that sets off promisingly with a fine melancholy theme, but dwindles shapelessly; an "alla tedesca" that might come out of a suite of *Ländler* by a third-rate Austrian; an Andante of no particular merit; a scatterbrained scherzo, and a furiously rushing "tempo di polacca" whose only achievement has been to earn the symphony its meaningless appellation: "Polish." It is difficult to evade the suspicion that Piotr Ilyich had some of this material lying about on his table or in his head and willy-nilly popped it into what he hoped would turn out a symphony. Parts of it have true Tchaikovskyan charm. As a whole it is artistic miles below the Second and unbelievable as predecessor to the Fourth. It is the only one of the six numbered symphonies in a major key (D), though even it has a minor introduction. Proof of its lack of organic construction is the fact that the order of its movements can be altered two or three ways (including that of leaving one or two of them out altogether) without either damaging or improving its symphonic unity.

Piotr Ilyich received two interesting communications shortly after his return to Moscow. One was a letter from Hans von Bülow, in the United States. This reported that on January 13 the music-lovers of Boston had tendered an "exceptionally warm reception" to a very fine and finished rendition of Piotr Ilyich's First String Quartet. The other was an official invitation to attend the first Bayreuth Festival, to be devoted to the first cyclic performance of *Der Ring des Nibelungen*. Piotr Ilyich dispatched replies at once, to Bülow thanks for disseminating his music abroad, and to Bayreuth acceptance of the invitation.

On March 1 Piotr Ilyich completed the mournful and elegiac E-flat minor String Quartet, Opus 30, dedicating it to the memory of Ferdinand Laub. It was first performed at Nikolay Rubinstein's house thirteen days later. Those present praised it extravagantly, but the composer was not satisfied. "It seems to me that I have written myself out a little," he wrote Modest. "I am beginning to repeat myself and can't think of anything new. Is it possible that my song is finished and that I shall go no farther?" He had been correcting unloved passages in *Vakula the Smith*, and now did the same for the quartet. In somewhat revised form it was used on March 28 to honour Grand Duke Konstantin Nikolayevich on a visit to the Conservatory, and was presented three times at public concerts. Its popularity was almost entirely due to one movement, an "andante funebre."

At the Crystal Palace, London, on March 23, 1876, the renowned Alsatian-English pianist, Wagnerite, and musicologist Edward Dannreuther, played the solo part in the first English rendition of Piotr Ilyich's Piano Concerto in B flat minor. An English critic described the work as distinguished by daring, by frequently felicitous and witty harmony, but also by diffuseness, verbosity, and the presence of supernumerary details. But the English public on that day had begun a love affair with the B flat minor that, for passion and endurance, has been exceeded only by the concerto's relations with the public of the United States.

Piotr Ilyich was not yet quit of *The Oprichnik*. On April 5, 1876 it was revived in Moscow "in a most disgraceful and compromising manner." He had been hard at work on *Swan Lake* [6] and was suffering from spiritual torpor. The botched *Oprichnik* was too much to bear. That day he wrote Modest that he was leaving Moscow for an Easter holiday, which he would spend with Shilovsky in the country. He planned to devote himself wholly to completing *Swan*

[6] A preliminary rehearsal of individual numbers from the first act of *Swan Lake* took place on April 4, 1876.

Lake. He carried out this plan, putting the final touches on the ballet on April 22 at Glebovo. He returned to Moscow somewhat refreshed after an absence of little more than two weeks. He was not in a charitable mood. Writing Modest, he told of hearing the music of an opera, *Count Nulin,* performed by its composer, G. A. Lyshin. "Heavens!" he groaned. "What tripe!"

By May 1876 Piotr Ilyich was so unwell that his physician ordered him to Vichy. He was financially able to carry out this prescription; he was beginning to collect considerable moneys from his compositions. His visit to Bayreuth was to be partly earned by writing articles, and his salary for the school year just closed had amounted to the equivalent of $1,237.50. From Kiev he wrote to Albrecht, asking that a book on *Der Ring des Nibelungen* be sent him. On June 16 he arrived at Kamenka, where he immediately became very ill. He told both Anatoly and his manservant, M. I. Sofronov, that he was having "terrible paroxysms of fever." He complained to Taneyev and Shilovsky that his head was empty: "Nothing can be squeezed out of it." The fever did not abate, and he was unable to read the *Ephraim* libretto Konstantin Shilovsky had sent him. On June 30, however, he was able to leave for Vienna.

In the Austrian capital, despite its being a city he liked, and despite hearing an "ideal rendition" of *Guillaume Tell,* he passed a week in what he called unutterable boredom. Thence he went to meet Modest at Lyon. Now for the first time he met Modest's deaf-mute pupil, Kolya Konradi, of whom he quickly became very fond. He spent six less unhappy days with them, and dragged himself unwillingly to Vichy. From there he wrote Anatoly that he was so overwhelmed by melancholy that he doubted his ability to remain the length of time required for the cure. A Vichy physician, nevertheless, persuaded him to allow for what Modest calls "a 'demi-cure,'" which seemed to alleviate his suffering. He had again been pondering future compositions and was mulling over the personages Modest had presented as candidates for a symphonic poem: Hamlet, Francesca da Rimini, Othello, and Lermontov's Tamara.

On July 24 Piotr Ilyich returned to Lyon for another visit with Modest and Kolya. The three of them, accompanied by Kolya's governess, took a river steamer down the Rhône to Avignon. From there they went on to Montpellier. August 13, the date set for the performance of *Das Rheingold* that was to introduce the first

Bayreuth Festival, was drawing near, and Piotr Ilyich had shortly
to be on his way to the little German town toward which a large
part of the aristocracy of Europe — both hereditary and musical —
was turning its attention. On the train to Paris he read Canto V of
the *Inferno* and settled the subject of his next big composition: it
would be the story of Francesca da Rimini.

"I found many prominent people here," Piotr Ilyich wrote Modest from Bayreuth, "and plunged directly into the vortex of the
festival, in which I revolve from morning to night like one possessed. I have also met Liszt, who received me most cordially.[7]
I called on Wagner, who no longer receives anyone. . . . Among
the people here whom you know are Rubinstein, with whom I live,
Laroche, and Cui. . . . Bayreuth is a tiny little town crowded,
at this moment, with several thousand visitors. . . . I am not
bored, but I cannot say I am enjoying my stay here. All my
thoughts and efforts are bent toward getting back to Russia, via
Vienna, as quickly as possible."

In his report to *Russkiye Vyedomosti* Piotr Ilyich included more
colourful details, and indeed gave one of the best descriptions of
the opening of the festival. "The village was in a furor. Mobs of
people — native and foreign — come together from the ends of the
earth, were rushing toward the railroad station to witness the Emperor's arrival. I saw this spectacle from the window of a near-by
house. First some brilliant uniforms passed by, then the musicians
of the Festspielhaus, in line, with the conductor Hans Richter at
their head. Next followed the fascinating figure of the Abbé Liszt,
with the fine characteristic head I have so often admired in por-
traits. And lastly, in a sumptuous carriage, a serene old man —
Richard Wagner — with his aquiline nose and the delicate, ironic
smile that lends its characteristic expression to the face of the
begetter of this cosmopolitan artistic festival. A rousing cheer re-
sounded from a thousand throats as the Emperor's train entered
the station. The old Emperor stepped into the carriage awaiting
him and was driven to the palace. The crowds greeted Wagner,

[7] More than one year later Tchaikovsky somewhat revised his account of the
cordiality with which Liszt had received him. In a letter of December 9, 1877
to Mme von Meck he wrote: "Last year I met Liszt. He was nauseatingly
polite, but on his lips there was an unchanging smile that expressed the
above words ['My condescension is such that I honour you with my attention
even though you are Russian'] rather plainly."

whose carriage was just behind the Emperor's, with equal enthusiasm. What pride, what overflowing emotions must have welled up at this moment in the heart of that little man who, by his powerful determination and great talent, has defied all obstacles to the final realization of his artistic ideals and audacious beliefs!"

Piotr Ilyich went on to say that everyone he encountered seemed to be searching anxiously for something. That something, he discovered, was food. Bayreuth was overcrowded, and only those who were quartered *en pension* with private families got their meals easily or on time. "As a matter of fact," he commented, "throughout the whole length of the festival, food formed the chief interest of the public. The artistic performances took second place. Chops, baked potatoes, and omelets were discussed much more eagerly than the music of Wagner."

Continuing, Piotr Ilyich reported that "the representatives of all civilized nations were assembled at Bayreuth. In fact, even on the day of my arrival I noticed among the crowd many European and American musical leaders. Yet the greatest of them all, the most famous, were conspicuous by being absent. Verdi, Gounod, Thomas, Brahms, Anton Rubinstein, Raff, Joachim, and Bülow were not in Bayreuth. Among the noted Russian musicians present were Nikolay Rubinstein, Cui, Laroche, Famintsin, Klindworth (who, as is well known, transcribed the Wagner trilogy for pianoforte), Mme Valtsek, Moscow's leading singing teacher, and others." Among the noted Russian musicians he might well have included himself. He told Modest that his artistic pride was flattered more than once: "It would seem that I am not so unknown in western Europe as I had thought."

Despite the best possible will and an ever obvious intention to be fair in his judgment, Piotr Ilyich could not like Wagner's Valhalla-storming epic. The distaste aroused in him by the saurian, dilated, and apparently endless operas appears in his report to *Russkiye Vyedomosti* and is openly expressed in letters. He fully appreciated their importance and never failed to think with wondering admiration of the devoted labour by which they had been created and brought to performance. What he could not like at all was *Der Ring des Nibelungen* itself.

"The performance of Das Rheingold took place on August 13 at 7 p.m.," he said in his article. "It lasted without an intermission for two hours and a half. The other three parts, Walküre, Siegfried, and Götterdämmerung, are given with an hour's intermission, and last from 4 p.m. to 10 p.m. Because of the singer Betz's illness Siegfried was postponed from Tuesday to Wednesday, so that the first cycle lasted a full five days. At three o'clock we took our way to the theatre, which is on a hill some distance from the village. Even for those who have managed to find strength in a good meal, that is the hardest part of the day. The way is uphill with absolutely no shade, so that one is directly in the scorching rays of the sun. Waiting for the performance to begin, the miscellaneous crowd camps on the grass near the theatre. Some dawdle over a glass of beer in the restaurant. . . . On every side one hears complaints of hunger and thirst mingled with comments on current or past performances. At four o'clock, on the dot, the fanfare is sounded, and everyone streams into the theatre. In five minutes every seat is occupied. Again the fanfare is sounded, the murmur of talk is cut off, the lights are turned down, and darkness fills the auditorium. From depths invisible to the audience, where the orchestra is sunk, float up the strains of the beautiful prelude. The curtains part on either side, and the performance begins. Each act lasts one hour and a half. Then there is an intermission, but a very disagreeable one, for the sun is still high, and it is difficult to discover a shady spot. The second intermission, on the other hand, is the most beautiful part of the day. The sun is near the horizon; in the air one can feel the coolness of twilight; the tree-covered hills around and the charming village in the distance are lovely. At about ten o'clock the performance ends."

It was to Modest that Piotr Ilyich confessed. Speaking of *Das Rheingold*, he wrote on August 14: "As a theatrical spectacle the work aroused my interest and charmed me by its wonderful staging. As music it is incredible nonsense, in the midst of which there are occasional flashes of extraordinary and amazing beauty." Some days after the curtains had closed on the first *Götterdämmerung*, he completed this confession: "With the last chords . . . I felt as though I had been set free from captivity. Perhaps the Nibelungen is a great masterpiece, but it is certain that there never was anything more boring and long-drawn-out than this spun-out composition."

Piotr Ilyich's final reactions to the *Ring* are remarkably close to those of many critics, operagoers, and musicians of today: "I brought away the impression that the trilogy contains many pas-

sages of extraordinary beauty, especially symphonic beauty —
which is remarkable, as Wagner has certainly no intention of writing an opera in the style of a symphony. I feel respectful admiration for the enormous talents of the composer and his wealth of
technique of a kind that has never been heard before. And yet I
have grave doubts as to the truth of Wagner's operatic principles.
. . . Yet if the Ring bores one at times, if much of it is at first incomprehensible and vague, if Wagner's harmonies are at times
open to objection as being too complicated and manufactured, if
his theories are false — even if the results of his vast labour should
at last disappear into oblivion and the Festspielhaus fall eternally
to sleep, yet Der Ring des Nibelungen is an occurrence of the
greatest importance to the world, and an epoch-making work of
art."

When that glittering audience dispersed, a weary and discouraged Piotr Ilyich took his way to Nuremberg and Kamenka. Whatever good the Vichy cure had done him had been undone by Bayreuth and its turmoil. He found Nuremberg lovely for one day,
but reached Kamenka and the Davidovs gratefully. He had become convinced that he must wholly change his manner of living
if he was to escape utter disintegration. The happy family life of
his sister, her husband, and their children stood in his imagination
as a beacon pointing the way to this change. He took loneliness to
be his ailment. He thought that intimate sharing of daily life with
another person would solve his problems. That, the world being
what it was, meant a woman. That, in turn, meant marriage. He
enjoyed children. Perhaps at Kamenka in that weary August he
decided that he must have children of his own. He was thirty-six
years old. On August 31 he wrote Modest a letter that must have
electrified that calm young man: "I am going through the most
critical moment of my life. Later on I shall write you about it more
fully. In the meantime I must tell you that I have decided to get
married. This is irrevocable."

This was not a passing desperation. It was an enduring one. On
September 22 Piotr Ilyich added that he had been thinking a great
deal of his future: "My predilections are my greatest, my most in-
surmountable obstacle to happiness. . . . I must fight against nature with all my might. . . . I shall do everything in my power to
get married this year. Should I lack sufficient courage to take such
a step, I shall, at any rate, discard my habits." In the same letter he

wrote: "Beginning today I shall seriously prepare myself to marry someone or other." A week later he enlarged on that fateful phrase: "someone or other," unconsciously retailing one of the chief reasons why he should not have considered marriage. "What comfort — I could almost say joy — there is in returning to my pleasant quarters and sitting down with a book in my hands! At this moment I detest, probably no less than you do, that beautiful, undiscovered being who will make me alter my manner of living. Don't be afraid that I shall rush into this matter; you can be certain that I shall approach it with great caution, and only deliberately." To Anatoly, who was not, as Modest was, homosexual, though he knew of his brothers' abnormality, Piotr Ilyich was not so frank. But to Alexandra Davidova he detailed his plan. There is reason to believe that he always told her everything with complete honesty and assurance of sympathy. Modest and Alexandra worried, pleaded, warned, and expostulated. He answered only that he would select a wife carefully and would wait until 1877 to marry. Otherwise he stuck to his rash resolution until he had carried it out.

In mid-September, Piotr Ilyich left Kamenka, where he had spent "two marvellous weeks," to go "tres à contre-cœur" to Usovo to borrow the equivalent of a thousand dollars. His friends always believed that his intermittent shortage of funds was due in part to his generosity. He could not say no to a request for money. Everything discernible in his character makes likely this unthinking generosity. It is more than possible, however, that on some occasions the rubles he handed to anonymous young men were payments of blackmail. An unscrupulous youth of sufficient attractions and lack of anything like the honesty of a whore or the sympathy of a human being could, supposing that he had been paid for his favours, have terrorized the timorous Piotr Ilyich into further purchases of silence. No documents reveal such transactions. Hints and omissions suggest their reality. Their existence, too, would suggest one more reason for a desperate decision to marry.

These problems were occupying Piotr Ilyich's mind in October 1876. On the 10th of that month, to Modest, he wrote the most naked of his surviving letters: "There are people who cannot help despising me for my vice, if only because they learned to love me before they had any suspicion that I was a man with a lost reputation. Sasha [Alexandra Davidova] is one of them! I know that she guesses everything and forgives everything. A similar attitude is revealed by many other people, who are either loved or honoured by me. Can you possibly think that the consciousness of their pity and forgiveness for actions for which I cannot be held responsible is not a difficult cross to bear? Or that the thought that those who love me may at times be ashamed of me does not torment me? And such occasions have arisen a hundred times and will arise a hundred other times. In a word, I want, through marriage or some other public bond with a woman, to shut the mouths of those contemptible creatures whose opinions I do not value, but who have it in their power to cause sorrow to those dear to me. . . . The realization of my plans is not nearly so imminent as you think. . . . I have sunk so deeply in the mire of my tastes and habits that to discard them at once, as one discards an old glove, is impossible. Besides, I am far from being the possessor of an iron character. Since my recent letters to you, I have already succumbed to my natural inclinations three times."

In June 1876, encouraged if not driven by Russian Pan-Slavists, Prince Milan Obrenovich IV of Serbia declared war on Turkey. What the Pan-Slavists — as well as Alexander II and his advisers — hoped to gain was a Turkish defeat that would enable Russia to regain much of what it had lost in the Crimean War, particularly the province of Bessarabia and dominance at Constantinople. A Russian general led the Serb armies, but the Turks defeated him and drove him back. Alexander intervened personally, temporarily freezing the war. But he could not stop what he had helped to start, and in 1877 was himself forced to declare war on Turkey. Although the war was successful in that Russia recovered Bessarabia (taking it from Rumania), it did not succeed in re-establishing the Tsar's lost position on the Bosporus, largely because England and Austria would not let it. When the Treaty of San Stefano was signed in March 1878, it looked as though Alexander had achieved his aims. But a Congress of Berlin held three months later revised the results in the Sultan's favour, and the Russo-Turkish War proved to have been a costly error for Russia.

Patriotic Russians naturally did not see the preliminaries of this war after the fact or objectively. On September 24, 1876 Piotr Ilyich wrote Lyov Davidov: "We expect a declaration of war any hour, and I was told by competent authority yesterday that today, the 24th, there will be a manifesto. It is at once terrifying and pleasant that our beloved country has at last decided to uphold its honour." A concert was to be given for the benefit of soldiers wounded in what was still called the Serbo-Turkish War. In a fever of jingoism Piotr Ilyich composed for it what was at first called the *Serbo-Russian March,* but which the world now knows as the *Slavic March* (or, in French, as the *Marche slave*). He completed this on October 6. It was performed under Nikolay Rubinstein's baton on November 17 and created what the composer described to his sister as "a whole storm of patriotic enthusiasm." When Cui heard it, he found it "perhaps the most wonderful of all interpretations, in any artistic field, of the state of mind aroused by the events we have been witnessing." The *Slavic March* is a superb occasional piece of bombast and inflation, and nothing more. Its undiminishing popularity has been caused by the catchiness of the melodies out of which it is fabricated — Serb or Slavonic folk tunes and the imperial Russian anthem.[8]

In mid-October, Piotr Ilyich was fretting over the glacial slowness with which rehearsals of *Vakula the Smith* were moving in St. Petersburg. He was once more doctoring the Third String Quartet, but this time only in moments he could steal from his new orchestral work, *Francesca da Rimini.* On October 26 he was able to write Modest that *Francesca* was finished. "I have worked at it with love, and the love, I think, has been quite successful. Regarding the whirlwind, perhaps it could correspond better to Doré's picture: it has not turned out exactly as I wished. However, an accurate estimate of the work is impossible as long as it has been neither orchestrated nor performed." He set to work on the orchestration at once, completing it on November 17. When he heard that Napravnik had scheduled the dances from *Vakula the Smith* for a forthcoming concert, he asked the conductor to substitute *Francesca* for them. But this did not please Napravnik, and the operatic dances were performed. *Francesca da Rimini* did not reach its *première* until 1877, and then in Moscow.

Vakula the Smith was presented at the Marinsky on December 6, 1876. Napravnik conducted, and the cast included the venerable Petrov and Fyodor Stravinsky, father of the composer. The house was sold out, and the large audience, better acquainted with the name and music of Tchaikovsky than when *The Oprichnik* had

---

[8] The *Slavic March* was introduced in the United States during the Boston Symphony Orchestra concert of February 24, 1883, with Sir George Henschel conducting.

been offered, was in a rippling mood of expectation. Everything possible to make *Vakula* a success had been done by an enthusiastic management, cast, orchestra, and conductor. Piotr Ilyich himself had not, for once, lost any of his enthusiasm during rehearsals. He believed it his finest opera and was more than hopeful of success; even Cui had bolstered his hopes.

After the Overture, applause was voluminous and prolonged. The first scene went well. Then the audience began to grow tepid. After the third act Piotr Ilyich was called to the stage, to be greeted by applause and by scattered, but insistent hisses. This was repeated after the fourth act. *Vakula* was a comic opera, and there was little laughter. As the curtains closed over the final scene, everyone involved in the production knew that it was not the success they had expected. The second performance, on December 11, was received with slightly increased signs of approval. But Piotr Ilyich wrote Taneyev that the opera had not pleased and was unlikely to survive for more than five or six repetitions. His explanation is pure Tchaikovsky: "I must freely admit that I am sharply jolted and discouraged. I have no complaint about anything in the mounting of the work. Down to the smallest detail it has been well thought out and prepared. The failure of the opera is my fault. It is overcrowded with needless detail, over-orchestrated, and unvocal. Now I understand why you were cool toward it when I played it for you at Rubinstein's. The style of Vakula is completely unoperatic: it has neither movement nor breadth."

Piotr Ilyich seldom attempted to shift blame onto his collaborators. Even less often, unfortunately, did he make apt criticisms of his own works while he was preparing them and they remained unperformed. The peculiarly subjective nature of his creative process, the hallucinated way in which he worked in a vacuum consisting of himself, his imaginative talent, and his visions, prevented him from taking up an objective stand before his compositions until too late. He could, and did, revise many of them in the light of his own severe criticisms and the suggestions of others. But revised music is seldom so satisfying to composer or listener as music polished and rounded before presentation. Piotr Ilyich did not, like Rimsky-Korsakov, revise because of a hounding desire to have everything he had ever done brought abreast, from year to year, of his current personality and wisdom. But his revisions were seldom happier than his friend's.

The reviews of *Vakula the Smith* were unusually mixed. Cui praised both opera and production, remarking that the success had been considerable, though not so great as had been expected. A few days later he analysed the reasons for its failure sharply. "First," he wrote, "the style of *Vakula* is unoperatic, symphonic; second, there is no correlation of the music and the action on the stage. As for the music, it is noble practically all the way, beautiful both thematically and harmonically." These sentences could have been — and were — repeated, with almost the same pertinence, of every opera Piotr Ilyich composed.

It was a bad period for Piotr Ilyich's music and pride. In Vienna, Hans Richter performed *Romeo and Juliet*. Probably because it was a novelty and because Richter was a renowned Wagnerite, the redoubtable, profound, and foolish Eduard Hanslick trained his siege mortars on it, demolishing it in the columns of *Neue freie Presse*. The audience had shared Richter's liking for the music, but Hanslick's was the voice heard in Russia, together with those of the few hissers who had supported his view. Further, on December 10 Jules-Étienne Pasdeloup had included *Romeo* on a program of his Paris *Concerts populaires*. Writing from Paris that day, Taneyev informed Piotr Ilyich that Pasdeloup had conducted so wrongly as to destroy passage after passage of the music. The only comfort Taneyev could offer was that he had played over the B-flat minor Concerto to Saint-Saëns, who was pleased with it, and that Parisian musicians in general were interested in Piotr Ilyich and his compositions.

Upset by the news of Pasdeloup's bungling, Piotr Ilyich wrote Taneyev to discuss a possible all-Tchaikovsky concert with Saint-Saëns. He suggested as conductor Pasdeloup's rival, Édouard Colonne. Lacking Colonne, he would journey to Paris to conduct such a concert in person. He worked at this idea for some time. On January 6, 1877 he addressed Colonne, asking for the use of his orchestra in the proposed concert. He invited Taneyev to take part in it, and to learn whether Pauline Viardot-García could be persuaded to appear and sing two or three of his songs. On February 10 he finally discarded the idea, writing Taneyev that he could not raise the essential funds.

Piotr Ilyich soon recuperated enough from the labour and disappointment of *Vakula the Smith* to work on his Variations on a Rococo Theme for cello and orchestra. This brightly attractive set clearly reflects his adoration of Mozart. Consisting of an introduction, theme, seven variations, cadenzas, and orchestral interludes, it is deft and melodic in a preponderantly classic style. More objectively and abstractly composed than most of his long works, it is masterly light music. It was written for, and dedicated to, the Russo-German cellist Wilhelm Karl Friedrich Fitzenhagen, who often played it both in Russia and abroad until his death in 1890.

As 1877 opened, Lev Nikolayevich Tolstoy visited Moscow. Piotr Ilyich's admiration for the great man's writings was so strong as to have developed into a cult in which the novelist figured as demigod. He was thrilled, flattered, and embarrassed when Tolstoy called on him and expressed interest in his music. In view of this he persuaded Nikolay Rubinstein to honour Tolstoy with an evening of music at the Conservatory. During this evening Fitzenhagen and the other members of the Conservatory's string quartet performed the *Andante Cantabile* from the D major Quartet. "Never in my life," Piotr Ilyich solemnly entered in his diary, "have I felt so flattered and proud of my creative ability as when Lev Tolstoy, sitting next to me, heard my andante with tears coursing down his cheeks."

The two men discussed music. Tolstoy, to Piotr Ilyich's embarrassment and anger, vituperated Beethoven and expressed distaste for Schumann and Berlioz. On the subject of Mozart they found agreement. But the younger man was upset to find his demigod prejudiced and expansive on subjects on which he was uninformed. He overcame his fear of Tolstoy — he had been afraid that the great writer would merely look at him and instantly know his innermost secrets — only to find him a garrulous and ordinary man ready to discourse banalities. He was more upset when a group of folksongs Tolstoy had promised to send him arrived from Yasnaya Polyana — and proved worthless.

Piotr Ilyich, in his disappointment over personal contact with his idol, reacted against Tolstoy's writings. *Anna Karenina* was appearing in serial form, and he found it "revolting and commonplace," asking Modest if he was not ashamed to praise it. As the dislocations caused in Piotr Ilyich's hierarchical scheme by Tolstoy's visit were healed, and as he persisted to the end of *Anna Karenina*, he revised his opinion, confessing to Modest that his first judgment had been wrong, that the novel was one of Tolstoy's best. He never met the novelist again. In 1886, however, after reading an article on Tolstoy's philosophy, he wrote his reactions into his diary. It is vicious criticism. "Why," he asks, "should this man, who more than any of his predecessors is able to inspire our soul with wonderfully melodic harmonies, who can probe our poor minds and penetrate the most hidden and complex turnings of our moral selves — why must he appear as a preacher and take it upon himself to propagandize and enlighten our befuddled and limited minds?" Later he lashed out against *What I Believe:* "Tolstoy says that in his earlier days, knowing nothing, he was rash enough to want to instruct men from his own ignorance. He regrets that. Yet here he is starting once more to teach. We must conclude, then, that he is no longer ignorant. Whence such self-confidence? Or is it silly presumption? The veritable wise man knows only that he knows nothing." As in his criticism of other men's music, so in his criticism of literature Piotr Ilyich, at times hopelessly biased, was at others brilliantly acute. It took more than passing attention in the 1880's to see that the philosopher-sage Tolstoy was rotten at the core, while the novelist Tolstoy was firmly ripe throughout.

It is likely that at about the time of his meeting with Tolstoy, Piotr Ilyich began his Fourth Symphony. Also the early weeks of 1877 were occupied, in addition to teaching, composing, and editing works for publication by Jürgenson, with rehearsals at the Bolshoi for the first performance of *Swan Lake.* This revolutionary work had a curious, ill-starred career. At the outset sections were omitted because the Bolshoi authorities found them undanceable. This gives the clue both to the revolutionary nature of Piotr Ilyich's ballet music and to the reasons for its unsuccess. It was quite simply more music than ballet dancers, choreographers, and balletomanes could handle. It is music of symphonic size — not great in itself, and seldom profound, but something wholly different from the routine rhythms and pedestrian harmonies of the Minkuses and Drigos and Pugnis who lorded it over Russia's dancing stages at the time. Taking hints from Delibes, who had produced *Coppélia* in 1870 and *Sylvia* in the very year of *Swan Lake's* composition, Piotr Ilyich had lavished craftsmanship and intellection on composing an extended ballet score that would be simultaneously serviceable and of interest in itself.

It is all but impossible for dance-lovers who have become used to such scores as *Daphnis et Chloë* and *Le Sacre du printemps* to think of the wistfully insouciant music of *Swan Lake* as revolutionary. It was precisely *Swan Lake,* none the less, with *Coppélia* and *Sylvia,* that did most eventually to sweep the trashy tinklings of fifth-rate composers from the pit at ballets and substitute for them the possibility of *Daphnis et Chloë* and *Le Sacre du printemps.* This does not mean, obviously, that good music had not been composed for dancing in earlier days. No one who has heard Gluck's *Don Juan,* to name but one example of many, could believe that. It does mean that by 1877 ballet in Russia had come largely to be danced to music written by hired automata of minuscule creative talent.

The first Bolshoi performance of *Swan Lake* was poor in every department. The choreography was by Julius Reisinger, a second-rater. The scenery and costumes were second-hand or worse, and the conductor could master neither score nor musicians. It was a benefit performance for a ballerina named Karpakova, otherwise unknown to fame. The "too difficult" numbers from the carefully constructed score were replaced with sections borrowed from other ballets, making the whole a pastiche. Through four acts — *Swan Lake* has a complex German fairy-story plot requiring the prima ballerina to dance and mime a dual role — it was a soggy failure. It was repeated a very few times and then dropped from the Bolshoi. True to himself, Piotr Ilyich blamed the score for what had happened, and for the rest of his life intermittently dawdled over the idea of revising it, without ever doing so.

Shortly after Piotr Ilyich's death in 1893, the great choreographer Marius Petipa, then over seventy, sent from St. Petersburg to Moscow for the original score of *Swan Lake.* Looking through it, he rose inflamed with enthusiasm — he had already made ballet history by his production of Piotr Ilyich's *Sleeping Beauty* — and asked the authorities to allow its restaging. In their rush to memorialize the recently dead composer, they permitted time only for Act II to be studied. Petipa sketched out the general choreographic scheme for this, though the details were worked out by one of his co-workers, Lyov I. Ivanov. The performance took place at the Marinsky on February 29, 1894. At last, again at the Marinsky, and again with Petipa-Ivanov choreography, the complete

Swan Lake Piotr Ilyich had composed was performed on January 27, 1895, as a benefit for the dazzling Italian ballerina Pierina Legnani.

Today, outside the Soviet Union, the complete *Swan Lake* is seldom performed, though it has been revived in England.[9] However, separate acts — and particularly pastiche acts including numbers from other acts — are a staple of every ballet company. One aspect or the other — at times both aspects — of the dual-personality role of Odette-Odile has been danced by a dozen outstanding ballerinas since Legnani, including Pavlova, Karsavina, Kshesinskaya, Spesivtseva, and, in our time, Danilova, Markova, Baronova, and Toumanova. The predominantly mime and support role of Siegfried has been done by Nijinsky, Mordkin, Lifar, Dolin, and Youskevitch, to name but a few. Without *Swan Lake*, balletomanes are agreed, ballet would not be ballet. It is a foundation of that art as understood today.

The music Piotr Ilyich composed for *Swan Lake* is marvellously atmospheric. Performed as a fragmented four-movement symphony, it would prove to consist of a multitude of brief evocations redolent of magic at once story-book and human, connected and separated by less numerous sections of mechanical time-beating. In character dances and national dances it has moments of brashness, of period trashiness. But in such sections as require it, potent charm of melody and harmony spread over it. As what it was designed to be — music to be danced and mimed as one means of projecting a story — it is superb. With it alone to his credit, Piotr Ilyich would outrank almost all other composers of ballet.

In March 1877, when that bedraggled staging of *Swan Lake* was presented to an indifferent public, Piotr Ilyich had started the most fateful and dramatic year of his life. He had already made the acquaintance of the two women who were to project themselves farther into the internal drama he lived than anyone else. One of them would turn that drama into suddenly concentrated tragedy. The other would lend him the most peaceful and carefree years of his maturity. The first was a Conservatory student he had scarcely noticed, Antonina Ivanovna Milyukova. The other was a rich widow he had never met, but with whom he had begun one of the

[9] At the Sadler's Wells Theatre, November 20, 1934, with Markova and Robert Helpmann. Margot Fonteyn has been identified with the dual role in later English performances.

most fantastic friendships-by-letter in history, Nadezhda Filaretovna Frolovskaya von Meck. Destiny and well-meaning friends
were joining forces to tear his life into blazing shreds. It would be
up to him, assisted by the same destiny and the same well-meaning
friends, to stamp out the flames and reweave his life.

VIII

A T the graduation exercises held in the Moscow Conservatory late in the spring of 1876 a medal was awarded to Yosif Yosifovich Kotek, who had shone in the violin class and in Piotr Ilyich's course in the theory of composition. Modest describes Kotek as "good-looking, big-hearted, enthusiastic, and a talented virtuoso." He had conceived a schoolboy crush on his composition teacher, whom he regarded as unable to be wrong in anything. While Kotek was still a student, their relationship became close friendship. After his graduation he was in desperate need of a teaching position to fill the interval until he would be prepared to besiege western Europe as a performing violinist. Nikolay Rubinstein found him a perfect situation.

The director of the Conservatory was substantially the sole visitor from outside her large family whom Nadezhda Filaretovna von Meck cared to receive in the period following her husband's death. She was passionately, undiscriminatingly infatuated with music, which she used as an anodyne to sorrow, loneliness, and a widow's state as another woman might use alcohol or narcotics. Nikolay Rubinstein was the logical man to serve as her contact with the musical world of Moscow. From her point of view, he was the leading figure in that world, director of the Conservatory and the local Russian Musical Society, a renowned pianist, and the most dynamic musical figure in the city. From his point of view, she was the richest woman in Moscow and a patroness of musicians. Neither of them ever abused the other's confidence; each was of value to the other.

Nadezhda Filaretovna Frolovskaya was born in 1831, nine years earlier than Piotr Ilyich, to middle-class parents in a small village southwest of Moscow. Her father was an amateur violinist and all-round musician, and her acquaintance with music was early and wide. At seventeen she married Karl Georg Otto von Meck, a member of a knightly German-Balt family of Riga. Their early years of married life were a time of something like poverty, prin-

cipally because several of the twelve children she bore him arrived
very quickly. At a date when she had already added five to the
family, their income was a government salary equivalent to $750
a year. Nadezhda Filaretovna was more ambitious than her husband. She prodded him into resigning his static position with an
eye to entering possibly more profitable private railroad work.
According to her statement, when he finally did resign they had
not more than the equivalent of ten cents a day for all expenses.

Nadezhda Filaretovna had been right, as she had a lifelong
habit of being. As a private railroader Karl von Meck became afflu-
ent and at last rich. In 1876 he died, leaving her with a vast fortune and eleven living children, seven of them — the youngest a
girl of four — still at home with her in a huge mansion on Rozhdestvensky Boulevard. She was genuinely grieved by her husband's
death, but relieved by the cessation of sexual demands on her. She
was later to tell Piotr Ilyich that she thought it too bad that human
beings could not be artificially produced, thus obviating the need
for marriage. Despite her twelve childbearings, her experience of
marriage had been that of a frigid or an unsatisfied woman. The
results of that abnormal state influenced the remainder of her life
and changed that of Piotr Ilyich. She encased herself in the Rozhdestvensky house like an eremite, rendering herself invisible by
one motion of her strong will. Emerging only to attend occasional
concerts and operas or to go on caravanlike hegiras abroad, she
existed in a universe of sons, daughters, grandchildren, servants —
and emotions stirred by music and sublimated into music.

Mme von Meck first became conscious of the existence of Piotr
Ilyich during a hearing of *The Tempest*. Whether she heard it in
concert, had it played for her in piano transcription, or played it
over to herself is unknown. "I cannot tell you the impression it
made on me," she later wrote Piotr Ilyich. "For several days I was
half-demented." Instantly identifying the music and the man who
had composed it, she instituted elaborate inquiries about him. She
began collecting, as if they were stray jewels, Piotr Ilyich's remarks and opinions as Rubinstein and others reported them. Beyond question she learned much about him from her caller and
friend Nikolay Rubinstein.

After her husband's death Nadezhda Filaretovna added to her
already enormous staff of servants a captive violinist. She herself
played the piano, and the staff musician's duties included playing

to her accompaniment and arranging music that she liked so that it could be so played. Nikolay Rubinstein recommended Kotek as qualified and deserving. That he was an admirer and friend of Piotr Ilyich would also have been in his favour. He was hired. It is to be taken for granted that among the first pieces Nadezhda Filaretovna had him play with her were compositions by her favourite composer, his teacher and friend. It is known that he was required to tell her in detail what he knew and could remember about Piotr Ilyich, who could have asked no more inflamed or devoted ambassador to her heart and attention.

One fact Nadezhda Filaretovna learned about Piotr Ilyich was that he always needed money. That a man whom she regarded as a genius should be irked by lack of what she possessed in abundance was intolerable to her. She determined to find a way of increasing his income. What better way than by giving him commissions, thus simultaneously benefiting his financial and artistic states and enabling herself to hear his music? She was a decisive woman, and she acted. Some time in December 1876 Piotr Ilyich received, through either Kotek or Nikolay Rubinstein, his first order from the fabulous recluse of Rozhdetsvensky Boulevard. It was for a violin-and-piano arrangement, of what we do not know. Piotr Ilyich produced the transcription speedily, and on December 30 Nadezhda Filaretovna wrote the earliest surviving letter of a correspondence unparalleled in musical history. It was formal and restrained:

HONOURED SIR:

Permit me to extend my sincere gratitude for your rapid execution of my commission. It would be superfluous for me to tell you of the enthusiasm I feel for your music, for you are doubtless used to receiving homage quite unlike any a person so insignificant, musically speaking, as I am could offer. It might, for that reason, appear to you absurd, and my admiration is something I value too highly to want it laughed at. Thus I shall make only one statement, which I ask you to accept as literal truth — your music makes life easier and pleasanter to go through.

The following day Piotr Ilyich answered, a brief note compared with the hundreds of long letters he would address to Nadezhda Filaretovna later on:

HONOURED MADAME:

Thank you most sincerely for the gracious and flattering things you have written me. For my part, I can assure you that it is a great comfort

for a musician, among all his failures and trials, to know of the existence
of a few people, of whom you are one, who are true and passionate
music-lovers.

For fourteen years post and private messenger were to carry letters back and forth between Nadezhda Filaretovna and Piotr Ilyich. What survives of that correspondence fills three large volumes published by the Soviet government. The salutations of the
letters become more friendly and intimate, culminating in "Dear
Piotr Ilyich," "Dear Nadezhda Filaretovna," and finally "Beloved,
incomparable Friend." Into her letters went, at last, all but the final,
innermost secrets that a nineteenth-century lady would share with
no one, though even they are between the lines in sympathetic ink.
Into his letters went everything he dared to tell her — and he
stopped only at the door to his erotic life. Did she move, with her
children, servants, animals, and endless impedimenta, from Moscow to her country estate or Riviera villa, every detail went into a
letter to her composer. Did he suffer or rejoice, receive praise or
rebuff, she knew it as soon as the post could cross the spaces between them. Yet they were never introduced to each other, never
held a conversation, never — except in a concert hall — spent time
under one roof. They saw each other less than a half-dozen times,
and then either by embarrassing accident or because she had gone
to a concert he was conducting. This relationship, constantly a
friendship of the most intimate sort, and at times blossoming into
love, existed for more than fourteen years without the propinquity
that is the essence of every love affair and almost every friendship.

Nadezhda Filaretovna wished it that way. Piotr Ilyich, learning
of her wish, granted it happily. She was infatuated with Tchaikovsky the composer, and confused him with Piotr Ilyich the man only
at times. She knew clearly that the two were not the same. She had
but recently been freed from a sexual relationship that had not
meant happiness to her, and she did not consciously want a lover.
A few times she blindly, in despite of her will, reached out to touch
Tchaikovsky the composer, unconsciously desiring to transform the
prolonged love affair she was carrying on with that ideal creator
of music into an actual and perhaps even erotic contact with the
living man who created the music. Another man than Piotr Ilyich,
a heterosexual man — or one less scrupulous — might have responded to one of those blind thrusts by her unconscious. Him
they merely terrified, for the condition of apartness she had im-

posed on their friendship was the only one under which he could have had any but the most superficial prolonged relationship with any woman near his own age. So, partly because he ignored her slips or gently rebuffed them, partly because she herself recognized and regretted them, she always withdrew again behind curtains of distance.

A field day for the psychoanalyst, professional or amateur, is offered by Nadezhda Filaretovna's letters. Indeed, they are often so inchoate, so clearly written instead of what her inmost being really wanted to say, that it is possible, without stretching analysis far, to read almost anything just below their surfaces. Piotr Ilyich's letters are less complex. He knew exactly what he dared to say and exactly what he must omit saying. Her side of the correspondence, that is, tells us all about her, while his only reveals his inner character when read in the light of facts found outside his letters. A biography of Nadezhda Filaretovna might be a book of endless fascination. But to a biographer of Piotr Ilyich her letters are of interest only when they give information about him and about those of her states of mind that affected him.

Some time before March 6, 1877 Piotr Ilyich conducted the *Slavic March* at the Bolshoi. He reported to Alexandra Davidova that he had been unskilful and faltering, but had scored a success. He added that he must seek out opportunities of conducting his works, as he planned to do so abroad and must conquer his "insane shyness." On March 9, at a concert of the Moscow Russian Musical Society, Nikolay Rubinstein conducted the *première* of *Francesca da Rimini*. It was brilliantly successful: the conducting was Rubinstein at his best. It was repeated in Moscow within the month. Despite this, and despite the prospects of his relationship with Nadezhda Filaretovna, Piotr Ilyich now fell into one of the worst of his spells of black depression. On April 1 he journeyed to Kamenka, possibly hoping to secure renewal and surcease among the Davidovs.

Although he was working desultorily on the Fourth Symphony and had given up *Othello*, Piotr Ilyich could not evade the vision of a successful opera. Stasov now had another suggestion: a libretto called *Cardinal*, drawn from Alfred de Vigny's *Cinq-Mars*. Piotr Ilyich thought this over and answered: "I have decided definitely that Cardinal does not satisfy the demands of my musical make-up. It is difficult for me to explain in detail exactly what my soul craves. I need a subject dominated by a single dramatic motive, such as love (maternal or sexual, it doesn't matter), jealousy, ambition, patriotism, etc. I should like a more intimate, more modest drama than the sweeping historical one in which the nobility and selflessness of Cinq-Mars, the craft of Richelieu, the feebleness of the King, the fickleness of Marie, the martyrdom of Grandiet, the devotion of the Abbot, the baseness of Père Joseph all combine into a colossal drama requiring a colossal talent and — should it be composed — a colossal theatre with a colossal cast." Piotr Ilyich could at times err about his own talents, but he knew absolutely that he was not Meyerbeer.[1]

From an unexpected source the idea he was seeking suddenly came. Visiting the home of the singer Yelizaveta A. Lavrovskaya, Piotr Ilyich took part in conversation about librettos. One of the guests made what he called "appalling suggestions." Mme Lavrovskaya herself asked: "What about *Yevgeny Onyegin?*" At the moment, Piotr Ilyich wrote Modest: "The idea struck me as wild, and I didn't answer. Later, while dining alone in a restaurant, I recalled her words, and on second thought the idea did not seem at all preposterous. I quickly made up my mind, and at once set off to find Pushkin's works. I found them with some difficulty. I was enchanted when I read the work. I couldn't sleep that night; result — a sketch of a delightful opera based on the Pushkin text. The next day I went to [Konstantin] Shilovsky, who is now at work feverishly on my sketch. You have no idea how mad I am about this subject. How grateful I am to avoid the banal Pharaohs, Ethiopian princesses, poisoned cups, and the rest of those tales of automata. What a wealth of poetry there is in Onyegin! I am not unaware of its faults. I know full well that it gives small scope for treatment, and will be poor in stage effects. But the wealth of poetry, the human quality and simplicity of the subject, expressed in Pushkin's inspired lines, will make up for whatever it lacks in other ways."

On June 18, writing to Modest from the Shilovsky estate at Glebovo, Piotr Ilyich had lost none of his enthusiasm for the Pushkin story. "I am in love with the image of Tatyana," he chanted. "I am under the spell of Pushkin's poetry, and am compelled to compose the music as if by irresistible attraction. I am lost in the

[1] Gounod's *Cinq-Mars,* an opera based on Vigny's romance, was presented in Paris in 1877.

composition of the opera." Tatyana, the ill-treated heroine of the story, was, in a very real sense, to be the third woman taking part in the uprooting of his life that was now full upon him. He was in love with her because of the way she was maltreated by Onyegin. He was to confuse her with a living woman to his own despair.

Just before May 15 Piotr Ilyich received from Nadezhda Filaretovna a commission for a violin-and-piano composition on the subject of reproach. On almost exactly the same day he received a letter from one of his Conservatory pupils, Antonina Ivanovna Milyukova. She wrote that she had long been in love with him. Here was a situation whole out of *Yevgeny Onyegin*.[2] He did not intend to act the brutal Onyegin. Furthermore, he wanted to get married. With one hand, he started inquiries into the character of Antonina Milyukova. With the other, respecting the warmth and sincerity of her letter, he wrote saying that all he could offer in return for her love was gratitude and sympathy. He did not explicitly attack her feeling for him. Simultaneously, his conscience began to bother him with regard to Nadezhda Filaretovna's commissions: he understood clearly that they were disguised charity. So a letter went forth to her also, refusing to supply the composition about reproach. He explained his refusal to write it, and asked for a loan equivalent to $1,500. He added — here the mixture of honesty and disingenuousness may be too tangled to unravel — that he was hard at work on the Fourth Symphony, which he wanted to dedicate to her. "I think," he explained, "that you will find in it echoes of your own inmost thoughts and desires."

Piotr Ilyich was hard at work completing the first draft of the third movement of his new symphony when he received from a friend a highly unfavourable report on Antonina Milyukova. We do not know what this report contained. She was twenty-eight years old, and if the report was accurate it added that she was reasonably good-looking and had a good moral reputation though she lived alone, apart from her mother. She was unintelligent to the

[2] Tatyana, infatuated with Onyegin, declares her love in a letter to him. Onyegin receives it and then meets her in a garden to say that he honours her for her frankness and honesty, but cannot be her husband, being profligate and completely unsuited to marriage. He tells her unfeelingly that a young girl's love is dream-stuff that can be willed away. This leads to a loveless marriage for Tatyana, to the death of her sister's lover at Onyegin's hands in a duel, and finally to Onyegin's fruitless discovery, years later, that he has ruined his own life.

point of stupidity and had firmly enthroned and dangerous delusions about being desired by all men. She was of a mind so unsound that it would eventually give way, and was an incipient nymphomaniac. The items of this after-the-fact report that were visible on the surface Piotr Ilyich must have known, while those that he could not see he might have deduced had it not been for Tatyana and Onyegin. To a man lost in an imaginary world in which a young girl declares herself passionately to a man who has showed no interest in her, a similar declaration addressed to himself by a real girl would not seem extraordinary. Nor would such a man be made wary when the girl's pursuit failed to slacken in the face of his own lack of response.

Antonina Milyukova's reply to Piotr Ilyich's first letter had been an invitation to call on her. He wanted to be married, and as he shortly later told Anatoly: "*She is as much in love with me as a cat.*" He accepted her invitation. Face to face with her, he repeated that he had nothing beyond gratitude and sympathy to offer her. Away from her, however, he began to examine his own conduct. In a letter to Nadezhda Filaretovna he later wrote: "If I did not care for her, if I wanted not to encourage her affection, why did I go to see her? . . ."

Life went on as it does when a storm is moving in. Piotr Ilyich spent some days with Shilovsky at Glebovo. He wrote Klimenko that he was thinking of "marriage or some other lasting union." He wrote to Antonina Milyukova listing many blemishes on his character. On May 28 she answered in a vague ramble that expressed understanding of how difficult it must be to read her letters. She had, she said, been forced to listen, one week before, to a declaration of love from a man "who has been in love with me almost since school days, and has remained true to me for five years." Possibly she was telling of a real occurrence. More likely, in view of her later delusions, she was making it up in such a way that she believed in it. One statement that she iterated and reiterated was a fact: she was passionately in love with Piotr Ilyich.

On May 30 Antonina Milyukova wrote a letter that is a shocking mixture of fiction, incoherence, and threat: "I sat at home all day, wandering from one corner to another like one half-demented, thinking constantly of the minute when I shall see you. I shall be prepared to throw myself on you, kiss you — but what right would I have to do that? You would consider me forward. You were frank with me, and I owe you similar frankness, but I must add that it would be very unfair if you misinterpreted this confession of my emotions. I assure you that I am a girl of good reputation. I have nothing to conceal from you. My first kiss will be yours and no one else's. Farewell, my dear one. Don't try to disillusion me about yourself, because you'll be wasting your time. I can't go on without you, and so it may be that I'll soon put an end to my life. Let me look at you and kiss you so that I may take that kiss with me into the other world. Good-bye. Eternally yours. . . ."

Whatever it was that Piotr Ilyich had so frankly told the girl in an attempt to disillusion her about himself had been unavailing. He had not damped the unreasoning passion she felt for him. Now she had threatened to commit suicide. On June 1 he went to see her, and there is evidence that he returned two days later. It is extremely likely that at some time near that date he told her, with what delicacy and internal shuddering can only be imagined, the fundamental reason why he would be a poor husband indeed. Either she did not believe him or she did not understand what he told her — or, and this is most probable, she was convinced that she could change him into the lover-husband she craved. When he saw that she was not to be diverted and was possibly at the edge of violence, he asked her to marry him. Without hesitation she accepted. This happened between June 4 and June 8. Nowhere, at any time, is there a word of evidence that he ever tried to convince himself or anyone else that Antonina Milyukova's infatuation was reciprocated, or that he felt toward her anything other than sympathy and gratitude.

Having taken this monumentally foolish step, Piotr Ilyich became suddenly calm. He wrote Nadezhda Filaretovna on June 8 that he had completed the first draft of the Fourth Symphony, and that he had decided to compose an opera on Pushkin's *Yevgeny Onyegin.* As though it were an afterthought, he added: "One small detail agitates me a great deal. I can write you nothing at present, but shall probably, in my next letter, explain what it is all about, and how it will end." It is difficult to decide whether this was an attempt to deceive himself or one to prepare Nadezhda Filaretovna for the news. Certainly his forthcoming marriage was not a "small detail." In no letter could he ever "explain what it is all about, and how it will end," for on neither point did he have sufficient information.

On June 10 Piotr Ilyich paid a short visit to Shilovsky at Glebovo. He worked hard and joyfully at *Yevgeny Onyegin*, describing his progress to Nadezhda Filaretovna, and staunchly defending Pushkin against her dislike. At last, on July 5, he came to the point of telling someone in his family of his engagement. On that date he wrote the news to Anatoly, enclosing a brief request for his father's blessing. "I have thought it over," he told Anatoly, "and am taking this step with a calm mind. You will realize how unshaken I am when I tell you that, with the prospect of the wedding before me, I have been able to compose two thirds of my opera. I am marrying a girl who is not so young, but quite passable, and who has one leading virtue: *she is as much in love with me as a cat.* She is poor, and her name is Antonina Ivanovna Milyukova. I now invite you to my wedding. With Kotek, you will be the only witness of the ceremony. Ask Father not to mention it to anyone. I shall write Sasha and our brothers myself." To his father he wrote reassuringly. A stranger reading these letters would have pictured Piotr Ilyich as an entirely calm, if unenthusiastic young man about to marry a somewhat unattractive girl of whom he was mildly fond. There is no agitation in them.

Back in Moscow, Piotr Ilyich, on July 15, faced the issue of informing Nadezhda Filaretovna of the step he had made without her advice, knowledge, or approval. With the wedding only three days away, he told her the unvarnished story of what had happened. It was in the process of writing this extraordinary letter that he himself was seized by a panicky sense of terror at what he had done and was about to do:

For God's sake, dear Nadezhda Filaretovna, forgive my not having written you earlier. Here, in brief, is the story of what has lately been happening to me.

Early in June, first of all, to my own astonishment, I became engaged. This is how it happened. Awhile back I received a letter from a girl I had seen and met. From it I learned that for a considerable time she had honoured me by being in love with me. The letter was written so sincerely and with such warmth that I was driven to answer it — a thing that in other similar cases I had always evaded. My reply held out no hope that the emotion could become mutual, but it started a correspondence. Without detailing what followed, I shall merely say that I finally called on her. Why did I do so? Now I believe that Fate attracted me to that girl. When we met I repeated that I could offer no more than

gratitude and sympathy in exchange for her love. After that I began
to consider how foolish my behaviour had been. If I did not care for
her, if I did not want to encourage her, why did I call on her, and
where would it all end?

Her next communication made me see that if I were suddenly to
cut off our relationship after having gone this far, I should make her
truly unhappy and drive her to a tragic end. I faced a painful choice:
I must preserve my freedom at the price of the girl's ruin (this is not
a mere word — she honestly adores me to distraction) or I must marry.
I could make only the latter choice. One factor that aided me in making this decision was the constant hope of my eighty-two-year-old
father and all my relatives that I would marry. Thereupon I went one
evening to my future wife, told her frankly that I did not love her, said
that I would be a devoted and grateful friend, described in detail my
character, irritability, unstable temperament, misanthropy, and, finally,
my financial status. Then I asked her if she would care to be my wife.
Of course her answer was yes. There is no way of describing the torture I went through following that evening — it must be imagined.
Naturally, having lived thirty-seven years with a distaste for marriage,
it is painful, all at once, to be changed by destiny into a man engaged
to a woman he does not love.

The letter proceeds to describe Antonina much as he had pictured her to Anatoly. It discusses *Yevgeny Onyegin* and Pushkin.
It assures Nadezhda Filaretovna that for her he feels tender friendship, love, and gratitude. He tells her that he is pleased to accede
to her request that his dedication to her of the Fourth Symphony
omit her name and read simply "Dedicated to My Best Friend."
Then there is a final paragraph:

And now farewell, my dear, sweet, good friend. Hope that I shall not
give way under the approaching new life. God knows I have the fullest
good intentions toward my future companion, and if we are unhappy I
shall not be to blame. My conscience is clear. I am marrying without
love, but I do it because circumstances left me no alternative. I stupidly
accepted the first declaration of love from her. I should never have
replied. Once I had encouraged her affection by replying and going to
see her, I could only do what I have done. At any rate, I say again that
my conscience is clear. I have not lied or pretended to her. I have told
her what she can expect from me, and on what she cannot count. Please
tell no one what led to my marriage. You are the only one to know.

Having objectified his perilous situation, and thus for a few hours
pushed it a little away, Piotr Ilyich at last informed Alexandra

Davidova and Modest of what was taking place. His letters to them are dated one day before the ceremony. He may have believed that they would oppose this particular marriage and, if given time, attempt to stop it. Neither of them was to know anything about it until it had been accomplished.

On July 18, 1877, at the Church of St. George on the Malaya Nikitskaya, Antonina Ivanovna Milyukova became the wife of Piotr Ilyich Tchaikovsky in the presence of Kotek and Anatoly. That evening the newly married couple left for St. Petersburg. They planned to visit old Ilya Petrovich and then, after returning to Moscow, to call on Antonina Ivanovna's mother, who lived near by in the country.

"As the train started," Piotr Ilyich wrote Anatoly two days later, "I was at the point of screaming, choked up with sobs. In spite of that, I had to talk entertainingly with my wife as far as Klin in order to buy the right to remain, alone with myself, in my own chair in the dark. . . . The only mitigation was that she did not understand or recognize my poorly concealed agony." If Antonina Ivanovna had hoped, despite warnings, to find her husband a lover on their wedding night, her hope was disappointed. He did not desire her, had never desired sexual contact with any woman, and in all probability never would desire it. The best thing he could find to write about her to Anatoly was that she agreed without qualification to his provisos, would be satisfied with merely fondling him and caring for him, and was not very bright. "A clever woman," he explained, "would terrify me. In relation to this one I stand so high and rule her so completely that at least I am not afraid of her."

With one hand Piotr Ilyich wrote Modest his belief that in time he would learn to love Antonina. With the other, three days later, he told Anatoly that she had become physically loathsome to him. His nerves, already raw, were being exacerbated by her nearness, her docility, her yearning love, and the constant, inescapable knowledge that she wanted, hoped, and perhaps expected that he would soon become her husband in act as well as in name. It is doubtful that he had one waking moment short of nervous terror from just before the wedding until he and Antonina Ivanovna returned to Moscow on July 26.

The visit to his mother-in-law had to be gone through, but what Piotr Ilyich could not face was remaining in Moscow with Antonina. Finding a letter from Nadezhda Filaretovna, a letter in which her sympathy proved big enough to encompass his marriage, he wrote her asking that she lend him another thousand rubles so that he could go away alone to think and rest. From a sum she had sent him earlier he had originally saved enough for a vacation in the Caucasus, but his marriage had used it up. He would, he wrote, tell her the entire story of his marriage and the torments he had been enduring, but could not do so in his excited, abnormal state of mind. All he now wanted was the means with which to get away from his wife, regain some of his lost peace of mind, and once again compose.

Nadezhda Filaretovna sent him the money and urged him to go to the Caucasus at once. All that she asked in return was that he think of her and, when in the proper state of mind, tell her what had occurred. On August 7, the visit to Antonina's mother accomplished, he wrote Nadezhda Filaretovna that he was leaving Moscow alone in an hour. He planned to break his trip at Kiev for several hours for the single purpose of writing her in detail all that had happened. "If I come out of this mortal spiritual battle victorious," he concluded, "I shall be beholden to you, and to you only. A few days more of this would have unhinged my mind. Farewell, my most beloved friend, my Providence." He was going, not to the Caucasus, but to Kamenka.

Piotr Ilyich kept his word. From Kiev, on August 9, he wrote Nadezhda Filaretovna a letter that is like bloody pulp torn from his body:

Nadezhda Filaretovna: here, in brief, is a history of everything I have gone through since July 18, the day of my marriage.

I wrote you that I was marrying without the urgings of affection because of circumstances I could not understand, circumstances that had placed me in a difficult dilemma. I had either to desert an honest girl whose love I had thoughtlessly encouraged, or to marry her. I took the latter course. In the beginning, I sincerely believed that I would fall in love with a girl so truly devoted to me. Also, I realized that my marriage was realizing the dreams of my aged father and other dear ones. The moment the wedding was over, and I found myself alone with my wife and realized that our future lot was to be inseparably united, I suddenly realized that I did not feel even ordinarily friendly toward her, but that I abhorred her in the fullest sense. I became certain that I — or, rather, music — the finest and perhaps the only fine part of my

being — had died for ever. The future appeared to me the merest vege-
table existence, a sordid comedy not to be endured.

My wife is not guilty at all. She did not ask me to marry her. It
would, therefore, be cruel and spiteful of me to make her understand
that I dislike her and look upon her as an unbearable nuisance. All I
can do is act a part. But to act a whole lifetime is unbearable. How
could I ever work? I was in despair, particularly as no one was near to
whom I could turn for support and encouragement. I wished fiercely
for death. Death seemed the only way out, but suicide was out of the
question. I love some members of my family — my sister, my two youngest brothers, and my father. If I decided on suicide and committed it,
I should be killing them. And there are many others, loved friends
whose affection binds me to life. And I have the frailty — if it can be
called one — to love life, love my work, love the prospect of success. I
have not yet said everything I have to say, all I want to utter before
the hour of my migration to oblivion. Death does not come to me. I
shall not, and cannot, go to death. What is left?

I have told my wife that I shall travel for my health during August,
as I am really unwell and need strict treatment. As soon as I had told
her that, my journey began to seem like an escape from prison, however temporary. I found the strength to endure in the thought that the
day of my departure was close. We were in Petersburg one week and
then came back to Moscow. There we found ourselves without money,
as one Kudryavsev had duped her when he had made her believe he
would sell her forest land. A new series of tortures and anguishes set in:
uncomfortable quarters, the need to arrange a new home, inability to do
so without funds, all possibility of getting away removed by the same
lack, worry, and a life of stupid idleness in Moscow (I had no im-
pulse to work, and our quarters were highly uncomfortable), no friends,
not a moment's respite from it all. I do not understand how I remained
sane.

Then I had to visit my mother-in-law. There my torments multiplied.
I detest the mother and the whole membership of the family I have entered. They have narrow ideas and freakish opinions and are constantly
quarreling. My wife (this may be unfair) became more abhorrent to me
each hour. I can scarcely describe, Nadezhda Filaretovna, the spritual
tortures I underwent. Before leaving for the country, in one desperate
attempt to get out of the terrible situation, longing to get away, I turned
to someone you know well, a sweet and loved friend living at Braïlov.
The idea that she would help me, the assurance that she would liberate
me from these terrible chains of grief and madness, supported me. But
would my letter get to her? Fear that my letter might go astray was
torturing me. We went back to Moscow.

That awful life dragged along for several days. I had two distractions: first, a good deal of wine, which made me dizzy and gave me some minutes of forgetfulness, and, second, cheering talks with Kotek. He is the only one besides yourself who knows all that I am writing you now. He is good in the true sense of the word. That sorrows do not come singly is a fact. I received word of the sudden death of one of my closest friends, Adamov. We were in school together, started our service together, and despite our paths' having parted, remained close friends until he died. He had every good fortune in life: flawless health, an excellent official position, money in his wife's name, an utterly happy family life, then, suddenly, death. It quite unnerved me.

Finally, one blessed evening, there was a letter from Braïlov. I began to cheer up a little. The remaining days were taken up by preparations for leaving and arrangements for future quarters, and on Tuesday at 1 p.m. I left. I don't know what I'll do next, but I feel as though I had awakened from a terrifying, painful nightmare, or, better, from a protracted illness. Like a man convalescing from fever, I remain very weak. I think consecutively only with difficulty. Even writing this letter has been a struggle. But what a sensation of sweet rest, and what an intoxicating sense of freedom and solitude!

If I understand my make-up correctly, it is altogether possible that when I have rested and quieted my nerves, I shall be able to return to Moscow and my customary routine, and regard my wife in a different light. In truth she has many qualities that can contribute to my future happiness. She likes me sincerely, and desires nothing more than my peace and happiness. I pity her.

I shall remain in Kiev one day. Tomorrow I go to my sister, and thence to the Caucasus. Forgive the incoherence and jumpiness of this letter, Nadezhda Filaretovna. My nerves and my entire spirit are so weary that I can scarcely bring two thoughts together. However fatigued my spirit is, it is not so broken that it cannot warm with unlimited, profound gratitude to the hundred-times-priceless friend who is saving me. Nadezhda Filaretovna, if God gives me the strength to get through the terrible present, I shall prove to you that this friend has not helped me in vain. I have not written one tenth of what I want to say. My heart is full. It wants to pour itself out in music. Who knows? It may be that I shall leave behind something really worthy of the renown of an artist of the first category! I have the daring to hope so. Nadezhda Filaretovna, I bless you for everything you have done for me. Farewell, my best, my most loved sweet friend.

P. T.

PS. I shall impatiently await a letter in Yessentuki.

On August 12 Piotr Ilyich arrived at Kamenka. He did not go on to Yessentuki in the Caucasus, but remained with the Davidovs for more than one month. It happened that Modest and Anatoly were both there, and their pleas that he drink the healing Yessentuki waters at Kamenka, added to Alexandra Davidova's urgings, changed his mind. At first he could not work. By about August 23, the well-loved peace, friendliness, and intimacy of the Davidov household had calmed his agitation so successfully that he sat down at a desk and began to orchestrate the Fourth Symphony, which he was to dedicate with reason and emotion to Nadezhda Filaretovna. She wrote him subtly inspiriting letters full of remarkable understanding, affection, and admiration. She was happy that he had not gone to the Caucasus, for she feared the Turks might somehow, some time invade it. She expressed gratitude for his honesty to her, telling him that he gave her great and profound happiness.

Piotr Ilyich, able to forget Moscow and Antonina Milyukova, raced ahead with the symphony. Writing to Nadezhda Filaretovna on August 24, he called the first movement complicated and long, but said it was the part he deemed best. He described the persistent pizzicato strings of the Scherzo and told of the hope he built on this novel effect. Not long after that, he was able to write her in Italy that he had again taken up work on *Yevgeny Onyegin*. By September 11 he had completed the orchestration of the first scene. On that day he formulated his artistic credo for Nadezhda Filaretovna and simultaneously assayed the future of his opera:

Now that my first ardour has passed and I am able to look at this composition objectively, it seems to me destined to failure and lack of public response. The contents are completely artless, there are no scenic effects, the music lacks brilliance and noisy, scintillating effects. Yet I believe that a few choice spirits may perhaps, while listening to this music, be moved by the emotions that excited me while I was composing it. I do not mean by this that my music is so good as to be inaccessible to the despised masses. In general I do not understand how it is possible to write beforehand for the crowd or the select few. In my opinion, one must write in obedience to one's immediate inclination, without thought of pleasing this or that section of humanity. And I composed Onyegin without burdening myself with any extraneous objectives. It merely turned out that Onyegin will not be interesting in the theatre. Therefore those for whom the first requisite of an opera is action will be dissatisfied with it. Those, however, capable of seeking in an opera musical re-creation of everyday, simple emotions, common to all humanity and far removed from tragedy and theatrical effects — they (I hope) will be content with my opera. In a word, it is written in all sincerity, and on that sincerity I rest all my hopes.

Could Piotr Ilyich have remained in the calm and happy atmosphere of Kamenka, he might have completed both the Fourth Symphony and *Yevgeny Onyegin* at that time. But the day was nearing when he could stay away from Moscow, from Antonina Ivanovna and the living-quarters she had prepared for their sharing, no longer. He began to suffer from nervous apprehension, from terror in advance. Writing to Anatoly, he said: "Tolya! I love you terrifically. But oh, what small love I feel for Antonina Ivanovna Tchaikovskaya! With what profound indifference that woman inspires me! How little does the prospect of seeing her cheer me!" Whistling in the dark, he added: "Yet she doesn't scare me — she is simply an annoyance."

With a dawdling stop at Kiev to hear a performance of *La Traviata*, Piotr Ilyich at last dragged himself back to his bride, arriving in Moscow on September 23. Antonina met him at the railroad station. She took him to the unpretentious rooms she had furnished as their home. By the next morning he was again a desperate man, rushing from wall to wall of the cage into which he had unwittingly stepped, searching wild-eyed for an escape. To Anatoly on the 24th he wrote baldly: "I am frightened." To Nadezhda Filaretovna, far off in Italy, he wrote: "To explain my feelings, all I need say is that my only wish is for the chance to run away somewhere. But how and whither? It is impossible, impossible, impossible!"

Kashkin says that Piotr Ilyich immediately made his appearance at the Conservatory. "He had an exaggeratedly carefree and bold manner, but that was obviously put on. . . . Noting his nervous state, we were all very careful, asked no questions, and waited for him to introduce us to his wife." At a supper given by Jürgenson, Kashkin met her. "She created a generally favourable impression both by her appearance and by her modest manner. I entered into conversation with her, and could not avoid noticing that Tchaikovsky stayed with us practically all the time. Antonina Ivanovna seemed either shy or a little at a loss for words, and Piotr Ilyich at intervals during forced pauses spoke for her or finished what she

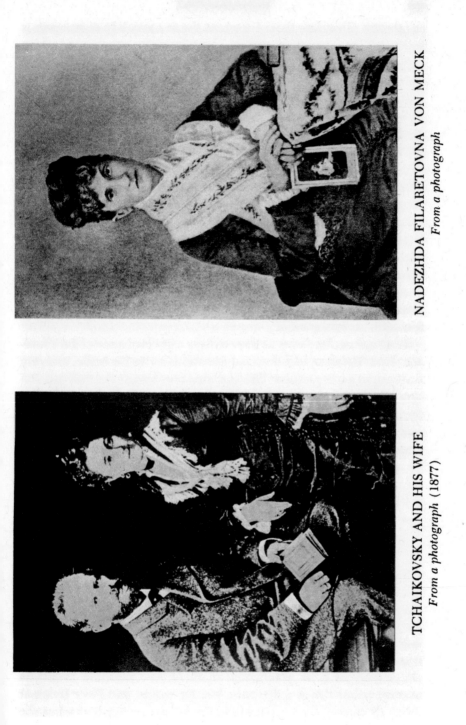

NADEZHDA FILARETOVNA VON MECK
From a photograph

TCHAIKOVSKY AND HIS WIFE
From a photograph (1877)

had left unsaid. The conversation, by the way, was so trivial that I would have paid no attention to Piotr Ilyich's interference had he not been so insistent each time his wife talked to anyone. Such attention was not quite natural and seemed to indicate a fear that Antonina Ivanovna would perhaps find it difficult to carry on a conversation in the proper manner. In general, our new acquaintance left . . . a somewhat colourless impression."

The days dragged on, and, worse than days, the nights. His friends noticed a peculiar, unpleasant look in Piotr Ilyich's handsome blue eyes. He was, had they but known it, holding to self-control and sanity by a prolonged, terrible, and losing effort. He hated his wife, loathed being near her, could find not an hour's peace for thinking, composing, or just sitting idle. He knew that he was approaching the moment when he would be unable to bear the strain. On an evening between September 29 and October 5 he walked, with his clothes on, into the ice-strewn waters of the River Moskva until they reached his waist. He stood there, a lost and half-mad figure, until the cold was a torture. Emerging, he was certain that he would soon die of pneumonia. When he understood at last that his strong physique had absorbed the icy shock without damage, that his attempted suicide had failed, he became more terrified and unbalanced than before. He realized completely that he was no longer a responsible person.

On October 5 Piotr Ilyich telegraphed St. Petersburg, instructing Anatoly to send him a wire, signing Napravnik's name, and demanding his immediate presence in the northern capital. Kashkin says that he turned up at the Conservatory the following morning in a visible state of excitement, explained that he had been summoned to St. Petersburg by Napravnik, hastily bade farewell to his colleagues, and departed. He left a note for Albrecht, stating that he would be back soon.

The man who boarded the St. Petersburg train in the Moscow station the night of October 6 was in utter nervous collapse. By no ordinary measure could he have been called either responsible or sane. Anatoly was at the Nikolayevsky Station to meet him the next morning, but at first did not recognize him, so much had his appearance changed in one month. Shocked and scared, Anatoly rushed him to a room in the Dagmar Hotel. There Piotr Ilyich suffered a violent nervous attack. Anatoly never told anyone, unless it was Modest, exactly what took place in that room. We do know

that, after a period of scarifying outburst, Piotr Ilyich went unconscious and remained in a coma for two days. A physician at first
thought that there was small chance of his living or, if he did live,
of his recovering sanity. But after the two days of healing uncon-
sciousness he began slowly to recover. He saw and talked to his
brothers and old Ilya Petrovich. The doctor prescribed what Piotr
Ilyich surely would have achieved without prescription: complete
change of surroundings and way of living.

Leaving the patient in St. Petersburg, Anatoly went to Moscow
to inform Nikolay Rubinstein of what had happened and to tell
Antonina Ivanovna that divorce was required. Kashkin states that
Rubinstein so feared Anatoly's kindly softness of character that he
decided to accompany him to Antonina Ivanovna. She greeted
them cordially and ordered tea. Brusquely Nikolay Rubinstein
went to the point, telling her of Piotr Ilyich's condition and the
doctor's recommendation of a divorce. She listened with what Anatoly called "amazing calmness," and then replied that for Piotr
Ilyich's sake she consented to everything. In the same breath she
offered Rubinstein and Anatoly the tea that had just been brought
in. When Rubinstein had gulped his, she escorted him to the foyer.
Returning to Anatoly, her face shining with pleasure, she said: "I
hadn't expected Rubinstein to be drinking tea here today!" Anatoly's amazement at her *sang-froid* was due to his not realizing that
she was stupid and mentally unstable.

By October 13 Piotr Ilyich was able to write Modest that he was
becoming himself again and "returning to life." Shortly thereafter,
accompanied by Anatoly, he left for western Europe. On the 14th,
the directors of the Moscow Russian Musical Society, at Nikolay
Rubinstein's suggestion, voted him a stipend for the "enormous
services rendered by him to both the Society and the Conservatory." His astonishing marriage, peculiar behaviour, and abrupt
departure were the subject of endless gossip and conversation in
both Moscow and St. Petersburg. Everyone was curious; many had
theories. Strangely, however, that marriage, a failure in every other
detail, had apparently succeeded in one: it quieted for a time the
whispers of his homosexuality. Had the gossipers known the facts,
it must have raised those whispers to a shout.

On October 16 Piotr Ilyich was in Berlin. From there, the next
day, he wrote Jürgenson requesting that the publisher commission
from him whatever he needed, "songs, compositions, transposi-

tions, translations." He felt that work would benefit him, but that he could not yet turn back to the Fourth Symphony and *Yevgeny Onyegin*. He went to Geneva, and on October 20 rented the Villa Richelieu at Clarens on the lake.

Piotr Ilyich's finances were once more severely straitened. He had money enough for only five or six weeks, and no immediate prospect of earning more except through commissions from Jürgenson — unless Nadezhda Filaretovna renewed her generosity. On October 22 *Vakula the Smith* was revived in St. Petersburg, but that did not supply immediate funds. Also he received from Karl U. Davidov, then head of the St. Petersburg Conservatory, the offer of an appointment as delegate to the Paris Exposition of 1878, a position that would carry a salary. It was an appointment of considerable honour, but also required prolonged effort and social contacts for which Piotr Ilyich would have been poorly equipped at any time and for which he was wholly unfitted in the autumn of 1877. He let the offer stand unanswered.

The need for funds was too pressing to permit delay. On October 23 Piotr Ilyich therefore wrote at length to Nadezhda Filaretovna. In this letter he detailed the events of his married life that had occurred after his previous letter. Speaking of his meeting with Anatoly in the Nikolayevsky Station, he said: "When I saw my brother, everything I had hidden in my heart during those two endless weeks burst out. Something awful occurred — what I do not remember. When I began to come to, I found that my brother had had time to get to Moscow, talk to my wife and Rubinstein, fix things so that he could take me abroad and send my wife to Odessa, of which last no one will be aware. In order to avoid scandal and gossip, my brother and Rubinstein decided to give out the story that I was ill, that I was going abroad, and that my wife would follow."

Piotr Ilyich tells Nadezhda Filaretovna how he fears returning to Russia and facing the criticism even of the Davidovs. "I must remain here awhile, rest, and let the world forget me," he concludes. "I need money once more, and once more I can ask no one but you. It is awful, it is painful and regrettable, but I have to do it, have again to tax your endless kindness. In order to get me here, my brothers obtained a small amount by telegraph from my sister. They are far from wealthy: to ask them again is out of the question. And funds had to be left with my wife. Several kinds of obligations had to be paid, the trip here paid for — and, as if by design, our exchange is low. I had been hoping Rubinstein would find it possible to forward something, but my hope was fruitless. In short, I am spending the last of my small means and have only you to turn to."

Unstrung and exacerbated as he was, Piotr Ilyich found some solace in the physical beauty of Switzerland. He began to orchestrate *Yevgeny Onyegin,* completing the first act on November 1. On that day he heard from Nikolay Rubinstein that the directorate of the Moscow Conservatory had decided to pay to him the balance remaining in the budgetary allowance for his classes for that year — a sum totalling between 1,200 and 1,300 rubles, or between $600 and $650. Replying gratefully, Piotr Ilyich suggested the staging of the first act and first scene of the second act of *Yevgeny Onyegin:* "Its performance at the Conservatory is my fondest dream. It is designed for an economy budget and a small stage."

Nadezhda Filaretovna, returning from Italy to Moscow, learned of Piotr Ilyich's flight to Switzerland before receiving his letter from Clarens. She sent for Nikolay Rubinstein and plied him with questions. She had already, from Venice, written Piotr Ilyich a letter (which he received in Clarens after having appealed to her), stating that she had decided to send him enough money to permit a visit of several months abroad. Hardly had he received this welcome news, forwarded to him from Moscow, when another letter arrived from that city, this time directly from Nadezhda Filaretovna. She had elected, instead of making him a further loan, to place at his disposal an annual income of 18,000 francs — about $3,475 — of which she enclosed the first instalment, a double one.

IX

WHEN Nadezhda Filaretovna finally received the letter in which Piotr Ilyich had asked for money, she was inclined to annoyance at its apologetic tone. "Are we really such strangers?" she asked. "Don't you understand how much I care for you, or how much good I wish you? In my opinion, it is not a tie of sex or relationship that gives these rights, but a sense of mental and spiritual kinship. You know how many joyful moments you have given me, how grateful I am, how indispensable you are to me, and how necessary it is to me that you should be just as you were created. What I do, therefore, is not for your sake, but for my own. Why should you spoil my satisfaction in caring for you, and make me feel that I am not very much to you, after all? You wound me. If I wanted something from you, you would of course give it to me — isn't that so? Very well, then, we cry quits. Don't interfere with my management of your domestic economy, Piotr Ilyich."

He was free, if he wished, to resign from the Conservatory, live abroad, and devote himself to composition. Best of all, he could stay far enough from Antonina Ivanovna so that she could not, in person, bother or frighten him. By letter, however, she continued to scare and enrage him. He had told Nadezhda Filaretovna that his wife was empty-headed, that, for example, despite her pretence of having been in love with him for several years, she did not know a single one of his compositions. "You may be curious as to how we passed the time when we were together," he continued. "She is very garrulous, but everything she said inevitably ended with the countless men who have been in love with her (which she reiterates constantly), mostly generals, nephews of famous bankers, noted actors, or members of the imperial family. The viciousness, baseness, and loathsome actions of her relatives — with every one of whom she is at war — she described with the most singular rage, most of it being directed particularly at her mother."

Anatoly, still with Piotr Ilyich at Clarens, received an ominous letter from Kamenka, where Antonina Ivanovna was temporarily

quartered on the Davidovs. In it his wife turned furiously on Piotr
Ilyich, accusing him of having deceived her, and vituperating him
generally. In the same letter, however, she had time to say that
while on the train to Kiev she had so attracted a colonel that he had
fallen in love with her. Piotr Ilyich, far from realizing into what an
uncomfortable position his sister had put herself and her family
by accommodating his wife, wrote Antonina what he foolishly
considered to be a final letter. He took all blame for the failure of
their marriage on himself and agreed to support her. What he did
not do, but would certainly have done had he been able to picture
the situation at Kamenka, was suggest that she take herself away
from there at once.

Kamenka was a comfortable and attractive household, and Antonina Ivanovna, unused to such luxury, had quite simply decided
to remain there. From sympathy for her — they were a little inclined to blame Piotr Ilyich — the Davidovs' attitude rapidly
changed to horror and detestation of her, swinging their momentarily unsettled partisanship in the quarrel back toward him. She
was a weeper, and sniffled constantly. She bit her nails, leaving
spots of blood wherever she sat. At last they could bear her no
longer. Lyov Vasilyevich addressed Anatoly (they had temporarily
broken off friendly relations with Piotr Ilyich), demanding that he
include Kamenka on his return route to St. Petersburg, take Antonina Ivanovna away with him, and leave her with her mother
outside Moscow.

This letter reached Anatoly in Venice late in November. On the
6th of that month Piotr Ilyich had written Nadezhda Filaretovna
of a change in his plans. Instead of remaining at Clarens, which he
found beautiful but somewhat depressing, he would go to Italy with
Anatoly in about two weeks. He assured her that "*our* symphony"
— the Fourth — would be completed by December. He told her,
an outspoken atheist, that his religious beliefs were agnostic and
pantheistic at once, and asked for her own religious philosophy in
detail. And then, on November 14, he wrote her from Paris, where
he had arrived the previous day. His dogged digestive complaint
had been stirred up once more by the agitation of the preceding
months, and he had rushed to France for treatment by a doctor
whom he regarded highly. The doctor was out of Paris, and he had
had to consult a substitute. When he had informed the strange
physician that he was a Russian, the reply had been: "*Le climat*

y est bien rude." Without allowing him the chance he craved to
describe his ailment and symptoms, the doctor, saying first that
the malady was incurable, had prescribed a regimen that would
guarantee his living to be a centenarian. It consisted of simple
medicine, curative water, baths, and a diet. Piotr Ilyich left his
consulting-room unconvinced.

From Paris, Piotr Ilyich set out with Anatoly for a most unhappy
visit to Italy. On November 16 they were in Florence, three days
later in Rome. No sooner did he arrive at one place than he could
not understand why he had gone to so loathsome a city. Difficult
as he found any work on his compositions, it was all that kept him
from sinking back fully into the despond because of which he had
fled first Moscow and then Russia and then Switzerland. "In Clarens, where I was leading a completely quiet life," he wrote Nadezhda Filaretovna on November 18, "I was often sunk in melancholy. Unable to explain these periods of depression, I attributed
them to the mountains. What puerility! I convinced myself that I
had only to cross the Italian frontier for a life of perfect happiness
to start! Nonsense! I feel a hundred times worse here."

Before his departure from Clarens, Piotr Ilyich had received a
most encouraging letter from Apukhtin. The poet begged him to
pay no attention to those who gossiped about his marriage. "That
you, of whose name the country in which you were born will be
proud, should bow your head before various X's and Z's is incomprehensible, senseless. . . . Leave them for the heights, the creative heights where you not only will be unable to see them, but
will be forced to ignore their very existence. From there fling another *Tempest* or *Romeo!* Let the weight of your fame crush this
scum."

From Rome, on November 19, Piotr Ilyich informed Nadezhda
Filaretovna that he continued to feel ill. "I know that my morbid
state lets me see only the bad side of Rome in all its viciousness,
while the city's beauties seem invisible to my eyes — but this is
poor consolation." He could not face continuing the tour to Naples,
he could not face returning to Clarens. He had decided to accompany Anatoly as far as Vienna. Not feeling able to be alone, he had
also sent to Moscow for his manservant — Alexey, the second of his
Sofronovs. The following day, writing to Nikolay Rubinstein, he
begged not to be recalled to the Conservatory before September
1878. He also expressed worry over Rubinstein's reception of that

portion (the first act) of *Yevgeny Onyegin* already sent to him,
and promised to forward the first scene of the second act shortly.
With that accomplished, he would attack the symphony "with
all zeal." He asked Rubinstein to save a place for it on the Musical
Society's programs.

En route to Vienna, Piotr Ilyich and Anatoly stopped at Venice,
moving into the "wretched" Grand Hotel on November 23. From
there he wrote Nadezhda Filaretovna of his struggles, in the
Rome post office, to locate a parcel forwarded to him from Clarens,
and containing his sketches of the Fourth Symphony. Delayed and
sent from office to office until he was cold with anxiety, he had
finally located the package. Venice, he wrote, pleased him so much
that he was considering renting quarters there and remaining for
some time. All that annoyed him in Venice was the newsboys' habit
of crying: "*Vittoria dei Turchi!*" whenever there was a skirmish
between the Turks and the Russians in the dragging war. On
November 30 he told her that the Venetian atmosphere was benefiting him so much that he was going to be able to send the all but
finished first scene of the second act of *Yevgeny Onyegin* back to
Moscow with Anatoly. He had taken a newsboy to task for his
Turkish victories, only to be greeted a day or so later with a lying
call of "*Gran combattimento a Plevna, vittoria dei Russi!*" "Can it
be that peaceful, lovely Venice, who once spent her own force in
fighting these selfsame Turks, is as full of hatred for Russia as the
rest of western Europe is?" he asked. He had told Nadezhda
Filaretovna with acute and self-deprecating humour: "Tomorrow
I shall look for a furnished apartment. If I succeed in locating one
— I shall be exactly as undecided as before." Despite that, he actually leased a very pleasant apartment on the Riva degli Schiavoni.

On December 1 the brothers arrived in Vienna. Piotr Ilyich continued the prolonged and loose-termed correspondence with Nadezhda Filaretovna concerning religious beliefs, pessimism, opti-
mism, and morality. He worried about Alexey Sofronov's trip from
Moscow to him, as Alexey could speak not a word of anything but
Russian. He had been to a performance of *Die Walküre*; it had
been excellent. "The orchestra outdid itself. The finest singers did
everything in their power — and still it was tiresome. What a Don
Quixote Wagner is! He uses up his entire strength pursuing the
impossible, and all the while if he would only follow the natural
direction of his extraordinary talent he could evoke a whole world

of musical beauties. In my opinion, Wagner is a symphonist by nature. He is gifted with a genius that has been wrecked upon his tendentiousness. His inspiration is paralysed by theories that he has himself invented and that he is determined to put into practice against all opposition. In his attempts to attain *reality, truth,* and *rationalism,* he leaves *music* quite out of the picture, so that in his latest four operas it is, oftener than not, notable for its absence. I cannot call music that which is made up of kaleidoscopic, flowing phrases that follow one another uninterruptedly and never come to a close, which is to say never allow the ear the smallest chance to grasp the musical form. Not one broad, rounded melody, not one minute of rest for the singer! The latter must always run after the orchestra and watch not to lose his note, which has no more importance in the score than some note for the fourth horn. But there is no question that Wagner is a marvellous symphonist. I shall prove to you by just one example how much the symphonic exceeds the operatic style in his operas. You have probably heard the renowned Ride of the Valkyries? What a huge and wonderful panorama! How we actually seem to see those fierce heroines soar on their magic horses through thunder and lightning! In the concert hall this selection makes an extraordinary impression. On the stage, in view of the cardboard rocks, the canvas clouds, and the awkward soldiers running about in the back — in short, seen in a very inadequate theatrical heaven that makes a poor stab at realizing the unending upper realms — the music loses all its expressive power. In this the stage does not enhance the effect, but instead acts as a wet blanket. Finally, I cannot comprehend, and never shall, why the Nibelungen should be thought a literary masterpiece. Perhaps as a national saga, but as literature — distinctly not! Wotan, Brünnhilde, Fricka, and the rest are all so impossible, so inhuman, that it is hard to feel any interest in their destinies. And how little life! For three entire hours Wotan lectures Brünnhilde on her disobedience. How boring! And with it all, there are many fine and exquisite sections of purely symphonic character."

Kotek, who had left Nadezhda Filaretovna's service to study with Joseph Joachim in Berlin, took a few days' vacation to join Piotr Ilyich and Anatoly in Vienna. With him Piotr Ilyich looked over Brahms's First Symphony, describing Brahms as "a composer the Germans praise to the skies," and adding: "He has no charms for me. I find him dark, cold, and pretentious, but lacking real profundity. All together, it seems to me that Germany is deteriorating musically. I think that the French are now coming to the fore. Lately I have heard Delibes's music for the ballet Sylvia, in its own style enormously clever. I knew this music in piano arrangement some time back, but its splendid performance by the Vienna orchestra quite fascinated me, especially the first part. Swan Lake is poor stuff compared with Sylvia. Nothing during the last few years has charmed me so greatly as this ballet by Delibes — and Carmen."

Piotr Ilyich had not forgotten that the Vienna performance of *Romeo and Juliet* had been vigorously hissed. When Kotek and Anatoly went to a Philharmonic concert to hear a program including Schumann's Third Symphony (a work Piotr Ilyich greatly admired), he remained at the hotel writing to Nadezhda Filaretovna. He feared that he might meet someone he knew, perhaps a musician, at the concert. And on December 10 he wrote to her again to say that Alexey Sofronov had arrived without incident the previous afternoon, that Anatoly had left for Moscow that morning with the nearly complete scene for *Yevgeny Onyegin* in his pocket, and that only the news of the fall of Plevna [1] cheered him at all. He remarked acutely that Austria did not seem pleased by the Russian victory and was upset by the surrender of the flower of the Turkish army.

Still discussing ethics and religion by mail, Piotr Ilyich denied Nadezhda Filaretovna's claim that she had found in a creed of her own a satisfactory substitute for the formal creeds she could not accept. His psychological insight was sharp, and he touched near the centre of their relationship when he wrote: "That yearning, that discontent, that aspiration toward some undefined ideal, that apartness from humanity, the admission that only in music — most ideal of the arts — can you discover any answer to these agitating problems, all proved to me that your self-made religion does not provide that complete peace of mind which is peculiar to people who have found in their religion a prepared answer to all the doubts that torture a meditative and sensitive nature. And, you know, it seems to me that you care so intensely for my music only because I am as full of such ideal longing as you are. Our sufferings are the same. Your doubts are as strong as mine. We are both

[1] A tiny Bulgarian town held by the Turks, to which, during the continuing Russo-Turkish War, the Russians attached an incomprehensible importance.

drifting in the unbounded sea of scepticism, seeking a harbour and not finding it. Aren't these the reasons my music touches you so intimately?"

To Kashkin, Piotr Ilyich wrote on December 8 that he was orchestrating the Fourth Symphony and *Yevgeny Onyegin* as though they were compositions by someone else. Still arguing by mail with Nadezhda Filaretovna on the subject of religion, he told her that when, in the depths of his suffering, he had written N. D. Kondratyev a letter that was a cry for help, the reply had ended: "Pray, dear friend, pray. God will show you how to overcome your sad state." Two days after Anatoly's departure Piotr Ilyich and Alexey arrived in Venice and took up residence in the apartment arranged for at the Hotel Beau Rivage. Within one week, the magic of the city had so worked on Piotr Ilyich that he was steadily forging ahead on the orchestration of the Fourth Symphony and happily absorbed in its development. Yet all was not well, for again his funds were running short. He had been spendthrift with his first annuity receipt, lending money to Modest and probably paying for Anatoly's trip. He found himself at one juncture down to ten lire, at another with only three. The awaited instalment did not arrive from Moscow. Instead he had word that Taneyev had played some of the score of *Onyegin* to Kashkin, Nikolay Rubinstein, and others, and that all had been left breathless with enthusiasm. Instead he received a telegram from Anatoly, dated at Kamenka, saying that Antonina Ivanovna had at last been persuaded to move on and leave the Davidovs in peace. Instead, by December 23, he received a warm letter from Alexandra Davidova, opening again the close relationship between them, explaining that her disapproval of his treatment of his wife had been mistaken. All these things would have cheered him, returned him to his desk in the mood to compose, but that he had no money.

Then the money came — again two months' instalments in one. His spirits blazed up. He had persuaded Kolya Konradi's father to let Modest and the boy join him in Italy. The only proviso had been that he must move to a place with a more healthful climate than Venice, and he had agreed to San Remo. There was to be an interval of time before that meeting, however, and he turned to work with renewed zest. On December 17, telling Nadezhda Filaretovna that the orchestration of the first movement of their symphony was nearly finished, he had said: "I can confidently state that this is my best composition." On December 21 he told her of coming upon the following, which he had scribbled on the first sketch during the worst days of his last stay in Moscow and had then forgotten: "In case of my death I desire this book to be given to N. F. von Meck." Three days later he wrote her that he had begun work on the second movement and that the task was becoming easier every hour. He was labouring in a remarkable concentration of speed, for he completed the second movement the next day and all but completed the third the day after that. On December 27 he admitted in a letter to Anatoly that he was tired.

Piotr Ilyich was more than tired, and this time the reason was not lack of money. Nadezhda Filaretovna had been slow in answering his letter, the one in which he had spoken of *Die Walküre,* Brahms's First Symphony, *Sylvia,* and *Carmen.* He was working well on the symphony he believed to be his best composition, and again he had plenty of lire in his pocket. Modest and Kolya were coming, his Moscow confreres were enthusiastic over *Yevgeny Onyegin,* Alexandra Davidova had forgiven him. All was well except that Nadezhda Filaretovna did not write. Why did she not write? To Anatoly he explained his fears: "With my usual tremblings I supposed that she had stopped loving me, that she had discovered *This* and wanted to break off the entire relationship. Up to this morning I was still certain of it, but I just received a letter from her, so sweet, so generous, with such sincere expressions of love!" His secret was safe. But for how long was it safe in the vindictive and unbalanced mind of Antonina Ivanovna?

En route to San Remo, Piotr Ilyich stopped in Milan, admired the Cathedral inordinately, and at the Teatro dal Verme heard a bungled performance of Filippo Marchetti's opera *Ruy Blas,* which raised before him the spectre of a poor staging of *Yevgeny Onyegin.* Already he had written Albrecht that what his opera required was "1. singers of average ability, but well trained and thorough; 2. singers who can act simply and well; 3. not too sumptuous a setting, but one thoroughly in keeping with the period of the story — the costumes must correspond faithfully to the dress of the period [the 1820's] during which the action occurs; 4. a chorus that is not a flock of sheep like those of the imperial opera, but real people participating in the plot of the opera; 5. a conductor who is not a machine or even a musician à la Napravnik, concerned only with the fact that a C sharp must not be played as a C, but a real leader

of the orchestra." Now, from Milan, he asked Nadezhda Filaretovna: "Where shall I find a Tatyana, the Tatyana depicted by
Pushkin, whom I tried to visualize musically? Where is the artist
who will approach, at least in some respects, the ideal Onyegin,
that cold dandy bespeaking worldly bon ton from head to foot?
Where is there a Lensky, an eighteen-year-old youth with thick,
wavy hair and the impetuous and eccentric impulses of a young
poet à la Schiller?" Into all this he read what was, for him, the
proper meaning, though one he could not act upon: "Composing
music for instruments alone is far more satisfactory, has fewer dis-
appointments."

On December 29 Piotr Ilyich went on westward to Genoa. There
he heard *L'Africaine,* which he called "the most boring of operas."
The execrable performance it was given did not quiet his fears for
his own new opera. He continued westward, arriving in San Remo
on the last day of 1877. Hardly had he accustomed himself to the
subtropical lushness of the Riviera when a communication from St.
Petersburg threw him into turmoil. It was his official appointment
by the Minister of Finance as Russian musical delegate to the Paris
Exposition. He had forgotten that he had not definitely refused the
position. Now, after a day of vacillation and of wishing for advice
he could not get in time, he refused it, writing Nikolay Rubinstein
to that effect on January 4. To Albrecht, more than two weeks later,
he sent a complete explanation of the refusal, basing it on doubt
that proper funds for the setting up of concerts would be forthcoming, painting the blackest picture of his own inability as a conductor, and repeating his repulsion by the idea of having to play
the social game. Curiously, in view of his former friendship with
Saint-Saëns, he wrote: "It would be unbearable to have to stand
humbly before Saint-Saëns and be honoured by his gracious condescension when in my heart of hearts I feel as far above him as
the Alps. In Paris my self-respect (very large despite my apparent
modesty) would be wounded hourly by my having to mingle with
all sorts of celebrities who would look down on me." On January
26 he received an angry letter from Nikolay Rubinstein, who had
been reaping in advance the glory that Piotr Ilyich's Parisian position would create for the Conservatory. Rubinstein stated that
Piotr Ilyich's illness was a pose, that he was pretending to be sick,
that he preferred the *dolce far niente* aspect of life, that he was
drifting away from his work, and that he (Rubinstein) regretted

having encouraged such indolence by too great a show of sympathy. Infuriated, Piotr Ilyich wrote his chief a hot reply. Rubinstein answered this outburst more calmly, and his enraged subordinate in turn quieted down, still sputtering:

"Possibly you may be right, and I am only *putting it on*. But that is exactly the nature of my disease. . . . I know how much I am in your debt, but in the first place your reproaches chill my gratitude, and in the second it aggravates me when you pose as benefactor in a matter in which you have proved yourself the opposite." Explaining the fields in which he recognized Rubinstein's benefactions, he added: "Not possessing gifts as a conductor, I should certainly have failed to establish my name had not so admirable an interpreter of my compositions been constantly at hand. Without you I should have been condemned to perpetual mishandling. You are the only man who has rightly understood my compositions. Your extraordinary artistic instinct has enabled you to take a difficult work and, without preparatory study, carry it through with only two rehearsals." He ended this honest statement with a plea for quick performance of the Fourth Symphony. But he was adamant in his refusal to represent Russian music at the Paris Exposition.

From the Pension Joli, San Remo, Piotr Ilyich told Anatoly how miserable the business of refusing this appointment had made him. He feared that it might vex his friends. "There is one thing I have hidden from you," he wrote Anatoly. "Since the day you left, I have taken several glasses of brandy at night, and during the day I drink a considerable amount. I can't do without it. I never feel calm except when I have taken a little too much. I have so accustomed myself to this secret tippling that I feel a kind of joy at the sight of the bottle I keep close by. I can write letters only after a nip. This proves that I am still not well." During the rest of his life Piotr Ilyich intermittently drank a little too much. He was never a sot or even a frequent drunkard. But the nerve-relaxing use of alcohol was a lesson that, once learned, he never forgot.

He must have taken several nips the next day before sending Nadezhda Filaretovna a lengthy reply to her question as to his opinion of the Five. He began by berating them all for their "horrible presumptuousness and wholly amateur conviction of superiority to all other musicians in the universe." His strictures on

Rimsky-Korsakov well explain what is least attractive in that composer's personality and music:

As a mere youth he fell into a coterie that first solemnly told him that he was a genius and then went on to convince him that he did not need study, that academies were destructive to all inspiration and dried up all creative activity. At first he believed it all. His earliest compositions bear the mark of striking ability and lack of theoretical training. . . . Rimsky-Korsakov is the only one among them who discovered, five years ago, that the doctrines propagated by his circle were without reasonable basis, and its contempt of the schools and the classical masters, its hatred of authority and of the masterpieces, were just boorishness. . . . From contempt for the schools, he [Rimsky-Korsakov] went over abruptly to the cult of musical technique. Shortly after that, his symphony and his quartet appeared. Both works are full of obscurities and, as you will justly observe, bear the stamp of dry pedantry. At present he appears to be passing through a crisis, and it is difficult to foresee how he will come out. Either he will turn out a great master or he will lose himself in contrapuntal complexities.

To Cui, Piotr Ilyich granted taste and musical instinct, but called him a gifted amateur and forecast posterity's judgment by calling his music graceful, elegant, and unoriginal. Borodin, he knew, possessed very great talent that had been defeated by the amount of time he spent in the chemistry laboratory. "He has not so much taste as Cui, and his technique is so poor that he cannot compose one measure without help." Mussorgsky, who as Piotr Ilyich talked of him had but four more miserable years to live, he correctly described, in repeating Nadezhda Filaretovna's words, as "used up." He recognized that Mussorgsky's gifts were the most remarkable of all, but accused him of a narrow nature and lack of any desire for self-perfection: in addition to having been misled by the anti-technical nonsense of the coterie, he had a positive liking for what was "coarse, untidy, and rough." Piotr Ilyich saw him playing with his lack of polish, taking pride in lack of skill, believing blindly in his instinctive infallibility. "As a matter of fact," he conceded, "his very original talent does flash out now and then." Balakirev, who had entered a period of mystical and muddleheaded retirement from the world, he regarded as a vivid and destructive personality. It was Balakirev who had blighted Rimsky-Korsakov's early career. It was Balakirev who had supplied the creed to this remarkable coterie that united "so many undeveloped, wrongly developed, or prematurely decayed talents."

Before closing on a note of hope with regard to young French composers, Piotr Ilyich summed up his charges against the Five — and, incidentally, the Germans: "What a sad phenomenon! So many talented men from whom, except for Rimsky-Korsakov, we hardly dare expect anything serious. But this is always Russia's trouble: vast forces impeded by the fatal shadow of a Plevna from taking the open field and fighting as they should. All the same, however, the forces exist. Thus Mussorgsky, for all his ugliness, speaks a new language. Beautiful it may not be, but it is new. We may reasonably hope that Russia will one day produce a whole school of forceful men who will open up new artistic paths. Our roughness is, at any rate, better than the poor, would-be serious pose of a Brahms. The Germans are irreparably played out. With us, there is always the chance that the moral Plevna will fall and our strength make itself felt. So far, however, little has been accomplished." Just as Nietzsche had upheld *Carmen* as the antidote to Wagnerism, so Piotr Ilyich now upheld it as the antidote to Balakirevism: "The music is not profound, but it is so fascinating in its simplicity, so charged with vitality, so sincere, that I know every note of it from beginning to end."

Musicians and critics of a later day, persuaded by propaganda spread by admirers of the Five, were to ridicule Tchaikovsky the composer as an imitative old fogy, Tchaikovsky the critic for blindness with regard to his contemporaries. Yet today Tchaikovsky the composer, who wrote exactly as he felt and held no all-embracing theory except that it was his duty to do the best work he could, endures. Cui and Balakirev are all but unheard, or are heard in one or at most two compositions each. Borodin's genius is no more evident than his tragic unfulfilment in the fragmentary *Prince Igor* and Third Symphony, which contain incomparably his richest inspirations. For all the great pages in *Boris Godunov* and *Khovanshchina*, it is evident that the full harvest of Mussorgsky's genius was stopped by the two elements Piotr Ilyich names: lack of skill, which made his progress snaillike, and naïve and stubborn faith in his own infallibility. It is not too fantastic to say that Mussorgsky killed himself with drink because he had not the ability to create satisfactory formal structures for the produce of his fiery musical imagination. Only with regard to Rimsky-Korsakov was

Piotr Ilyich altogether wrong — and *The Golden Cockerel* was not composed until 1906. Rimsky-Korsakov turned out neither a great master nor a man lost in contrapuntal complexities. He turned out a surpassing second-rater, a master of surface glitter and story-book illustration. Piotr Ilyich himself had not the innate genius of Mussorgsky, and was not in that same respect, perhaps, superior to Borodin. He was a better all-round craftsman than any of the Five save Rimsky-Korsakov, and far excelled that self-confessed pretender in æsthetic sincerity.

Hard work, Piotr Ilyich always realized, was one indispensable component of good music. When his mental poise was momentarily firm, he turned from opinions to his own work. On January 6 he wrote Anatoly that he was composing without rising from his desk. He completed the orchestration of the Fourth Symphony the following day. On the 8th he went to Milan to meet Modest and Kolya. They planned to go to the theatre, but news was received of the death of Victor Emmanuel I, and the theatres were closed. So Piotr Ilyich bought a metronome, put the final indications in his score,[2] and sent it off by post to Nikolay Rubinstein. "What is in store for this symphony?" he wondered. "Will it remain alive long after its creator has disappeared from the face of the earth, or will it at once fall into the abyss of oblivion?" As always, he saw his work clearly as soon as it was done. "I am certain that, in scoring and form, it represents a forward step in my development, which is very slow. In spite of my mature years I am still far from that point of development beyond which my talent cannot go."

Piotr Ilyich, Modest, Kolya, and Alexey Sofronov were back in San Remo on January 12. Piotr Ilyich was still ruminating on his symphony. The Scherzo in particular worried him. "The third part is all played pizzicato," he told Nikolay Rubinstein. "The quicker the tempo, the better — but I'm not quite certain in how fast a tempo pizzicato can be played." He stated that he would revise the metronome marks for publication in view of Nikolay Rubinstein's experience while performing the symphony. On the same day he wrote Nadezhda Filaretovna that on his return to San Remo it had been from her telegram that he had first heard of the Turkish surrender at the Shipka Pass — the defeat that was to lead, a

[2] In view of the exacting care with which Tchaikovsky wrote agogic and tempo indications into his scores, there is no excuse save ignorance for playing, conducting, or singing his compositions other than as he intended them.

few weeks later, to the armistice ending the war. It proved an empty victory for Russia, as Alexander II, wanting to force on Turkey stringent terms not approved by Austria and England, found that the Germany of Wilhelm I, the nation in whose formation he had had some influence, would not back him up.

On January 14, besides starting to orchestrate the third act of *Yevgeny Onyegin*, Piotr Ilyich wrote to Taneyev, asking him to transpose the Fourth Symphony for piano duet. He also answered some criticisms Taneyev had made of the opera:

If it isn't theatrical, don't put it on and don't play it. I composed this opera because one beautiful day an inexpressibly strong desire to set to music all that in Onyegin cries out for music overwhelmed me. . . . I worked with indescribable delight and enthusiasm, worrying little about motion, effects, etc. I don't give a fig for effects! What are they? If you find them in Aïda, I assure you that I couldn't compose an opera on such a subject for all the world's wealth, for I need people, not puppets. I should gladly undertake any opera that, though lacking strong and startling effects, contained human beings like myself who experience emotions I experience and understand.

The emotions of an Egyptian princess, a Pharaoh, some sort of mad Nubian, I neither know nor understand. Some instinct informs me that these people must have moved, talked, and had feelings, and therefore must have expressed their feelings in some special way completely different from ours. Therefore my music, which despite me is permeated with Schumannism, Wagnerism, Chopinism, Glinkaism, Berliozism, and all the other latest isms, would have as much relation to the protagonists of Aïda as the elegant and polite speeches of Racine's heroes, who address one another in the second person plural, bear to the real Orestes, the real Andromache, etc. It would be a lie, and it is this lie that disgusts me so. . . . You will ask what I do want, then. I shall tell you. I don't want kings and queens, popular uprisings, battles, marches — in a word, anything that is an attribute of grand opera. I am looking for an intimate but forceful drama built on the conflict of circumstances experienced or seen by me, a conflict that can move me vitally. Neither do I reject the fantastic element, for there are no obstacles in that, and the realm of fantasy has no limits.

When Piotr Ilyich found what he wanted — as in *Yevgeny Onyegin* and *The Queen of Spades* — he composed operas full of beautiful, expressive, and emotional music, however faulty they may be as stageworthy entities from an impresario's point of view. When he did not, when he filled his stage with kings, battles, and

marches, as in *The Maid of Orleans,* he produced operas inferior
to *Rienzi* and *Les Huguenots,* however superior some of the separate numbers in his pseudohistoric opera may be to any in Wagner's or Meyerbeer's. His tragedy as a composer of opera was that
he never found a libretto as good as the one Halévy and Meilhac
gave Bizet for *Carmen* or the ones Boïto gave Verdi for *Otello* and
Falstaff.

Piotr Ilyich had written Jürgenson that he did not demand royalties on the Fourth Symphony. What he did want was its publication in fine format. On January 21 he received from Nadezhda
Filaretovna 1,500 francs with which to assure this. She was as interested in having "our" symphony present a good face as he was. He
at once asked Jürgenson for its publication "in irreproachable
form," and stated that he had decided not to demand royalties on
Yevgeny Onyegin either. His finances were in better order than
they had ever been, and he sent Anatoly the draft of a letter to
Antonina Ivanovna, promising to pay her a monthly alimony and
to liquidate one of her debts amounting to 2,500 rubles (about
$1,250). In this letter, however, he asked that she turn over their
piano to him.

On January 25, 1878 death diminished the size of Piotr Ilyich's
immediate family for the first time since 1854. His half-sister,
Zinaïda Ilyinishna Olkhovskaya died in Orenburg at the age of
forty-nine. He had not seen her for many years. Indeed, at thirty-
seven he was not on intimate relations with her or with his elder
brothers, Nikolay and Ippolit. He was close to his eighty-three-
year-old father. But his family ties were strongest with Modest and
Anatoly, and with Alexandra Davidova and her family at Kamenka.

Piotr Ilyich worked in a fever of enthusiasm at the remaining
unfinished portions of *Yevgeny Onyegin,* sending reports on his
progress to Anatoly and to Nadezhda Filaretovna almost daily. He
completed the orchestration on February 1 and immediately began to make a clean copy of the entire score, including the libretto.
On the 13th he wrote Anatoly that he had completed the score
and sent it to Moscow. It was to be a long time before he knew
what his friends and colleagues there thought of it. His own opinion was clear and unshakable — it was the most deeply and sincerely felt and the best-written opera he had composed. He was
certain of that much, and he expressed this certainty to others.
He was, as was eventually proved, exactly right.

On February 11 Piotr Ilyich received a letter from Nikolay Rubinstein in which that redoubtable quarreller announced that the Fourth Symphony was being scheduled for performance on February 22. As Rubinstein would conduct it himself, Piotr Ilyich was satisfied that it would be played impeccably. He was still worrying about the Scherzo, that "pizzicato ostinato" by which he set such store. "I think I have already written you that the faster it is played the better. Now I suddenly begin to think that it should not be played so fast. However, I rely completely on your intelligence."

Letters full of money continued to arrive from Nadezhda Filaretovna. The one Piotr Ilyich received on February 12 contained 1,000 rubles more than he had expected or she specified. "I wish that this could be the last grant," he told Anatoly. "I don't know why, but this time the realization that I am exploiting the astonishing generosity of this woman really oppresses me." Such a mood recurred from time to time, but when he really considered the matter coolly he knew that nothing, unless it was his music, gave the unhappy, lonely woman so much satisfaction as her largess toward him.

Hearing that Azanchevsky was coming to visit him in San Remo, Piotr Ilyich spent the designated day in Monaco. He explained this uncivil flight to Anatoly: "In general, I have made up my mind to disregard all proprieties, all civilities, all the unavoidable observances of social forms when they are burdensome to me. I have tortured myself long enough. It is time for me to begin living the remainder of my life as I want to live, freely, without submitting to the tyranny of social relations." In general, as he said, Piotr Ilyich carried out this resolution, putting it progressively into effect during the next few years and receding from it only when events drove him into blind corners.

From time to time Piotr Ilyich went hopefully to San Remo's opera house and to similar establishments in near-by cities and towns. A performance of *La Favorita* he found so bad as to be laughable. Rossini's *Il Barbiere di Siviglia*, with a Russian Rosina, was better. A Pisa staging of *La Forza del Destino*[3] he called horrible, remarking with disgust that the tenor's figure was exactly like Apukhtin's. What he enjoyed more than operas was wandering into

[3] Tchaikovsky does not seem to have been present at the world *première* of *La Forza del Destino* — in St. Petersburg on November 10, 1862.

the surrounding mountains with Modest and Kolya, or with Kolya alone. He wrote Anatoly in pleased excitement about a most enjoyable trip on donkeyback to the mountain church of Santa Maria di Guardia.

Piotr Ilyich's letters from San Remo brim, and all but dance, with good spirits, good health, and happy peacefulness. He wrote Nadezhda Filaretovna that people had not been altogether incorrect in stating that he had been out of his mind. He himself realized that during his last days in Moscow he had been mentally affected. "To you," he concluded, "and to my two dear brothers, *to all three of you,* I owe not only my life, but my mental and physical recovery." Again on February 13 he was in an unaccustomed mood of bubbling gaiety — "rose-coloured," he called it. "Glad the opera is finished, glad spring is at hand, glad I am well and free, glad to feel secure from unpleasant encounters, but gladdest of all to have, in your friendship and my brothers' affection, such certain supports in life and to be aware that I may eventually perfect my art. I have faith that this feeling is no self-deception, but a correct appraisal of my powers. I thank you for everything, for everything."

As the end of the stay at San Remo approached, Piotr Ilyich entered upon a protracted series of letters discussing Schopenhauer, women, and love. Suddenly Nadezhda Filaretovna asked him if he had ever experienced love otherwise than in its Platonic form. "Yes and no," was his answer, written from Florence on February 21. "If you had phrased your question differently, if you had asked me whether I had ever discovered complete happiness in love, I should have answered no, and no again. Besides, it seems to me that the reply to that question is to be heard in my music. If, however, you ask me whether I have ever experienced the entire power and inexpressible tension of love, I must answer yes, yes, yes. For time and again I have laboured to render in music all the anguish and ecstasy of love." This was an honest answer, as honest as any he could make to Nadezhda Filaretovna. Whether it answered her question to her satisfaction or not, it is the deepest glimpse into Piotr Ilyich's erotic-amorous life that she — or anyone but perhaps Modest, Anatoly, and some whose names are unknown — was ever allowed.

Piotr Ilyich was in a Florentine hotel, resting after a tiring tramp through the Uffizi, when Nikolay Rubinstein, the night of

February 22, 1878, conducted in Moscow the world *première* of
the Fourth Symphony. Its composer's impatience for news of its
reception had mounted to agony. He had sent it to Moscow more
than five weeks before and had received no comment on it from
anyone. He believed in it, went as far as saying that he secretly
valued it above *Yevgeny Onyegin*. What would be the audience's
reaction? What the critics'? It was fortunate for him that the first
word he received was a telegram from Nadezhda Filaretovna, for
the symphony had been indifferently received and was to be neglected by the critics until Napravnik conducted it in St. Petersburg more than nine months later.

That Moscow audience's reception of the Fourth Symphony and
the critics' neglect or misapprehension of its character provide one
more futile lesson in the humility and care necessary in approaching a new work of art. One of the few writers who did report the
performance said in *Moskovskiye Vyedomosti* of March 1 that
"this time also" Tchaikovsky had proved himself entirely worthy
of his reputation as a symphonist. What could that *also* have
meant? That the Fourth is worthy of the Third, the Second, and
the First? No one in that audience, at least no one vocal except
Nadezhda Filaretovna, realized that he was hearing the greatest
extended piece of orchestral music a Russian had ever composed,
and a piece of music likely to become loved and familiar throughout the world. No one realized that Piotr Ilyich Tchaikovsky, in
being himself — and therefore a Russian and a suffering man and
an eclectic and much else besides — was uttering in a fateful,
large manner pieces of musical speech beyond the uncertain tongue
of an Anton Rubinstein, beyond the capabilities of all the Five
save Mussorgsky and perhaps Borodin, and more accessible and
meaningful to the generality of music-lovers than any Russian
symphonic work yet composed. Not even Piotr Ilyich, perhaps,
would have guessed that the symphony he had dedicated to Nadezhda Filaretovna would challenge the popularity of Beethoven.

With Nadezhda Filaretovna's warm, laudatory, and appreciative
telegram on February 24 there arrived another signed by Nikolay
Rubinstein and several others. It said that the symphony had been
played, and nothing more. Perhaps his colleagues wanted to spare
him the pain that an honest report of its reception would have
caused him. As it was, they merely increased his anxiety and postponed his pain. In thanking Nadezhda Filaretovna he stuck to

his guns: "In my heart of hearts I feel sure that this is the best thing I have ever done."

Piotr Ilyich visited the Palazzo Vecchio. He composed a song that was to be one of the six in Opus 38 and a piano piece called *Interrupted Reveries* that was to become No. 12 of Opus 40. This latter contains a middle section based on a song sung under his window in Venice every day. He saw the renowned Salvini in *Hamlet* and disliked the actor for being too old, unattractive, and mannered. He looked at the Medici Chapel and compared Michelangelo to Beethoven. He asked Nadezhda Filaretovna to pick out some poems suitable for songs from the works of Alexey Tolstoy, Fet, Mey, and Tyutchev. He informed Jürgenson that he would compose a suite of children's pieces (Opus 39) and a liturgy (Opus 41). He advised Anatoly not to aim higher than his innate abilities, saying that he himself wanted to be the best composer in the world, a first-class conductor, a very clever and wise man, and an elegant and fashionable star of the salons. "How much time I have needed to come to the conclusion that I belong to the category of the people who are not unintelligent — not to that of those whose intellect displays extraordinary qualities! How many years I required to understand that even as a composer I am merely a talented man and not some exceptional phenomenon!" He decided to write one composition each day, and complained that Italian music had fallen upon evil days and that Florence had no opera house.

At last, on March 1, there arrived a letter in which Nadezhda Filaretovna opened her heart on the subject of the Fourth Symphony. She knew — Piotr Ilyich had told her — what had been in his heart and mind while he composed it, and now she was able to say that while listening to it she had felt just as he had during its birth. His music, as ever, went, not to her head, but to her heart. As that was precisely where he wanted it to go, Piotr Ilyich was as happy over her reaction as he would have been over an enthusiastic review by Laroche or Cui, or over praise from Hans von Bülow.

In her letter Nadezhda Filaretovna inquired whether or not Piotr Ilyich had had a specific program in mind while composing the symphony. He answered her in detail in one of the longest and most curious letters he ever penned. Through this document outsiders are enabled to learn how one composer worked. The possibility that Piotr Ilyich may have thought up some of the specific details of his program after the fact does not lessen its value, for even though such specific pictures and ideas may not have floated through his imagination as he worked, they clearly might have, and are in all probability very like the ones that were there:

You ask me if this symphony has a definite program. In reply to this sort of question in reference to a symphony I usually answer no, none. And it is really very difficult to answer such a question. How can one express the indefinable sensations one experiences while writing an instrumental composition that has no definite subject? It is a purely lyrical process. It is a musical confession of the soul, which is full to the brim, and which, true to its nature, unburdens itself through sounds just as a lyric poet expresses himself through poetry. The difference lies in the fact that music has far richer resources of expression and is a more subtle medium into which to translate the thousand shifting moments in the soul's moods. In general, the seed of a future composition appears suddenly and unexpectedly. If the soil is ready — that is to say, if the disposition to work is present — it takes root with astonishing force and swiftness, shoots up through the surface, puts out branches. leaves, and finally blossoms. Only by this metaphor can I describe the creative process. The great problem is that the seed must appear at a favourable moment; the rest takes care of itself. I would try vainly to express in words that unbounded sense of bliss that comes over me when a new idea opens up within me and starts to take on definite form. Then I forget everything and behave like one demented. Everything inside me begins to pulse and quiver: I hardly begin the sketch before one thought begins tumbling over another. In the midst of this magic process it often happens that an interruption from outside awakens me from my somnambulistic condition: someone rings the bell, a servant enters, or a clock strikes, reminding me that it is time to stop. This kind of interruption is truly horrible. Sometimes it breaks off the inspiration for a considerable time, and I have to search for it again, frequently in vain. In such a case cold reason and technical knowledge have to be levied on for assistance. Even with the greatest masters there are often moments when the organic sequence breaks off and a skilfull jointure has to be manufactured so that the sections appear to be completely one. But that cannot be avoided. If the state of mind and soul that we call inspiration lasted without interruption for a long time, no artist could survive. The strings would snap and the instrument shatter into fragments. It is already a good thing if the central ideas and the general pattern of a composition come without intense mental activity, appearing as a result of that supernatural and inexplicable force we call inspiration.

However, I have wandered away from the answer to your question. In *our* symphony there is a program. That is, it is possible for me to outline in words what it attempts to express, and to you, to you alone, I want and am able to communicate the meaning of the whole, as well as of the separate sections. This I can do, of course, in general terms only.

The introduction contains the germ of the entire symphony, without question its central idea:

This is Fate, the fatal force that prevents our striving for happiness from succeeding, that jealously watches to see that felicity and peace shall not be complete or unclouded, that hangs over the head like the sword of Damocles and constantly, unswervingly poisons the soul. It is invincible, it can never be mastered. One must submit to it and take refuge in futile longings.

The unconsolable, hopeless feeling is growing stronger and more consuming. Would it not be better to turn away from reality and immerse oneself in dreams?

Oh joy! A sweet, tender vision has appeared. A blessed, luminous being flies by and beckons somewhere.

How wonderful! How distantly already sounds the importunate first theme of the Allegro. Little by little, dreams have completely enveloped the soul. All that was gloomy and joyless is forgotten. Happiness is here, it is here!

But no! They were only dreams, and Fate awakens us harshly.

And thus all life is an incessant shifting between grim reality and fleeting visions and reveries of joy. There is no haven. We are buffeted by the waves hither and thither until the sea swallows us. That, approximately, is the program of the first movement.

The second movement of the symphony expresses another phase of longing. This is the melancholy feeling that suffuses you toward evening when you are sitting alone, weary from work. You have taken a book, but it has fallen from your hands. A host of memories appears. And you are sad because so much is already past. It is pleasant to remember one's youth and to regret the past, but there is no wish to begin again. Life has tired you out. It is pleasant to rest and cast a backward glance. Many things flit through the memory. There were happy moments when young blood pulsed warm and life was gratifying. There were also moments of grief, of irreparable loss. It is all remote in the past. It is both sad and somehow sweet to lose oneself in the past.

The third movement expresses no definite sensations. It is a capricious arabesque, fleeting apparitions that pass through the imagination when one has begun to drink a little wine and is beginning to experience the first phase of intoxication. The soul is neither happy nor sad. You are not thinking of anything; the imagination is completely free and for some reason has begun to paint curious pictures. . . . Among them you suddenly remember some muzhiks on a spree, and a street song. Then somewhere in the distance a military parade is moving along. These are the disconnected images that pass through our heads as we begin to fall asleep. They have nothing in common with reality, they are strange, exotic, incoherent.

The fourth movement. If you cannot discover reasons for happiness in yourself, look at others. Get out among the people. Look, what a good time they have, surrendering themselves to joy! A picture of popular merriment on a holiday. You have scarcely had a chance to forget yourself when indefatigable Fate appears once more and reminds you of herself. But the others pay no attention to you. They do not even turn around, do not even look at you, do not notice that you are alone and sad. Oh, how gay they are! How fortunate they are that their emotions are direct and uncomplicated! Upbraid yourself and do not say that all the world is sad. Strong, simple joys exist. Take happiness from the joys of others. Life is bearable after all.

I can tell you nothing more, dear friend, about the symphony. My description is naturally neither clear nor satisfactory. But that is the peculiarity of instrumental music — it cannot be analysed. As Heine said, "Where words leave off, music begins."

There is more to the letter, remarks about Florence and about a visit to the popular comic theatre. As he was about to post it, Piotr Ilyich started a little to regret having been so specific and detailed. He added a postscript:

PS. As I was putting this letter into the envelope, I started to read it over and felt misgivings about the chaotic and incomplete program I am sending you. For the first time in my life I have tried to put into words and phrases my musical thoughts and sensations. I have not been successful. I was in very low spirits last winter all the while I was writing this symphony, and it is a true echo of my feelings at the time. But only an echo. How can one reproduce it in clearly defined language? I don't know. I have already forgotten a lot. Only a general impression of my intense and grief-filled experiences remains with me. I am very, very eager to know what my Moscow friends will say of my composition.

Too often, non-Teutonic music in large forms has been attacked for not copying the satisfactory architectural designs developed out of centuries of experiment by the Mannheim school, Karl Philipp Emanuel Bach, Haydn, Mozart, and Beethoven. This sort of criticism finds all Latin and Slavic symphonies nonsymphonic, or even antisymphonic, because they do not achieve the kind of unity the great German and Austrian masters won by means, largely, of sonata form. This sort of criticism has meaning only if one of two postulates is accepted in advance as axiomatic. The first is that the sonata-symphony form, found near perfection in such works as the later symphonies of Haydn and Mozart, is the only ideal toward which all extended orchestral compositions in several sections should aspire. The second is that it is impossible to build a satisfactory plural-movement work by any other means. Neither of these postulates, it is scarcely necessary to say, is a law handed down by the goddess of music. As a method by which Haydn, Mozart, and at times Schubert and Beethoven succeeded in achieving something like perfect form, the machinery of statement, secondary theme, development, recapitulation, and so on is a miracle of constructive intellection. As a measure applied unthinkingly to the works of later — and earlier — composers, it leads straight into nonsense. To find Bach's suites inferior to Mozart's symphonies because they are not in symphonic form is idiocy, and exactly the same is true of criticizing the Russian composers — or any composers later than Beethoven — for building by other methods works they chose to call sonatas or symphonies or concertos.

Here we have, in fact, an obfuscatory argument over names. If a composer sets out to imitate the structure of the classical sonata or symphony and fails to create it, he has failed in imitation. But his failure may have nothing at all to do with the æsthetic value of the work produced. It may be nothing more important than failure in wholly extraneous detail or nomenclature. If the resulting composition, be it called sonata, symphony, symphonic poem, fantasia, or rhapsody, successfully supports and displays the composer's materials, that should be all that matters. To think otherwise is to ignore the true value and meaning of structural form. An extended composition, to succeed, must avoid monotony, achieve unity within its separate sections and as a whole, and have movement. To require that it achieve those qualities by means native to composers who lived from roughly 1717 to 1827 is to misread the meaning of musical form and stultify its present and future.

Piotr Ilyich's Fourth Symphony is a failure only if measured by the classical model. In his monumental book *Music in Western Civilization,* Paul Henry Láng, usually ready to judge any composition by its own merits, goes astray in exactly this direction. "The Fourth Symphony," he says, "is still largely antisymphonic. While some of its thematic material is engaging and well presented and the orchestration is interesting throughout, there is no trace of development in the symphonic sense, but merely a succession of repetitions and a sequence of climactic runs that often become hysterical. The slow movement has one of Tchaikovsky's typical songlike melodies, presented with dignity and simplicity; the scherzo fascinates with its clever orchestration, but all the good is lost in the coarse band music of the last movement, swelling an innocent Russian dance tune into a wild Sarmatian bedlam." This judgment — which, be it said, is prefaced to praise of the Fifth and Sixth symphonies — is one of criticism's typical muddles.

Mr. Láng, by giving the wrong criticism of the Fourth Symphony first, and the right criticism second, has muddied the issue and weakened his argument. Despite its many beauties, the symphony somehow fails in detail and as a unit. So much need not be denied. But it fails, not because it has "no development in the symphonic sense," but because some of its germinal materials are cheap, bombastic, or trivial, and because, hypnotized precisely by the classical models, Piotr Ilyich failed to find for his best ideas their own adequate form. He submitted them instead to half-hearted attempts at development and recapitulation. Two of the symphonies he was yet to compose turned out greater works, not because they leaned closer to the classical models, but because he found better materials with which to build them and ways of handling those materials more hospitable to their innate natures.

The first movement of the Fourth Symphony is too long. Aside from the possibility of simply exhausting a listener's ability really to listen, a piece of music can be too long for only one of two reasons: it stretches insufficient material out to intolerable thinness and monotony or — in the case of one section of a work in several parts — it overbalances the other movements by sheer bulk and thus unhinges the structure. This "andante sostenuto, moderato con anima" commits both sins. Note, however, that the question of whether or not it is strictly in the sonata-allegro form required of the classical imitation is irrelevant. If Piotr Ilyich had been in better command of his materials, he would have cut it by one third. Had he been such a belated seeker of Beethoven's form as Brahms was, he might have given us, instead, derived secondary themes and cleverly concealed connective passages, producing as admirably correct and musically sluggish a movement as the first of Brahms's Second Symphony.

The second movement of Piotr Ilyich's Fourth Symphony is an unqualified success. It is reared largely on two exceedingly beautiful and malleable melodies. It is exquisitely proportioned. It is of exactly the right length. And it is superbly orchestrated. The slight touches by which repetitions of its principal melody are varied and given new significance are miraculous. The use of wind instruments, from the opening oboe theme throughout, is of creative originality. The structure approximates one of the several allowed to second movements by the codifiers — three-part song form. It succeeds, however, not because Piotr Ilyich has successfully worked recalcitrant matter into such an approximation, but because he has squeezed from excellent melodies all that was in them — and not one measure more.

The third movement of the Fourth Symphony — Piotr Ilyich's beloved "pizzicato ostinato" — is a light stroke of genius comparable to the gossamer fairyland music of Mendelssohn and Berlioz. As third to the revelry of the first movement and the lyric meditation of the second, it is perfect contrast, all swift motion and points of light. It is in the reliable A–B–A form, and is a scherzolike frolic. The man who wrote it was a sovereign of the orchestra. It could be analysed for ever without giving up one iota of gloom, hysteria, or rotund oratory.

It is impossible to avoid the conviction that Piotr Ilyich's mind and imagination, battered and exhausted by the frightening occurrences in his private life, no longer functioned at their best when he set down the concluding movement. Taking a theme (a folksong with words beginning "A birch tree stood in the fields"), Piotr Ilyich built on it a series of variations, not realizing that it was substantially unvariable. To it he added a blustering march. The whole, mistaking volume and muscularity for true size, he enlarged and loudened. It is like a man shouting weak arguments to give them force. The abstract form is conventional enough. The flaw lies not in deviation from the Mozart canon or the Beethoven canon, but in poor materials and lapses of taste. The unfortunate result is that the Fourth ends in a roar of spurious glory.

Yet — and this is an important test of the validity of a long composition — Piotr Ilyich's Fourth Symphony creates an over-all effect of unity, power, and beauty. It is not a suite of disjunctive pieces. Nor is it unified by the mere presence of the Fate theme. Its unity resides in a pervasive conception, an inner sense of stress and balance that is tested severely only by the excessive length of the first movement. The melodic invention, the harmonic and instrumental variety, above all, the emotional power of the Fourth assured its future, which is now the present, and today seems to assure it another future.

X

WHILE still in Florence, Piotr Ilyich remembered a young boy he had formerly heard singing in the street there. On December 28, 1877 he had written Nadezhda Filaretovna: "One evening Anatoly and I suddenly heard someone singing in the street and, noticing a crowd, joined it. The singer was a boy of ten or eleven accompanying himself on the guitar. He sang in a marvellously rich, full voice, with such warmth and finish as are rarely heard even among professional artists. The intensely tragic words of the song had a curious charm on his childish lips." Now he asked other street singers about the boy. They promised to produce him on the Lung' Arno. When they did so, Piotr Ilyich doubted that it was the same boy. "When I begin to sing," the boy said, "you will be convinced that I am the one. Give me a silver piece of fifty centesimi first." The beauty of the boy's speaking voice all but convinced him. "What I felt when he began to sing is beyond all words!" he told Nadezhda Filaretovna. "I cried, I trembled, I was flooded with pure delight. He sang again: 'Perche tradirmi, perche lasciarmi.' I do not remember that any simple folksong ever made such an impression on me. This time the lad sang a charming new melody that I want to have him sing again so that I can note it down for my own use on some future occasion." The new melody Piotr Ilyich heard on this occasion, and which the boy sang for him again two days later, was to become the basis of one of his most attractive songs, the sixth of Opus 38, *Pimpinella*.

On March 8, 1878 Piotr Ilyich, accompanied by Modest, Kolya, and Alexey Sofronov, was in Geneva, and the next day the four of them returned to Clarens. There he found no letter from Rubinstein, no word about the Fourth Symphony from any of his musical friends in Russia. Only indirectly, through Kotek, had he received any report on its reception, except that from Nadezhda Filaretovna. Kotek said that a student at the Conservatory had enjoyed the work. That was all. Piotr Ilyich was inescapably and rightly irritated and depressed. So Nadezhda Filaretovna wrote him comforting letters: his pupils missed him, the public had been unable to comprehend the symphony in one hearing, its future was sure. She herself was especially pleased by the Russianness of the symphony, and asked him whether he had put it there consciously. In his answer he showed himself wiser than many of his subsequent critics:

As to the Russian element in my works, it is true that I often start to compose with the idea of using some popular song or other. Sometimes, as in the finale of our symphony, I do this without intent, quite unexpectedly. As to the Russian element in my music generally, its melodic and harmonic relation to folk music — I grew up in a quiet place and was drenched from earliest childhood with the wonderful beauty of Russian popular songs. I am therefore passionately devoted to every expression of the Russian spirit. In brief, I am a Russian through and through.

Rimsky-Korsakov, Borodin, Ippolitov-Ivanov, and a host of other lesser men have composed music that is more Russian at first glance than any of Piotr Ilyich's. Not one of them, as he saw, was more Russian than he. The difference lies in his having absorbed the superficial aspects of highly coloured folk music into himself, in his having transformed it there by the alchemy of personality into an individual musical idiom, and in his having expressed himself with the directness of speech while the nationalists expressed their own personalities only by indirection. There is no question of superior or inferior methods here, for all methods that produce good music are superior. The point is that to deny Piotr Ilyich's pervasive and ineluctable Russian quality is to confess having listened to his music with prejudiced or insensitive ears. Stravinsky, not making that mistake, said flatly: "Tchaikovsky was, of all of us, the most Russian."

Kotek was visiting Clarens, and with him Piotr Ilyich was playing over scores he did not know. He enjoyed Lalo's new work, the *Symphonie espagnole*, lately introduced by Sarasate. But nothing distracted him from composing. He was at work, he told Nadezhda Filaretovna, on a piano sonata and a violin concerto. He was also developing several small piano pieces. The sonata caused him difficulty: "Even the thinnest and trashiest ideas I have to squeeze out of myself," he told her, "and I ponder over each measure." With complete blindness to his limitations, he failed to understand that a piano sonata was outside his capability. He laboured over it with determination but without joy. The mammoth work, the forty-five-page Sonata in G major, opus 37, is an unmitigated failure, a vast and desolate ruin. Only in combination with other instruments did Piotr Ilyich often conceive viable piano music. Here it is poor and strained. The writing is unpianistic in the extreme, difficult without reason. The Tchaikovskyan gestures appear, but communicate little. Year after year the few yellowing copies of the G-major Sonata remain in dusty bins. Not even Piotr Ilyich's staunchest admirer could wish them elsewhere.

Indeed, in the midst of composing the sonata, Piotr Ilyich became so engrossed in work on his Violin Concerto that he turned away eagerly from the unfinished piano composition. Kotek, a violinist, was at hand and could give advice on the solo writing. In the midst of telling Nadezhda Filaretovna of his happy work on the concerto, he stopped to thank her for sending him a marked copy of Alexey Tolstoy's poems. He particularly liked an excerpt in *Don Juan* and stated that he would set it. This became the first and finest of the six songs in Opus 38. As *Don Juan's Serenade* it has remained one of the most popular of all Piotr Ilyich's vocal works. Three of the other songs in Opus 38 are also to Tolstoy words, the fifth is Lermontov, and the last is the Florentine song, *Pimpinella.* Only *Don Juan's Serenade* is first-rate among them. It was favored by Édouard de Reszke, whose powerful projection of it James Gibbons Huneker described as "satanic." In spite of it, however, Opus 38 does nothing to prove that Piotr Ilyich was natively or by effort a true composer of songs.

Kotek lingered at Clarens. With Piotr Ilyich he played four-hand arrangements of *Francesca da Rimini* and the Fourth Symphony. In far-away Moscow the B-flat minor Piano Concerto was performed on March 22, while on the 28th Nikolay Rubinstein played its solo part to Karl U. Davidov's conducting in St. Petersburg. By that time, too, Napravnik had led the northern capital's first performance of *Francesca,* which was received enthusiastically and reviewed well — one critic ranked it next to *Romeo and Juliet.* Work on the Violin Concerto went ahead rapidly, and by the 29th Piotr Ilyich had begun to copy it. He had found time to chide Nadezhda Filaretovna for her lack of appreciation for Mozart, telling her that *Don Giovanni* was the most beautiful opera ever composed, and its Donna Anna "the most superb and wonderful human character ever depicted in music." It was at the end of this letter that he said: "It is thanks to Mozart that I have devoted my life to music."

Piotr Ilyich also made time to answer Nadezhda Filaretovna when she inquired whether or not he would like the idea that a statue be erected to his memory after his death. He did not care for this prospect and moralized on the fleeting quality of sudden fame. "I, perhaps, am so indifferent to my modest lot because my faith in the fair judgment of posterity is unshakable. While still alive, I am already enjoying in anticipation that portion of fame which the future histories of Russian art will allot to me." He rested on his sincerity and his honest labours, and posterity has fully justified his faith.

On April 1 Piotr Ilyich was able to tell Nadezhda Filaretovna that he had played over with Modest and Kotek the completely copied first movement of the Violin Concerto in D major. Modest and Kotek were enraptured by it. Two days later he said that Kotek had played the solo part so well that he could have given a public concert of it at a moment's notice. On the 3rd both the violinist and Modest were dissatisfied with the Andante. Piotr Ilyich set himself to compose a new one, which he completed in one day to their entire satisfaction. On the 6th he began the orchestration of this, completing it in five days.

At last Taneyev, a musician whose opinion Piotr Ilyich valued, wrote him a detailed opinion of the Fourth Symphony. The young pianist found the first movement so disproportionately long as to seem an independent symphonic poem to which the other movements were unnecessarily added. He sensed a program in the trumpet fanfares. He found the Andantino charming, but criticized the trio of the Scherzo. He reported that Nikolay Rubinstein liked the Finale best, but himself dissented from that opinion, saying that to him the variations on a folksong appeared neither important nor interesting. In general he felt that the symphony had one serious defect: it contained numerous phrases sounding like ballet music. He could not hear it without seeing a prima ballerina in his mind's eye, a vision that put him in poor humour and spoiled his pleasure in the symphony's many beauties.

Taneyev's chief charge against the Fourth Symphony has been made so often since March 30, 1878, when he sent it to the composer, and has been levelled against so many of Piotr Ilyich's large works, that it must be considered seriously. One answer to it is that it is thinking in reverse, that it is the best ballet music — Piotr Ilyich's own — that sounds like his symphonies. The paragraphs in which he himself answered Taneyev are interesting:

I have no idea what you consider "ballet music," or why you should object to it. Do you look upon every melody in a lively dance rhythm as "ballet music"? If so, how can you reconcile yourself to most of Beethoven's symphonies, in which you will find such melodies on every page? Or do you intend to say that the trio of my Scherzo is in the style of Minkus, Gerber, or Pugni? To my mind, it does not deserve such criticism. I can never understand why "ballet music" should be used as an epithet of contempt. The music of a ballet is not invariably bad, for there are good works of this class — Delibes's Sylvia, for example. And when the music is good, what difference does it make whether Sobyesichanskaya dances to it or not? I can only think that certain parts of my symphony displease you because they recall the ballet, not because they are intrinsically bad. Perhaps you are right, but I do not understand why dance tunes should not be employed episodically in a symphony, even with the announced purpose of lending a touch of coarse, everyday humour. Again I appeal to Beethoven, who frequently had recourse to such effects. I must add that I have racked my brains vainly to recall in what section of the Allegro you can possibly have discovered "ballet music." It remains enigmatic.

With what you say as to my symphony having a program I wholly agree. But I do not understand why this must be a mistake. I am much more afraid of the contrary: I wish no symphonic work to emanate from me that has nothing to express and is made up merely of harmonies and a purposeless pattern of rhythms and modulations. Of course my symphony is program music — but it would be impossible to present the program in words: it would seem ludicrous and cause only smiles. Should not this be true of a symphony, the most lyrical of all musical forms? Should it not express all the things for which words cannot be found, which nevertheless arise in the heart and demand expression? Besides, I must tell you that in my simplicity I imagined that the plan of my symphony was so obvious that everyone would understand its meaning, or at least its salient ideas, without a definite program. I beg you not to imagine that I want to swagger before you with profound emotions and lofty ideas. Throughout this work I have made no effort to express a novel thought. In reality my work is a reflection of Beethoven's Fifth Symphony: I have not copied his musical content, but only borrowed the central idea. Has the Fifth Symphony a program? What do you think? Not only does it have a program, but one so clear that there cannot be the smallest difference of opinion as to its meaning. Much the same lies at the base of my symphony, and if you have failed to grasp it, that simply proves that I am no Beethoven — on which point I never had any doubt whatever.

Piotr Ilyich added that there was no line in the Fourth Symphony that he had not felt, or that was not an echo of the true emotions he had felt. Then he qualified this: "The only exception is the middle section of the first movement, which contains some forced passages, seams, gluings — in a word, artificialities." His unwavering honesty is admirable. When Taneyev later remarked that he had found the influence of *Der Ring des Nibelungen* in *Francesca da Rimini,* Piotr Ilyich acknowledged the accuracy of the judgment. "I was myself aware of this while composing," he wrote. "Isn't it curious that I succumbed to the influence of a work of art to which I am in general antagonistic?"

On April 18 Piotr Ilyich was in Lausanne, two days later in Vienna, on the 23rd with the Davidovs at Kamenka. He had been away from Russia more than six months. He still did not wish to return to Moscow, and still must think of avoiding Antonina Ivanovna. Again Nadezhda Filaretovna came to his assistance, offering the use of her estate at Braïlov for several weeks. She specified that she herself would not be there, and he gratefully accepted. His activity while he remained at Kamenka proved what he had written from Vienna, that he was returning "a sound, sane man, full of renewed strength and energy." He was working on the Piano Sonata and the *Twelve Piano Pieces of Moderate Difficulty,* opus 40. He was starting the twenty-four pieces of the *Children's Album,* opus 39, and was considering the composition of a liturgy, probably that of St. John Chrysostom. He was likewise waiting to begin a large work, probably to a libretto by Modest based on his old favourite, Zhukovsky's *Undine.* He also notified Jürgenson that he had composed a *March of the Volunteer Fleet* for piano, and asked that it be published with a pseudonym.[1]

On May 25 Piotr Ilyich stopped in Kiev. Four days later he reached Braïlov, in the Ukraine, where the land begins to rise south and west toward the Carpathian Mountains. The stay at Kamenka, despite full reconciliation with Alexandra Davidova, had not been entirely happy. He had seen Anatoly there, but only

---

[1] Jürgenson respected this request, issuing the *March* as the work of P. Sinopov.

for the few days before that faithful brother rushed off to Moscow to see what could be done about persuading Antonina Ivanovna to sue for divorce. As Piotr Ilyich moved on to beautiful Braïlov, he did not know what the proceedings had in store for him. Nadezhda Filaretovna's estate proved to be beauty and comfort beyond his imaginings. At his absent hostess's orders, he was waited on, catered to, watched over like a precious, breakable object. He managed to relax in the midst of so much care, and actually put together a house-gift for Nadezhda Filaretovna, an unrelated trio of pieces for violin and piano that he called *Souvenir of a Loved Place*. Consisting of the discarded original Andante of the Violin Concerto and two trifles composed on the spot, this colourless effusion was published as his Opus 42.

He was bathing in the vast loveliness of the Ukrainian countryside when word arrived from Moscow. It was a letter from his wife. He described it to Anatoly as "filled with incredible nonsense," but he fairly shouted the news that in it his wife had agreed to divorce. This meant that at last, after eight months, he must return to Moscow, see people, face the stares of the curious, and somehow take up once more the ravelled fabric of his usual life. Four days before leaving Braïlov he played over almost the entire score of *Yevgeny Onyegin* for his own ears alone. To Modest he wrote: "I am ashamed to confess it, but so be it, I shall tell you confidentially. The audience was borne away by the music to the point of weeping, and paid the composer myriad compliments. Oh, if future audiences would only be as moved by this music as was the composer himself!"

After he had put the finishing touches on the six songs of Opus 38, he and Alexey Sofronov went to Moscow, arriving on June 13. To his horror, he then learned what he had forgotten, that the following day was Nikolay Rubinstein's birthday. His presence at the birthday breakfast was mandatory. Steeling himself, he attended it. He was terribly uncomfortable despite, or perhaps because of, everyone's cordiality and friendly inquisitiveness. He felt that Rubinstein had not forgiven him for turning down the position of delegate to Paris. "He doesn't," Piotr Ilyich remarked to Nadezhda Filaretovna, "like those who do not feel in his debt: he would prefer everyone around to be known as his creations. In brief, I am *persona non grata* to him, and he couldn't hide it."

It was necessary, if Piotr Ilyich was to be divorced, that he see

Antonina Ivanovna. He was spared that ordeal of terrible moment, for she could not be found. He stood the game of hide-and-seek as long as he could and then again left Moscow, going first for a brief stay with Kondratyev at Nizi and then back to the Davidovs at Kamenka. Meanwhile the patient and sympathetic Jürgenson instituted a search that finally discovered the hiding woman. To the astonished publisher Antonina Ivanovna announced that she did not wish a divorce, and that if the matter came to trial and tales of Piotr Ilyich as an adulterer were advanced, she herself would proclaim his innocence. This made divorce impossible, as adultery was, in Russia, the only legal ground for divorce.

Piotr Ilyich wrote Nadezhda Filaretovna that he would not need the 10,000 rubles she had kindly proffered to pay for his divorce. He believed, however, that about one third of the sum might persuade his wife to remove her distasteful presence from Moscow and thus again make it possible for him to live there. He had begun to hate her with so violent a passion that he confessed a momentary desire to do her physical harm. "While I write these things to you, the hated vision rises before my eyes, and I become agitated and suffer. I am angry, and hate her — and myself no less. Last year, one September evening, I was very close — oh, within one step — of that blind, insane, sick loathing that can lead to crime. I assure you that only a miracle saved me, and now, thinking of her, I feel the same sensation churning within me, and it makes me afraid of myself." Perhaps this "crime" was the suicide he had attempted. There is also the possibility that, at the peak of the terror he had endured during his weeks with his wife, he had been tempted to kill her. Such a temptation has been hinted at — somewhat more graphically than documentary evidence allows — by writers on Piotr Ilyich. This letter is their best evidence.

As though to clear his desk for more important activities, Piotr Ilyich began his visit at Kamenka by making final corrections in all the compositions he had recently completed and then making clean copies. Nadezhda Filaretovna asked him a series of questions about his methods of working. In answering, he divided his compositions between those he had written on his own initiative and those that had been commissioned. He pointed out to her that not all his successful works were in the first class, nor all the unsuccessful ones in the second. Citing Glinka as a perpetual dilettante who worked only when no more attractive activity was offered, Piotr Ilyich asked: "What would have occurred had Glinka been born on another social level, had he lived under other conditions, had he laboured as an artist who, understanding his powers, feels that his duty is to exploit his talent to its utmost limit rather than to write music as an amateur simply because he has nothing better to do?" Later in the same letter he added:

I trust, my friend, that you will not find me vainglorious if I tell you that my turning to inspiration is never fruitless. I can only state that this power, which I have called an uncertain guest, became customary with me so long ago that we are now inseparable, and she leaves me only when she feels out of place because my workaday human living has intruded. Always, however, the shadow removes itself and she reappears. I may therefore say that in my normal mental condition I compose music constantly, anywhere, at each moment of a day. Sometimes I look curiously at this productive flow of creativeness which, entirely by itself, separate from any conversation I may at the moment be participating in, separate from the people with me at the time, goes on in the region of my brain that is given over to music. Sometimes it is a working-out, a melodious detail of some small work thought out in advance, at other times a wholly fresh, original musical idea that I try to remember. Its source is a mystery.

This letter, detailing his *modus operandi* for the greedy eyes of Nadezhda Filaretovna was already long when he interrupted it to eat dinner. But an even longer section follows, headed: "Two o'clock." Much of it he had stated before — indeed, had written to her before. But he knew that she could never learn too much, know too much for her own taste, of how his music came to be. Occasional phrases of real insight and value crop up. "No melody ever comes to me without its related harmony. Generally speaking, these two elements of music, plus rhythm, are impossible to conceive separately: each melodic germ carries with it inescapable harmony and rhythm." She had asked him about orchestration. "If one is composing for orchestra, the musical idea includes the proper instrument for its projection, though one often changes the instrumentation later." He was clear on the relation between music and verbal text: "Words must never be written to music, as it is the text that summons up its proper musical expression." She had asked whether he used only established forms, and his answer was that of any honest artist above the status of automaton: "Yes and no." Even this long, two-part letter — it runs to more than two thousand words — did not satisfy Piotr Ilyich that he had made himself clear either to himself or to Nadezhda Filaretovna. The next day, therefore, he continued the argument:

Talking with you yesterday about the process of composition, I failed to describe clearly the labour that follows the first sketch. This part is particularly important: what has been written emotionally must now be examined critically, amended, extended, and — most important of all — condensed to fit the necessities of form. Sometimes one must act contrary to one's nature in this, be unsparing in the destruction of things that were composed with love and inspiration. I cannot complain of poor powers of invention and imagination, but I have always had to endure lack of skill in managing form. Only by prolonged hard work have I been enabled to achieve forms corresponding to some extent to contents. In the past I was careless in not understanding the very great importance of critically examining my rough drafts. It is because of this that successive sections were loosely put together and bastings were always visible. That was a grave fault, one it took me years to begin correcting. But my compositions will never be models of form for the reason that I can only *alter* what is wrong with my musical character — I cannot basically change it.

It is characteristic of Piotr Ilyich to blame his own nature for his unquestioned lack of formal mastery, rather than the tyranny of outdated patterns. What he never realized fully was that his formal sins were results of mistaken compromise and wrongheaded reverence. His was not a musical imagination likely to produce themes, harmonies, and rhythms perfectly apt to classical forms. In his worship of Mozart, he himself to some extent repeated the cardinal error of criticism. He believed that Mozart combined the highest powers of musical imagination with perfect grasp of form. He did not take the further step, to realize that Mozart had lived in a musical ambience, at a musical hour, when instrumental materials from the highest levels of musical imagination were likely to be conceived in relation to sonata-symphony style. He realized only dimly and without assurance that he himself lived at no such musical hour. Had he done so, and had he possessed the integrity and strength required, he might simply have swept aside whatever of the classical machinery was sterile for his materials. That would have required the lonely, rare ability to build unique forms wholly from within, and it is sure that, except at moments, he lacked that ability. When he failed, it was seldom from lack of care and effort. It was because he was not wholly conscious of his own problems and therefore straddled their central issues.

Wanting Nadezhda Filaretovna to see with her own eyes how he worked, Piotr Ilyich presented her with the original sketches for *Yevgeny Onyegin*, suggesting that she compare them with the arrangement for piano and voices, which was to be published in the autumn. She at first demurred, asking that he accept 500 rubles ($250) for the sketches, but at last guiltily accepted them as a gift. "I am far from being so famous that my handwriting has value," he told her. The values he placed on his works are revealed in a bill he sent to Jürgenson on August 10, 1878, shortly after dispatching to the publisher all the pieces of which he had made clean copies:

Sonata	50 rubles
12 pieces at 25 rubles	300 rubles
Collection of children's pieces at 10 rubles each	240 rubles
6 songs at 25 rubles each	150 rubles
Violin pieces at 25 rubles each	75 rubles
The Liturgy	100 rubles

"A total of 915 rubles," he wrote, "or, to make a round figure, 900 rubles. But in view of the fact that I composed so much all at once, I am letting you have everything for 800 rubles. . . . Are you willing to accept the opera [*Yevgeny Onyegin*] in payment of my 500-ruble debt to you? For the Violin Concerto I should like 50 rubles. . . ." He had shortly before written Jürgenson that the Violin Concerto was to be dedicated to Leopold Auer, then a prominent violinist of thirty-three. It is to be understood, of course, that Piotr Ilyich's entire income from his compositions was not derived from these flat sums paid in advance, but was increased in many instances by performance fees.

By August 13 Piotr Ilyich had completed correcting the score of *Yevgeny Onyegin*. On that date he played it through to the assembled Davidovs. The following day he sent the corrections to Jürgenson, requesting that the title page be made to read *Yevgeny Onyegin, Lyrical Scenes in 3 Acts*. He wanted by this phrase exactly to describe the opera, and perhaps to forestall the criticism that he had not achieved dramatic vigour or theatrical unity. Now, at last, he had no incomplete works on hand. "Regretting the past and hoping for the future without ever being satisfied with the present: that is how my entire life is spent," he wrote Anatoly. He eagerly accepted another invitation to make use of Nadezhda Filaretovna's unoccupied estate at Braïlov. Blazing with flowers, the exterior of the house delighted him. Its well-stocked library was a joy. He read George Sand's *Histoire de ma vie* and Alfred de Musset's *Andrea del Sarto* and *Les Caprices de Marianne,* which last made him shout with pleasure and consider using it as a libretto. Nothing he read, saw, or did could for very long be unrelated to music.

At Braïlov, surrounded by Nadezhda Filaretovna's flowers, books, and dogs and lapped in the luxuries she had commanded for his care, Piotr Ilyich sketched his First Suite for Orchestra, opus 43, starting with the Scherzo. Having, after about ten days, returned to Kamenka for a final visit before going to St. Petersburg and Moscow, he rushed ahead with the suite, sketching movement after movement. Even before he had set them down roughly on paper, they were, he told Modest, whirling in his head. Something else that had been whirling there was slowing to a stop that would be a final decision to resign from the Moscow Conservatory. The decision had been made when he left Kamenka on September 9. What Piotr Ilyich did not know was that on that same day the first Russian concert given in connection with the Paris Exposition had taken place at the Trocadéro, and that Nikolay Rubinstein had given a clamorously successful performance of the B-flat minor Piano Concerto, thus increasing his sense that the composer was bound to him by artistic indebtedness.

On September 13 Piotr Ilyich arrived in St. Petersburg to visit his father and Anatoly. He saw Apukhtin every day, going to the French theatre with him. Unquestionably he discussed Antonina Ivanovna, divorce, his decision to leave the Conservatory, and the myriad problems of his future. In Berlin Benjamin Bilse was conducting *Francesca da Rimini,* and in Paris Nikolay Rubinstein was playing the eternal *Song without Words* and conducting *The Tempest.* Stasov, who was in Paris, called the piano piece "a thin, scrofulous imitation of Chopin," but recognized value in *The Tempest.* On the 15th Piotr Ilyich spent the morning on a letter that he described to Modest as an attempt to prepare Nadezhda Filaretovna for news of his resignation from the Conservatory. On the 18th he presented that news to her in unvarnished form. Nor was he going to accept the position of professor of theory at the St. Petersburg Conservatory, offered to him by its director, Karl U. Davidov.

Piotr Ilyich was never wholly unconscious of the social and political forces moving around him. He and Nadezhda Filaretovna had recognized and discussed the repressive measure that had been the reaction of Alexander II and his government to their diplomatic defeat, chiefly at the hands of Disraeli, after the Turkish War. The atmosphere in St. Petersburg in September 1878 seemed to Piotr Ilyich ominous and unhealthy. "We are living through terrible times," he wrote Nadezhda Filaretovna, "and if one stops to meditate on the present, one is terrified. On one side, a completely panic-stricken government, bewildered to such an extent that Aksakov is exiled for bold and upright words; on the other side, ill-fated, mad youths, thousands of them exiled without trial to lands where not even a crow flies; and between these two extremes the masses, indifferent to everything, waist-deep in the mire of their egotistic interests, watching everything without a sign of protest." It did not require acute political wisdom to know that trouble was gathering, but it is notable that Piotr Ilyich, who thought it best to take refuge in the world of art, and who was conservative in his political sympathies, could see the destruction toward which Alexander II was hurrying.

At the third Russian concert in Paris, on September 20, Nikolay Rubinstein conducted Piotr Ilyich's *Melancholy Serenade,* opus 26, and his *Waltz-Scherzo,* opus 34, the soloist being a Polish violinist, Stanislav Bartsevich. One week later, at the final concert, Rubinstein repeated the Piano Concerto, knowing from experience that he could guarantee success by its presence. The enthusiasm expressed by its audiences was said to have exceeded any in Parisian memory.

Meanwhile, on September 22, Piotr Ilyich had returned to Moscow, taking an apartment opposite the Alexandrovsky School. The next morning he lectured to his first class of the season. To Modest he stated that the Conservatory was hateful to him, appeared to him "a dirty, fetid, disgusting jail." That night again Laroche dined with him, as he did on the 24th, this time accompanied by Kashkin. To Nadezhda Filaretovna, Piotr Ilyich referred to these two old friends as "people . . . in whose society I once took pleasure." He had made up his mind to leave Moscow. Nothing in it could please him.

Hailed as a victorious proconsul, Nikolay Rubinstein arrived from Paris on October 4. At the dinner given in his honour he made a fulsome speech about Piotr Ilyich, who must have squirmed in his chair at the knowledge that he was about to deal this man a blow. "He said that my compositions made a tremendous impression in Paris," he wrote Modest, "and that the Conservatory is fortunate in possessing so great a celebrity as myself. Everyone congratulated me, Samarin wept publicly from emotion — in brief, a comedy thoroughly repugnant to me took place." The next day he bearded Rubinstein in his den and told him that the Conservatory would have to do without him after December. When he had word from Nadezhda Filaretovna warmly supporting his decision to give up teaching, he wrote Taneyev, asking the young pianist to take over his piano class so that later he could do the same for the class in theory without the change being too noticeable.

On October 6 Piotr Ilyich had word for Nadezhda Filaretovna of, not Antonina Ivanovna, whose whereabouts he did not know, but "that person's mother." "Her mother bombards me with letters made up of protestations of the most tender love! She asks me to visit her, even wants me to stand godfather at her daughter's wedding. She says that my blessing will bring good fortune!!! Oh God! to be away from this all! If only a letter from you would arrive! I can't do anything before I know your opinion."

On October 14, Piotr Ilyich was still more impatient to be quit of the Conservatory, Rubinstein, his other colleagues, and Moscow. It was to Anatoly that he wrote: "A stroke of genius occurred to me: now that there is someone [2] to take my place at the Conservatory, it is entirely unnecessary for me to continue performing this boring chore until December or November. I completely overlooked the fact that in general I owe no particular loyalty to the Conservatory and need not be especially squeamish." Four days later he taught a Conservatory class for the last time. It was twelve years and ten months since the January day in 1866 when, a student of twenty-five himself, he had first lectured. The next day he wrote Lyov Vasilyevich Davidov how happy his departure was making him. On the 19th he was tendered a farewell dinner, among those gathering to honour him being Nikolay Rubinstein, Albrecht, Jürgenson, Kashkin, and Taneyev. That night as he boarded the St. Petersburg train, a repeat performance

[2] Here Tchaikovsky seems to have had in mind, not Taneyev, but Hubert.

Salon in the Moscow Conservatory of Music during the Tchaikovsky Centennial Exposition (1940)

of *Francesca da Rimini* was being conducted in Berlin by Bilse.

When his determination to abandon teaching had resulted in the severing action, Piotr Ilyich accepted Nadezhda Filaretovna's long-standing invitation to him to visit her house on Rozhdestvensky Boulevard. Her majordomo admitted him, and he spent two hours wandering about the house. The following day he wrote her that the formal salons were, of course, delightful, but that what had most pleased him was the private apartments. She had suggested that he make use of them during her absence, but he pointed out that any discovery that he was living in her house would blow up a scandal. He tried her pianos, admiring a Steinway and the Bechstein. He played her pedal organ. He even examined her bathroom. It is possible to imagine only part of what she must have experienced in far-off San Remo as she read the words that allowed her to picture Piotr Ilyich in her home.

Piotr Ilyich could not bear St. Petersburg for more than three weeks. Too many invitations, too many dinners and festivities tired him. He wanted quiet and the calm in which he could compose. A revival of *Vakula the Smith* he found distasteful. "Good God!" he exclaimed by mail to Nadezhda Filaretovna. "How many unforgivable mistakes there are in this opera, mistakes I alone could have made! I have done the best I can to neutralize the effect of every situation that might have been calculated to please. If only I had held my purely musical inspiration in check and kept the scenic and decorative effects in view! The whole opera suffers from a plethora of details and tiresome use of chromatic harmonies. *C'est un menu surchargé de mets épicés.* . . . I think that *Yevgeny Onyegin* is a step forward."

Tolstoy had not forgotten Piotr Ilyich or his music, for on November 8 he said, in a letter to Turgenyev: "What about *Yevgeny Onyegin*? I haven't heard it yet, but am very much interested." Napravnik, who had had the score for some time, wrote to thank Piotr Ilyich for it, but remarked that he had found time to glance only at the libretto.

Piotr Ilyich was going to Kamenka. He stopped in a Moscow hotel two nights, spending his waking hours correcting the Liturgy. Although Nikolay Rubinstein scheduled the Piano Concerto for the November 15 Russian Musical Society concert, the composer left the city on the 14th, arriving in Kamenka on the 16th. He remained only eleven days, but found the quiet so conducive to the work he loved that he sketched the last two movements of the First Suite in that time. He was dismayed by the discovery that he had left the first three movements in St. Petersburg, and from Kamenka began a protracted attempt to recover them, an attempt that he was to give up as fruitless just before — months later — he finally recovered the missing manuscripts.

On the day Piotr Ilyich left Kamenka for Vienna, Turgenyev, writing from Paris, answered Tolstoy's question about *Yevgeny Onyegin*. "Tchaikovsky's piano score of *Yevgeny Onyegin* has been received here," he said. "Mme Viardot has begun to study this composition evenings. It is undoubtedly remarkable music, the lyrical, melodic parts are particularly good. But what a libretto! Imagine, Pushkin's verses describing the actors are put into the mouths of the actors themselves. . . . Tchaikovsky's fame has increased a good deal since the Russian concerts at the Trocadéro; in Germany he has long received, if not esteem, at least attention. In Cambridge a certain Englishman, a professor of music, told me seriously that Tchaikovsky's is the most remarkable musical personality of our times. I gaped."

Stopping only briefly in Vienna, Piotr Ilyich went on directly to Florence, where he was to remain about four weeks. This visit was an act of daring, for he was going to live in an apartment rented for him by Nadezhda Filaretovna, who was herself in Florence, living in the luxurious Villa Oppenheim, only half a mile away. He knew that she would not try to see him, but must have suspected that it would be impossible for a meeting not to occur accidentally. He was given entire freedom. He found a note from Nadezhda Filaretovna awaiting him, a welcoming letter in which she detailed the exact time of her morning walks, thus telling him how to avoid running into her. She also stated that she was going away in three weeks, and Piotr Ilyich wrote Anatoly that they would probably not encounter each other once.

On the day of his arrival, Piotr Ilyich sent Nadezhda Filaretovna a note praising his new surroundings as ideal for work. He would orchestrate those parts of the suite which he had with him. He had decided to compose another opera, this time on the subject of Joan of Arc. He understood that Verdi's *Giovanna d'Arco*, produced at Milan in 1845, was weak, and he also understood that it had failed partly because it was not based on Schiller's psychologically powerful drama, *Die Jungfrau von Orleans*. He felt that he would have to go to Paris in order to do some research on materials for his libretto.

One day while out walking, Piotr Ilyich encountered a carriage in which Nadezhda Filaretovna was riding. It was the first time they had been face to face. For even here in Florence all communication between them was carried on by letter, by notes carried back and forth by Alexey Sofronov and Nadezhda Filaretovna's chief manservant, and through Vladislav A. Pakhulsky, Kotek's successor in her service. On this occasion it is not certain that she recognized Piotr Ilyich, but even when she did recognize him at several musical performances, they both refrained from approaching each other and never spoke. In their notes, they joyfully mentioned seeing each other and commented on each other's appearance and minor conduct. Piotr Ilyich's nervousness over her propinquity gradually relaxed, and when she left Florence he felt depressed. Whatever her intimate feelings were, she kept her part of their bargain to the letter. Once she suggested that Pakhulsky show him around the Villa Oppenheim when she was out, but she took his refusal in good grace. Piotr Ilyich was giving Pakhulsky harmony lessons, and talks with this young man who had been with her guest down the avenue were the closest Nadezhda Filaretovna came to knowing Piotr Ilyich face to face.

The first three movements of the First Suite still had not turned up, and Piotr Ilyich was limited to orchestrating the sections he had with him. Unexpected news of great cheer arrived. A telegram from Modest in St. Petersburg informed him that on December 7 Napravnik had conducted the Fourth Symphony to outstanding success. Piotr Ilyich at once forwarded the telegram to the Villa Oppenheim and waited for the post to bring him the reviews. When they came, he could have read in them a heartening fact: he was established in St. Petersburg as a composer of the first importance. The reviews were all but unanimously praise.

On December 17 Piotr Ilyich informed Nadezhda Filaretovna that "with fear and agitation, and not without trepidation," he had begun the composition of *The Maid of Orleans*. As he did not yet have a complete libretto, it is difficult to know exactly what he was doing at this time, but it seems likely that he was elaborating either sketches for the libretto or sketches for purely orchestral interludes. Nadezhda Filaretovna sent him a French book on Joan of Arc. When he had read it, he wrote Modest: "On reaching the trial, abjuration, and execution (she screamed terribly while they were leading her out, and begged that they cut off her head rather than burn her at the stake), I wept copiously. I was suddenly filled with intense pity, intense pain for all humanity, and inexpressible sadness." When he reached the point of identifying himself thus closely with the protagonist of his story, there was never any doubt that in a brief time he would be devoting himself to the work in a frenzy.

First, however, he had to pass the time before his departure for Paris and Clarens. He went to the theatre, analysed various pieces of music for Nadezhda Filaretovna, continued their discussion of program music, commented on Pakhulsky's talents and future, wrote a poem called *Lilies of the Valley*, and received a farewell message from the Villa Oppenheim. Commenting on Nadezhda Filaretovna's departure to Anatoly, he said: "How recently I was embarrassed by her close proximity — and now I miss her!"

All his reading of books and plays about Joan of Arc — including the libretto Jules-Paul Barbier had supplied August Mermet for his opera *Jeanne d'Arc*, produced in 1876 — served to convince Piotr Ilyich that Schiller's drama was unequalled. He therefore decided to write his own libretto, using chiefly Zhukovsky's translation into Russian of *Die Jungfrau von Orleans*, but taking a hint or two, particularly with regard to the last act, from the librettist of *Faust*, *Mignon*, and *Le Pardon de Ploërmel*. Fifteen years later, just before his death, Piotr Ilyich was considering a revision of the libretto of *The Maid of Orleans*, a revision that would have been wholly faithful to Schiller.

From Paris, on January 7, 1879, Piotr Ilyich informed Anatoly that he had become reconciled to the loss of the manuscript sketches for the First Suite. Characteristically, he had become so engrossed in a new, large work that he had all but lost interest in the smaller composition on which he had been working, and which remained incomplete. Two days later he left for Clarens, but was detained at Dijon by a storm and did not reach the Villa Richelieu until the 11th. The very next day he started to compose the opera in earnest. He was to do substantially nothing else but that work until the opera lay complete on his table fifty-two days later. He was, as always, convinced that he was at work on his best composition: he had forgotten his own advice to himself on the subject of kings, battles, and concourses. Faith in his operatic powers must have been heightened by receipt of an article by Laroche, published in *Golos,* in which his critic-friend, having examined the score of *Yevgeny Onyegin,* said: "Never has the composer been so much himself as in these lyrical scenes. . . . Tchaikovsky is an incomparable elegiac poet in sound."

Piotr Ilyich's plan of work on *The Maid of Orleans* was simple and singular. He did not write out the libretto first. Contenting himself, as to over-all design, with what was in his head, he devoted about two hours before supper each day to writing as much of the text as he could compose the next morning. Devoting mornings to the music, he moved ahead. As relaxation he read articles on Russia's past in an antiquarian magazine, and revelled in a translation of *Little Dorrit.* On January 16 a package arrived and proved to contain the missing manuscript pages of the First Suite. He was too occupied with the opera to do more than write Anatoly of his joy at refinding them. Further work on them would await completion of *The Maid of Orleans.*

England and the English had never been favourites with Piotr Ilyich. This dislike was largely derived from political considerations, and had been intensified by Disraeli's triumphant insistence on a complex balance of power after the Russo-Turkish War. Now, inevitably, his dislike of the English was becoming hatred of the murderers of Joan of Arc. In a letter to Anatoly, in which he described *Little Dorrit* as a work of genius, he added: "In general, Dickens and Thackeray are the only people I forgive for being English. I should add Shakespeare, but he belongs to a time when this corrupt nation was not quite so vile." When *Little Dorrit* had been read, he bought piano transcriptions of several Beethoven and Mozart quartets and rested by playing through one of them each evening.

Piotr Ilyich's spirits soared as he worked. One day, returning from a stroll, he sat down on the balcony of his villa to read letters he had brought back. "Having gone through the letters," he wrote Modest, "and having raised my eyes and seen the wonderful view before me lighted in the hot, springlike sun, I suddenly experienced such a surge of quiet ecstasy, the ecstasy that only nature can create, that I sat enraptured for two hours without moving." The day before, he had written in jocular mood to Jürgenson:

As you are well aware, there are three remarkable personages whom you know intimately: the feeble poetaster N. N.,[3] who has scribbled a few verses for your editions of Russian songs; B. L.,[4] formerly music critic of Russkiye Vyedomosti, and the composer and ex-professor Mr. Tchaikovsky.

An hour or two ago Mr. Tchaikovsky asked the other two gentlemen — who live with him — to go with him to the piano, and played for them the second act of his new opera, The Maid of Orleans. Mr. Tchaikovsky, who is very intimate with Messrs. N. N. and B. L., overcame his timidity without much difficulty and played his new work with great ability and inspiration. You should have seen the enthusiasm of the two gentlemen! You might have supposed, seeing how they stalked about the room and praised the music, that they had had some part in composing the opera. At last the composer, who had been struggling to keep his modesty intact, was carried away by their enthusiasm, and the three of them ran out on the balcony as though demented, to cool their disordered nerves and control their wild eagerness to hear the balance of the opera as quickly as possible. Messrs. N. N. and B. L. vainly tried to persuade Mr. Tchaikovsky that operas could not be tossed off like pancakes, and the latter began to despair at the feebleness of human nature and the impossibility of getting onto paper in one night all that had long been seething in his mind. Finally the good men persuaded the unbalanced composer to calm himself, and he sat down to write to a certain Moscow publisher.

On February 18 Piotr Ilyich arrived in Paris. For the first few days he did no work. But his always enormous correspondence continued unthinned. He kept up his frequent letters to Nadezhda Filaretovna, making them slightly less frequent only when she wrote that headaches and eye strain forced her to cut down her correspondence. He had no way of seeing in this reasonable remark one of the minor forces that, matured and abetted by others, was eventually to snap off their relationship completely.

He could not work on the First Suite because he could not stay away from *The Maid of Orleans*. On February 25 he wrote Jürgenson that he was living the life of an anchorite, going out only to eat and to take a little exercise. "Last Sunday, however, I enjoyed a true musical treat. Colonne conducted one of my favourite works — Berlioz's Faust. The performance was excellent. It was

[3] Tchaikovsky signed these initials to his translations into Russian of German texts Anton Rubinstein had set to music.

[4] The initials signed to Tchaikovsky's reviews.

TCHAIKOVSKY IN 1879
From a photograph

so long since I had heard any good music that I was steeped in happiness, the more so as I was alone, with no acquaintance at my side. What a work! Poor Berlioz! While he lived, nobody wanted to hear of him. Now the papers call him 'the mighty Hector.' . . . Oh God! How happy I am! Did I ever dream that I should enjoy life so much?"

His patroness asked why Piotr Ilyich did not call on Turgenyev, who was likewise in Paris. He answered by telling her the story of his meetings with Tolstoy. "The company of a fellow creature is pleasant only if enduring intimacy of common interests makes all effort unnecessary. Except in such cases, society is a burden nature did not intend me to bear. . . . As to spending time with famous people, I know from experience that their works, musical or literary, are far more interesting than their personalities." He informed her, too, that he was admiring sections of *The Brothers Karamazov,* and had appreciated a performance of Berlioz's *Symphonie fantastique* even though he had not remained to its end.

On March 5 Piotr Ilyich unexpectedly completed *The Maid of Orleans.* Then, having put the manuscript in order, he set to work again on the First Suite. One evening, against his will, he went to a performance of the dramatization of Zola's *L'Assommoir.* He found it loathsome both because of its subject matter and because wholly inept comic relief had been introduced. "Zola long ago became repugnant to me . . ." he wrote Anatoly. "Of course, I shall not devote one moment more of my life to reading his scurvy abominations." On March 6 Piotr Ilyich told Modest that Colonne would conduct *The Tempest* at a concert the following Sunday. "I know beforehand that it will not be well played and will be hissed by the audience — the invariable fortune of all my works abroad." The event turned out as he had foreseen it, and on the 10th he wrote an intensely characteristic letter to Modest:

Yesterday was a most exciting day. In the morning, at the Châtelet Concert, my Tempest was played. That a country life is the one I endure best was proved by the agony I went through. What used to be a pleasure — hearing one of my own works — has now become a reason for misery. The evening before, I began to suffer from colic and nausea. My agitation continued increasing, crescendo, until the first chords, and while the piece was progressing I thought I should die from the pain in my heart. It was not fear of failure with the public, but that of late the first hearing of one of my own compositions has brought me the keenest disappointment. Mendelssohn's Reformation Symphony preceded The Tempest, and all the time I was admiring that fine masterpiece. I have not yet reached the position of a master. I still compose like a gifted youth from whom much can be expected. What chiefly astonished me was that my orchestration sounded so poor. Of course, my reason told me that I was exaggerating its faults, but that was small consolation. The Tempest was not played badly. The orchestra took pains, but displayed no warm enthusiasm. One member of the band (a cellist) kept staring, smiling, and nodding, as if to say: "Excuse our playing so curious a work. It isn't our fault: we were ordered to play it, and we obey." After the last measures had died away, there was some weak applause mingled with two or three audible hisses, at which the whole hall broke out with exclamations of "Oh! Oh!" intended as kindly protests against the hissing.

Despite his disappointment Piotr Ilyich — who had not notified Colonne that he was in the audience, or even in Paris — wrote the conductor a thank-you note. He thanked him for the fine interpretation and splendid playing, and then added: "As to the feeble applause and rather energetic hissing with which the audience greeted my unlucky Tempest, they affected me intensely, but failed to surprise me — I expected them. If some degree of prejudice against our Muscovite barbarism had something to do with this, the intrinsic faults of the composition were also to blame. The form is diffuse and lacks proportion. In any case, the performance — which, as I have said, was excellent — had nothing to do with the failure of the work." In writing Modest of the event, he said merely: "I have become reconciled to it, as after completing the opera and the suite, I intend to compose something exemplary for orchestra." The fundamental healthiness of his attitude toward his chosen profession was never better expressed.

Picking up Rousseau's Confessions, into which he had never looked before, Piotr Ilyich was absorbed. He read as though bewitched. Then he diffidently recommended the book to Nadezhda Filaretovna, remarking that "it contains much cynical matter making it all but unfit for a woman's eyes." Nevertheless, he honestly stated that he had found in it, and for the first time, much of his own character revealed and detailed. "He tells of things wonderfully comprehensible to me," he explained to Anatoly, "things I have never spoken of to anyone — for I couldn't express them. And suddenly I find them completely expressed in Rousseau." Only the last sections of the *Confessions,* in which Rousseau became "merely a petty and bilious gossip," disappointed him.

On or about March 21 Piotr Ilyich arrived in St. Petersburg. From the happy, dynamic, and almost frolicsome man who had displayed himself in letters from Clarens and Paris, he immediately turned into the whining, complaining, and truly unhappy person he always was when his chosen routine of life was interrupted and he could not work. He derived some pleasure from an article on himself by Bülow, published in translation in *Golos,* referring to "this young master whose knowledge grows with each new work," and calling him "a true poet of sound." The world *première* of *Yevgeny Onyegin* was scheduled to take place in Moscow on March 29. He had expected to arrive just in time for it, but a telegram from Jürgenson summoned him to the final rehearsal.

Piotr Ilyich arrived in Moscow with only enough time to reach the Maly Theatre as the rehearsal started. Hiding in a seat in the dark auditorium, he listened undetected. He found the performance generally satisfactory. The soloists, he noted, could have been much better, but orchestra and chorus were splendid. After the rehearsal Nikolay Rubinstein expanded to say that he had fallen in love with the opera. Taneyev, trying to express his enthusiasm, burst into tears. Piotr Ilyich later described these few hours in the Maly Theatre as the only pleasant ones of his Moscow visit.

On the Saturday of the *première* — March 29, 1879 — the arrivals from St. Petersburg included Modest and Anatoly, and, paying a grudging tribute at last, Anton Rubinstein. Piotr Ilyich spent a fevered day of nervous anticipation, having promised Nikolay Rubinstein that he would appear to accept applause if necessary. Before the curtains parted, Piotr Ilyich was bidden to come backstage. There, to his horror, he found the staff of the Moscow Conservatory. Nikolay Rubinstein made a speech, and presented a wreath to Piotr Ilyich, who forced himself to respond. Then, almost two years after he had begun to work with Konstantin Shilovsky on its libretto, the curtains parted on *Yevgeny Onyegin.* "I noticed no special enthusiasm in the audience," Piotr Ilyich wrote Nadezhda Filaretovna two days later. "I draw this conclusion

from the fact that it was always myself — not the performers —
who received the calls."

After the performance Piotr Ilyich wanted to go somewhere
with Anatoly and Modest for a quiet talk before retiring for the
night. Instead he had to attend a supper being given in his honour
at a café. Even Anton Rubinstein was present, though he spoke no
single word of praise or blame for *Yevgeny Onyegin* to its creator.
Not until four a.m. was Piotr Ilyich, his head painfully aching, able
to go to bed.

XI

YEVGENY ONYEGIN had pleased its first audience no more than Piotr Ilyich thought. The applause had been for himself and not for the opera. It had been performed by Conservatory students and was therefore a semi-amateur production. Audiences were unused to seeing operatic treatment of a period so close to their own — it was not yet sixty years since the time of Pushkin's story. Connoisseurs of that story found Piotr Ilyich overbold in daring to place such classic and all but hallowed figures as Tatyana and Lensky on the stage. They said that he had been ill advised to alter the poem the little he had altered it. All together, as he had foreseen and predicted, it failed to arouse enthusiasm because of its lack of dramatic impact and obvious theatrical effects. Anton Rubinstein's reactions were typical. Returning to St. Petersburg, he told his wife that it was futile throughout and entirely lacked grand-opera style. Years later, grown accustomed to the opera's lyricism, he expressed admiration for it. His wife could not resist reminding him of what he had said after the *première*. "What do you know about it?" he answered. "Nobody brought up on gypsy songs and Italian opera can rightfully criticize such a composition."

Piotr Ilyich did not wait in Moscow for the critics to speak. Wanting above all to avoid riding with Anton Rubinstein, he took the mail train to St. Petersburg the day after the performance and was hard at work orchestrating the First Suite when the first critical notices of *Yevgeny Onyegin* appeared in Moscow periodicals. The majority were favourable, none was laudatory throughout. One anonymous writer objected to the opera's realism — by which he meant that the protagonists spoke as real people might speak. But it was the critic of *Russkiye Vyedomosti* who proved a seer: "In spite of its lack of dramatic life, Tchaikovsky's work will probably become one of the most popular pieces of our operatic repertoire, thanks to its national subject and excelling music."

Yevgeny Onyegin eventually became a staple of Russian opera houses. It has survived all changes of style, regime, and taste. It was the preferred opera of at least one Tsar. Josef Stalin, heading a government that has delighted in honouring Piotr Ilyich's memory, has declared that it is, with *The Queen of Spades,* his favourite opera. Its melodies are as familiar to Russians as those of the last three symphonies are to the rest of the world. It has been produced in every civilized country, and excerpts from it — in particular Tatyana's "Letter Scene" and Onyegin's aria from Act I, the waltz and Lensky's aria from Act II, and the polonaise from Act III — have been performed by great artists and amateurs throughout the musical world for more than sixty years.

For the purpose he had conceived, Piotr Ilyich's libretto is more than adequate. It actually preserves some of the literary distinction of Pushkin's original. The music is sensitively modulated between the lyrical and the dramatic. Its melodiousness is stanchless. Why, then, has it failed to become a fixture of the standard repertoire outside Russia? The answer is that it is too small for the expensive barns that customarily house opera in world capitals. It is a chamber opera, an opera whose effectiveness depends on close *rapport* between performers and audience. Like Mozart's greatest operas, like *La Traviata* and *Falstaff* and *Pelléas et Mélisande* and a dozen other similarly delicate compositions, it is given adequately only when a cast of intelligent actors, singing it in the language to which it was composed, performs it simply in a small theatre. Lacking that, and produced halfheartedly — even though with stars on the stage and high prices at the box office — it will always rattle unhappily in its shell, appear puny because it has been placed in a box many times too large for it.

During the first days of his stay in St. Petersburg, a number of storm warnings put Piotr Ilyich's nerves on edge. While he was out, a servant informed him, a lady several times came to call. She had also been standing outside, eyeing the house. It was unquestionably Antonina Ivanovna. One afternoon Piotr Ilyich returned to find her awaiting him. She was herself the storm, a tempest of passion and incoherent words about love. She talked high-pitched nonsense for more than two hours, while in the next room Anatoly listened. At the edge of his control, Piotr Ilyich told her to take a trip to Moscow, and gave her money. This calmed her, and the rest of her talk was of new conquests among the men of the city. When Anatoly and Modest at last entered the room, she acted the role of a loving sister-in-law. Again a torrent of words came from her. The sense to be gathered from it was that she believed Piotr Ilyich to be in love with her. They were being kept apart, she asseverated, by someone who was himself also in love with her. It must have crossed the minds of the three Tchaikovsky brothers as they confronted her that this unfortunate and unhappy girl was insane. Certainly she was dangerous.

Now Piotr Ilyich was scarcely ever free of Antonina Ivanovna. She wrote him disjointed, meandering letters. She moved into a house where he was temporarily sharing a small apartment with Anatoly. He went to Kamenka to avoid her — and she followed him as far as Moscow, forcing her way into his room there and demanding money. He gave her money. Then, when he was where she could not see him, her letters began again, letters that maddened him and kept him in cold fright, as they were to keep on doing for another several years.

Piotr Ilyich had remained in St. Petersburg only a short time. It was April 21 when he arrived at Kamenka, and he waited only one day to turn his entire attention to completing both the orchestration and the four-hand piano transcription of the First Suite. Both were accomplished by May 4. "Either I am much mistaken, or this work will be popular, catching on quickly. It is very modestly and easily orchestrated," he wrote Jürgenson. Later he added: "I am beginning to be proud of my works now that I see what an unusual effect some of them make. Everyone here is mad about the Andante, and when I played it as a piano duet with my brother, one girl fainted (this is a fact!). To make the fair sex faint is the loftiest triumph any composer can achieve."

From Kamenka on May 10 Piotr Ilyich wrote Vladimir Shilovsky a letter that lights up a little the obscurity of their relationship and silently comments on their respective characters:

Volodya!
I have learned from reliable sources that you are complaining to the whole world of my ingratitude, adding that you have given me 28,000 *rubles!!!* I would be lying were I to say that I am completely indifferent to *the rumours you are spreading.* I find them unpleasant — but accept them as just punishment for my indiscriminate methods of *obtaining money* and for my genuine interest in you. In rare instances similar money transactions between friends — one of whom is rich, the other poor — entail neither punishment for the recipient nor poisonous accusations and misunderstandings from the giver. Ours evidently is not

one of those rare instances. I am guilty, therefore, not because I took
the money (I see nothing *dishonourable* or *shameful* in that), but because I took that money from *you;* that is, from a man who I well knew
would sooner or later tell of it à qui voudra l'entendre.

And so the fact that you are now revealing our money relations to all
and sundry wounds me to some extent, but does not surprise me in the
least — I have always expected it. I am, however, greatly astonished by
the arbitrary figure with which you so generously endow your gifts to
me. I have of course no legal means of preventing you from spreading
about me whatever wild tales you choose, or of forcing you to make an
accurate reckoning of the sums of money you have given me in the
ten years we have known each other. But I do not consider it superfluous to point out that you have magnified the sum total of your generosity — and proportionately the degree of my black ingratitude — most
unsparingly. I have an exceptionally fine memory in such matters, and
I shall tell you to a kopeck exactly how much I got from you. You can
later verify my reckoning from your ledgers. You will find I'm not even
an iota wrong. However, I warn you that I do not consider as debts
either the things you gave me when you left for Nice in 1869 — the piano,
bed, screen, etc. — costly though they were, nor the money you spent
on our trips abroad in 1868 and 1870. In 1868 I accompanied you as
your teacher working for a specified salary, and in 1870 in the capacity
of something between companion, teacher, and uncle. The cost of my
Dec[ember] 1871 trip to Nice, however, I am including in my reckoning. And so I begin, recalling to you after each figure where and how
it was given to me. . . .

[Here the reckoning is detailed.]

That's all. I leave it to you to make the most thorough check-up, in
complete confidence that if I have made some insignificant mistakes,
they are in your favour. For inst[ance], I am not quite certain whether
you gave me 1,300 or 1,500 rubles in 1875, while the two suits and coat
that you bought at Zimmerman's for me cost, I believe, less than the
150 rubles I have allowed for this item.

I shall now make the final reckoning. 100, 100, 300, 900, 600, 150, 300,
200, 600, 1,500, 2,000, and 800 — altogether *7,550 silver rubles.* This is
both a great deal and very little. A great deal from the point of view
of the absolute value of money. Very little if one takes into consideration the innumerable spiritual tortures this money cost me; very little
when one remembers that you are a rich landowner and I a poor artist;
very little indeed when one recalls your endless protestations of love
and readiness to make sacrifices for my sake; and, finally, it amounts to
but a zero when compared with your everlasting promises! Do you know,
once (in May 1872) you definitely promised me an annual income of

20,000 rubles within a few years? You of course do not remember this
— but it's a fact, an indubitable fact. Tell me, please, what is 7,500 rubles
handed out during a ten-year period compared with such a sum? Nevertheless, I shall do you complete justice: when you gave me the money,
you did so out of a sincere desire to help a friend; you rescued me from
great difficulties, and God knows I was grateful to you then and still
am grateful. At the same time, I submit, is it becoming a gentleman to
brag of having been my "benefactor," and, while doing so, to sin so
against truth by magnifying the sum *fourfold!*

However, the purpose of my letter is not to reproach you, but to
ask a favour. Since I took from you a total of 7,550 rubles only, a sum
which you arbitrarily increased to 28,000, I consider, not without basis,
that 20,450 rubles are still coming to me. However, I shall be more
modest in my demands. I need much less. The fact is that now (when
I depend only on the sporadic earnings from my morceaux malingres et
rachitiques), I am not in a position to be of as great and dependable
assistance to Bochechkarov [1] as I was. And so it occurred to me to ask
you to give him a life pension of 300 silver rubles a year (i.e., 25 rubles
a month). Do please grant this request. Nik[olay] Lvov[ich] is today
a poor, pitiful, and sick old man. And for you the sum is so insignificant!
As for my gratitude to you, it will be so great, I promise not to be in the
least offended should I hear that you continue to spread the rumours
of having given me 28,000 rubles and of the blackness of my soul. Good-
bye. I hope you have a pleasant summer.

P. Tchaikovsky

Piotr Ilyich interrupted the long task of writing out the full score
of *The Maid of Orleans* at Nadezhda Filaretovna's invitation, moving again to Braïlov. This time, however, the place failed to work
its miracle on him, and he did nothing creative during ten days
there. He complained to Anatoly of the number of letters he had
to write — "this has, of course, nothing to do with my letters to
you." By May 20 the desuetude into which he had fallen no longer
seemed pleasant idling. To Anatoly he admitted that he was getting no pleasure from life in Braïlov and was horrified to note that
all his thoughts were directed toward killing time. He returned
with little regret to Kamenka.

While Piotr Ilyich was lost in work, his Liturgy was sung in the
chapel of the University of Kiev, and *Yevgeny Onyegin* was given

[1] Nikolay Lvovich Bochechkarov was an elderly Muscovite whom Tchaikovsky first met in 1869. He gave the old man considerable material assistance
until his death in August 1879. In later years Tchaikovsky often spoke
warmly of Bochechkarov.

a special performance in honour of Grand Duke Konstantin Nikolayevich at the Moscow Conservatory. The singing of the Liturgy
was followed by a telegram from Jürgenson. In 1878 the director
of the Imperial Chapel had confiscated the composition under an
old regulation that no religious work not recognized by the chapel
could be sold or performed. Jürgenson had sued the director for
damages, and had now won his case. Piotr Ilyich, who had long
recognized the low estate of music composed for the Church, saw
this as a victory of principle and a harbinger of good tidings for
Russian composers.

Good news came piling in. Colonne wrote most respectfully to
state his determination to put Piotr Ilyich on his programs again
in spite of Paris's cold reception of *The Tempest*. Fitzenhagen
wrote from Germany that the Variations on a Rococo Theme, which
he had played at the Wiesbaden Festival, had been most warmly
received. Liszt had said: "Here, at last, is music again." A letter
from Bülow was best of all, for it announced that the pianist had
won enormous success with the B-flat minor Piano Concerto in both
Wiesbaden and London.

Further instalments of *The Brothers Karamazov* had cooled
Piotr Ilyich's liking for Dostoyevsky. "Every one of the characters
is mad," he told Modest. "Generally speaking, Dostoyevsky is to
be borne only for one section of a novel. After that he becomes
absurd." The orchestration of his opera was growing well, and he
went to Nizi to spend two weeks with Kondratyev, returning to
Kamenka on July 19. Kotek paid him a visit, but that did not long
interrupt incessant work at *The Maid of Orleans*. Completing Act
III by August 18, he went to Simaki, a small house on Nadezhda
Filaretovna's Braïlov estate, where she was occupying the large
house. After he had been there a few days, Pakhulsky told him
that he was bringing Lyudmila, Nadezhda Filaretovna's youngest
daughter, the next time he came over from the large house. Already Piotr Ilyich had found his hostess's proximity disturbing,
and he now quickly quashed this suggestion:

"Forgive me, dear friend, and make fun of my mania if you
wish — but I shan't invite Milochka [Lyudmila] here, for this
reason: my relationship with you — as it exists now — is my chief
joy, and is of the utmost importance to my well-being. I do not
want it changed one hair's breadth. The entire charm and poetry
of our friendship lies in your being so near and dear to me, while

at the same time I do not, in the ordinary sense of the word, know you at all. This state of things must include your nearest belongings. I shall love Milochka as I have hitherto loved you. If she came before me — *le charme serait rompu!* Every one in your family is dear to me — particularly Milochka — but, for God's sake, let things stay as they are. What could I answer if she were to ask why I never go to see her mother? I should have to start our acquaintance with a *lie*." Nadezhda Filaretovna understood; Pakhulsky did not take the girl to Simaki.

The date on which Piotr Ilyich, after more than nine months of labour, completed the full score of *The Maid of Orleans* is not certain. It seems to have been about September 5. By then, too, he had composed a new section for the First Suite and had orchestrated that entire composition. As he saw his desk less cluttered, he felt the need for new distraction and asked Nadezhda Filaretovna to send him books, particularly Tolstoy, Dostoyevsky, and Dickens. He left Simaki on September 12.

On October 1 Piotr Ilyich was again in Moscow. Nikolay Rubinstein and Jürgenson breakfasted with him, and that evening he dined at the publisher's home, "where they drank and drank. I can't tell you how painful and odious it was for me to immerse myself in this Moscow atmosphere of drunkenness," he told Anatoly. Soon he set off for Grankino to visit Modest. From there he wrote Nadezhda Filaretovna that the gloom that had borne down upon him during his visits to St. Petersburg and Moscow had lifted as soon as the southbound train left Moscow. He found a letter from her, including news that the piano transcription of the Fourth Symphony had been issued — a fact the distracted Jürgenson had failed to tell him. She had played it, replayed it, and played it again. For two nights, as a result, she had been sleepless and feverish. The symphony revealed her to herself, and she could not let it remain silent. Now, stirred by it, and momentarily off guard, she unwisely put on paper the dammed-up emotions of more than two years:

I doubt that you can ever understand how intensely jealous I am of you despite the absence of personal contact between us. Do you know, I am jealous in the least forgivable way, as a woman is jealous of the man she loves? Do you know, when you married, it was intensely difficult for me, as though some part of my heart had broken? The thought that you were near that woman was bitter and unbearable. And do you realize how wicked I am? I was glad when you were unhappy with her! I blamed myself for that feeling. I don't believe that I gave myself away at all, and yet I could not quell my feelings. They are not to be commanded. I hated that woman because she did not make you happy, but I should have hated her a hundred times more if you had found happiness with her. I believed that she had robbed me of what should be mine alone, what is rightfully mine for the reason that I love you more than anyone and value you above anything else in the world. If knowing this upsets you, forgive my unintentional confessions. I have said them. The symphony was the cause. Still, I think that it is better for you to realize that I am no such idealist as you picture. And then, it can't alter any part of our relationship. I want no change. I should like to be assured that nothing will be altered as I come to the end of my life. . . . But that I have no right to say.

Replying as he prepared to leave Grankino, Piotr Ilyich once more expressed his intense gratitude for all that Nadezhda Filaretovna had done for him. He reaffirmed the multitudinous reasons that justified the dedication of the symphony. He felt for her, he said, "love too powerful to be expressed otherwise than through music." Even allowing for differences in national character and period, differences that make much intimate nineteenth-century correspondence appear overwrought to the twentieth century, it is difficult to believe that Piotr Ilyich was not deliberately fending off the threat unconsciously implied by Nadezhda Filaretovna's ardour. His reply could not have been better, for it restated the solid basis on which their epistolary intimacy had grown and flourished. It did not chide or dampen her, but it refrained from taking cognizance or advantage of the covered and quickly self-denied invitation to another sort of intimacy.

Nadezhda Filaretovna, about to leave Braïlov for western Europe, responded with an offer to subsidize a Paris *première* of their symphony under Colonne. When Piotr Ilyich agreed to the idea, though insisting that the work would have no success in France, she took Pakhulsky, her children, her servants, and her load of impedimenta, and went straight to Paris. At Kamenka, meanwhile, Piotr Ilyich was correcting proofs of the First Suite and was enjoying the absence of other guests from his sister's home. "I find it most pleasant here," he wrote Anatoly. "We all sit and sew. I have hemmed several towels and have marked the linen." That was October 19. But simple domesticity was not long for him. That same day, in fact, he wrote Nadezhda Filaretovna that he was about to compose a second piano concerto.

On October 22 Piotr Ilyich began work on the massive, and now unreasonably neglected, Piano Concerto in G major, opus 44. He was pleased by word from Paris that Colonne, in a talk with Pakhulsky, had agreed to play the Fourth Symphony. "Does Colonne actually want to be remunerated for doing the work?" he asked Nadezhda Filaretovna. "It would gratify me to know that his readiness to perform the symphony was not based on pecuniary considerations." The truth was that the performance would cost her a considerable sum, as Parisian conductors of that day found the presentation of entire symphonies costly and risky.

Although he told others that he was finding composition easy, Piotr Ilyich wrote Anatoly that work on the new concerto was hard. He had no great inclination to work, but kept at it because experience had shown that he could not exist without activity. By November 1 the first movement was complete. That was as much of it as he could compose at Kamenka, for events in the two capitals began to occupy his mind. The music season was being inaugurated with repetitions of his works — and he had begun to long for Italy and was planning to go there. *Vakula the Smith* was unsuccessfully revived in St. Petersburg. The First String Quartet was played there. On November 2 Nikolay Rubinstein gave the first public performance of the Piano Sonata at a Russian Musical Society chamber-music concert. It was well received, and Rubinstein announced his intention of playing it again at his own recital later in the season. A reviewer who had examined the score before the performance saw it joining the B-flat minor Piano Concerto, *The Tempest*, and *Francesca da Rimini* in a sweep of the globe.

At Kamenka, Piotr Ilyich came upon a pack of the letters he had sent home to his parents during his preparatory studies at the School of Jurisprudence in 1850 and 1851. Reading them, he became so stirred as to be almost sick and had a sleepless night. Twenty-five years after her death he could not think of his mother without the most scarifying and painful grief. Life had brought him no one and nothing to fill the awful space she had left. Not Désirée Artôt, not Antonina Ivanovna, not Nadezhda Filaretovna — and surely not the shadowy figures in whose arms he may have found sexual release — had repaid him for that loss. Part of himself had been in her grave for a quarter of a century, and he would never be whole again.

In Moscow, visiting Nikolay Rubinstein, Piotr Ilyich was amazed and delighted by the great pianist's performance of his Piano Sonata. Then, his business affairs attended to, he proceeded to St. Petersburg. There, at two a.m., he sat down to write to Nadezhda Filaretovna: "The journey was not unpleasant. Proofreading occupied two whole days in Moscow, and I saw all the Conservatory people, including N. G. Rubinstein, who wanted me to hear his interpretation of my sonata. He plays it marvellously; I regret that you couldn't hear it. I was simply amazed by the artistry and astonishing force with which he plays this rather dry and complex piece." Success and fame were not clouding Piotr Ilyich's self-criticism.

About all that Piotr Ilyich did in St. Petersburg was to send Rubinstein thanks for that performance, visit his father and Anatoly, and obtain from Bessel a score of the Second Symphony, which he intended thoroughly to revise. On November 23 he was in Berlin attending a performance of Thomas's *Hamlet*, an opera of which he was fond. Paris was his next stop. Nadezhda Filaretovna was also there, and soon Pakhulsky and other messengers were busy carrying letters between her apartment and the Hôtel Meurice, where Piotr Ilyich was staying. He went to a circus and was bored. The next morning, however, a fine Erard piano was in his room, and he began again to work on the new concerto, tackling the finale before the second movement.

On December 3 Alexey Sofronov went to church, returning to tell his master that Grand Duke Nikolay Nikolayevich and his entourage had been present in full uniform. At breakfast, picking up a Paris paper, Piotr Ilyich discovered the reason: a terrorist had attempted to assassinate Alexander II. The nihilist ferment seethed in the corners of repressed Russia. "So long," Piotr Ilyich wrote Nadezhda Filaretovna, "as all of us — the citizens of Russia — are not called upon to take part in our country's government, there is no hope for a better future." A few days later he interrupted work on the piano concerto to answer her question about his opera *The Voivode*. He told her honestly that it was very poor. Not *Undine, The Oprichnik,* nor *Vakula the Smith,* he admitted, had equalled his intentions. "I find this branch of art very difficult!" As always, he was in love with his youngest child. "Perhaps I deceive myself, but it seems to me that The Maid of Orleans finally fulfils every requirement. If this is not so, if it becomes plain that I have failed to achieve true operatic style even in this work, I shall then be convinced of the justice of the judgment that I am a symphonic composer by nature and should not try dramatic music. In that case I shall give up all attempts at opera." *The Maid of Orleans* might have proved it to him, except that he could never give up one more trial. He was to make four more attempts, of which only *The Queen of Spades* approaches the operatic vitality of *Yevgeny Onyegin*.

During the three weeks Piotr Ilyich remained in Paris, he attended a performance of *Die Zauberflöte* (as *La Flûte enchantée*) at the Opéra-Comique, and twice heard sections of Berlioz's *Les Troyens*. The first, excerpts from *La Prise de Troie*, was part of a Pasdeloup concert, the second a Châtelet concert at which Colonne conducted this entire second part of the mammoth opera, the part Berlioz had died without hearing. Piotr Ilyich found the Pasdeloup performance bad, the opera itself weak and tedious. "Berlioz," he wrote Nadezhda Filaretovna, "was a man of lofty mind who conceived beautiful things, but lacked the strength to fill out his conceptions." When she wrote him that Liszt had spoken well of *Paraphrase*, a set of variations on *Chopsticks* by Rimsky-Korsakov, Borodin, Cui, and Lyadov, he replied by saying that the work was an amusing game, nothing more. "As for Liszt," he remarked, sagely anticipating posterity, "he is an old hypocrite who answers with the most overblown flattery the submission of any composition to his august judgment. He is kindly by nature — in fact, he is one of the few renowned artists never stung by jealousy or the temptation to interfere with the success of his confreres. Wagner and — in part — Anton Rubinstein owe their success to him, and he has done a lot for Berlioz. But he is too hypocritical to be trusted to criticize sincerely."

Neither Nadezhda Filaretovna nor Piotr Ilyich remained to hear Colonne's performance of the Fourth Symphony. She returned to Russia. He, planning to revise his Second Symphony (which had never been printed), was going to Italy with Alexey Sofronov to meet Modest and Kolya Konradi. He completed the first draft of the Piano Concerto in G major on December 15 and left for Rome two days later. On the day he arrived there, Nikolay Rubinstein, in Moscow, conducted the *première* of the First Suite.

The work was well received, and was treated approvingly by the critics as exactly what it was, light music of mild charm. Piotr Ilyich himself admitted that he had not written it "from the heart." Today it is all but unknown. Its revival would not alter its composer's fame or popularity. Its six movements — Introduction and Fugue, Divertimento, Intermezzo, Military March, Scherzo, and Gavotte — are, collectively, far too long for the little weight of musical thought they have to convey. The entirety suffers from diffuseness and — a serious fault in one of Piotr Ilyich's works — lack of subjectivity. Some of it is adept. None of it is spoken in the unmistakable voice of Piotr Ilyich.

From Rome, Nadezhda Filaretovna received the information that the First Suite was to be dedicated to her, and that Piotr Ilyich was launched on a complete revision of the Second Symphony. In Moscow, as they both knew, rehearsals were being held for a revival of *The Oprichnik*. What they did not hear until much later was that, on January 10, 1880, the opera was ordered dropped from the official Moscow repertoire for an indefinite period. Political events were slipping toward a crisis, and inflammatory ideas had been found in the libretto. In Rome, meanwhile, in the loved company of Modest, Kolya, and Alexey, Piotr Ilyich was finding the city admirable. He visited the Via Appia, St. Peter's, Santa Maria Maggiore, San Pietro in Vincoli, where Michelangelo's *Moses* fascinated him, the Colosseum, and the Sistine Chapel. "Michelangelo's frescoes at the Sistine Chapel are no longer Greek to me," he crowed to Anatoly, "and I am beginning to marvel at their originality and powerful beauty."

Learning that Nikolay Rubinstein had found untoward difficulties in the First Suite, Piotr Ilyich wrote to Taneyev, who explained what they were. This was dangerous ground: it summoned memories of Rubinstein's first reactions to the B-flat minor Piano Concerto. This time Piotr Ilyich reacted by letter to Taneyev: "One or the other. Either I have never understood an orchestra or his criticism of my suite is a pendant to N. G.'s positive pronunciamento of 1875 that it was impossible to play my concerto. However, what was impossible in 1875 became possible in 1878!"

On January 20 Piotr Ilyich heard from Anatoly that their father was seriously ill. Two days later morning brought him a telegram from St. Petersburg announcing that Ilya Petrovich had died there the day before. The peaceful old man had lived to eighty-five, long enough to realize that one of his sons was a famous man. Piotr Ilyich had loved him and paid his death the tribute of sincere sorrow. But this was in no light such a blow as Alexandra Andreyevna's death had been, and he accustomed himself to it with ease.

Colonne's letter sent to inform Piotr Ilyich that the Paris *première* of the Fourth Symphony would occur on January 25 did not reach Rome until January 24. This infuriated the composer, who had to wait in Rome for word of the public reaction. While he waited, he began, on the 28th, to compose the *Italian Caprice,* which he wanted to be "something on the order of Glinka's Spanish fantasies." He completed the first draft in exactly one week and then told Nadezhda Filaretovna that he foresaw a bright future for this composition.

When news came from Paris, it was not good. Colonne had suavely sent Piotr Ilyich a congratulatory telegram right after the concert. But the letter he sent later made clear that the Fourth Symphony had failed. Yet Piotr Ilyich's international reputation was at last on the verge of measuring up to his worth. Even in Paris the newspapers had to report that performances of the *Melancholy Serenade* and the Third Quartet had awakened enormous enthusiasm. In New York, on January 17, the Symphony Society had brought out the First Suite, and Leopold Damrosch was addressing the composer to inform him of its unmistakable success with the New York public, a success that unquestionably had influence, a decade later, on Walter Damrosch's invitation to Piotr Ilyich to decorate the opening of Music (later Carnegie) Hall. Berlin was becoming familiar with the Piano Concerto in B flat minor, having heard two performances by Bülow and one by Albert Friedenthal in a short time. Budapest had enjoyed the concerto. New York had listened with rapt attention to its performance at the hands of Franz Rummel.

Now the official Russian world of music reached out to interrupt the peaceful interlude in Rome. From Karl U. Davidov, Piotr Ilyich had word that he had been commissioned to compose music for one tableau of several to be staged in St. Petersburg in honour of the twenty-fifth anniversary of Alexander II's accession. He had to telegraph his acquiescence. "My tableau represents 'Montenegro receiving the Russian declaration of war,'" he wrote to Nadezhda Filaretovna. "You can imagine what an inspiration that will be!" He completed this unwelcome job in three days and then, on February 11, wrote Anatoly: "Naturally, I wasn't able to contrive any-thing better than the most abominable noise and crashing."

Despite Nadezhda Filaretovna's dislike of this whole project — she consistently wanted Piotr Ilyich to compose only what would express him — he mailed the music to Russia. It was not performed. Another attempt on the Tsar's life made celebrations untimely. Before some other pretext for its use could be found, the score was lost. No trace of its "great noise of drums and trombones" has been found.

With the commission off his hands, Piotr Ilyich returned to the new piano concerto, completing its transcription for two pianos and advancing its orchestration a little. He wrote chiding Na-dezhda Filaretovna for her continuing efforts to persuade Colonne to play his compositions. He appreciated her intentions and gener-osity, but gently asked her to let his works make their own way — or fail to make it — without the bribing of conductors. She could not understand this delicate point. She wanted to hear the music, and to have others hear it. Colonne was the man to teach it to Paris. What difference could it make to Piotr Ilyich that he had to be paid? When Piotr Ilyich insisted, she sputtered a little and then let the subject drop.

Piotr Ilyich had been examining the score of Brahms's Violin Concerto, not yet two years old. It was to Nadezhda Filaretovna that he wrote:

The concerto of Brahms pleases me no better than his other works. Certainly he is a great musician, even a master, but in his case the mastery smothers the inspiration. So many preparations and circum-locutions for what ought to appear and charm us instantly — and noth-ing appears but ennui. His music is not lighted by genuine emotion. It lacks poetry and makes great pretence to profundity. These depths con-tain nothing: they are empty. For example, take the opening of the concerto. It is an introduction, a preparation for something excellent, an admirable pedestal for a statue. But the statue is not there; we get merely a second pedestal placed on the first. I don't know whether I have expressed my thoughts on Brahms — or, rather, the feelings his music arouses in me — clearly. I mean to say that he never expresses anything, or, when he does, fails to express it wholly. His music is made out of fragments of some undefinable *something*, skilfully welded to-gether. The design lacks definite shape, colour, vitality. But I must confess simply that, apart from any definite accusation, Brahms as a musical personality is antipathetic to me. I can't abide him. No matter what he does, I remain unmoved and cold. This is an entirely instinctive reaction.

Just before leaving Rome, Piotr Ilyich spent part of a day in the Sistine Chapel, gazing long and intently at the frescoes. Modest had for years been trying to make him share his own intense reactions to painting and sculpture. Piotr Ilyich had liked only those plastic expressions that related themselves to music or could be misapprehended in musical terms. This time, however, he proudly wrote that a miracle had come to pass: "I experienced, probably for the first time in my life, a truly artistic rapture from painting." He had enjoyed Raphael and Domenichino and a half-dozen other painters, had liked sculptures by Michelangelo and disliked those of Bernini. But it was the universal drama of the Sistine that at last penetrated to that area of his consciousness customarily touched by music alone.

On March 11, 1880 Piotr Ilyich once again arrived in Paris. With his old friend Kondratyev he went to the theatre. They found the play so dull that they left before its third act. The next day, at the Variété, Meilhac and Halévy's La Petite Mère was better. "Its hero is a young symphonic composer," Piotr Ilyich informed Modest, "with long hair and neurotic sensibilities. I have never seen anything more entertaining in my life, nothing truer despite a certain element of caricature. During one scene when, in a dressing-gown, he is composing the second part of his symphony at the piano, I almost burst with laughter." At the Comédie Française, during a performance of Corneille's Polyeucte, he seems to have revised his formerly harsh opinions of the classic French drama. Where earlier he had found its severely stylized dialogue unbearably artificial, he now found its lines packed with beauty, strength, and lofty artistic verity. He had matured beyond insistence upon workaday verisimilitude.

In Berlin on March 15 Piotr Ilyich heard a Bilse concert. The next day he attended a performance of Der fliegende Holländer, finding it "terribly noisy and dull." His education in painting continued. "Teniers, Wouvermans, and Ruysdael please me far more than the famous Rubens, who represents even Christ as healthily

robust, with unnaturally pink cheeks," he advised Modest. "One
thing makes me begin to see myself as a *great* connoisseur. I recognize Correggio's brush before I see his name in the catalogue. But
then, Correggio has his own manner, and all his male figures and
heads look like the Christ in the Vatican, his women like the
Danaë in the Borghese Palace."

Continuing northward, Piotr Ilyich reached St. Petersburg on
March 19. There he learned that he, Kotek, Pakhulsky, and possibly Nikolay Rubinstein were not the only musicians who had received largess from Nadezhda Filaretovna. The able Polish violinist Henri Wieniawski was mortally ill, no longer able to support
himself by concerts and lessons, and the generous woman had supplied him with sufficient funds so that he could die in comfort. On
March 22 Piotr Ilyich wrote her that this benevolence had touched
him deeply. He spoke with admiration of the violinist's *Legend* and
parts of his A-minor Violin Concerto. Eleven days later Wieniawski died in Moscow at the age of forty-four.

St. Petersburg meant incessant activity to Piotr Ilyich. He visited his father's grave. He dickered with the pestiferous Bessel
about publishing the Second Symphony. He wasted an entire night
discussing music with a student son of Grand Duke Konstantin
Nikolayevich. He heard Lavrovskaya in *Le Prophète*. On March
26, when he would have preferred to be in Moscow, he was at the
Alexandrinsky Theatre for a performance of *Camille*, which he
found "terrible." In Moscow that night Nikolay Rubinstein played
Piotr Ilyich's Piano Sonata in G major, a paraphrase of airs from
Yevgeny Onyegin, and Liszt's transcription of the polonaise from
the same opera. Two days later a reviewer in *Moskovskiye Vyedomosti*, writing particularly of the sonata, described Piotr Ilyich as
"evidently at the crossroads: he is fearful of succumbing to Wagnerism, but on the other hand senses, despite himself, the irresistible force of the times." The fashion of finding Wagner in everything new, the lazy dodge that so plagued Verdi, had taken on
among Russian critics.

Jürgenson had submitted a score of *The Maid of Orleans* to the
St. Petersburg opera authorities, and Piotr Ilyich took this chance
to make a few corrections in it. Social engagements dogged his
days and exhausted him. The musicians of the northern capital
vied in honouring him. On March 30 a quartet including Karl U.
Davidov and Leopold Auer played his Second String Quartet at

a concert. He was given an ovation and presented with a wreath. "This is very flattering," he wrote Modest, "but, good God, how tired I am and how I hate everything here!" Grand Duke Konstantin Nikolayevich, to whom the composer had been presented at a soirée, stopped his carriage in the street to greet him and invited the frightened man to tour the world with him on a Russian battleship. Piotr Ilyich waited upon officials, crying out to Nadezhda Filaretovna that he did it only for *The Maid of Orleans.* He even had to attend a dinner the Grand Duke gave. There was no time for composing, none for finishing the orchestration of the Second Piano Concerto.

Piotr Ilyich had looked forward to Moscow as a promise of rest. No sooner had he arrived there, however, than he encountered his nemesis, the Grand Duke. This meant that others in the city would hear of his presence. He had to waste a whole day in pointless visits. But he would not remain in Moscow long. He settled numerous business matters with Jürgenson, made corrections on some final proofs, and left for Kamenka on April 23. There his sister and her husband took advantage of his visit to go away for a short time, leaving him with the responsibility of their five children. Nadezhda Filaretovna wrote him, renewing a suggestion that she had made earlier — a union of their families through the marriage of her son Nikolay Karlovich to one of his nieces. Which one of the four Davidov girls would he suggest? One of the older two? He replied offhandedly that it might be best for Kolya to choose the one he preferred.[2] He was finding the children a series of interruptions to his work. Yet he completed the orchestration of the Second Piano Concerto on May 10, that of the *Italian Caprice* two weeks later. He slaved away at corrections in *The Maid of Orleans.* The children were bothersome, but the country was quiet and beautiful, and he could work.

How far Piotr Ilyich had removed himself from the callow young man who had composed the First Piano Concerto is made clear by the letter with which he sent the Second to Nikolay Rubinstein. He merely asked the pianist to look it through. "If you find anything that needs changing," he wrote, "entrust the revisions to Taneyev." Also, he had just been offered the directorship of the Kiev Russian Musical Society and its attached school, and had

[2] The marriage Nadezhda Filaretovna desired eventually took place. Nikolay Karlovich von Meck married Tchaikovsky's niece Anna Lvovna Davidova.

rejected the offer unhesitatingly. Now he was an established composer, a man who could without vanity apologize to Taneyev for having himself made the four-hand transcription of the *Italian Caprice,* thus depriving the pianist of that task.

In June, Piotr Ilyich improved the time by composing the six vocal duets of Opus 46. He dedicated them to his eldest niece, Alexandra Lvovna Davidova. The extreme heat weakened him, he complained, but he worked on. A letter from Anatoly informed him that *The Maid of Orleans* had been passed for Marinsky performance. This news came while he was still correcting the proofs of the opera, a task through which he fought, struggling all the way. With it still incomplete, he accepted Nadezhda Filaretovna's invitation to visit Braïlov, arriving there on July 14. In his room he found a present, a costly gold clock with Joan of Arc, Apollo, and two muses.

A prolonged interchange of letters with Nikolay Rubinstein was dragging on. His former chief wanted him to compose a piece of official music for (1) a forthcoming exposition, (2) the Tsar's twenty-fifth anniversary, or (3) the dedication of the Church of Christ Saviour. In one letter Piotr Ilyich told Jürgenson that the entire prospect filled him with extreme distaste. "Neither the jubilee of the eminent personage (for whom I have always had quite an antipathy) nor the church (which I don't like at all) offers anything that could inspire me." This was not to be the end of Rubinstein's insistence.

Taneyev wrote from Paris that he had played *Yevgeny Onyegin* for a young French composer, Vincent d'Indy, who had been fascinated. This was flattering. Not so soothing to Piotr Ilyich's ego was an examination of a complete collection of his own works in Nadezhda Filaretovna's library. "How much I have composed," he exclaimed to Modest, "but how imperfect it all still is, how weak, how uncraftsmanlike! And what printing in the larger part of my works! Terrible! I have decided not to compose anything new for some time and to devote myself solely to correcting and reprinting my old compositions." Some part of the latter section of this resolution was to be carried out, but the first part naturally went by the board. In less than two months, with none of his earlier works corrected, Piotr Ilyich was to be at work on the Serenade for String Orchestra, opus 48.

By insisting that Piotr Ilyich was a symphonist when at his best, and by reiterating that his most considerable accomplishments were to be located in his symphonies, his contemporaries may have done posterity a serious disservice. There is no doubt that he took this insistence as a challenge. His inmost determination was to prove his critics wrong, make them confess error. He was always composing an opera or a suite or songs or a concerto to prove that he could, without composing a symphony, rise into the loftiest altitudes to be borne by a man of his talent. And so eleven years were to elapse between the Fourth Symphony (1877) and the Fifth Symphony (1888). During that period, he wrote, besides the *Manfred* Symphony, much else that remains viable. But his contemporaries were correct — his best music is in his symphonies. Perhaps they would have served music better if they had repeatedly told him that he could compose anything but a symphony. Then, being Piotr Ilyich, he might have left nine or a dozen symphonies instead of seven.

Besides his own works, Piotr Ilyich found in the Braïlov library a collection of dances by Glinka that was unknown to him. Telling Nadezhda Filaretovna of this discovery, he remarked that Glinka's Memoirs revealed "a nice, friendly, rather commonplace man," whom it was hard to picture writing the "Slavsya" chorus in *A Life for the Tsar*. After speaking most enthusiastically of *Ruslan and Lyudmila* and Glinka's overtures, he added: "How amazingly original is his Kamarinskaya, from which all succeeding Russian composers (myself included) continue to this day to borrow contrapuntal and harmonic combinations the moment they have to develop a Russian dance tune! This is done unconsciously; but the fact is that Glinka managed to concentrate in one brief composition what a dozen second-rate talents would have created only by the entire expenditure of their powers." This is acute criticism and should help to re-establish Piotr Ilyich's judgment in the eyes of any who find his cold reaction to Brahms incomprehensible.

Later in this letter Piotr Ilyich summed up Glinka as a man: "Glinka is a gifted Russian aristocrat of his epoch, and has the flaws of his type: petty vanity, limited culture, intolerance, ostentatiousness, and morbid sensitivity to — and impatience of — all criticism. These are usually the characteristics of mediocrity; how they come to exist in a man who should — so it appears — dwell in calm and modest pride, certain of his ability, is beyond my understanding! In one page of his Memoirs, Glinka writes that he had a bulldog whose conduct was not irreproachable, and that his servant had continually to be cleaning the room. Kukolnik, to whom Glinka gave the Memoirs for revision, remarked in the margin: 'Why put this in?' Underneath, Glinka pencilled: 'Why not?' Isn't that highly characteristic? Yet, all the same, he did compose the 'Slavsya'!"

From Simaki, on July 20, Piotr Ilyich wrote Modest that he was swimming in an ocean of happy sensations. Then there came a letter from his wife. "Just the sight of her script on the envelope, with my address written by her, makes me really ill, not only mentally, but physically," he wrote Nadezhda Filaretovna. Antonina Ivanovna's letter agreed to a divorce, but made it clear that she would not agree to accept the only possible grounds on which she could sue for divorce — adultery. Worse, her letter contained another covert threat. She accused her husband of gossiping about her faults — an unlikely activity for Piotr Ilyich — and cuttingly asked why he never mentioned his own "awful vices." The letter was demented nonsense. Or was it? Immediately he suffered from sharp pains in his feet. As Catherine Drinker Bowen pointed out, the symbolism of frustrated flight in these pains is obvious — too obvious, perhaps, to be credible.

There was musical labour to calm his nerves and recall the peace Antonina Ivanovna had driven off. Third press proofs of *The Maid of Orleans* required four days' work. Clean copies had to be made of the Six Duets, opus 46, and there were the Seven Songs, opus 47. After playing over the first two acts of the opera, Piotr Ilyich wrote his hostess that, though not the best of his compositions, it was likely to prove the most popular. How this man, who could judge an orchestral effect to split-second nicety, became blinded by the paraphernalia of opera! No popularity has ever accrued anywhere to *The Maid of Orleans*. Only the peculiarly poignant drama of Joan's "Farewell, forests," keeps its name green.

When he was ready to return the proofs, Piotr Ilyich sat down at the piano and played *Carmen* straight through. None of the original delight it had aroused in him was lost. In letters to Nadezhda Filaretovna and Modest that delight welled up in long paragraphs of praise — deserved praise not unmixed with criticism. He recognized the elements of the merely pretty in Bizet's masterpiece (could he have meant Micaëla's music or the *"air de fleur"*?).

He called it "a *chef d'œuvre* in the complete sense of the phrase; that is, a work destined to reflect in the highest degree the musical tastes and aspirations of an entire epoch." Summing up this little essay, he said: "Bizet is an artist paying tribute to the spoiled tastes of his century, but one warmed by genuine, sincere emotions and inspiration."

Modest had written the suggestion that Piotr Ilyich should read Victor Hugo's *L'Homme qui rit*. "Don't you know the story of my relations to Victor Hugo?" he replied. "I once began *Les Travailleurs de la mer*. I read and read, growing more and more angry at his grimaces and tomfoolery. At last, after a whole series of short, meaningless phrases consisting of exclamations, antitheses, ellipses, etc., I lost my temper, spat upon the book, tore it into bits, jumped on it, and ended by throwing it out of the window. Since then I have not been able to bear the sight of the name Hugo on the cover of a book. . . ." This man, whose judgments of music, his own included, eventually were based on a reasonable amalgam of emotion and intellect, had purely emotional reactions to the written word. In his criticism of Hugo (even though some of its specific points be just) is to be found the reason why he could not, except by accident, select a fitting opera libretto. Yet he was studying English, the language of a people he detested, solely in order to read Shakespeare, Dickens, and Thackeray in the original. Jürgenson later told Modest that Piotr Ilyich persisted at his study long enough to read *Pickwick Papers* and *David Copperfield* in English. His knowledge of that language proved valuable to him during visits to the United States and England.

On August 12 Piotr Ilyich was back at Kamenka. Taneyev had written him a half-joking letter saying that his misanthropy was insincere, and jokingly making the suggestion that if he really cared as little for glory and fame as he pretended, he had only to leave his compositions unsigned. Piotr Ilyich replied in solemn vein: "I want, I desire, I love to have people interested in my music, to have them praise it and love it, but I have never been concerned with their interest in me personally, my appearance, my conversation. Not to sign my compositions because of my unsociable nature would be silly and stupid, for I must somehow distinguish myself from contemporaries speaking the same language. . . . I want a name, whether my own or a pseudonym, to serve as the label distinguishing my wares from those of others, and I want that label to be valued, to be in demand on the market, and to have recognition."

The directorate of the imperial theatres notified Piotr Ilyich that *The Maid of Orleans* was accepted for performance. The censors had reluctantly passed the libretto after demanding that the archbishop in the story be called a pilgrim. Realizing that this silly alteration had been required from fear that the character might be taken as referring to a Russian archbishop, Piotr Ilyich asked the publisher to persuade the chief censor to let the cleric become a cardinal. (There are no cardinals of the Orthodox Church.) This variant was accepted by the censors.

Nikolay Rubinstein kept reminding Piotr Ilyich of the promised occasional piece for the silver-jubilee exposition, and the composer at last settled on the Napoleonic invasion of 1812 as its subject. By October 18 he was able to tell Anatoly that the Overture, *The Year 1812*, opus 49, was done, the Serenade for String Orchestra all but done. To Nadezhda Filaretovna he expressed his habitually frank opinion of the works, which he said he had composed very rapidly. "The Overture will be very loud and noisy, but I wrote it with little warmth or love; therefore it will probably have small artistic worth. The Serenade, on the other hand, I wrote from inner compulsion: I felt it, and therefore venture to hope that it does not lack artistic quality."

Nadezhda Filaretovna had news for Piotr Ilyich, too. She had hired a new musician, a talented French boy who had been recommended to her by Marmontel of the Paris Conservatoire. On October 20 she wrote Piotr Ilyich that she had asked the young man to make four-hand piano arrangements of the Spanish, Neapolitan, and Russian dances from *Swan Lake*. The young man's name, she added, was Debussy, though she came to refer to him as "our little Bussy." The first published work of the great French composer was to be those same transcriptions from Piotr Ilyich's ballet. As far as can be ascertained, however, the two men never met. They would have disagreed on musical subjects, particularly later, when Debussy's admiration for Mussorgsky became one of the motivating forces in his own composing.

Piotr Ilyich's variable health was poor in the autumn of 1880. He suffered from what Modest describes as "neuralgic headaches." Yet he worked unceasingly. On November 8 he wrote Jürgenson that he had "unexpectedly" composed a string serenade. "Whether because it is my latest child or because in reality it is not bad, I am terribly in love with this serenade, and can scarcely wait to have it presented to the world." Two weeks later he went to Moscow. He visited the Conservatory, seeing his ex-colleagues. On December 3 his Liturgy of St. John Chrysostom was privately performed at the Conservatory. "The chorus sang superbly," he informed Nadezhda Filaretovna, "and I experienced one of the sweetest moments of my musical career." He discussed the Bolshoi mounting of *Yevgeny Onyegin* with the new conductor there. This was Enrico Bevignani, later of the Metropolitan Opera House, New York.

Piotr Ilyich seemed to be avoiding *premières* of his compositions. Had he remained in Moscow ten days longer, he could have attended the December 18 Russian Musical Society concert, at which Nikolay Rubinstein conducted the first performance of the *Italian Caprice*. Instead he went to St. Petersburg, and returned to Moscow on the 20th just in time to watch a rehearsal of *Yevgeny Onyegin*. The Moscow critics were taken in by the *Italian Caprice*, eulogizing it in terms that should be reserved for better music. When this shallow, tuneful, and vividly orchestrated potpourri was performed in St. Petersburg under Napravnik on January 7, 1881, Cui and one or two other critics saw through it. Cui stated accurately that it had a brilliant surface, but was poor in internal content.

After a rehearsal of *Yevgeny Onyegin* the composer wrote Modest: "I was enraptured by the soloists' performance of the first act, and couldn't refuse Bevignani's urgings that I attend the orchestral rehearsals and the performance." The censor's ban on *The Oprichnik* had been lifted, and it was currently occupying the Bolshoi stage. Piotr Ilyich told Modest that its third performance had been enthusiastically applauded. "The audience tenaciously called for me — but I wasn't there." Moscow was enjoying a veritable Tchaikovsky festival. His songs and chamber music were receiving constant performance. Public demand required a repetition of the *Italian Caprice,* and the composer was persuaded to attend a rehearsal of it. "It sounds marvellous," he told Modest. "The Second Symphony of Borodin, who has come to Moscow for the event, and who was at the rehearsal in a general's uniform, with the Cross of St. Vladimir around his neck, is also to be played at this concert."

Daring the ecclesiastical prejudice against concert performances of sacred music — indeed, against performance of any sacred music not commissioned by or approved by ecclesiastical authorities — the Moscow Russian Musical Society gave a public performance of Piotr Ilyich's Liturgy on December 30. Its composer was altogether pleased. "Capacity house," he told Modest, "and despite the prohibition of applause, an uproarious and unexpected ovation, as well as the presentation of some sort of foliate lyre from an unknown." On January 15, 1881 an article written by Amvrosy, Bishop of Moscow, but signed "An Old Moscow Minister of the Church," appeared in *Rus*. It was a virulent attack on Piotr Ilyich for having composed the Liturgy. The Bishop was attacking the public's favourite composer: *Moskovskiye Vyedomosti* suggested that the last week of the musical season of 1880 should, in all fairness, be called "Tchaikovsky week."

Alexey Sofronov, Piotr Ilyich's loyal, invaluable, and beloved manservant, had been called up for military service, much to his master's annoyance and sincere grief. On December 31 the composer visited him in his barracks and as a result had what he described to Modest as the worst nervous attack he had ever experienced. He wrote of feeling so sorry for Alexey that he lacked words to express his feelings. The wildly emotional tone in which Piotr Ilyich wrote about and to Alexey forcibly suggests that, whatever the private relations between master and servant were, his personal feeling was not far from love.

Returning to Moscow on January 19, after a two-week visit to Kamenka, Piotr Ilyich found his restlessness undiminished. "Heavens!" he wrote in his daybook. "How unhappy I am in Moscow — which, by the by, I love to distraction! Where is the glowing past? Or does it merely appear glowing now? But everything here is poisoned for me. . . . It is terrible!" On the 22nd he attended the dress rehearsal of *Yevgeny Onyegin* at the Bolshoi, and the next night was present at its Moscow *première*, conducted by Bevignani, whose benefit night it was. "At first the public was very reserved," he wrote Nadezhda Filaretovna the next day. "By degrees, however, the applause increased, and finally all went well. The performance and mounting of the opera were satisfactory. . . ." In truth, second-hand scenery had been adapted to this new use, only two members of the cast were adequate, and only the costumes and the orchestra were good. A minority registered enthusiasm, which gradually increased during further performances, until *Yevgeny Onyegin* established itself permanently in the repertoire.

The reviews were a mixed bag of praise and of attack directed against the opera's small structure, lack of breadth, and weak theatrical impact. Having read them, Piotr Ilyich went to St. Petersburg, arriving there just in time to attend the first orchestral rehearsals of *The Maid of Orleans*. He was worried about Nikolay Rubinstein, who was seriously ill and who was ignoring the advice of his physicians that he go away to rest. He was fretted by the halfhearted production being given his new opera at the Marinsky, noting that the directors, having just spent 10,000 rubles on a new ballet, were refusing to spend a kopeck on *The Maid of Orleans*.

Piotr Ilyich was intensely displeased with most of the singers who had been assigned roles in his opera. The prime donne were squabbling. The directors were openly unfriendly. Napravnik was cutting the score, demanding alterations. Only the composer's familiar unruffled assurance that the public would like his new opera buoyed up his spirits. His revised Second Symphony was performed on February 12, but he did not attend, writing Nadezhda Filaretovna: "I wasn't there. I hear that it was liked." Modest remarked that not one of the critics who reviewed the concert seemed to have realized that the symphony had been changed and that the whole first movement was new. The public, however, was enthusiastic.

Despite the emotional strain of rehearsals and the related struggle with various individuals involved in the production of his opera, Piotr Ilyich found time to go to theatre. On February 13 he saw Minkus's ballet *Zoraya, or The Moorish Maid in Spain*. On the 18th he attended the first performance of *The Benefactor*, a comedy drama by Modest Ilyich Tchaikovsky, now a promising playwright. On the 21st he concluded with Jürgenson a contract by which he received 7,000 rubles (about $3,500) for the outright sale of thirty-seven minor pieces. This is a reliable indication that his songs and piano pieces were in demand and were having a wide sale. Jürgenson was a true lover of music and a true friend to Piotr Ilyich, but he would not have paid so large a sum for compositions of dubious commercial value.

After one postponement *The Maid of Orleans* was presented at the Marinsky on February 25. In the cast it is interesting to find the role of Dunois played by Fyodor Stravinsky, father of that Igor Stravinsky who became a great composer and one of the most intelligent admirers of Tchaikovsky. Napravnik conducted. When the opera was over, the composer was certain of its success: the applause, thin at first, had waxed as the evening progressed, until the fourth act had been approved noisily. With this pleasant misapprehension in his mind, Piotr Ilyich started for Italy, travelling through Vilna to Vienna. In a copy of the *Neue freie Presse* that he picked up in Vienna, he read a telegraphic account stating that *The Maid of Orleans,* despite the St. Petersburg public's enthusiasm, was "uninspired, tiresome, and monotonous." This was a tiny sample of the abuse that the critics, marshalled by Cui, were hurling at the opera. One of them, hesitating to decide whether it was a step forward or a step backward for its composer, found sections of it reminiscent of *Aïda, Le Prophète, La Juive, Faust,* Mendelssohn's songs, and works by Moniuszko and others. Harsh words were levelled against its vocal writing; praise was awarded only the orchestral parts. The officials at the Marinsky reacted abruptly by withdrawing the opera despite increasing public support at the box office.

XII

ON March 5, 1881 Jürgenson wrote Piotr Ilyich a letter that was to release him from the worst of his fears. The publisher had been watching the movements and activities of Antonina Ivanovna and now triumphantly retailed a major discovery. That lady had taken a lover named Bolkov, had had a child by him, and was living with him in Moscow. This welcome, but not surprising news meant several things. If Piotr Ilyich wanted divorce proceedings instituted, he no longer had to trump up a plausible adultery involving himself. A blameless wife could no longer accuse him of hidden vices. The balance of justice must, in the eyes of his friends and relations, now tip back wholly in his direction.

But Piotr Ilyich never sued for divorce; probably and rightly he feared revelations Antonina Ivanovna still had the power to make despite her own guilt. He continued until his death to pay for all or part of her support. After the spring of 1881, however, he referred to her, even in his intimate letters to Anatoly and Modest, less and less often. From time to time, news reached him that she had given birth to another illegitimate child, whether by Bolkov or another no one was ever certain.[1]

During a brief sojourn in Rome, Piotr Ilyich was in demand among the resident Russian nobility, playing his compositions at luncheons and soirées at the homes of the Ambassador, a countess, and a grand duke. "I did not expect to live this sort of life in Rome," he wrote Nadezhda Filaretovna. "I shall have to leave, as there will no doubt be other invitations that I can't refuse. Out of fear of offending someone, I am always weak enough to accept. I haven't the strength of will to refuse all such engagements." He kept his word, leaving Rome on March 12 for a week's stay in

---

[1] In 1896 Antonina Ivanovna became so patently insane that she could no longer be left at large and was confined to an asylum. She continued to send wandering, inconsequential letters shot through with the same amorous delusions of seduction and conquest that had troubled her otherwise vacant mind even before she had married Piotr Ilyich. She died in 1917, at the age of sixty-eight.

Naples. There still another Russian nobleman called to inform him that, on March 13, one more attempt to assassinate Alexander II had achieved its purpose.

Alexander II had emancipated the serfs. His relatively liberal policies, however, had been reversed at the discovery that his half-measures did not still nihilist and other revolutionary activity. He had already enacted severe repressive measures when a series of attempts on his person made it appear to him necessary to assert autocratic powers ruthlessly. In 1880 his wife, Marya Alexandrovna, died during the twenty-fifth year of their reign. He fell subject to profound mental depression. A secret marriage to his mistress, Princess Dolgoruki, did not brighten his outlook, and he gradually delegated powers to his chief advisers. Early in 1881 they persuaded him to try abating the terrorist movement by a ukase creating commissions to suggest reforms. On March 13, after signing this ukase, the Tsar went for a drive near the Winter Palace and was wounded by the explosion of small bombs thrown at his carriage. He died a few hours later. The Tsarevich, Nikolay Alexandrovich, having died in 1865, Alexander would be followed by his second son, the thirty-six-year-old Alexander Alexandrovich.

"At such moments being abroad is miserable," Piotr Ilyich told Modest. "I long to be in Russia, closer to the source of news, and to have a part in the demonstrations tendered to the new Tsar . . . in short, to be in living touch with my own people. It seems so curious, after receiving such news, to hear people chattering at table d'hôte about the beauties of Sorrento, etc." He had scarcely recovered from that mood when he heard by telegram from Jürgenson that Nikolay Rubinstein was dying in Paris. On the heels of the first telegram another arrived stating that death was a matter of hours. Then a final one stated that Rubinstein was dead. Piotr Ilyich went to Paris immediately, arriving on March 25.

"Mentally, I suffered the tortures of the damned during my trip," he wrote Modest. "I must, to my shame, confess that I suffered less from my sense of irreparable loss than from horror of seeing in Paris — and at the Grand Hotel, too — the body of poor Rubinstein. I feared that I should be unable to bear the shock, though I exerted my whole will-power to conquer this shameful cowardice. My fears were vain. The body had been taken to the Russian church at six o'clock this morning."

Returning from Rubinstein's funeral, Piotr Ilyich wrote Na-

dezhda Filaretovna a singular letter. It is about God and the
Christian way of life and being humble before God's will. "I often
pray to Him with tears in my eyes (where He is, what He is, I do
not know; but I do know that He exists), and implore Him to
grant me love and peace, to pardon and enlighten me; and it is
sweet to say to Him: 'Lord, Thy will be done,' for I know His will
is *holy*." Line upon line the letter expresses faith Piotr Ilyich could
not feel. He was wrestling with himself in the darkness of Rubinstein's death, and the result of his struggle is a brave flow of religious phrase, nothing more.

Gloom deepened about Piotr Ilyich. When he had last been in
Moscow, rumour had said that Nadezhda Filaretovna was under-
going financial reverses. He wrote to her begging to know the
truth. She answered that rumour was right, that her losses had
mounted to millions of rubles. He need not think, she added, that
the small amounts she sent him were of importance compared
with her losses: she wanted to continue his annuity. "But you see,"
he wrote Modest, "that this pension is no longer a certainty, and
that therefore, soon or late, I must return to my teaching. All this
is far from cheering." Whatever blows circumstance had directed
against the Von Meck millions were to have no immediate effect
on the flow of funds from Nadezhda Filaretovna to Piotr Ilyich.
She continued, too, to keep a composer-performer attached to her
staff of servants.

To Anatoly, Piotr Ilyich wrote the honest report of his reaction
to Nikolay Rubinstein's death. "I have always held a high opinion
of Nikolay Grigoryevich as a worker, but have had no affection
for him (especially lately) as a man. Now, of course, I have forgotten all but his good points, and they outnumbered his weak ones.
I am not even considering his significance as a citizen. Terror lays
hold of me when I am confronted with the impossibility of replac-
ing him." To Nadezhda Filaretovna, on April 1, he explained why
he had watched Rubinstein's body put on the train without following it to Moscow for the second funeral. At the preliminary service
held in Paris on March 25 he had been present, as had Anton
Rubinstein, Massenet, Lalo, Viardot-García, and Turgenyev. Anton's apparent indifference to his brother's death had aroused all
Piotr Ilyich's enduring resentments. They had decided him: he
would not accompany Anton to Moscow. He waited in Paris five
days.

Moskovskiye Vyedomosti of April 4 carried a long article on Nikolay Rubinstein by Piotr Ilyich. It contains the details of the Paris funeral, and implies a judgment of Nikolay that would place him above Anton as both pianist and conductor. What was occupying Piotr Ilyich's mind most constantly was that the Moscow Conservatory, which he loved in direct ratio to his detestation of teaching, was without a chief. The position was offered to him, and offered again, and he found the strength of will to refuse. His own candidate was Taneyev, then only twenty-five years old. No decision was reached, however, and by May 11 Piotr Ilyich had left both St. Petersburg and Moscow behind once more and was at Kamenka.

On May 17 Piotr Ilyich wrote Karl U. Davidov asking that the director send him *Poltava*, a libretto that had been prepared for his use, but which he had never set. Davidov complied at once, writing: "I am happy that a subject that once attracted me so much is now in the hands of so talented an artist as you." This was eventually, in modified guise, to become Piotr Ilyich's seventh completed opera, under the title of *Mazepa*. During the spring and early summer, however, he found himself devoid of inspiration or lacking the compulsion to compose. He wrote Nadezhda Filaretovna that he had begun to "study housekeeping." He hit upon the idea of harmonizing a vesper service,[2] and studied with great care the liturgy and ceremonials of the Church.

Jürgenson had suggested that Piotr Ilyich edit for him the religious works of Dmitri Stepanovich Bortnyansky. He forwarded the enormous mass of material to Kamenka, where Piotr Ilyich looked at it with despair. Yet his finances, despite the continuation of his pension from Nadezhda Filaretovna, the sale of compositions, and performance fees, were — as ever — limited. He accepted the commission, writing Anatoly to discuss the honorarium with Jürgenson. "I feel that without a sizable honorarium in view, my patience would give out and I shouldn't have the strength to conquer my distaste." Bortnyansky was not a composer likely to engage his most sincere interest. Yet the Jürgenson edition, when he finished it, comprised ten large volumes. When Nadezhda Filaretovna heard of his work on Bortnyansky and understood that he

---

[2] Jürgenson had won another suit with regard to a private publisher's right to issue religious music.

loathed the task and was doing it only for money, she was enraged. She sent him an extra present of money, begging him not to perform musical tasks that did not respond to some inner need. He had given his word to Jürgenson, however, and he plodded ahead until the edition was complete and the proofs read and corrected, some time in August 1882.

Piotr Ilyich addressed a petition to K. P. Pobedonostsev, former tutor and now court minister to Alexander III, asking him to intercede with the Tsar in the matter of a grant of 3,000 silver rubles. Exactly nineteen days later, on June 19, he again addressed the minister, this time to express thanks for helping him get the grant. Thus easily did the new Tsar divert national funds to a composer whose music was well loved in every large town and city of all the Russias. It was not only his own pocketbook that Piotr Ilyich watched over: he wrote Anatoly that he planned, in the future, to compose works that would bring a profit to "poor Piotr Ivanovich" [Jürgenson], and specifically mentioned a collection of children's songs.

Piotr Ilyich was still supporting Taneyev for the position of director of the Moscow Conservatory. When the young man argued that it was Piotr Ilyich's duty to accept a professorship there, the composer became extremely agitated. "I didn't sleep the entire night, or slept badly," he told Modest, "and that with the help of some wine. No. It is better to die in poverty than to make a stupid sacrifice." In replying to Taneyev on September 6, he casually mentioned that he had the libretto of *Mazepa* in his possession and had already composed four numbers to it in spare hours. The extreme heat could keep him from the monotony of Bortnyansky, but not from another foredoomed attempt to compose an immediately successful opera.

On September 16 Jürgenson again had news for Piotr Ilyich. The Violin Concerto, completed more than three years before, had never been performed. Leopold Auer, to whom he had originally dedicated it, had pronounced it too difficult and radical to perform. Kotek had announced his intention of attempting the solo part, but had likewise dropped the project. Now Adolf Brodsky would play it in Vienna at a Philharmonic concert, with the renowned Wagnerian, Hans Richter, as conductor. According to his own statement, Brodsky had looked longingly at the concerto for more than two years before finding the courage to learn it. Suddenly he made his decision and then learned it as though in a fury.

On October 30 the St. Petersburg Russian Musical Society, with Napravnik conducting, gave the first performance of the Serenade for Strings on a program that also included *The Tempest*. The conductor wrote that the Serenade had had considerable success, and that its second movement, a waltz, had had to be repeated. The same sort of reception awaited it in Moscow. The critics were all but unanimous in calling it delightful, and in nominating it one of Piotr Ilyich's most successful works. All four of its movements are written superbly for massed strings, and at least two of them — the opening "Piece in Sonatina Form" and the "Elegy" — have substantial melodic materials subtly and nobly harmonized. The popular second movement, the "Waltz Tempo," is so light in character as to be out of place, and the "Finale (Russian Theme)" is no more than adequate. The Serenade as an entity disappoints the expectations its best sections arouse. Its two best movements are often performed separately, suffering not at all by divorce from the other two.

Vera Lvovna, the Davidov daughter Nadezhda Filaretovna had selected as the future wife of her son Kolya, was married on November 16 to a member of the Rimsky-Korsakov family — not a suspect musician, but a naval man in the lofty family tradition. This upset Nadezhda Filaretovna, far away in Florence. Piotr Ilyich suggested another Davidov daughter, Anna, whom Kolya von Meck eventually married. But Anna had been away at school and might have modern or even radical ideas, and Nadezhda Filaretovna needed a good deal of convincing. At last, however, she consented. Neither Anna Lvovna nor Kolya von Meck, still a student, was in the slightest aware of these plans for their joint future.

On November 25 Piotr Ilyich was in Vienna, two days later in Venice, three days after that in Florence. Although he knew that Nadezhda Filaretovna was again at the Villa Oppenheim, he stayed in Florence only two days, writing her a note to say that he was full of half-formed and indecisive projects, and then went happily on to Rome and Modest. There he awaited news of Vienna's reception of his Violin Concerto, which was conducted by Hans Richter, with Adolf Brodsky as soloist, on December 4.

Liszt, temporarily resident in Rome, had been seventy years old on October 22. A concert to honour that occasion was given tardily

Scenes from THE NUTCRACKER (*above*) *and* YEVGENY ONYEGIN, *Act III*
(*below*) *as mounted in 1940 at the Bolshoi Theatre* (*Moscow*)

on December 6. Sgambati was the pianist, and Piotr Ilyich was present. "The program was made up exclusively of his [Liszt's] works," Nadezhda Filaretovna learned. "The performance was worse than mediocre. Liszt himself was present. It was touching to watch the ovation that the enthusiastic Italians tendered to the venerable genius, but Liszt's compositions leave me cold. They have more poetical intention than actual creative strength, more colour than form — in short, despite being effective on the surface, they lack deeper qualities. Liszt is the direct opposite of Schumann, whose huge creative strength does not harmonize with his colourless manner of expression." This was not the opinion of Liszt held by most of his later contemporaries, but it is exactly the judgment posterity has increasingly tended to make. Whatever else happened to Piotr Ilyich, time did not dull the edge of his sensitivity to other men's compositions.

The reviews of the world *première* of the Violin Concerto ranged from the phrase "barbarously terrible" to "one of the most original and effective compositions for the violin," from Theodor Helm's "the wildest Russian nihilism" to Max Kalbeck's "the strangeness of the composition mystified many." The review that stabbed Piotr Ilyich so fiercely that the wound troubled him always was by the awesome critic of the *Neue freie Presse*, Eduard Hanslick. At fifty-six Hanslick had already sat for his portrait as Sixtus Beckmesser, and he was at his most malicious and silly when he dipped his pen in vitriol to write of the Violin Concerto:

For a while it advances in customary fashion, is musical and not uninspired. Then crudity gains the upper hand and reigns to the end of the opening movement. The violin is no longer played, but torn apart, pounded black and blue. Whether it is actually possible to project these terrifying difficulties clearly I do not know, but I am sure that Herr Brodsky, in trying to do so, brought martyrdom to us as well as to himself. The Adagio, with its tender Slavic melancholy, calmed and charmed us again, but this breaks off abruptly, only to be succeeded by a Finale that plunges us into the brutal, deplorable gaiety of a Russian holiday carouse. We see savages, vulgar faces, hear coarse oaths, and smell fusel oil. Friedrich Fischer, describing obscene painting, once said that there existed pictures one could see stink. Tchaikovsky's Violin Concerto brings us face to face for the first time with the revolting thought: may there not also exist musical compositions that we can hear stink?

Brodsky's story of the *première* of the Violin Concerto agrees
with the glimpses of the occasion in the criticisms. When the work
was finished, a riotous demonstration burst forth in the hall. There
was insistent and prolonged applause that gradually drowned out
very determined catcalls. The violinist had to return to the stage
three times to make bows. Much of the applause was directed at
him, and all of the hissing was for the composition. Today, when
the D major has become so familiar as to be almost without impact,
it is impossible to turn back to the frame of mind of Hanslick and
the other Viennese tradition-defenders. Reading their wildly im-
probable phrases now merely calls up again the truth that critical
experience is seldom armour against the bruises of novelty.

Piotr Ilyich's gratitude to Brodsky increased in direct ratio to
the amount of abuse heaped on the concerto. Auer, he learned, had
not only refused to play it, but had dissuaded the brilliant young
French violinist Émile Sauret from doing so. Kotek had weakly
given up the idea at the first sign of opposition. Karl U. Davidov,
who, much to Piotr Ilyich's disgust, had succeeded Napravnik as
conductor in St. Petersburg, was opposed to performing the concerto. Brodsky, unmoved by the critical barrage, fulsomely announced that he would like to go on playing it for ever. He fully
deserved the dedication, which, expunging Auer's name, the composer awarded him. Auer lived to repeat the cycle of Nikolay Rubinstein's reactions to the B-flat minor Piano Concerto: he changed
his mind and became one of the Violin Concerto's champions. Indeed, when he abandoned violin-playing to become the most celebrated modern teacher of violinists, he taught its performance to
more than half of the soloists of yesterday and today.[2a]

Nadezhda Filaretovna had once suggested to Piotr Ilyich that
he compose something for violin, cello, and piano. He had replied
that he desired to please her, but disliked this combination of
timbres too much. As 1881 drew to its close, he wrote her that, to
his own surprise, he had begun to compose such a piano trio. He
expressed reservations, but said that he was led on by a desire to
please her and by the resolution to conquer the difficulties inherent in combining the three instruments. When he completed it, on
February 9, he had composed a tribute to the memory of Nikolay
Rubinstein, the massive Trio in A minor, opus 50, far and away the

[2a] I learn from Mr. Joseph Szigeti that "most of the D major Concerto interpretations we hear . . . are based on Auer's 'emendations,' cuts and so on!"

best-achieved chamber work to come from him. Dedicated "To the memory of a great artist," this exceedingly thoughtful, richly melodious, and persuasive music has challenged the capabilities and strength of soloists to this day and has retained an important place in the snobbish company of recognized chamber works.

On January 28, 1882, at a concert of the Moscow Russian Musical Society, Max von Erdmannsdörfer, its new conductor, brought out the Serenade for Strings. Although this first Moscow performance seems to have been good, and though the composer later became friendly with Erdmannsdörfer, he was to miss Nikolay Rubinstein in Moscow even more than Napravnik in St. Petersburg. In Rome, meanwhile, he was working on the Trio, on Bortnyansky, and on ideas for the vespers and a future opera — which latter, quite definitely, would now be *Mazepa*. On February 3, he wrote to thank a friend for sending him E. T. A. Hoffmann's fairy tale *The Nutcracker and the Mouse King*, saying that he had greatly enjoyed it. A work to be composed a decade later was being forecast.

Late in January, Modest, who was in Rome with Piotr Ilyich, was sick for some time, and the composer was therefore called upon to spend many hours with the deaf and dumb Kolya Konradi. This seriously delayed his work. On February 9, nevertheless, he dated the manuscript of the Trio as complete. Two days later he sent it to Jürgenson with the request that Taneyev, I. V. Grzhimali, and Fitzenhagen play it over before it was published. "I should very much like that, as a work composed in memory of Nikolay Grigoryevich, it should be published in some splendid format," he added. In the same letter he asked Jürgenson to hurry his decision with regard to a request from the editor for whom *The Seasons* had been composed for six brief piano pieces to be paid for at the rate of one hundred rubles each. Jürgenson demurred despite Piotr Ilyich's having made it plain that he could well use the six hundred rubles. "From your point of view you are quite right," the composer sputtered, "and your arguments are well founded. Nevertheless, this annoys me a little."

"This season I have no luck," Piotr Ilyich detailed to Jürgenson on January 16. "The Maid of Orleans will not be repeated; Onyegin ditto; Auer intrigues against the Violin Concerto; no one performs the Piano Concerto [in G major]; in short, things are bad. But what infuriates me and mortifies me most is that the directorate, which would not spend a kopeck on The Maid of Orleans, has granted 30,000 rubles for the mounting of Rimsky-Korsakov's Snyegurochka. Isn't it equally distasteful to you to feel that 'our subject' has been taken away from us, and that Lyel will now sing new music to the old words? It is as though someone had forcibly torn a piece off me and presented it to the public in a new and brilliant setting. I could cry with mortification." *Snyegurochka* was not the only Tchaikovskyan subject that Rimsky-Korsakov was to adopt: shortly after Piotr Ilyich's death he was to compose his *Christmas Eve* to the Gogol story on which *Vakula the Smith* had been based.

In February, Anatoly sent Piotr Ilyich a letter announcing his marriage to Parasha V. Konshina. In replying, on February 19, Piotr Ilyich said: "When you have completely calmed down — that is, after your wedding — read Anna Karenina, which for the first time I recently read in a state of ecstasy bordering on fanaticism.[3] What you are now experiencing is there excellently expressed in connection with Levin's marriage. . . . There is a need for a certain type of endearment and care that only a woman can satisfy. I am sometimes possessed by a mad desire to be caressed by a woman's hand." Neither the passing years nor the awful experience of Antonina Ivanovna had destroyed Piotr Ilyich's intense need for a woman to replace his long-lost mother. Nothing in whatever fleeting and secretive intimacies he enjoyed with other men satisfied that need.

On the way from Florence to Vienna, Piotr Ilyich began to try his carefully learned English on a reading of *Bleak House*. He lingered in the Austrian capital a few days, writing Modest that he had never been so reluctant to return to Russia. "Perhaps when I am actually in Russia this will pass, and I shall regain the ability to be intoxicated with the Great Russian spirit, but at this moment it is hateful to me." Nor did Moscow, after he arrived there, prove bearable. There were endless breakfasts, dinners, and suppers in honour of Anatoly and his fiancée, chiefly given by her family, and all irritating to Piotr Ilyich. An evening spent quietly with his sister, her husband, and their daughters Tatyana and Anna was a little relaxing. But on April 16 there was all the confused excitement of the wedding. When that was over, he managed to settle

[3] Tchaikovsky had read the book some years earlier, at first with detestation — he rebuked Modest for reading such trash — but later with admiration.

down to some necessary labour for Jürgenson, hacking away at
further details of the Trio, *1812*, and Bortnyansky. By about May
5 he was so weary that it was with the keenest pleasure that he
left for Kamenka, passing his forty-second birthday at Kiev on the
way.

Hans Richter, who had conducted the Vienna performance of
the Violin Concerto, had not been discouraged by Hanslick and
his confreres. With Brodsky again as soloist, he now presented
the work in London. It was "a tremendous success," the violinist
informed Piotr Ilyich. This news brightened a little and momentarily the gloom of inaction in which Piotr Ilyich was existing at
Kamenka. Doing no work at first, and then trifling lackadaisically
at *Mazepa*, he was bored, telling Modest that during each evening
he awaited the time to go to bed "with sick impatience." He worried because he was occupying a room needed by the Davidov
children's tutor, and asked Modest to invite him to Grankino as
quickly as possible. For his work on *Mazepa* he felt not one twentieth of the inspiration and love he had experienced while working on earlier compositions. It was a difficult and trying expenditure of energy. He wrote apologetically about it to Nadezhda
Filaretovna.

On May 30 Anton Rubinstein conducted the first symphony concert given in connection with the Moscow Exposition of Industrial
Arts. The novelty of the occasion was Piotr Ilyich's Piano Concerto in G major, with Taneyev as soloist. This long, variegated,
and extremely difficult work attracted thunderous applause, but
those present had little doubt that the noise was directed toward
the performers and the composer rather than the composition. No
lack of peculiarly Tchaikovskyan colour or abundant melody has
militated against the G-major Concerto. Its disappearance from
concert programs is without sense or justification.[4] Critics have
often damned it as a symphony with piano obbligato — there is
nothing intrinsically distasteful about that form. It is in reality
a triple concerto, for there are long, important passages for solo
violin and solo cello. When have the first-desk string men of an
orchestra refused to shine? The piano part is of unexampled difficulty (Huneker records that when the New York Philharmonic
Society played the concerto under Anton Seidl's direction in 1892,

[4] Contemporary ballet enthusiasts may have heard the concerto as the excelling score of Balanchine's *Ballet Imperial*.

the "iron-handed" Franz Rummel had to cut the solo passages). Today there are a dozen pianists who could perform it without strain. Decidedly the G major must and will be revived. Beyond a doubt it would repay effort. Each of its three movements contains excellent musical ideas put into action with assurance and originality. To perform it once to every ten playings of the B-flat minor would be to hurt no one and to increase the musical enjoyment of many.

Piotr Ilyich was writing Modest that he had just finished *Bleak House* and had cried a little out of pity for Lady Dedlock, reluctance to abandon characters with whom he had been living for two months, and gratitude to "so great a writer as Dickens," when the first of the few reviews of the Second Concerto appeared in *Moskovskiye Vyedomosti*. It was favourable. Five days later, writing to Jürgenson, he requested that Fitzenhagen or Grzhimali put the markings into the string parts of the Trio before its publication. He also asked that, if the Violin Concerto were to be included in the Exposition programs, the solo part be given to Brodsky, and not to Kotek.

The Serenade for Strings was to be played first, with Anton Rubinstein conducting. At the first rehearsal Jürgenson wrote: "Jupiter [Rubinstein] said to me: 'This, I think, is Tchaikovsky's best work.' He praised it just as unconditionally to others, and at the final rehearsal said to me: 'You may congratulate yourself on the publication of this opus.'" On June 11 the Serenade was a true and spontaneous success, and Jürgenson informed the composer that it had pleased public and musicians equally. With this gladdening news, Piotr Ilyich left for Grankino on June 15. He sharply missed his former visits to Braïlov and Simaki, which Nadezhda Filaretovna had sold after her financial setbacks. At Grankino, situated in endless steppe country, he found some of the same peace and sense of contentment that her hospitality had formerly brought him. He began once again to work at *Mazepa*.

The first performance of a Tchaikovsky opera outside Russia occurred on July 28, when *The Maid of Orleans* was staged in Prague in a Czech translation. Alexandra Davidova, returning from Karlsbad, stopped off to hear it and reported to her brother that it had been staged in a summer theatre built like a barracks, and that both mounting and performance had been poor. The opera awoke small interest, though the few scattered reviews were favourable and Jürgenson wisely wired the composer that it had had a "brilliant success."

An all-Tchaikovsky program was scheduled for August 20 as part of the Exposition festivities, and the composer agreed to attend. The Violin Concerto was to have its first Russian hearing, and it was with annoyance that Piotr Ilyich — leaving Grankino with Modest and Kolya — learned that Kotek and Brodsky had both been invited to Moscow. Back in Kamenka, he worked a few days more at *Mazepa*. Then, the day before the concert, he was in Moscow with Modest. The program of August 20 was: *The Tempest*, Lelya's songs from *Snyegurochka*, the Violin Concerto, the *Italian Caprice*, two songs, and *1812*. Ippolit K. Altani was the conductor, Brodsky the soloist. The large audience was happy throughout, and after the concerto called Piotr Ilyich to the stage many times.

When Modest had left the city again, Piotr Ilyich found great pleasure in spending time with Anatoly and Parasha. "I consider Tolya's marriage the greatest of blessings for both him and me," he wrote Modest. Alexey Sofronov, still in military service, was sick in a hospital, and there Piotr Ilyich visited him almost every day. Rimsky-Korsakov and his wife — the latter an intense admirer of Piotr Ilyich — were in Moscow and made fulsome displays of friendship. "Exceedingly strange, this 'mighty handful,'" Piotr Ilyich wrote Modest. "They are constantly at me with mawkish tenderness — and that does not in the least correspond with their actions toward me." He was undoubtedly thinking of Cui, least mighty of the handful. The only complaint he could have against Rimsky-Korsakov was with regard to his use of *Snyegurochka* as an opera subject.

From the day of his arrival at Kamenka right after September 1, Piotr Ilyich worked on *Mazepa* steadily for eight months. His letters during the period seldom fail to contain some report on the opera's progress. Either he is finding the composing and arranging tiresome and slow or he is working at them feverishly. The inner buoyancy with which he had composed *Yevgeny Onyegin* and *The Maid of Orleans* is altogether lacking. His hopes for *Mazepa's* success are tinctured as though with foreknowledge of failure. The truth was that he had begun the opera halfheartedly and was writing it the same way, continuing only because the possibility of dropping it altogether did not occur to him — or, if it did, seemed to him an accusation of defeat.

On September 27 Piotr Ilyich wrote Jürgenson that he had completed the first draft of *Mazepa* and was embarking on its orchestration. In complete ignorance of the prolonged effort it would
cost him, he told Modest that the orchestration would be, not
labour, but pleasure. With the opera and six piano pieces behind him, he felt what he called "an extraordinary mental and
moral well-being that at once manifested itself in my physical appearance." He wrote Jürgenson that he would like to arrange a suite
from the music for *Swan Lake,* and asked that an orchestral score
and piano score of the ballet be sent him. Unfortunately, he never
carried out this project: the suites now played are the work of others and customarily omit much of the ballet's most attractive music.
Only for *The Nutcracker* did Piotr Ilyich himself arrange a suite
from one of his ballets.

Balakirev, emerging from his mystic withdrawal, wrote Piotr
Ilyich that he had in mind a program that would serve excellently
as the basis for a new Tchaikovsky symphony. It was conceived
about the semi-mythical figure of Manfred, and had been offered
Berlioz during his visit to Russia in 1868. After examining it, Piotr
Ilyich wrote Balakirev that it left him utterly cold: "If the heart
and imagination aren't set afire, it is scarcely worth while to start
a composition." However, the idea sank into his mind to germinate,
coming to the surface three years later to produce the huge *Manfred* Symphony, opus 58.

On October 30, at the season's opening chamber-music concert
of the Moscow Russian Musical Society, the Trio received its first
public performance. It was played, as the composer had desired,
by Taneyev, Grzhimali, and Fitzenhagen. A few days later Piotr
Ilyich received a copy of the Trio, which had been sumptuously
published. This gave him great pleasure, and he told Jürgenson
that not one of his other compositions had been so perfectly
printed.

The audience ungrudgingly gave the Trio a tribute of sincere
and prolonged approval. The critics mingled unwilling praise with
captious and niggling attack. Taneyev and Jürgenson, however,
were enthusiastic over the public's reaction, which clearly required
a repetition in the immediate future. The Trio became, in Russia,
and has remained, the most popular of Piotr Ilyich's chamber
works. Its great length has sometimes operated against its performance. But its combination of rich abundance in musical ideas with

brilliant execution and firm sincerity has endeared it to performing musicians and listeners alike. In view of the composer's original dislike of the combined timbres of piano, violin, and cello, its successful achievement approaches the miraculous. On its own plane it is one of his most consistently structural compositions, giving, as not many of his long works do, the satisfaction of architectonic solidity.[5]

Taneyev wrote, asking that Piotr Ilyich send the libretto of *The Voivode* to young Anton Stepanovich Arensky, who might compose an opera to it. "Since you have destroyed this opera, and will probably never recompose it, you will, I think, have nothing against his using this libretto." Piotr Ilyich quickly answered that the libretto could be obtained from the Jürgenson office. "How happy I am that from now on I completely cease to be the author of *The Voivode*. Memories of this opera, and also of *The Oprichnik*, are like memories of some capital crimes I committed."

Tatyana Davidova, Piotr Ilyich's niece, was at this time a sore problem to her family. Already, at twenty-one, a narcotic addict, she had become pregnant by her music teacher. In mid-November, when she heard that he intended to go to Moscow, she announced that she would go with him. This so upset him that he complained bitterly to Modest: "Not only can I not spend two days travelling with her, but even here, among many people, I feel positively sick as soon as she comes into the room."[6] He finally avoided her unwelcome company by pretending that he was leaving Kamenka only to go with Jürgenson to Prague, where there was in truth to be a revival of *The Maid of Orleans*.

On December 26 Piotr Ilyich arrived in St. Petersburg. He was unwell, attributing his sickness to "a combination of cold and nervous breakdown." He received a curious communication that brought him a voice from the long-dead past when he had been a child of five in Votkinsk. A Mme Longinova wrote to say that she had before her marriage been Marya Markovna Palchikova, his first music teacher. She needed money and asked him for help. He wrote to Jürgenson that he owed her a great deal, and instructed the publisher to send her fifty rubles.

[5] In an orchestral arrangement the Trio has been used for one of Massine's "symphonic" ballets, *Aleko*.
[6] Tatyana's illegitimate child, a boy later adopted by her brother Nikolai Ilyich, was born in Paris while Piotr Ilyich and Modest were there, on April 26, 1883.

Piotr Ilyich left on January 9, 1883 on what had become his annual winter trip to western Europe. Bogged down in the orchestration of *Mazepa,* and put on guard by Napravnik's criticisms of passages he had examined, Piotr Ilyich had sent the libretto to the conductor. If there were to be changes or contractions, he said, let Napravnik indicate them at once. As for him, he would not begin to orchestrate the second act until he had received Napravnik's judgment. In Berlin he heard his first *Tristan und Isolde,* and the thoughts and reactions it stirred up in him went entire into a letter to Nadezhda Filaretovna:

The work gives me no pleasure, though I am glad to have heard it, for it has greatly enforced my early opinions of Wagner, which — until I had seen performances of all his works — might not, I sensed, be well grounded. In brief, this is my opinion: despite his large creative gifts, despite his poetic talents and his wide culture, Wagner's contributions to art — and in particular to opera — have been only of a negative kind. He has proved that the older forms of opera lack every logical and æsthetic *raison d'être.* But if we may no longer compose opera on the old models, must we compose as Wagner does? I answer with an emphatic no. To compel people to listen for hours at a stretch to an unending symphony which, however rich in orchestral colour, lacks clarity and directness of thought; to keep singers all these hours singing melodies that have no autonomous existence, but are merely notes belonging to the symphony (in spite of lying very high, these notes are often drowned in the orchestral thunder), this is certainly not the ideal at which modern musicians should aim. Wagner has moved the centre of gravity from the stage to the orchestra, which is an obvious absurdity, and for that reason his much talked-of operatic reform — if viewed separately from its negative accomplishments — comes to nothing. With regard to the dramatic interest of his operas, I find them poor, frequently naïve to childishness. But I have never been quite so bored as by Tristan und Isolde. It is the most tedious and emptily spun-out tale, without motion, without life, utterly incapable of holding the spectator or of calling forth any emotional feeling for the protagonists. It was clear that the audience, even though German, was bored. But they applauded loudly after each act. How can one explain this? Perhaps by patriotic feeling for the composer, who actually devoted his entire life to hymning the praise of Germanism.

Hardly had Piotr Ilyich reached Paris before he began indulging himself in performance after performance of *Le Nozze di Figaro* at the Opéra-Comique, where the wife of Léon Carvalho, its manager

— Marie Miolan-Carvalho, still a great soprano at fifty-six — was singing the Countess. Between January 16 and the middle of April he heard Mozart's comic masterpiece seven or eight times, always with a mixed feeling of rapture and adoration. After the first performance he was so refreshed and stimulated that he worked at his desk six hours a day for two days running. For diversion he went to the theatre, seeing Alfred de Musset's *On ne badine pas avec l'amour* and Sardou's *Fédora*. The latter, with Sarah Bernhardt playing "like an arch-genius," seemed to him full of lies about Russia and Russian customs.

"I have just come from the Opéra-Comique," Piotr Ilyich wrote Nadezhda Filaretovna on January 23, "where I heard Le Nozze di Figaro. I should go every time it is performed. I know that my worship of Mozart astonishes you, dear friend. I, too, am often amazed that a broken man like myself, sound neither in mind nor in spirit, should still be able to enjoy Mozart, who possesses neither the profundity and force of Beethoven, the warmth and passion of Schumann, nor the brilliance of Meyerbeer, Berlioz, Wagner, etc. . . . . Mozart is not oppressive or agitating. He captivates, delights, and warms me. To hear his music is to feel that one has done a good deed. It is hard to say exactly wherein this good influence lies, but it is unquestionably beneficial. The older I become, and the better I know him, the more I love his music."

In February, when he had completed the hackwork connected with arranging the "Slavsya" chorus from *A Life for the Tsar* so that it could be sung in the open air by 7,500 Moscow students, Piotr Ilyich sent the manuscript to Jürgenson with a comic bill attached. The publisher had told him that the city of Moscow would pay him for the work. "For simplifying sixteen measures of choral and instrumental music, to be repeated thrice, three rubles; for the composition of eight connecting measures, four rubles; for four additional lines to the third verse, at forty kopecks a line, one ruble and sixty kopecks. Total, eight rubles, sixty kopecks. This sum I present to the city of Moscow," he concluded. "Jokes aside, it is ridiculous to talk of payment for such a job, and to me, most unpleasant. These things should be done for nothing or not at all."

The pitiable figure of Antonina Ivanovna was not altogether out of Piotr Ilyich's mind, for on March 12 he wrote Jürgenson that he was worrying about her. If she was in need, he said, the publisher was to give her money. News arrived that the seventy-year-old Wagner had died in Venice. The three outstanding Parisian conductors — Colonne, Lamoureux, and Pasdeloup — devoted entire Sunday concerts to his works. "It is necessary to die in order to attract their attention," Piotr Ilyich remarked to Nadezhda Filaretovna. He well knew the history of Paris's treatment of Wagner in the past and himself in the present. He turned doggedly back to the glacially slow work on *Mazepa.*

On March 20 Piotr Ilyich received the official order to compose, to a Maikov text called *Moscow,* a cantata for the coronation. He began making notes that same day. The municipality of Moscow, too, asked him to compose a march for a celebration to be staged in Sokolniki Park in honour of the Tsar. This commission, too, he accepted, beginning work on both occasional pieces on March 21. This meant that he could not go to Italy. "I shall have to spend about six weeks working to exhaustion, go through sleepless nights, and tire myself out completely," he wrote Nadezhda Filaretovna. But his finances were, as always, straitened, and while he would accept no remuneration for the *Coronation March,* he was to be handsomely rewarded for *Moscow.*

Welcome news arrived from Jürgenson. The Paris publishing house of Namelle had asked for the French rights to the Trio. Expecting instantaneous refusal, Jürgenson set the price at 1,000 francs. Namelle accepted, asking only that the *Melancholy Serenade,* the Violin Concerto, the Waltz-Scherzo, opus 34, and Balakirev's *Islamey* likewise be sold to them. That Paris, in which his music had won real appreciation only under Nikolay Rubinstein's baton, should pay well for his music was joyful news to Piotr Ilyich.

Ten years after Piotr Ilyich had composed the *Six Pieces on One Theme,* opus 21, and dedicated them to Anton Rubinstein, that moody and unpredictable pianist played them at his St. Petersburg concert of April 16. This performance created a demand for the sheet music, and Jürgenson was nettled because Bessel, who had published it, was reaping the reward. "You reproach me because the pieces Rubinstein played belong to Bessel," Piotr Ilyich wrote him. "I'm very regretful, but I must say, in self-justification, that if I had had any suspicion twelve years ago [7] that it would in the least be a deprivation for you not to own anything by me, I should under

---

[7] The date of Bessel's publication of *The Oprichnik* was evidently unclear in Tchaikovsky's memory. The contract had not been signed twelve years before, as it is dated June 8, 1872.

no condition have been faithless to you. . . . At that time I had no idea that I could hurt you by going to Bessel. Now I would give anything to get the pieces back again." At the end of the letter he added: "What a curious man, this Anton Rubinstein! He could pay no attention to my piano compositions ten years ago. Would he perform a single note of mine then? What a service that would have been! I am nevertheless grateful to him even now, but the difference is great."

The evening before Modest's departure from Paris, Piotr Ilyich went with him to the Opéra-Comique to hear *Lakmé*. Then, alone in the city, he spent his days on *Mazepa,* many of his evenings in theatres, until on April 28 he told Modest that the full score of the new opera was complete, the piano score begun. On that day, too, his shrunken pocketbook was fattened by the receipt of 2,500 francs from Jürgenson. A disturbing telegram from Moscow informed him that the authorities there had not received the score of *Moscow.* Too upset by this appalling news — he had sent off the full score some time before, and the recomposition of the cantata was unthinkable even if it were not too late — he could not work. He found some surcease from agitation in reading Maupassant, a writer who enchanted him. The very next day, however, a second telegram brought the welcome news that the missing cantata had been located.

Piotr Ilyich left Paris on May 22. Two days later, from Berlin, he wrote Nadezhda Filaretovna that the German capital seemed to him, after Paris, to be like a desert, "as if I had left a capital for some backwoods province." Lingering just long enough for a performance of *Lohengrin,* which he continued to consider Wagner's masterpiece, he arrived in St. Petersburg on May 27.

XIII

PIOTR ILYICH evidently was not present at the Granovi-
taya Palace when Napravnik conducted *Moscow:* more
than a week later he wrote Nadezhda Filaretovna that
he had been told it had been sung admirably and had
won Alexander III's approval. He likewise avoided the
June 4 Moscow performance of his *Coronation March,* included in
the celebrations there. At the beginning of July, however, he was
to receive a tangible token of imperial approval when the coronation committee notified him of an order by the Tsar that a gift
of 1,500 rubles be given him for the cantata and the march.

By July 9 he was at work again, writing Nadezhda Filaretovna
that he was occupied in correcting proofs of *Mazepa* and in composing a new suite for orchestra. This was to be his Suite No. 2,
opus 55.

But the interminable task of proofreading *Mazepa* interfered
with his resolution to compose a suite "at all costs." When he had
been at work on the proofs for more than three weeks, he wrote
Modest that his distaste for the music of the opera was beyond
belief, a nightmare. He could not compose. He could not continue
his study of English. He could not, as he had planned, play over
those compositions of Mozart that were still unknown to him. He
had to go on grinding away at *Mazepa.* Already he was suffering
from insomnia. Then two blows fell at once. The Tsar's gift arrived and proved to be a diamond ring rather than money. It was
a large diamond, and he pawned it on August 6. Hardly had he
left the pawnbroker, however, when he lost both the pawn ticket
and the 375 rubles in cash. He returned to Podushkino in a sour
mood.

There he found a letter from Jürgenson including the information that he would be paid 1,000 rubles for *Mazepa.* This put him
into a black rage. He wrote Jürgenson that this was severe under-
payment for an opera on which he had lavished two years and
three months of perseverance. The momentary strain caused in

their composer-publisher relationship was added to by well-meaning friends who assured Piotr Ilyich that Jürgenson was taking advantage of him. It eased when the publisher immediately agreed to Piotr Ilyich's price of 2,400 rubles and added that he was very happy that the composer himself had named the sum. On August 24 Piotr Ilyich wrote Modest: "We have already seen each other several times, and our relations do not seem to have changed, but I cannot forget that he wanted to take advantage of my irresponsibility, and that I have never paid any attention to the advice of numerous people who told me that he was exploiting me." Despite undocumented and tendentious hints on the part of Soviet editors, there does not appear to be the smallest proof that Jürgenson ever had the slightest intention of underpaying or otherwise taking advantage of Piotr Ilyich.

On August 21 Piotr Ilyich had conferred with the directorate of the Moscow theatres about the mounting of *Mazepa*. The newly appointed director of the opera house, Ivan Alexandrovich Vsevolozhsky, was an intense admirer of his music, and the resulting change in the attitude toward him astonished the composer. He told Nadezhda Filaretovna that in the past he had begged to have his works performed, while now St. Petersburg and Moscow were clamouring for his new opera. The very next day he wrote her again to say that the madness of composing had so taken hold of him that he was devoting every available moment to the new suite, which he expected to finish quickly. The news in Moscow was good — *Mazepa* was enthusiastically accepted for performance. Someone cared for his music, after all, and he could put heart into more of it. The suite sped on. The proofs for *Mazepa* were completed and returned to Jürgenson. Not even a continuing bout with some undiagnosable fever could delay him.

Completing the orchestration of the Second Suite at Kamenka on or about October 22, and the four-hand transcription with Hubert's help on the 25th, Piotr Ilyich had been working an average of six hours a day. Nevertheless he had kept up the unending spate of his enormous correspondence. "Not without pleasure," he played over Rimsky-Korsakov's opera *May Night*, Serov's *Judith*, and *Carmen*, the last three times in what he described as "a fit of passion." From day to day he sent Anatoly, Modest, Nadezhda Filaretovna, and a half-dozen others detailed reports on the state of the new composition. As soon as he completed it, he sketchily reworked his First Symphony, which was to be revived in Moscow early in December.

Early in December, too, Piotr Ilyich played a piano version of the newly completed suite to a group of Moscow musicians and wrote Nadezhda Filaretovna that it "earned great praise." The next day was wholly flattering to his self-esteem. While in St. Petersburg, at the season's second Russian Musical Society concert, Auer was conducting the Second Symphony, the composer himself was at a Moscow concert of the Society at which, after fifteen years, his First Symphony was successfully reborn, with Erdmannsdörfer conducting. He was volubly called to the stage, where he found the audience's enthusiasm, as ever, both painful and flattering.

Mazepa was a three-act opera. Payment by the state theatres was calculated partly by the number of acts a work contained. So Piotr Ilyich requested that *Mazepa* be regarded as a four-act work. The theatre directors transmitted this report to the proper imperial minister, who refused the composer's request. When Piotr Ilyich heard of this refusal, he became intensely offended — in part because of the curt style of the official communication — and considered withdrawing the opera altogether. Friendly persuasion changed his mind, and he contented himself with writing the theatre directors a letter in which he protested the insulting rejection of his request. Just before the first Moscow performance took place, he received word that a second report to the minister had elicited permission to pay the ten per cent royalties he had originally requested.

Still another journey to St. Petersburg and back had to be made, this time for the marriage of Anna Lvovna Davidova to Nadezhda Filaretovna's son, Nikolay Karlovich von Meck, which took place on January 23. The groom's mother was absent. Napravnik urged Piotr Ilyich to remain for the rehearsals of *Mazepa*, but he refused. He felt more certain that his opera was safe under Napravnik's hand than that it would receive adequate attention in Moscow from Altani. So back to Moscow he went and was present at the first Bolshoi rehearsal. At the start everything about the production left him dubious and dissatisfied. In a few days, however, having discovered that the singers knew their parts and were zealous in taking direction, he began to feel better. He was especially pleased with the prima donna, Emilia Karlovna Pavlovskaya.

Word from G. P. Kondratyev that the Marinsky rehearsals were
at last about to begin also and that the composer's presence in St.
Petersburg was imperative failed to shake Piotr Ilyich's determination to keep close watch at the Bolshoi. Too, he was suffering
acutely from nervous fatigue, and could not face the prospect of
still another journey north.

From February 6 on, *Mazepa* was concurrently rehearsed in
St. Petersburg and Moscow. By then Piotr Ilyich was so wearied
by all the complex manœuvres needed that he began to suffer
from nightmarish obsessions that he was about to die. He swore
roundly that he would never compose another opera, "although
you must admit," he added in a letter to Nadezhda Filaretovna,
"that opera possesses the advantage of reaching the musical feelings of the *masses*, whereas the symphony appeals only to a smaller,
if more select, public. . . ."

The Bolshoi dress rehearsal, on February 13, did not dissatisfy
Piotr Ilyich from a musical point of view, but he found the stage
direction execrable. Modest, arriving in Moscow two days later,
found him fearful, nervous, and unwell. He was altogether down-
cast about *Mazepa*. He was intensely depressed because Alexey
Sofronov was still in military service and would therefore be unable to accompany him on his forthcoming trip abroad. That night,
however, February 15, while he "almost lost his mind from nervousness and fear," *Mazepa* appeared to triumph on the boards of
the Bolshoi. A brilliant audience recalled the quaking composer
numerous times and showered applause on its favourite singers.
Piotr Ilyich correctly sensed that this favour was for himself and
the performers. The opera, despite unprecedented magnificence
of scenery and costumes, was a failure. The next day, after thanking Pavlovskaya by letter for her "indescribably marvellous" rendition of the role of Marya, he left for western Europe. His
departure infuriated Erdmannsdörfer, who at almost the very moment the train pulled out was lifting his baton to conduct the
première of the Second Suite.

On February 19 the Marinsky *première* of *Mazepa* was received
with cold politeness by an audience disappointed that Piotr Ilyich
himself was absent. The critical reviews of the opera in both St.
Petersburg and Moscow were temperate and mixed. There can be
small doubt that had it been by another composer or had it been
less lavishly staged, it would have been damned out of hand. As

matters stood, it was a bare *succès d'estime*. Because of Piotr Il-yich's nervous condition, Modest and others tried, by letter and telegram, to make him believe that it had conquered. About all that was true in their glowing reports was that Alexander III had remained to the end of the Marinsky performance.

The Second Suite fared differently. Something like unanimous praise was its critical reception. The melodic inventiveness, youthful verve, and instrumental deftness that marked it were played up against the flaws of *Mazepa*. Consisting of five movements — *Play of Sounds*, Waltz, *Burlesque Scherzo*, *A Child's Dreams*, and *Baroque Dance in the Style of Dargomizhsky* — it is music with enormous surface attractions. Compounded of melodically rich materials, composed with care and distinction, it is music that should be heard often. By one of the meaningless vagaries of chance, however, it is never played at all. Its reappearance on concert programs would do something to dispel the altogether unfair legend that, especially in his later years, Piotr Ilyich was exclusively a poet of frustration and melancholy.

While the critics were weighing *Mazepa* and the Second Suite, Piotr Ilyich was tarrying in Berlin and Paris. In the German capital he was so sharply lonely that he could only with difficulty decide where to go next. From Paris he wrote Modest gratefully for the lies his friends had told him about the "grand success" of *Mazepa* in St. Petersburg: "But you did well to lie, for the *truth* would have been too heavy a blow had I not been prepared for it by various signs. Only yesterday I learned the worst in a letter from Jürgenson, who not only was cruel enough to blurt out the whole truth, but also reproached me for not having gone to Petersburg. It fell on me like a thunderbolt, and all day I suffered as though some dreadful catastrophe had taken place. Of course, I am exaggerating, but at my age, when one has nothing more to hope from the future, a small failure assumes the size of a shameful fiasco. Were I different, could I have forced myself to go to Petersburg, I should no doubt have returned crowned with laurels."

Nothing in Paris tended to calm Piotr Ilyich's nervous condition. He found Massenet's *Manon* "very graceful, very finished, but without one moving, enchanting, or gripping moment." Most of the plays bored him, though he derived some small release from the Comédie Française, particularly from Molière's *L'École des femmes*. Paris itself was a chill, damp, and windy city in the grip of Wagnerism. He decided to leave it, return to Kamenka, and compose a symphony. Then notice came that Alexander III planned to confer a decoration on him, and that he must be in St. Petersburg to receive it. Napravnik wrote also that choral rehearsals for the *Yevgeny Onyegin* authorized by the Tsar would start on March 11. There was nothing for Piotr Ilyich to do but crush back his tingling nerves as best he could and face the ordeal of an imperial audience. He travelled by way of Berlin and Vienna to Kamenka for a short respite and arrived in St. Petersburg on March 15.

On Saturday, March 17, Piotr Ilyich went to bed with a nervous chill. By dosing himself liberally with bromides, he recovered enough to appear at the Gatchina Palace on the following Monday. He had foreseen being presented only to the Tsar, but learned from a palace official that the Tsarina — the beautiful daughter of Christian IX of Denmark, for whose wedding he had, eighteen years earlier, composed his *Festival Overture on Danish Themes* — had expressed a wish to meet him. The Tsar received him in a calming and friendly way and conferred on him the Order of St. Vladimir of the Fourth Class. "I think it is necessary to look into the Tsar's eyes but once in order to remain for ever his most loyal adherent," Piotr Ilyich wrote Anatoly, "for it is hard to express in words all the charm and sympathy of his manner." Nevertheless, while being escorted to the apartment where Marya Fyodorovna awaited him — on its very doorsill, in fact — he had to take another bromide for fear that his nerves might give way completely, that he might even faint. He found the Tsarina "bewitching." Still his trial was not over. His old friend Grand Duke Konstantin Nikolayevich required his presence and invited him to sit in the imperial box two days later at a Conservatory rehearsal of *Die Zauberflöte*. At last the shattered composer was free to return to his room, describing himself as "tired, but satisfied with the reception."

To his pleased amazement, Piotr Ilyich began to encounter musicians and constant operagoers who had been delighted by *Mazepa*. Despite the opposition of much of the press, and despite the jealous envy of not a few musicians, many influential people in St. Petersburg were not only well disposed toward him, but enthusiastic about his operas. Nothing could have lifted his spirits more certainly or quickly. To find the Tsar leading what he called "the friendly section" was perhaps best of all. "It turns out that I have no right to complain," he wrote Nadezhda Filaretovna. "I ought, rather, to thank God, who has shown me such favour."

Piotr Ilyich had managed to read a manuscript copy of Lev Tolstoy's *Confessions*, which, despite having appeared in print, had been banned by the censor. "They made a deep impression on me," he told Nadezhda Filaretovna, "because I, too, know the torments of doubt and the tragic perplexity that Tolstoy has undergone and so well described in the Confessions. But *enlightenment* came to me sooner than to Tolstoy; perhaps because my mind is organized more simply than his, and perhaps because of my continual need to work I have suffered less than Tolstoy. Every day, every hour, I thank God for having given me this faith in Him. What would have become of me, with my cowardice, my capacity for depression, and — at the least lapse in courage — my desire for *nonexistence*, had I been unable to believe in God and submit to His will?"

This was Piotr Ilyich on an upswing from depression. Soon he was telling Nadezhda Filaretovna that he was full of energy and burning with impatience to begin a new composition. On March 28, too, he heard the welcome news that Alexey Sofronov had been released from military service and was ready to take up his former duties as manservant and irreplaceable factotum. Then not even a two-week bout with stomach trouble and an incessant sensation of fatigue could depress his spirits. He was able to perform the thousand small activities of daily life in comparative calm. The necessity to make still further revisions in *Mazepa* for additional St. Petersburg performances did not appear too hard.[1]

On April 24 Piotr Ilyich arrived at Kamenka. The next day he went to the Davidov house for tea. When his brother-in-law went out, he remained behind "to strum and to think of something new." He considered a third piano concerto, but realized that the musical idea that had come to him was poor and not new (it was eventually to be used in the Concert Fantasy for Piano and Orchestra,

---

[1] From late in the 1870's Tchaikovsky intermittently kept a diary, a sort of daybook in which he noted his activities and thoughts. In 1891, however, he burned most of the volumes of this record, leaving only some sections from April 1884 on. As 1884 saw some small diminution of his letter-writing — with the exception of communications to his family and to Mme von Meck — it is from this so-called diary that much of the information concerning his whereabouts and thoughts from 1884 has been derived.

opus 56). That day, too, he played over Massenet's *Hérodiade* and read part of Jahn's *Life of Mozart*. For two days more he dallied in unhappy desuetude, for which he was inclined to blame the presence of his friend of nearly twenty years before, Vera Vasil-yevna Davidova, now Mme Butakova. Then, on April 28, he noted in his diary that he had strolled in the garden and sowed the seeds of another orchestral suite. Thenceforward he was constantly jotting down musical ideas for it. "They are somewhat thin and unimportant," he wrote Modest. "I am, in general, passing through a period of doubt in my creative powers." Instead of labouring steadily and seriously at the new composition, he continued to study English "furiously." He had made up his mind, he told Nadezhda Filaretovna, to compose a suite rather than a symphony because the looser form offered him the freedom to discard traditional rules.

That financial matters were still bothering Piotr Ilyich is proved by his having requested a loan of 300 rubles from the Fund for the Aid of Musicians on May 6. On that same day, in a letter advising Jürgenson to issue a selected rather than a complete edition of his piano pieces, he asked the publisher to send him Balakirev's *Tamara* and a piano score of *Le Nozze di Figaro* "if it is a Jürgenson edition." His forty-fourth birthday found him going through one of his periodical summations of himself. The tally dissatisfied him. The chief decision he came to as a result was that the hour had arrived for him to live alone and as he liked, to have a house suited to him in which he would be his own master.

The Third Suite was to occupy Piotr Ilyich off and on until July 31. During the first part of May he noted in his diary: "Played four hands with my little darling, the incomparable, wonderful, ideal Bobyk." Bobyk was the family nickname for Vladimir Lvovich Davidov, his young nephew, of whom he grew increasingly fond. No records survive to show whether or not Bobyk manifested so early the morbid streak that was at last to drive him to suicide. Certainly some community of feeling existed between him and his famous uncle from the time he was a child. "Bobyk, the suite, and English" were "the three ornaments" that made life in Kamenka bearable.

Kamenka, Braïlov, Simaki, Nizi, Grankino, Glebovo — none was Piotr Ilyich's own home. From early in 1884 on he was constantly looking for a piece of country property that he might be able to buy or rent, where he could set himself up to compose as he liked, his comfort watched over by Alexey Sofronov. He would ask Modest to examine a small property of which he had heard. Or he would himself go to inspect one. Nothing definite resulted immediately, but the prospect obsessed him. "I want no land," he told Nadezhda Filaretovna, "but only a small house with a pretty garden, *not too new*. A *stream* is most desirable. Proximity to a forest would be an attraction. The house must stand by itself, not in a row of country villas, and — most important of all — must be within easy reach of a station, so that I can get to Moscow at any time. I can't afford more than two or three thousand rubles."

On May 29 Piotr Ilyich played over some Mozart. As always, it soothed and fascinated him. In his diary he wrote the phrase: "An idea for a suite from Mozart." This was to mature, nearly four years later, in the last of his orchestral suites, *Mozartiana*, opus 61. He noted that he could read English with considerable ease, but still could understand nothing when Miss Eastwood, governess to the younger Davidov children, spoke that language. He wrote Jürgenson that he was making selections for the forthcoming edition of his piano pieces, and also that he was dedicating the Third Suite to Erdmannsdörfer "to pacify him . . . for my flight from Moscow."

Mme Butakova continued to trouble Piotr Ilyich. She constantly harked back to the past with evident regret. "But everything that she recalls is obnoxious to me, and I would not wish its return," he noted in his diary. Another time he surmised that she had not in two decades changed her feelings toward him. He read with Bobyk, and when Modest invited him to Grankino, he wrote in his diary: "Strange — I am terribly unwilling to leave here. I think it is Bobyk." By June 23, nevertheless, he was at Grankino. From there he jocularly informed Jürgenson on July 2: "A work of greater genius than my new suite never was!!! My opinion of a newborn composition is always confidently optimistic!" He wrote Nadezhda Filaretovna that it would be difficult to find a pianist to replace Nikolay Rubinstein in performing his pieces. There was a young man named D'Albert, however, who seemed to him "a pianist of genius, Rubinstein's legitimate successor." Taneyev would do "if only he had that vein of virtuosity in which resides the secret of the magic spell that great interpreters exercise over the public."

The ailing Laroche used Piotr Ilyich as amanuensis, dictating to him a long article on Mozart, a subject so sympathetic to him that the composer found the task entirely pleasurable. He was at first apprehensive and then horror-struck to find Laroche's talent and imagination grown slightly dim. But he wrote Nadezhda Filaretovna that Laroche, despite this deterioration, could still write about music better than anyone else in Russia. He and Laroche had fallen into the habit of reading Maupassant aloud after supper. As the time came for Piotr Ilyich to return to Kamenka, he more and more disliked the prospect of having again to mingle with so many people. He asked Nadezhda Filaretovna to let him spend some time at Pleshcheyevo, the smaller estate with which she had replaced Braïlov. She eagerly agreed, and all arrangements were completed at once. He arrived at Pleshcheyevo on September 15, settling down there to complete the Concert Fantasy.

During his first five days at Pleshcheyevo, Piotr Ilyich made acquaintance at the piano with *Khovanshchina* and *Parsifal*. In the former he found "pretensions to realism, oddly understood and adapted, pitiful technique, poverty of imagination, some talented episodes here and there, but in a sea of harmonic incoherence and mannerisms peculiar to the musical circle of which Mussorgsky was [2] a member."

Parsifal [he continued to Nadezhda Filaretovna] leaves exactly the opposite impression. Here we are dealing with a great master, a genius, even if one gone somewhat astray. So luxuriant, so enormous, is his wealth of harmony that it finally tires even a specialist. What, then, must be the feelings of an ordinary mortal who has struggled for three hours with this flow of complex harmonic combinations? . . . If the singer may not *sing*, but — amid the deafening roar of the orchestra — is expected to declaim a series of set and colourless phrases to the accompaniment of a gorgeous, but disjunctive and amorphous symphony, is that opera? What astonishes me, however, is the solemnity with which this philosophizing German set the most inane subject to music. Who can be moved, for example, by *Parsifal*, in which, rather than men and women like ourselves in temperament and emotion, we find legendary beings who might do in a ballet, but not in a music drama? I can't comprehend how anyone can listen without laughing or being bored to those unending monologues in which Parsifal, Kundry, and the rest complain of their misfortunes. Can we sympathize with them?

[2] Mussorgsky had died in St. Petersburg on March 28, 1881, leaving both *Khovanshchina* and *The Fair at Sorochinsk* incomplete.

Can we love or hate them? Certainly not. We remain unmoved by their
passions, emotions, triumphs, and misfortunes. That which is unfamiliar
to the human heart should never be the source of musical inspiration.

At the Bolshoi on October 31, under Napravnik's experienced
conductorship, *Yevgeny Onyegin* had its first professional St.
Petersburg performance. The singers gave excellent account of
themselves, and Pavlovskaya in particular acted with fire. Piotr
Ilyich, in the audience, saw the first scene received with mingled
applause and hisses. The second and third scenes began the triumph. The scene of the ball in Larina's house (containing the renowned Waltz) was an unqualified and noisily received success.
Many times Piotr Ilyich was clamorously summoned to the stage.
Finally he was presented with a wreath of laurel. The excitement
became so intense that he had a severe attack of nerves while
still in the theatre. It may be that he mistook the reception he and
the singers were given for the sort of personal tribute he had experienced before. But this time the enthusiasm was for the opera
itself. The night of October 31, 1884 marked the permanent estab-
lishment of *Yevgeny Onyegin* in the active repertoire of Russian
theatres, from which it has never fallen and in which it continues
today to hold first place in esteem and popularity.

After a visit to Kotek, who was dying of tuberculosis in Switzerland, Piotr Ilyich returned to St. Petersburg, arriving there on
December 19. Three days after his return he attended the twelfth
consecutive Bolshoi performance of *Yevgeny Onyegin*. The next
day, while at the Alexandrinsky Theatre he attended the *première*
of Modest's play *Lizaveta Nikolayevna*, St. Petersburg was hearing
its seventeenth performance of *The Maid of Orleans*, which G. P.
Kondratyev described succinctly in his diary by the words: "Many
calls, little intake." Rimsky-Korsakov, who late in November had
conducted a St. Petersburg repetition of the First Piano Concerto,
gave Piotr Ilyich a copy of his *Textbook of Harmony* inscribed:
"To the dearest and kindest Piotr Ilyich Tchaikovsky from the
compiler, with the request to examine and discuss this book with
its compiler, N. R. Korsakov, December 26, 1884." Three days later,
having done little but hear *Yevgeny Onyegin* and *La Traviata* and
see Modest's play launched, Piotr Ilyich was in Moscow.

Hans von Bülow, his fame as conductor of the Meiningen Orchestra now larger than his renown as a pianist, was visiting Russia. His passion for Russian music, and for Piotr Ilyich's in par-

ticular, was at flood. He called on the composer and played for him, writing to his wife on January 6, 1885: "Tchaikovsky was much moved when I played his compositions for him, and said: 'You transmit my thoughts magnificently.'" When Bülow announced his eagerness to conduct the *première* of the Third Suite, Piotr Ilyich joyfully agreed. His contentment over the way things were proceeding was ruptured by word from Davos that Kotek had died there on January 4. Before leaving Davos, Piotr Ilyich had had a confidential interview with Kotek's physician, who had assured him that the patient's condition, though grave, was not necessarily fatal. Piotr Ilyich had made a financial arrangement to assure Kotek comfort and peace of mind. Now he was saddened by Kotek's death, but relieved and grateful that he had visited Davos.

Discovering that little had been done to put the score of the Third Suite in performable condition, Piotr Ilyich fumed and raged and then settled down in Moscow to correct both score and parts. He would much have preferred to be in St. Petersburg on January 10 when Bülow conducted the *Slavic March*. Instead he had to remain shut up for days at a time working on the proofs "with fury, rancour, and strain." He barely had time to agree to a request from the St. Petersburg Slavonic Welfare Society that he compose something in honour of the millennial of St. Mefodyi. When he had a free hour or two, he inserted an advertisement in *Politseiskiye Vyedomosti* for a summer house to rent, wrote Nadezhda Filaretovna that all his thoughts were directed toward finding a permanent country abode, and told Modest that work on the proofs of the Third Suite had at least prevented him from brooding over Kotek's death.

Free at last, Piotr Ilyich took a train to St. Petersburg and rushed directly from the station to a rehearsal of the Third Suite. Its *première*, on January 24, with Bülow conducting, was described by Modest as a veritable triumph for his brother. "Never before had any of his works been received with enthusiasm so unanimous. This was undoubtedly due partly to the admirable way in which it was interpreted." Piotr Ilyich himself reported the success to Nadezhda Filaretovna: "I could see that the entire audience was moved and grateful to me. Such moments are the finest ornaments of an artist's life. For their sake it is worth living and labouring." Critics matched the audience's enthusiasm, hailing the Third Suite as a masterpiece in small. Concertgoers of today, if they know the suite at all, know only its last movement, a sombre, malleable theme in G major and twelve variations, the last a brilliant polacca. Each of its first three movements — *Elegy, Melancholy Waltz,* and *Scherzo* — contains music of spontaneous charm and deft lightness. The entirety is not so long but that it would amply repay revival. Music of no great depth and no pretension, this finest of Piotr Ilyich's four orchestral suites deserves to be heard.

On January 28, at the Bolshoi, the fifteenth consecutive performance of *Yevgeny Onyegin* was signalized by the presence of Alexander III, Marya Fyodorovna, and members of their family. The Tsar summoned the composer to his box and engaged him in lengthy conversation. He asked numerous questions about Piotr Ilyich's life and work and then conducted him to the Tsarina. She, in turn, paid the composer what he described as "the most touching attention." When the imperial party had left, Vsevolozhsky told Piotr Ilyich that the Tsar had granted permission for him to use Pushkin's *The Captain's Daughter* as an opera subject if he wished. This was a remarkable sign of favour for the reason that the Pushkin work deals with the celebrated Pugachev rebellion against Peter the Great. Piotr Ilyich never took advantage of it.

Piotr Ilyich and Modest left St. Petersburg on January 29. In Moscow, Modest spoke of *The Enchantress,* a play by I. V. Shpazhinsky that he thought suitable for operatic treatment. Piotr Ilyich at once bought an illustrated edition of the play and read one scene — the meeting of Kuma and Knyazhich — that Modest had described. This inflamed him with immediate desire to compose and at once settled the question of his next opera. Bülow was to visit Moscow, and Piotr Ilyich asked the authorities to put *Mazepa* on the bill for February 2 so that the German, who was to leave on the 3rd, could hear it. On January 31, Moscow heard the Third Suite. Erdmannsdörfer's interpretation was described by Modest as lacking "the inspiration by means of which Hans von Bülow had electrified his audience," but the new composition was well received none the less. On the same program Bülow performed the solo part in the Concerto in B flat minor to Piotr Ilyich's entire satisfaction and the audience's vocal delight.

Piotr Ilyich invited Shpazhinsky to write for him a libretto based on *The Enchantress,* and the dramatist answered by letter that there was no one with whom he would prefer to collaborate. Piotr Ilyich called on him, and they held several long conferences with

regard to the libretto. Then Piotr Ilyich began in earnest his search
for a suitable country house. One he examined belied what he had
been told of it, and this so discouraged him that he momentarily
decided to give up the search, go abroad, and take up the revision
of *Vakula the Smith*. Moscow life, he wrote Nadezhda Filaretovna,
was insupportable. It wearied him, allowed him no time to compose. His days were overfull of visitors. Then he heard of a furnished house for rent at Maidanovo, a village on the Sestra River
not far from Klin, and sent Alexey Sofronov to look at it and, if it
met with his approval, to rent it for one year.

Negotiations with the owner of the Maidanovo house — he was
to pay 1,000 rubles rent per annum — were completed on February
17. They settled the question of the neighbourhood in which for
the rest of his life Piotr Ilyich would live while in Russia. Part way
from Moscow to St. Petersburg, the Klin district had the landscape
he particularly loved, fields and forests, villages and streams. It is
close to Moscow, and St. Petersburg is easy of access from it. For
Piotr Ilyich's taste it was somewhat spoiled by numerous country
villas of recent construction, but the charm of its scenery and the
handiness of its location were enough. He accepted Alexey Sofronov's word as to the beauty and luxuriousness of the furnishings
of the house he had rented, and worried only about heating its several rooms in winter. When he first entered the house, he was
sharply disappointed, feeling that the very things Alexey had considered comfortable and even splendid were grotesque and in bad
taste. It would do, however. The pleasure of having a home of his
own was deep, and there was a fine view of woodland from the
windows. He met the cook, the houseman, and the laundress Alexey
had hired. That whole day, he wrote Modest, was passed in "a
very pleasant state of mind."

Before visiting Maidanovo for the first time, Piotr Ilyich had
had to go to St. Petersburg. He had been unanimously elected a
director of the Moscow Russian Musical Society, a responsible
honour he accepted with little reluctance — and so had to visit
Moscow too. Also, rehearsals for the first performance of the Concert Fantasy, with Taneyev as soloist, had begun under Erdmannsdörfer. The first musical work Piotr Ilyich initiated at Maidanovo
was the revision of *Vakula the Smith*. When, on February 29, he
received a letter from Jürgenson suggesting that he compose a
hymn for four voices in honour of Saints Mefodyi and Kyrilla, he

answered: "What hymn? What for? Who needs it? However, I
shall be in Moscow Thursday and will talk to you." He had forgotten his promise to the Slavonic Welfare Society.

Writing to Pavlovskaya on March 4, Piotr Ilyich commented on
his revision of *Vakula the Smith:* "I have composed some completely new scenes; all that was bad I threw out. What is good, I
have left, lightening the massiveness and weightiness of the harmonies — in a word, I have done whatever is necessary to save the
opera from the oblivion . . . it has not deserved." He was ready
to orchestrate the new scenes. Two days later he was present at
the *première* of his Concert Fantasy. Moscow received it with
more show of enthusiasm than it had granted the Third Suite, but
Modest saw that the applause was for Taneyev, who gave a superb
performance of the taxing and ungrateful solo part. Nowhere at
any time has the Concert Fantasy had more than a flash of success.
It is difficult, involved, and vacant, and the solo part resembles an
obstacle race in futilities. Its revival, unlike that of the Second
Piano Concerto, could not be justified except on historical grounds.

On March 16 Piotr Ilyich asked Modest to devise a new title for
Vakula the Smith. "I don't want Vakula the Smith or Christmas
Eve ³ or The Tsaritsa's Shoes — I need something different. . . .
The work isn't going very rapidly, but how satisfied I am with it!
How pleasant to think that my Vakula is rising from the river of
oblivion!" When Jürgenson sent him a Czech hymn in honour of
Saints Kyrilla and Mefodyi, Piotr Ilyich used it as a model, and
himself worked out a Russian text for his own setting. "I struggled
some six hours over the verses. The rhymes are all right, but without the music they are precisely verses and nothing more." His
chief efforts during the latter half of March and the beginning of
April were toward completing the revision of *Vakula the Smith,*
which he finally decided to rename *Cherevichki,* indicating a type
of high-heeled boots worn by Ukrainian women.⁴ On April 4 the
revision stood complete. After spending Easter week in Moscow
"not very gaily," Piotr Ilyich went to St. Petersburg to obtain from
Polonsky, author of the original libretto, permission to publish the
opera in its new form.

³ Title of the Gogol story and of the opera (1894–5) Rimsky-Korsakov based
on it.
⁴ In its revised form this opera has also come to be known as *Oksana's Caprices,* Oksana being the heroine's name.

At the request of Alexander III, Piotr Ilyich composed several a cappella church songs, eventually published as parts of the *Nine Liturgical Choruses*. In the midst of completing them he found it "pleasant to devote a whole day to leisure, drinking, and idleness," when Jürgenson, Kashkin, and Laroche dropped in at Maidanovo. About one week later he went into Moscow to discuss the mounting of *Cherevichki* with the opera directorate. "The Cherevichki affair was settled beautifully," he informed Nadezhda Filaretovna. "The charming Vsevolozhsky answered the hesitations of the local directors by ordering that Cherevichki be staged with the greatest splendour. I was there at the meeting over which he presided, and at which the mounting was discussed. Valts (the scenic designer) is being sent to Tsarskoye Selo so that he can faithfully reproduce the amber drawing-room and a special palace hall. I am very pleased." While in Moscow, Piotr Ilyich likewise attended a meeting of the Russian Musical Society directorate. The St. Petersburg branch notified him that 260 rubles due him (he received 310 from the Moscow branch) for performances of his works during the 1884–5 season had, at his request, been turned over to the Society for the Aid of Musicians. He celebrated his forty-fifth birthday with a dinner at Anatoly's, later in the evening being honoured at a Conservatory supper. The St. Petersburg opera season closed on May 12 with the twenty-second consecutive performance of *Yevgeny Onyegin*. G. P. Kondratyev, who had commented in his diary on each performance, noted: "A full house as always."

As a director of the Moscow Conservatory, Piotr Ilyich had to attend the annual examinations late in May. He took constant interest in the institution's work and fortunes and regarded his position as a serious trust. He was pleased that, despite Nikolay Rubinstein's death, the Conservatory continued its excellent work, thus fulfilling a real need. He breathed a sigh of relieved tension that he had not agreed to become its head. Soon he decided that the hour for appointing someone had arrived. Lacking Rimsky-Korsakov, he felt that Taneyev would be the best choice. So ardently did he then champion Taneyev's cause that he threatened to resign from the directorate if another man were chosen. His insistence carried the day. "I spent three whole weeks at the Conservatory examinations," he told his cousin Anna Petrovna Merkling, "learned its true condition and needs, and accomplished a complete reorganization — that is, raised Taneyev to the position of director."

On June 13 Piotr Ilyich returned to Maidanovo "with the pleasant consciousness of having performed my duty, and confident that I have benefited the Conservatory." He told Nadezhda Filaretovna that he had decided to return as a professor so as to support Taneyev. Learning that the rules prevented him from acting simultaneously as professor and member of the directorate, he asked Taneyev to decide in which position he would be more valuable. Taneyev agreed wholeheartedly with Piotr Ilyich's implied belief that he would serve better as a director.

Piotr Ilyich had begun haphazardly to sketch ideas for *Manfred* on odd pieces of paper and correspondence late in April. Now he turned to the composition in earnest. He had no urgent wish in the matter at first, but felt that, having carelessly promised Balakirev to compose it, he would have no peace before it was done. Soon, however, he was writing Nadezhda Filaretovna that he had become so absorbed in it that he could not start *The Enchantress* for a very long time. The necessity of reading proofs on *Cherevichki* interrupted him, but he pressed ahead with *Manfred* until early in October. As the expiration of his one-year lease on the Maidanovo house drew near, he made inquiries about a more attractive country place. Through Nadezhda Filaretovna he asked Pakhulsky to find out if there was a house in Dubrovitsy, near Podolsk, "with a separate garden, a pretty view, suitable for winter residence." He visited the village of Koshelevo, later describing it to Taneyev as "a very solitary, charming corner." In the end he came to an agreement with his landlady and stayed on at Maidanovo.

Late in July, at the request of the other directors, Piotr Ilyich invited Vasily Ilyich Safonov, then teaching at the St. Petersburg Conservatory, to join the Moscow Conservatory staff. Safonov, in later years conductor of the New York Philharmonic and the New York National Conservatory, accepted the bid, remarking that it touched and excited him especially because it came from Tchaikovsky. He remained on the teaching staff throughout Taneyev's directorship, and in 1889 succeeded the younger man as chief of the Conservatory. He became renowned as one of the ablest propagandists of Russian music, and in particular that of Tchaikovsky.

"The symphony [*Manfred*] has turned out to be huge, serious, and difficult," Piotr Ilyich wrote Pavlovskaya on August 1. "It absorbs all my time, sometimes wearing me out completely. But an inner voice tells me that my labour is not in vain and that this composition will perhaps turn out to be my best symphony." On the manuscript, on August 12, he wrote: "And today is the 12th of August, and oh, how far away the end still is!" He felt gloomy, he wrote Nadezhda Filaretovna, for the work on *Manfred* was changing him into a Manfred too. "Terribly, incredibly tired," he stole two days away from his desk to go to Pleshcheyevo with Modest and Anatoly for a brief vacation. A week later he complained that he had been feeling sick, nervous, and irritable. "I ascribe this to my work, which is exceedingly wearing. Nothing has ever been so difficult for me or has cost me so much effort as the symphony I am now composing." When only a few details of orchestration were missing from *Manfred*, Piotr Ilyich turned at once — "without delaying an hour," he told Pavlovskaya — to *The Enchantress*. "Ah, what a man that Shpazhinsky is, and what a fine collaborator fate sent me in him!" he added. "The first act, the only one I have at present, is superb, full of fire and action." He could not work at the new opera without interruption, for four days after the letter to Pavlovskaya he was writing Anna Merkling: "I am finishing the labour to which I have devoted the entire summer. . . . [It] cost me inexpressible exertion and effort, for the task was very complex. . . . Under the influence of the gloomy Manfred, I was nervous and full of spleen all summer long." Only on October 4 did he put the last touch on the huge four-movement symphony.

Some days of absence from his desk were absolutely necessary. Wanting something to read, he accidentally picked up Zola's *Germinal*. He began it, became fascinated, and reached the last page late at night. "I was so upset by it that my heart began to palpitate, which kept me awake, and the following day I was completely sick. And now I think of this novel as some horrible nightmare," he told Modest.

On October 9 Piotr Ilyich wrote Nadezhda Filaretovna that he had completed Act I of *The Enchantress*. Continuing a discussion of several years' standing with regard to the comparative values of opera and instrumental music, he said:

You are quite correct in regarding this insincere form of art [opera] with suspicion. But for a composer opera has an irresistible attraction. It alone . . . offers him a way to get in touch with the masses. My Manfred will be played once or twice, and will then disappear for a long time; with the exception of the few connoisseurs who attend symphony concerts, no one will know it. Opera, on the other hand — and only opera — brings us closer to our fellow men, inoculates the public with our music, and makes it the possession, not of a small circle only, but — circumstances being favourable — of all peoples. I do not think that this tendency is to be condemned; that is, Schumann, when he composed *Genoveva*, and Beethoven, when he composed *Fidelio*, were not actuated by ambition, but by a natural wish to enlarge the circle of their hearers and to penetrate as far as possible into the heart of humanity.

Nadezhda Filaretovna was not to be convinced of this any more than of Mozart's greatness. She insisted on the exalted character of symphonic and chamber music and the vulgarity of opera. On October 23 Piotr Ilyich returned to the attack:

As regards the lofty significance of symphonic and chamber music when compared with opera, let me add only that to abstain from composing operas is the work of a hero, and we have only one such hero in our time — Brahms. Cui has justly remarked in a recent article that Brahms, both as man and as artist, has followed only the highest ideals — those worthy of respect and admiration. Unfortunately, his creative gift is thin and does not correspond to his lofty aspirations. Nevertheless, he is a hero. This heroism is not in me, for the stage and all its glitter beckons me irresistibly.

On December 21 Piotr Ilyich wrote Modest that Shpazhinsky's libretto for *The Enchantress* continued to delight him. He had completed composition of the first act. Working hard on the proofs of the *Manfred* Symphony, he was more and more inclined to judge it the best work he had ever created. While he enjoyed the Russian winter, he was full of plans that would take him away from Maidanovo. He had to visit Moscow to decide the fate of *Cherevichki*, still unpresented. He would spend the holidays in St. Petersburg. He would go to Italy in the spring. "I am considering going by sea from Naples to Constantinople," he told Nadezhda Filaretovna, "then to Batum, and thence by train to Tiflis, where my brother Anatoly already is expecting me." To Taneyev he wrote of looking forward eagerly to hearing concerts in Moscow. "Imagine! I am exulting at the thought of hearing Beethoven's First Symphony. I was scarcely aware that I loved it so much. The reason must be that it is so like my deity, Mozart. Remember that on October 27, 1887 the centenary of Don Giovanni will be celebrated." [5]

[5] Tchaikovsky was slightly in error. *Don Giovanni* was first given, in Prague, on October 29, 1787.

XIV

THE Paris music-publisher Felix Mackar had unexpectedly bought from Jürgenson the right to issue Piotr Ilyich's compositions in French editions. The original sum paid seems to have been 20,000 francs, half of which, though under no contractual obligation to do so, Jürgenson handed over to the composer. Mackar was an energetic promoter. Having acquired Piotr Ilyich Tchaikovsky as a property potentially of great value, he set about systematically fomenting interest in his new acquisition. He instituted a series of free concerts of Piotr Ilyich's works, enlisting the assistance of the eminent Belgian violinist Martin-Pierre-Joseph Marsick and the popular French pianist Louis Diémer. He persuaded Piotr Ilyich — who had already been elected to membership in several Paris musical societies — to join the Society of Composers and Publishers, a protective association formed to enforce payment of performance fees.

When Jürgenson approached Piotr Ilyich for both Mackar and himself with the question of payment for the *Manfred* Symphony, the composer answered that he had decided to ask nothing for it from either. "Even were Manfred a work of the greatest genius, it would still be a symphony that because of its unusual complexity and difficulty would be played only once a decade. It therefore cannot bring any profit to either you or Mackar. On the other hand, I value it highly. How is the material value of such a work to be set? I may be wrong, but it seems to me my best composition, and a few hundred rubles would not repay me for the labour and worry I have put into it. If you were very rich, I should unhesitatingly demand a very large payment on the grounds that you could recoup your loss on other pieces — but you are not at all rich. As for Mackar — to speak frankly — I am deeply touched by his cheerful self-sacrifice, for he can surely have made but very little out of my works in France. Having just received 20,000 francs from him, we must not show ourselves too grasping, especially as we realize that not much is to be made out of Manfred. In short, I have decided to ask nothing from Mackar or from you, and have already told him this. I ask also that you do not demand the promised thousand francs from him."

The holiday season passed rather unpleasantly for Piotr Ilyich. In St. Petersburg he was depressed over finding none of his operas on the boards. There were no plans for presenting the *Manfred* Symphony. The mounting of *Cherevichki* had been postponed. He returned to Maidanovo on January 25 with eagerness to learn the progress of a nonmusical activity that had been engaging his attention for some time. He had been disturbed at noticing that the village children had no school and were constantly idle. Consulting the local priest, he had learned that the institution of a school would be possible only if a dependable source of income could be found. He himself guaranteed the funds. He took great pride in this project. The school was opened on February 1, 1886, to his entire satisfaction. He maintained his annual contribution to its support until his death.

On the day when he completed the second act of *The Enchantress*, Piotr Ilyich wrote in his diary: "How much remains to be done! How much to be read! How much to learn! How terribly unwilling I am to die as yet, though sometimes it appears to me that I have lived in this world for, oh, so long a time." That day in Moscow, during a concert that also included his *Slavic March*, Piotr Ilyich's *Lullaby* (opus 54, no. 16) was sung by a young Polish soprano already famed throughout Europe and in New York, Marcella Sembrich. Piotr Ilyich was not present, for on the following day he was still at Maidanovo, composing the orchestral prelude for *The Enchantress*.

Off and on for more than two weeks Piotr Ilyich had been trying parts of Anton Rubinstein's opera *Nero*. It irritated him. At last, on March 13, his daybook received this outburst: "I am still amazed at the composer's insolent unceremoniousness. Oh, you ridiculous fool! By God, anger seizes my soul when I look at this score. However, I play this vile composition because the consciousness of my superiority, at least as far as sincerity goes, sustains my energy. You think your writing is vile. Then you look at this vapid stuff, which nevertheless was performed as a serious work, and your soul feels lighter. I am ashamed to show anger over such a publication, but there is no need to cover up one's feelings in a diary."

At last *Manfred* was to be performed, and on March 14 Piotr

ANTON GRIGORYEVICH RUBINSTEIN
From a photograph (1870's)

Ilyich went into Moscow both for the rehearsals and concert and to attend a conference of the Russian Musical Society directors. The rehearsal of March 21 left him dissatisfied and ashamed. But the next day he pronounced himself satisfied. At the final rehearsal the members of the orchestra applauded the composition. That evening, March 23, Erdmannsdörfer led its public *première* during a concert dedicated to the memory of Nikolay Rubinstein. "My nervousness," Piotr Ilyich jotted in his diary. "Half successful. Still, an ovation." To Nadezhda Filaretovna, after apologizing for having been so long in writing her — their correspondence had begun a little to thin out — he wrote: "The performance was excellent, but it seemed to me that the audience was unintelligent and frigid, though they gave me quite an ovation at the close. I think that this is my finest symphonic composition." Modest testifies that Piotr Ilyich did not hold to this high opinion of *Manfred,* but eventually came to consider the second half of it as poor as *The Oprichnik,* finding worth only in its first two movements. Its most ardent champion, after the occasion of its first St. Petersburg presentation, nine months after the Moscow one, was César Cui.

The *Manfred* Symphony is justly dedicated to Balakirev, who had supplied its program and urged its composition. With equal justice it might have been dedicated to the memory of Hector Berlioz or (if Piotr Ilyich had waited only a little more than four months) to that of Franz Liszt. Formally, it is the child of the *Symphonie fantastique* (its "Manfred theme" recurs constantly, like Berlioz's *idée fixe),* the *Dante* Symphony, and the more programmatic of Liszt's symphonic poems. It is narrative and pictorial, evocative and theatrical. Each of its four large movements has a literary superscription.[1] Its lack of inherent unity is not mitigated by the program, which is fragmentary in the extreme. Constant Lambert's remark that *Manfred* "shows more organic unity than his pseudo-classical symphonies" is not to be taken seriously as either positive or negative criticism. Here and there — and particularly in the first and last movements — it is meaty and expan-

[1] "1. Manfred wanders in the Alps. Tormented by the fatal anguish of doubt, rent by remorse and despair, his soul is victim to nameless sufferings. 2. The fairy of the Alps appears before Manfred in the rainbow of a torrent's spray. 3. Pastoral. The simple, free, and peaceful life of the mountaineers. 4. Ahriman's subterranean palace. Manfred appears in the midst of the bacchanal. Evocation of the shade of Astarte. She predicts the end of his earthly troubles. Death of Manfred."

sive with pure Tchaikovskyan materials. Had Piotr Ilyich carried out his intention, mentioned in a letter to Grand Duke Konstantin Nikolayevich, to condense the four movements into a symphonic poem, we might have had a worthy companion to *Romeo and Juliet, The Tempest,* and *Francesca da Rimini.* However flawed *Manfred* remains, it deserves performance. An epoch that can find resources and reasons for a radio festival of Mahler's nine symphonies, not infrequent mountings of the *Faust* Symphony, and even an attempt at resuscitating Berlioz's *Roméo et Juliette* neglects *Manfred* only out of ignorance and snobbishness. Like the Second Piano Concerto and *The Tempest,* it contains enough music of a high order to overbalance its flaws and difficulties, enough to make its performance certain of artistic reward.

Devoting only one day to the third act of *The Enchantress* at Maidanovo, Piotr Ilyich went to St. Petersburg to attend a Russian Musical Society concert on March 27. Hans von Bülow, conducting most of it, took his place at the piano in a performance of the B-flat minor Piano Concerto. "An ovation," records the daybook. The next entry reads: "Supper. Apukhtin, Guitry." The latter was Lucien Guitry, the French actor for whom Piotr Ilyich was to compose the Fantasy Overture and incidental music to *Hamlet.* After a day or so of what he labeled "social successes," Piotr Ilyich returned to Moscow and Maidanovo to prepare for his long-planned visit to Tiflis.

On April 6 Piotr Ilyich arrived at Taganrog, on the Sea of Azov. He spent two days with his brother Ippolit, whose ship was temporarily stationed there. Then, travelling along the coast, through Rostov, and along the banks of the Sinyavka River, he went into the Caucasus, arriving at Vladikavkaz [now Ordzhonikidze] on April 9. Between Vladikavkaz and Tiflis stood the peaks of the Caucasus Mountains. Early on April 11 he set off in a post-chaise drawn by four horses and accompanied by a guard. To Modest he wrote:

I had not slept the night before on account of the horrible bed and the bugs (when I think of the *finest* hotel in Vladikavkaz I feel quite nauseated), and thought that the beauties of the Georgian Road might therefore make little impression on me. The road, however, is so grand, so amazingly beautiful, that I never considered sleeping during the whole day. The variety of impressions kept my attention from flagging a moment. At first the approach to the peaks was slow, though they seemed quite near, and yet we still rode on and on. Then the valley of the Terek became narrower and we entered the wild and gloomy Daryal Gorge. Later we ascended into the region of snow. Shortly before I started on my journey, there had been an avalanche, and hundreds of miserable-looking natives were occupied in shovelling the snow away. At last we were driving higher and higher between great walls of snow, and we had to put on our furs. By six o'clock we were descending into the Aragva Valley, and we passed the night at Mleti. I occupied the *imperial rooms*. After the filth of the Vladikavkaz hotel, I found the clean rooms, good beds, and daintily set table quite delightful. I dined, took a short stroll by moonlight in the gallery, and went to bed at nine o'clock. Next morning I started off again. Already we could sense a breath of the south in the air: the mountainsides were cultivated, and picturesque villages and all kinds of houses came into sight constantly. The descent was made at a terrifying pace considering the curves in the road. Not far from Dushet, such a wonderful view burst on us that I almost cried with delight. The farther we went down, the more the influence of the south wind was noticed. At last we reached Mtskhet (noted for the ruins of its castle and the celebrated Cathedral), and at five thirty arrived in Tiflis.

Now Piotr Ilyich was the guest of Anatoly and Parasha. On his first day in Tiflis he strolled about the town, noting with surprise that its lively principal streets were lined with splendid shops and had a European air. He enjoyed the native quarter with its bazaar-stalls, its ways as mean and narrow as those of Venice. He saw Ippolitov-Ivanov and Genary Korganov, a young Armenian composer. That night, on the edge of Asia, he must have wondered how, in far-away St. Petersburg, an audience was reacting to his Third Suite as led by Hans von Bülow. On April 14 he attended a concert of the Tiflis Russian Musical Society. The program consisted of Beethoven's "Eroica" Symphony, Borodin's *On the Steppes of Central Asia,* and his own Serenade for Strings — played, he wrote Nadezhda Filaretovna, to a public conspicuous by its absence. He found the orchestra small and bad, but judged Ippolitov-Ivanov a good conductor.

On the evening of May 1 the local Russian Musical Society honoured the composer's presence with a program entirely of his works. "At eight o'clock," Piotr Ilyich wrote Modest, "accompanied by Pani [Parasha], I entered the director's box, which was decorated with flowers and foliage. The whole audience stood up, and amid great applause I was presented with a silver wreath and

many others.[2] A deputation from the Musical Society read an address. Then the concert — which consisted entirely of my works — began. There were endless cheers! I have never experienced anything like it before. After the concert, a subscription supper, with many toasts. A most exhausting evening, but a glorious memory."
When this honour, paid him in an outpost of the Empire, was added to the unquestionable success of *Yevgeny Onyegin,* a decoration from the Tsar, constant performance elsewhere throughout Russia, and ever increasing performance abroad, Piotr Ilyich could no longer doubt that he was successful and famous. This assurance that there was public value in what he had already accomplished had as much influence on the remaining seven years of his life as did any of the more outwardly dramatic events with which those years were marked. Cheers from a Tiflis audience meant that not merely one coterie in St. Petersburg and another in Moscow, but the musical audiences of Russia loved what he had done. He never found more durable or intense satisfaction.

As the time for his departure for Paris drew near, Piotr Ilyich summed up his impressions of Tiflis in letters. To Jürgenson's son he wrote: "Tiflis itself is unusually attractive and original, particularly because here Europe and Asia brush shoulders at every step, blend, and piquantly contrast each other. . . . No matter how much one learns, how much one tramps around, one continues to stumble upon new, original aspects." He found his plan of going by steamer from Batum to Naples, and then from Naples to Paris by train, rendered impossible by a cholera epidemic at Naples. On May 11 he therefore left Tiflis for Batum, there to board a Marseille-bound steamer that would omit any stop in Italy.

The *Armenia,* sailing westward through the Black Sea, stopped at Trebizond, which attracted Piotr Ilyich, summoning to his mind pictures of a city in an Eastern fairy tale. On May 16 it dropped anchor again, this time at Constantinople. He was glad to get off for a day, having discovered that none of the passengers aboard interested him. "The captain talks to me about music, and infuriates me with his inane ideas," he wrote back to Anatoly. "A French doctor from Trebizond also considers himself a music-lover, and thinks it his duty, since discovering that I am a musician, to discuss with me this hateful art that seems to have the ability to interest

[2] In letters to Jürgenson and Mme von Meck, Tchaikovsky also mentioned many precious silver gifts.

everyone." In Constantinople he put up for the night at a *maison meublée* that he described as "horribly and meagrely furnished." St. Sophia "delighted and amazed" him, but he was not delighted by Constantinople in general, and the city's notorious dogs made him feel unwell. On May 17 the *Armenia* weighed anchor and steamed from the Bosporus.

Now an Englishman among the passengers cornered the composer to ask information on his preferences among the songs of Tosti and Denza. The French doctor from Trebizond described to him in detail a piano of his own invention, a monstrous instrument having separate keys for each sharp, flat, double sharp, and double flat. Not only did this self-hypnotized Frenchman talk about his invention; he also presented the exacerbated composer with pamphlets about it, expecting him to read them and give his opinions on their contents before the voyage was over. Piotr Ilyich wrote him down as "wild and strange." He was happy to retire to his cabin, the only place guaranteeing privacy, to read Paul Bourget's *Un Crime d'amour*, which moved him deeply, in part because it recalled Turgenyev and Tolstoy.

As the *Armenia* passed the heel of Italy and entered the Strait of Messina, Piotr Ilyich wrote to Modest: "Etna is smoking a little, and on the left there is a terrible column of smoke and fire that excites everyone very much. The captain is unable to say certainly what it signifies, and seems rather upset by it. In consequence, I too feel a little fearful." Continuing this letter the next day, he added: "The column of smoke and fire I wrote about yesterday turns out to be a terrible eruption of Mount Etna, not at the top, but on the side. This eruption was clearly visible at a distance of three hundred versts [almost two hundred miles], and the closer we approached, the more interesting the sight. Alexey awoke me at two o'clock in the morning so that I might see this unique spectacle. We were in the Strait of Messina. The sea, which had been entirely smooth all day, was now extremely rough. I cannot describe the beauties of the moonlight, the fire from Mount Etna, and the swelling waves. At 3 a.m., I returned to my bed, and at 5 the captain sent a sailor to wake me so that I might see the town of Messina, the sunrise, and the eruption from the other side. Later we passed between the volcano Stromboli and a tiny new island giving out smoke — at least the captain, who knows these seas well, has never suspected a volcano at this spot and thinks that it may portend a serious eruption. Today the weather is glorious and the sea much smoother."

Arriving in Marseille on May 23, Piotr Ilyich walked about its streets, admiring the Cannebière as foreigners have always admired it, but describing the city by the curious phrase "very pretty." He stayed four days, looking into the local theatres, zoological garden, and *palais de cristal,* and then went to Paris on May 27. He was to remain there exactly four weeks. Aside from making the acquaintance of Mackar, his enterprising French publisher, Piotr Ilyich does not seem to have had urgent reasons for remaining so long. Modest states that he went to Paris "on important family business," but no details are to be found. He went to the theatre, concert, and opera to his heart's content, met most of the important men in French musical life, and even, for ten days, worked on Act III of *The Enchantress.*

On the 12th Piotr Ilyich met one of the most interesting musicians in the city, Pauline Viardot-García. Although he described her, in a letter to Parasha, as seventy, the great mezzo-soprano was only sixty-five. She had already outlived her famous father by fifty-four years, and Malibran — her even more famous sister — by fifty. Her brother Manuel Patricio, aged eighty-one, was still London's leading voice teacher. She herself, having made her debut nearly half a century earlier, and having been absent from the stage for almost twenty-five years, was enjoying in retirement the fruits of a brilliant mind and enduring interests. All the leading musicians and intellectuals of the day were her devoted friends, and she was rumoured to have been Turgenyev's mistress.

Piotr Ilyich found Viardot-García "enchanting," adding: "She is extremely lively, amiable, gay, and sociable, and was able to make me feel at home from the beginning." To his overwhelming pleasure, she allowed him to examine a treasure her husband had purchased thirty years before, the original manuscript of *Don Giovanni.* "I am incapable of expressing the emotion that seized upon me when I examined this sacred musical relic!" he wrote. "It was exactly as though I had pressed Mozart's hand and talked to him." Viardot-García spoke at length of Turgenyev and described how she and the novelist together had written *The Song of Love Triumphant.*

Marmontel, still dictating at the Conservatoire at seventy, and "touchingly kind to me," entertained for Piotr Ilyich. The crowd of guests gathered in his honour on June 17 included newspaper critics, writers, artists, and musicians. There were discussions about Russia and about Wagner, the latter leading to what Piotr Ilyich wrote down as "Quarrels. Screams." He particularly enjoyed a tête-à-tête with Ernest Guiraud, the New-Orleans-born composer who is still represented on the opera stage by his revision of *Les Contes d'Hoffmann* and his recitatives for *Carmen*. Two evenings after Marmontel's party a wealthy half-Russian lady gave a dinner and musicale in Piotr Ilyich's honour, introducing him to, among many others, Fauré and Lalo. "Fauré pleased me exceedingly, both as man and as musician," he noted, adding that a Fauré quartet played during the evening was excellent. Delibes called, and finding Piotr Ilyich not in, left a card with a flattering inscription certain to please a man who regarded him as the most talented French composer after Bizet.[3] Ambroise Thomas, whose austerity and fearsome personality struck many with awe, was paternal toward the visiting Russian. Colonne expressed a desire to conduct an all-Tchaikovsky concert. Lamoureux was "amiability itself, and made me a thousand promises." Finally, in the last few days of his visit, Piotr Ilyich called on Delibes, who was in, and Gounod, who was not. On June 24 he left for Russia. On the train the next day he entered in his diary: "Anniversary of mother's death." Thirty-two years had done little to compensate him for that loss.

Piotr Ilyich was once again at home in Maidanovo on July 30. He had been away three months. Except for the usual number of excursions into Moscow and St. Petersburg, he was to remain at work on *The Enchantress* until August 30. His first visitor was Lyegoshin, the manservant of his ailing friend Nikolay Kondratyev. "What a pleasure Lyegoshin's constant presence gives me!" the diary records for July 5. "He has such a wonderful personality. Good heavens! And to think that there are people who turn up their noses at a servant because he is a servant. I know nobody whose soul is purer and nobler than Lyegoshin's. And he's a servant! Man's equality irrespective of his social position was never given such positive proof as in this case." The following day he went to Kondratyev's bedside with Lyegoshin.

To Nadezhda Filaretovna, Piotr Ilyich told his happiness at being home again and at finding the little house, which he had left

[3] Tchaikovsky did not encounter the young Debussy, for that unwilling prize-winner was fretting away his time at the Villa Medici in Rome.

banked in deep snow, bowered in foliage and flowers. He was working well when, on July 10, a letter arrived from Antonina Ivanovna. "What can one do with this madwoman?" he asked his diary. The next day he was ill, had hemorrhoid pains, was completely out of sorts — and himself recognized his wife's letter as the cause. He spent an entire day attempting unsuccessfully to draw up a reply to her, noting that he was going through a mixture of emotions, including strong moral suffering, hatred, and pity. When, on July 13, he at last managed to finish a letter to her, he hoped fervently that he had performed the difficult task of simultaneously not offending and not indulging her. He could not work that day and spent it at the piano, playing *Parsifal*, which he did not like. In his diary two days later he wrote: "The incident with Antonina Ivanovna begins to disappear into the realm of the past. My conscience is clear — nevertheless, despite everything, despite even the fact that she is the worst piece of trash in the world, I feel sorry for her. She has no luck, poor woman."

The writings of Tolstoy had again been in Piotr Ilyich's mind. It was Tolstoy that he had discussed with the sick Kondratyev. One of the longest entries in his diary, dated July 11, runs in part:

When one reads the autobiographies of our best people, or reminisces about them, one constantly encounters emotions, feelings, and general artistic sensitivity that one has often experienced and that is completely comprehensible. But there exists one man who is not understood, who cannot be reached, who remains alone on his unattainable heights. Not unseldom does he arouse my anger — hatred almost. Why, I wonder, does this man, who can, as no one else before him ever could, attune our souls to the highest and most miraculously euphonious melody, this writer who was gratuitously granted from on high the power never before granted anyone, to enable us, dull-witted creatures that we are, to penetrate the most inaccessible alleys of our secret moral life — why has this man become addicted to teaching, why obsessed by the mania of preaching and enlightening our dark or limited minds? In the past, his depiction of, as it seemed, the simplest and most ordinary scene created an unforgettable impression. The highest love for mankind, the highest pity for its helplessness, limitations, and insignificance could be read between the lines. One wept, hardly knowing why. . . . Because for a fleeting moment, through his intervention, one came into contact with an ideal world of absolute goodness and humanity. . . . Now he annotates his texts, and claims to have the sole monopoly on understanding the problems of faith and ethics (or whatever); but a cold wind blows from all his present writings. . . . The former Tolstoy was half divine — the present one is a priest. And in essence priests are teachers only by the grace of a role they have themselves assumed, not through the power of an irresistible vocation.

Reading and pondering Tolstoy, working intermittently on *The Enchantress*, making an occasional sortie into Moscow, Piotr Ilyich passed the summer. Antonina Ivanovna again wrote to him, this time what he called "a strange, wild letter," asking that he dedicate something to her, and also that he undertake the care of her children. One day he walked through the neighbouring community of Klin, and there looked at a large grey house that was eventually to become his home and, after his death, the Tchaikovsky Museum. He heard some of his *Cherubim Songs* both at the Uspensky Cathedral and at the Moscow Choral Society. When Mme La Mara, compiling her *Musik Briefe aus fünf Jahrhunderten*, asked Jürgenson for suitable letters to represent Piotr Ilyich in the collection, the publisher discovered that not one of those in his files would serve her purpose. Piotr Ilyich agreed with him and added:

Isn't it strange that it should be hard to find an appropriate letter from a man who has been carrying on — and still carries on — the largest correspondence, dealing with not only business details but artistic effort? I constantly exchange letters with four brothers, a sister, several cousins, and many friends, in addition to a quantity of casual correspondence with persons of whom I've often never heard. The need to give so much of my time to letter-writing is such a burden to me that from the bottom of my heart I curse all the postal systems of the world. The mail often causes me sad moments, but it also brings me the greatest happiness. One person plays the leading role in the story of the last decade of my life: she is my good genius; to her I owe all my prosperity and the ability to devote myself to my beloved work. Yet I have never seen her, never heard her voice. All my intercourse with her is by mail. I can certainly say that I flood the earth with my correspondence and yet am not in a position to help you out of your difficulty.

This letter requires some comment. The "good genius" was Nadezhda Filaretovna, beyond doubt. But Piotr Ilyich did not owe all his prosperity to her, unless he meant that, by giving him freedom earlier she had made possible his ability to earn large sums later on. Surely it was not true that he had never seen her — again unless he meant that he had never met her formally face to face.

Piotr Ilyich began composing the twelve songs that make up his Opus 60. He wanted to dedicate something to Tsarina Marya Fyodorovna, and though inspiration for a round dozen of songs did not come to him readily at the moment, he persisted until that number was reached, believing that no smaller number would suffice. The task occupied him off and on for three weeks, and produced, in *The Song of the Gypsy Girl*, to a Polonsky text — number 7 of the set — one of the best of his brief vocal works. Playing over *The Enchantress*, Piotr Ilyich was horrified to find that its acts were very long — "and long operas are good for nothing." He did some excising. On September 30, however, he was still confiding to his diary that the opera needed shortening. The following day he began its orchestration.

Piotr Ilyich's diary for October 2 contains a long, revealing entry. Beginning with the observation that Tolstoy never published his opinions of other great writers, he remarked that his own musical predilections and prejudices would be of interest to posterity, especially because he had seldom spoken them.

I shall start with Beethoven, whom it is customary to praise uncritically, and whom one is commanded to worship as if he were a god. And so what do I think of Beethoven? I bow to the grandeur of some of his compositions — but I do not love Beethoven. My attitude toward him reminds me of my childhood feelings toward the God Jehovah. I had toward Him (nor have my feelings changed) a feeling of wonder, but also of terror. He has created heaven and earth, and though I kneel before Him, I do not love Him. Christ, on the other hand, calls forth only the emotion of *love*. He is God, but He is also Man. He has suffered like ourselves. We pity Him and in Him love the ideal part of man's nature. If Beethoven holds in my heart a similar place to that held by the God Jehovah, I love Mozart as the musical Christ. This comparison does not to me seem blasphemous. Mozart was pure as an angel, and his music is rich in divine beauty. Speaking of Beethoven, I arrive at Mozart. It is my profound conviction that Mozart is the culminating point of musical beauty. Nobody has so made me weep and tremble with rapture at knowledge of nearness to what we call the ideal. Beethoven has also made me tremble, but rather from something like terror and painful longing. I am unable to analyse music and shall not go into details. I shall, however, note two details: 1. I love Beethoven's middle period, and sometimes the first, but in general I hate the last period, particularly the last quartets. There are glimmers here, but nothing more. The rest is chaos, over which — encircled by impenetrable mists — hovers the spirit of this musical Jehovah. 2. In Mozart I love everything, for we love everything in those we love truly. More than anything else, I love Don Giovanni, for through it I learned what music is. Until then (until I was 17), I knew only the Italian semi-music — which, by the way, is attractive. Of course, in loving all of Mozart, I shall not begin insisting that each unimportant piece of his music is a chef-d'œuvre. No! I know, for example, that not one of his sonatas is a great composition. Nevertheless, I love every one of his sonatas because it is his, because his sacred breath was breathed into it. As to the forerunners of these two artists, I can say that I play Bach willingly because to play a good fugue is entertaining, but I do not recognize in him (as others do) a great genius. Handel I consider wholly fourth-rate, for he is not even entertaining. Gluck, despite the relative poverty of his creativeness, I find attractive. I like some things of Haydn. But all four of these masters are amalgamated in Mozart. Whoever knows Mozart knows also all that was good in these four, for, being the greatest and most potent of musical creators, he did not disdain to take even them under his wing and save them from oblivion. They are rays of the sun Mozart.[4]

Piotr Ilyich had promised to conduct the Moscow staging of *Cherevichki*. Realization of his inability to conduct had been tormenting him for years. He thought this weakness contemptible. Yet, he told Nadezhda Filaretovna, he feared that again he would arrive at the moment of mounting the podium only to discover that his courage had left him. A telegram from Napravnik stating that circumstances had forced postponement of *The Enchantress* merely gave him time to fuss further at the opera, tinker with the orchestration and piano score, and mark sections for further condensation. Late October found him overtired to the point of actual illness. Playing a Brahms symphony with Laroche, he was irritated into calling the composer "the scoundrel," and into comparing him unfavourably with Raff and Rubinstein. His only remark on Massenet's *Le Cid*, after he had examined it, was: "Heigh ho! It's all the same." Massenet, he thought, had written himself out. Again and again he levelled that charge against himself.

Rimsky-Korsakov had announced a performance of *Romeo and Juliet* at the fourth of a series of concerts he was conducting under

---

[4] It is difficult to know how Tchaikovsky could have been acquainted with Handel in performance. Likewise, his knowledge of Bach and Gluck must have been small or confined to transcriptions. His appalling dicta must be excused as a worshipper's excesses.

the sponsorship of Mitrofan Petrovich Belyayev. On November 11 Piotr Ilyich wrote him a note regarding Arensky, who had been very ill. This note suggested, as a measure that might hasten Arensky's recovery, that Rimsky-Korsakov substitute one of the younger man's compositions for *Romeo and Juliet*. "In concluding," Piotr Ilyich wrote, "I must add that your *Spanish Caprice* is a colossal masterpiece of instrumentation, and that you may regard yourself as the greatest master of the present day." On the 17th an all-Tchaikovsky program of chamber music — the Trio, one of the string quartets, and some small pieces — was presented to honour Piotr Ilyich. The enthusiasm of the listeners was sincere and the composer left the hall "choked with emotion and gratitude," as he wrote Nadezhda Filaretovna. He had planned to leave for Maidanovo three days later, but received from Vsevolozhsky an invitation to call and discuss the possibility of composing a new ballet.

Summoned to Moscow for rehearsals of *Cherevichki*, Piotr Ilyich felt so sick that he all but summoned a doctor and sent word that he could not attend the rehearsal. Half an hour later the headache that had been tormenting him for ten days vanished suddenly and completely. "Isn't this a curious pathological case?" he asked Modest. He got to Moscow on December 1, and went immediately to the rehearsal, which he described as "so-so."

As the day for the first orchestral rehearsal of *Cherevichki* drew near, Piotr Ilyich, who had promised to conduct rehearsals as well as the performance, found himself with a desire to carry out the promise. He solemnly took lessons from Altani. On December 16 he mounted the podium, baton in hand, and conducted the rehearsal. It had required an internal struggle lasting days, a struggle he had several times been on the edge of losing and had won only with help from vodka, but he performed the task cleanly and with dispatch. "In the end I mastered myself," he wrote Modest later that day, "was received with enthusiasm by the orchestra, found strength to make a brief speech, and raised the baton. Now I know that I *can* conduct. I shall not be nervous at the performance." This was an important victory for Piotr Ilyich: his ability as a conductor of his own works was to have practical influence on the rest of his life.

At the Bolshoi, Piotr Ilyich "got a little mixed up in the conducting" at a rehearsal of *Cherevichki* on January 19. He underwent the usual days and nights of nervous irritation at his own ineptitudes. On the 26th, however, he wrote Nadezhda Filaretovna: "Conducting is, of course, somewhat difficult for me, and strains my entire nervous system. But I must confess that it also gives me great pleasure." When all seemed ready for the opera's opening performance, it became clear that the prima donna was too ill to enact her role, and it was therefore necessary to rehearse another soprano — whom Piotr Ilyich did not like — in the role. The first performance occurred on January 31, and the following day the composer-conductor wrote Pavlovskaya that it had, in general, been a satisfactory one.

On February 2 a reviewer in *Moskovskiye Vyedomosti* said of the *première:* "The opera's music abounds in many beauties. . . . As conductor of his opera, Tchaikovsky displayed an aspect of his talent new to us. He proved to be an experienced and confident conductor, who not only informed the players of his composer's aims, but also inspired both the stage performers and the orchestra." News had arrived of the death of his niece, Tatyana Lvovna Davidova, and it was with "a heavy feeling" and "in a terrible mood" that Piotr Ilyich conducted the second performance of *Cherevichki.* His only surcease from personal grief and sceptical fear about his conductorial powers came from attending two piano rehearsals by Eugen d'Albert, whom he described as " a young genius."

The first few audiences for *Cherevichki* varied in their reactions to the opera. To Modest, on February 10, Piotr Ilyich wrote: "I think that, like Onyegin, Cherevichki won't meet with any noisy reception, but little by little they will learn to love this opera, too. The love I myself feel for it makes me certain that the public will also learn to love it some day." When, after his return to Maidanovo, he heard from Altani that *Cherevichki,* attracting full houses, was considered a success, he noted: "Terribly happy." What he did not understand, but what reviewers clearly saw, was that he was not most at home among the comic situations of Polonsky's libretto. Where the music should be brittle and gay, what one writer called "the involuntary notes of sadness and hesitancy" crept in and dissipated the mood. There are many pages of beautiful music in *Cherevichki,* but the whole has no musicodramatic unity, no overall life, and it has had few stagings, fewer than a dozen operas of less melodic richness and greater integrity.

On February 23, by working throughout the day until he had a headache, Piotr Ilyich completed the piano score of *The Enchant-ress*. The following day Alexey Sofronov carried it to Jürgenson in Moscow while his master settled down "with difficulty" to orchestrate Act II of the opera. While he laboured away at this task, he received a letter from Mackar stating that a Paris concert devoted wholly to his compositions had been very successful. This news he reported with great pleasure to Nadezhda Filaretovna. Then he had to go to Moscow and on to St. Petersburg, where he was to conduct an all-Tchaikovsky program for the Philharmonic Society. On the 12th he faced the orchestra for his concert, conducting it through the first rehearsal. "Nervousness. Terror," he wrote in his diary. "Then nothing. Ovation from the artists." At the third rehearsal, which he thought he conducted tolerably, he noted that the large group of onlookers included Balakirev. The program of the March 17 concert included the first St. Petersburg performance of the Second Suite, both vocal and instrumental excerpts from *The Enchantress*, two movements of the Serenade for Strings, *Francesca da Rimini*, small vocal and piano pieces, and *1812*. "Complete success," records the diary. "Enormous pleasure. But why is there a spoonful of tar in this barrel of honey???" The concert was widely reviewed, generally with enthusiasm, and there was no doubt that Piotr Ilyich had established himself as a conductor of talent.

Ippolitov-Ivanov was visiting St. Petersburg. Piotr Ilyich saw him often. He believed that the young composer would go far, "if only because he possesses something of his very own, and in addition what he possesses of his own is most sympathetic." In his *Memoirs* Ippolitov-Ivanov recorded that during this visit to the northern capital he was out for a walk with Piotr Ilyich. Unconsciously he was singing over and over a theme from one of Liszt's piano concertos. At last Piotr Ilyich interrupted him irritably. "Please don't recall that comedian to me," he said. "I can't stand his insincerity and affectations." The volatility of Piotr Ilyich's moods also shows in a diary entry for March 28: "I need not hide from myself that, in essence, all the poetry of life in the country and in solitude has for some reason disappeared. *Nowhere do I feel so abominable as at home.*"

Piotr Ilyich noted his own birthday in the following way: "47! hm! hm! A lot to have lived through." A visit from Taneyev brightened the day for him, lifting a little the gloom caused by word that the serious illness of his friend Nikolay D. Kondratyev was incurable. Finally, on May 18, he was able to note in his diary that *The Enchantress* was done: "Worked well . . . finished everything!!!" Three days later he went to St. Petersburg to the bedside of the dying Kondratyev. For six days he made daily visits to his friend's sickbed, and then had to return to Moscow to attend the annual Conservatory examinations.

On June 1, having stopped briefly at Maidanovo, Piotr Ilyich left for Tiflis and Borzhom, where he planned to spend the summer with Anatoly and Parasha. The following day he transferred to a river steamer at Nizhni-Novgorod. On the 3rd he went ashore in Kazan, walking about the city, which he described ambiguously as "very beautiful from a distance." The next day it was Samara (now Kuibyshev), where he found posters everywhere announcing a performance the previous evening of *Yevgeny Onyegin*. There were stops at Syzran, Khvalynsk, Volsk, Saratov, Kamyshin, and Tsaritsyn (now Stalingrad). The last place he disliked. "Rather strange!" he noted. "In the midst of some huge, deserted, infirm square, for instance, where one's feet sink in the sand, one suddenly encounters an enormous house in Viennese style!" Astrakhan pleased him more. As he transferred to a Caspian Sea steamer, he wrote Nadezhda Filaretovna that he had greatly enjoyed the river trip. "Mother Volga is truly a grandiose, majestically poetic spectacle."

In expansive mood Piotr Ilyich acted as accompanist during a musical evening by the steamer's passengers. A conservatory singer, not realizing who her vis-à-vis was, asked him if he had ever heard Pavlovskaya in *Yevgeny Onyegin*. An elderly gentleman told all who were listening that the composer Tchaikovsky had been so pleased by the singer Lody's rendition of Orlik in *Mazepa* that he had kissed him for it. The gentleman was unaware that Lody, a tenor, could not have sung the bass role of Orlik. "In general, a very gay evening." Descriptions of what he was seeing went into his diary and into letters to Nadezhda Filaretovna. On June 11 he arrived in Tiflis.

While in Tiflis, Piotr Ilyich saw performances of *Camille*, Shpazhinsky's *The Enchantress,* and plays by Ostrovsky. He looked over a score of Verdi's *Otello,* and attended a concert at which part of the program consisted of a potpourri of selections from *Yevgeny Onyegin.* He heard with pleasure that the city had supported an "exemplary performance" of *Mazepa* the previous year. On June 22 he went from Tiflis to Borzhom, with which, he wrote Nadezhda Filaretovna, he fell in love for ever. Calling on a physician, he was tapped and prodded, feeling pain in places. "He found that my liver has gone somewhere it has no business being. Immediately began to take the waters," he noted. Modest shortly joined him in Borzhom. Although still complaining of "complete lack of desire and ability to work," he began to sketch a sextet and also to orchestrate part of *Mozartiana*. "I think this suite, because of its successful choice of compositions and its originality (the past in a contemporary work) will have an excellent future," he wrote Jürgenson. "Should it win approval, I shall later do another one, and perhaps even a third."

In his diary on July 9 Piotr Ilyich noted: "It seems to me that letters are never entirely frank. I am judging, at any rate, by my own. No matter what or to whom I write, I always worry about the impression my letter will make, not only on my correspondent, but even on some accidental reader. It follows, therefore, that I am showing off. Sometimes I try to make my letters sound simple and sincere, so, that is, that they should give such an impression. But in no letters except those written under emotional stress am I ever myself. For that reason the latter sort of communication always remains a source of regret and repentance, at times even painful. When I read the letters of famous people, published after their death, I am always worried by an indefinable feeling of falseness and lies." In the same mood, he felt irritated at having been called, for the first time, a "venerable composer."

Having received word that the dying Kondratyev was going abroad in the hope of a cure, Piotr Ilyich decided to join him in Aachen. After a few days' more work on *Mozartiana*, and after composing a chorus — *The Golden Cloud Slept* — he left on July 18, getting to Batum that day. The city seemed to him to have degenerated since his visit one year before. "The merchants look very melancholy," he wrote Modest, "the streets are deserted." Now his route lay through Feodosiya, Yalta, Sevastopol — where he visited Mme Shpazhinskaya — and Odessa. At a service in Odessa Cathedral he found the singing "not very good, while the selection was simply abominable. As always, I was irritated by the singing. Only in a village of deacons can one listen to such singing without irritation." From Odessa he went via Vienna to Cologne, where he twice visited the Cathedral. He arrived in Aachen the evening of July 27.

For six weeks Piotr Ilyich remained in Aachen. He visited the sick Kondratyev daily, attended to his needs and wants, and tried to comfort him. Kondratyev was irritable and capricious, and his swift changes of mood and unceasing complaints eventually brought the composer near to nervous collapse. On August 3 his diary reads: "Sitting at home repenting of something. The gist of this repentance is as follows. Life is passing, nearing its end, yet I have come to no conclusions, and even brush aside any fatal questions that arise, or run away from them. Is it thus that I live? Am I right in doing so? Take, for example, this moment. Here I am, and everybody is admiring my *sacrifice*. But there is no sacrifice. I sit here placidly, stuffing myself at the *table d'hôte,* do nothing, spend my money on trifles, when others are in need of the bare necessities of life. Am I not a pure egoist? Even with those close to me I am not what I should be." By August 9, none the less, he had completed *Mozartiana.*

In mid-August, Piotr Ilyich broke his Aachen stay with one day in Paris. On the 24th he began the *Pezzo Capriccioso* for cello and orchestra. Finishing it in rough draft two days later, he asked the cellist A. A. Brandukov to look it over and polish the solo part. He wanted to put the final touches on it, but could not. On August 27 his diary reads: "Horrible, infernal homesickness and impatience to the point of despair to get away. Ten more days of this hell." The next day it was: "Oppressed by *horror* and *homesickness* the whole day, but no feeling of *pity.*" The invalid was unsettling him altogether, and he found "a ray of freedom" in knowledge that he would shortly be able to leave. While he tried to force himself to work on revisions in the *Pezzo Capriccioso,* he was shaken by news that Arensky was mentally unwell. "What frightens me in Arensky's illness," he wrote Taneyev, "is the fact that it is not merely a sharp attack of madness, but a religious mania." At last, on September 4, someone arrived from Russia to take Piotr Ilyich's place at Kondratyev's deathbed. The following day — "farewells without tears" — he left for Berlin and St. Petersburg.

XV

Having called on Kondratyev's wife at Peterhof, Piotr Ilyich went on to Maidanovo. From there, on September 11, he sent Jürgenson the *Pezzo Capriccioso*, asking him to have Fitzenhagen examine the cello part and put in all special notations. During a week at home, Piotr Ilyich spent considerable time playing over Schumann's ill-fated opera *Genoveva*. He also looked about the neighbourhood for a more attractive house. Having searched two near-by villages, he wrote: "Dirt and mediocrity. 1,500 rubles!!!" He even considered buying a stretch of woodland and building a house to suit his own wishes. "There are some nice places, and I like the site for a house. Decided to buy (and money???)." To Modest he wrote: "I don't think of Aachen. The place appears to me only in dreams, as some horrible nightmare." Kondratyev died on October 3, and the news reached Piotr Ilyich in Moscow the next day. It threw him into the gloomiest of moods, despite which he sat through a Bolshoi performance of *Robert le diable.*

Three events were to round out 1887 for Piotr Ilyich. The first performance — and failure — of *The Enchantress*, the conducting of his first Moscow concert, and his departure on his first international tour as composer-conductor were to end one period of his life and launch him on his last five years of enormous activity and worldwide fame. He was to become simultaneously something of a recluse and something of a newspaper celebrity, a man who delighted in the quiet seclusion of a country home and a man whose face and figure were known to thousands of concertgoers in western Europe and the United States.

Piotr Ilyich conducted the first orchestral rehearsal of *The Enchantress* at the Marinsky on October 12, 1887. Napravnik had prepared the way for him with careful attention, and he found himself "very well satisfied with the artists." For eighteen days rehearsals proceeded. Settings and costumes, he found, were to be magnificent, but Pavlovskaya unfortunately had too little voice left for the leading role. The *première* (with Igor Stravinsky's father again in a prominent role) occurred on November 1. The composer, both on his podium and on the stage, was given an ovation. At first he seems to have believed the opera a success. By November 25, however, he had realized its failure and was complaining by letter to Nadezhda Filaretovna: "The public doesn't care for my opera, and it isn't really successful. As for the Petersburg press, it greeted me with such malice and ill will that I haven't come to my senses yet, nor can I understand the reasons why and wherefore."

It was the familiar story. One critic, describing the weakness of *The Enchantress* as "its inability to convey dramatic situations in music," summed up the proper case against all of Piotr Ilyich's stage works except *Yevgeny Onyegin*, *The Queen of Spades*, and the ballets. Cui, surgically dissecting the opera, said that the best performer in it was the composer himself, "an excellent, first-class conductor." This was less than consolation to a man who had no wish at all to be a conductor and every wish to be a successful composer of opera. He patiently led three more performances of the opera, the last on November 14, and then left it to someone else's baton. Its seventh performance, attained on November 29, was given to a Marinsky only half full. Although it was mounted with more success in six performances at Tiflis late in December and early in January, the opera soon fell into complete disuse. Today, outside the Soviet Union, *The Enchantress* endures only in an excerpt or two, notably the heroine's fourth-act aria: "Where are you, my beloved?"

With the opera behind him, Piotr Ilyich turned his mind to preparing his first Moscow appearance as the conductor of an entire concert of his own works. Rehearsals for this nervous debut took from November 20 to 25 and kept him in Moscow when he would have preferred to be seeking out a new country home. The program of the Russian Musical Society concert of November 26 consisted of *Francesca da Rimini*, a selection from *The Enchantress*, the Concert Fantasy (with Taneyev as soloist), the Fourth (*Mozartiana*) Suite in its *première*, two songs, and *1812*. One movement of *Mozartiana* had to be repeated, and the concert was a series of triumphs for Piotr Ilyich as both composer and conductor. It was repeated at a popular concert the next day. "In the morning," Piotr Ilyich wrote Nadezhda Filaretovna, "I felt terrible, and thought I should have to abandon the concert. However, I forced myself to go. Just before the concert I had an attack of hysterics. When that was over, I came out and sensed that I was conducting better than I had ever conducted before. Never have I encountered such enthusiasm or had such a triumph." His popularity had begun to attain the proportions in which modern music-lovers know it.

Piotr Ilyich left for western Europe on December 27 with the knowledge that he was secure among the first musicians of Russia, and by no means last among them. Berlin was the first brief halt on Piotr Ilyich's tour. Having settled himself at a hotel, he visited bookshops, returning with a mass of French books. He visited a museum, enjoyed himself, and especially admired a Murillo *St. Anthony*. Hearing that Berlioz's *Grande Messe des morts* was being sung — German admiration for Berlioz continued to express itself more actively than that of his countrymen — Piotr Ilyich obtained a place in the theatre, where he met the young composer-pianist Franz Xaver Scharwenka. During the evening a stout, distinguished-looking woman of more than middle age attracted his attention and proved to be Désirée Artôt de Padilla, whom he had last seen nearly nineteen years before. He spoke to her. Her reply was extremely friendly, and they looked forward to other more extensive meetings. Little more than one month later, at a party given in Berlin in his honour, Piotr Ilyich again met her, this time with her husband. "Artôt was there," he told Modest. "I was unspeakably happy to meet her again. We re-established our friendship immediately without reference to the past. Her husband, Padilla, embraced me heartily. Tomorrow she gives a dinner. As an older woman she is as fascinating as she was twenty years ago."

From Berlin, after a pleasant visit with Karl U. Davidov, Piotr Ilyich went on to Leipzig. At the railroad station there were Brodsky, Siloti, the prodigious young pianist Arthur Friedheim, and the German pianist Martin Krause. Brodsky took the composer to his home for dinner, where Piotr Ilyich was delighted by the sight of a typically German Christmas tree and by the charm of Brodsky's wife and sister-in-law, whom he described to Modest as "really good Russian women." The following day, January 1, 1888, he went for a walk. When he returned to Brodsky's, some unfamiliar composition was being played in the music room. A "handsome man, rather short and fat," at the piano proved to be the composer of this new trio, Johannes Brahms. "He was very friendly to me," Piotr Ilyich wrote Modest. "Then we sat down to eat. Brahms enjoys a good drink. Grieg, fascinating and sympa-

thetic, was there too." One of the other guests was a slightly eccentric English girl of twenty-nine, an example of that rarity, a
female composer. She was Ethel Mary Smyth, who by the time —
thirty-two years later — that she became a Dame of the British
Empire was to have become one of the most prominent serious
composers of her sex in history.

After dinner the group proceeded to the Gewandhaus, where
the excellent orchestra, conducted by Carl Reinecke, performed
Beethoven's Fifth Symphony (Piotr Ilyich thought the tempo too
slow) and where the St. Timothy Choir, a cappella, performed
several works, including a Bach motet, so perfectly as to fill the
visitor with astonished delight. The featured composition was
Brahms's new Concerto for violin, cello, and orchestra, with the
solo parts played by Joseph Joachim and Robert Hausmann, the
composer conducting. The "Double" Concerto was destined to be
the last of Brahms's large compositions, and even it had been fabricated largely of materials he had been unable to fit into a symphony. Joachim, Brahms's friend since they had met under Schumann's eye thirty-five years earlier, did not like the work, but had,
with Hausmann, played its first performance at Cologne shortly
before the Leipzig concert. Piotr Ilyich wrote Modest: "I sat in the
conductor's box, and met so many people that I could not keep up
with them all." He suffered acutely throughout the evening, and
emphatically did not care for the Brahms "Double" Concerto.

Expanding his impressions of Brahms in his *Diary of My Tour in
1888,* Piotr Ilyich wrote: "Brahms is a shortish man, suggests a
kind of bigness, and has a most sympathetic appearance. His fine
head — almost that of an old man — reminds me of that of a handsome, kindly, elderly Russian priest. His features certainly are not
characteristic of German good looks, and I cannot understand
why some learned ethnographer (Brahms told me this himself
after I had spoken of the impression his appearance made on me)
chose to reproduce his head on page one of his book as being
highly characteristic of German features. A certain softness of
outline, pleasing curves, rather long and somewhat grizzled hair,
kind grey eyes, and a heavy beard freely sprinkled with white —
all this reminded me immediately of the type of pure Great Russian
so often found among our clergy. Brahms's manner is very simple,
devoid of vanity, his humour jovial, and the few hours I spent with
him left me with a most agreeable impression."

The *Diary* contains the following impression of Grieg as Piotr
Ilyich encountered him at Brodsky's home: "There entered the
room a very short, middle-aged man, exceedingly fragile in appearance, with shoulders of uneven height, blond hair brushed
back from the forehead, and a very slight, almost boyish, beard
and moustache. This man's features were not particularly striking,
but his manner at once attracted my sympathy — it would be impossible to call him handsome or his features regular. But he had
an uncommon charm, and his blue eyes, not very large, but irresistibly fascinating, recalled the glance of a charming and candid
child. I rejoiced in my inmost heart when we were introduced and
it turned out that this personality, so inexplicably sympathetic
to me, belonged to a musician whose warmly emotional music had
long before won my heart. It was Edvard Grieg."

Early the following morning Piotr Ilyich went to the Gewandhaus for the first rehearsal of his forthcoming concert. Reinecke
presented him formally to the men, and he responded with a short
speech in German. Despite the fears through which he had been
passing — he had "spent a terrible night" — the rehearsal was encouraging. "Brahms was there," Piotr Ilyich wrote Modest, "and
yesterday and today we have been together a lot. We are ill at
ease because we do not really like each other, but he makes a real
effort to be kind to me. Grieg is charming. Dined with Siloti. Quartet concert at night. The new trio of Brahms. Homesick. Very
tired. You cannot imagine a finer room than at the Gewandhaus.
It is the best concert-room I have ever seen."

The public rehearsal was held on January 4. Despite nervousness, Piotr Ilyich won a success he found particularly flattering.
The Russian visitor was astounded to discover how superior this
first-rate German orchestra was to the best Russian ensembles.
When the rehearsal was over, he found a card from Grieg, who
had been in the audience, congratulating him warmly on the performance. Writing to Jürgenson the next day, he was still discussing Brahms. "He is by no means a total abstainer, but he is very
pleasant, and not so vain as I had expected. But it is Grieg who
has altogether won my heart. He is most taking and sympathetic,
and his wife equally so."

Piotr Ilyich's part in the January 5 concert was to conduct his
First Suite. This went off exceedingly well. There was applause
after each of the six movements — not as much, however, as there

had been at the public rehearsal, when the audience had consisted almost wholly of musicians and students. After the concert Reinecke gave a banquet in honour of the visiting composer-conductor. Piotr Ilyich was much interested by his host's reminiscences of Schumann, and generally found the occasion "not so dull." From the banquet he went on to a party given in his honour by Russian students and did not get to bed until very late.

On the morning of January 6 the Liszt-Verein presented an all-Tchaikovsky program in the auditorium of the old Gewandhaus. Piotr Ilyich sat next to Grieg and his wife. The program contained the Trio, played by Siloti, Karl Halíř, and Alwin Schroeder, the First String Quartet, played by a group headed by Henri Willem Petri,[1] and an arrangement of the barcarolle and fantasy from *Yevgeny Onyegin,* played by Siloti. Those present were highly enthusiastic, and the composer found the renditions exemplary. At the end he was presented with a wreath by the Liszt-Verein.

The fearsome Leipzig critics bent backwards to be polite to the Russian visitor. They were unanimous in preferring the learned fugue with which the First Suite opens to its other movements, which the *Signale* critic described as recalling the "tea-caddy-decoration style of art." They were equally one in preferring both the Trio and the First String Quartet to the suite, and the "andante cantabile" movement of the quartet to everything else. The critic of the *Neue Zeitschrift für Musik,* after accusing the composer of lapses of taste, went so far as to compare this single movement to "a slumbering lily of the valley." No one, however, went so far as to find any of the music noisome, and it was evident at once that Piotr Ilyich Tchaikovsky was taken seriously as both composer and conductor in the very inner sanctum of German music.

Stopping in Berlin on January 8 just long enough to attend a Philharmonic concert, Piotr Ilyich went to Hamburg. There he heard Hans von Bülow conduct superbly — "it would be impossible to play Beethoven's 'Eroica' any better." Freed from duties and engagements for a few days, Piotr Ilyich visited Lübeck. While there, he saw a performance of Shakespeare's *Othello* and one of *L'Africaine.* More important, he received from Vsevolozhsky a telegram with the news that Alexander III had granted him a life pension of 3,000 rubles (approximately $1,500) a year. "I am, of course, deeply happy," he noted in his diary, "but I am also, so to

[1] Father of Egon Petri.

speak, overgrateful. That is, my conscience bothers me, as though I didn't deserve it."

The first rehearsal in Hamburg took place on January 17. "My agitation was going crescendo all the time." Leading off with the Theme and Variations from his Third Suite, Piotr Ilyich found his shyness gradually disappearing. The members of the orchestra were both sympathetic and co-operative, and he was shortly enjoying himself. The next day there were what he called "disorders in the piano concerto," but the rehearsals went generally well. Vasily Sapelnikov's playing of the B-flat minor Piano Concerto delighted orchestra men and composer alike.

The night of January 20, at the Conventgarten, after a hearing of Haydn's "Oxford" Symphony, Piotr Ilyich stepped before the Hamburg public as composer-conductor. The pieces were the Serenade for Strings, the Piano Concerto in B flat minor, and the Theme and Variations from the Third Suite. He noted that he conducted well, that the Serenade won great applause, the concerto — performed superbly by Sapelnikov — less, and the Theme and Variations still less. An appreciable section of the audience began to leave the hall during the final noisy apotheosis in the Variations.[2] When Piotr Ilyich had read the reviews, which were at once vitriolic and stuffily academic, he began to wonder whether he had composed properly to please Germans. They found his music wild, untutored, full of theatricalisms, and missed in it the earnest theoretical graces of their own composers.

The attitude of the Hamburg critics was summed up and all but caricatured by a well-meaning octogenarian who was to be rewarded for his attentions by receiving the dedication of Piotr Ilyich's Fifth Symphony. This was Theodor Ave-Lallemant, chairman of the board of directors of the Hamburg Philharmonic Society. He bluntly told the composer that he did not care for the Tchaikovsky works he had heard, that he could not endure their noisy instrumentation, and that, in particular, he disapproved their use of percussion. He nevertheless conceded that the barbarous Russian had in him the materials out of which a truly good German composer might be moulded. Earnest to the verge of tears, Ave-Lallemant begged Piotr Ilyich to give up Russia and settle in

---

[2] Tchaikovsky gleefully wrote home to Russia that a critic had stated that one of the variations depicted a sitting of the Holy Synod, another an explosion of dynamite.

Germany, "where classical conventions and traditions of high culture could not fail to correct my faults, which were easily explained by my having been born and educated in a country so unenlightened and so inferior to Germany." Piotr Ilyich argued with him, attempted to light up Ave-Lallemant's profound ignorance of Russia and to correct the misinformation he had garnered from Russophobes. He parted from the old gentleman on the friendliest terms. He had no way of realizing that he had just seen a symbolic incarnation of the deaf German prejudice that would continue for another half-century to exalt, not merely great German music, but third- and sixth- and tenth-rate German music at the expense of any music whatsoever composed by such outland savages as Russians, such mere tunesmiths as Italians, such frippery-mongers as Frenchmen.

In Berlin, on January 23, Piotr Ilyich for the first time heard a composition by a young man whom Bülow rated high. It was the Symphony, opus 12, of Richard Strauss. "Bülow has taken him up just at present," he told Modest, "as he formerly took up Brahms and others. To my mind, such an astonishing lack of talent united to such pretentiousness never before existed." At first he thought Strauss's Symphony trashier than the trashiest work of Russia's trashiest composer, but one day later he had begun to think that perhaps he had merely not understood it. He met the young Strauss (who was about to compose *Don Juan*), but had nothing to say of him.

Originally Piotr Ilyich had included *Francesca da Rimini* on the program he was to conduct in Berlin on February 8. On the advice of Bülow and others, he decided to omit it. With the program settled, he went for a few days to Magdeburg. There he saw *Tannhäuser*, which he labelled "a boring opera," tramped the streets filled with admiration for the city's beauty, and read a Bourget novel. In Leipzig, on January 27, he saw an opera near his heart — *Don Giovanni*. There, too, he met Ferruccio Busoni, liked him personally, admired his pianistic power, and even found much to admire in one of his quartets. Grieg, however, continued to interest him more than any of the other musicians he met: he thought Grieg's new sonata worth enthusiasm, and described the Norwegian to Modest as "enormously talented."

On the eve of his Berlin concert Piotr Ilyich attended a Siloti recital. Then he went to Artôt's, again finding Grieg among the guests. "I shall never forget this evening. Both the personality and the art of this singer are as inimitably enchanting as in the period long since gone." He was in good spirits because that day's rehearsal had been particularly good, while Bülow had made a special point of attending and showing the kindest disposition. The concert itself, on February 8, consisted of *Romeo and Juliet,* the B-flat minor Piano Concerto — with Siloti as soloist — the first movement of the First Suite, the *Andante Cantabile* of the First String Quartet, four songs, and *1812.* Siloti's performance was wholly to the composer's liking, and created vibrant enthusiasm among the audience. Piotr Ilyich noted honestly that "the First Suite and the 1812 overture were liked most of all." The next day, preparing to return once more to Leipzig, he was introduced to Moritz Moszkowski, "whose personality I found as attractive as his musical gifts."

The Berlin critics were altogether the friendliest who had passed judgment on Piotr Ilyich in Germany. In high spirits he went to Leipzig, where, at his request, *Die Meistersinger* was being presented. The excellent performance was led by the young first conductor of the Hofoper, Arthur Nikisch. In letters Piotr Ilyich described Wagner's comic masterwork as "very interesting," about the most laudatory phrase he ever applied to any Wagnerian work except *Lohengrin.*

Now Piotr Ilyich was to visit Bohemia, having been invited to conduct in Prague. He was understandably worried over information that the Czechs were planning to make use of his visit, and particularly of his concert, as the core of anti-German demonstrations. Slavophile that he was, Piotr Ilyich nevertheless admired the Germans, and had, in any case, little desire to be involved in political disturbance. Arriving with Siloti in the Prague railroad station on February 12, he found himself face to face with an organized gala reception. He was presented to Antonin Dvořák and then rushed off to the opera to hear Verdi's *Otello.* The following day Dvořák called, remaining for two hours, and the composers became friends at once. Then the days were full of rehearsals, sightseeing, receptions of official delegations, and visits to concerts and operas. Piotr Ilyich heard chamber works by Smetana, dead only four years, and by Dvořák, a performance of *The Bartered Bride,* and much else. He was serenaded by students, honoured in the Rathaus, and generally treated as a distinguished vis-

itor from the greatest of Slav nations to one of its smaller friends.
Dvořák gave him the manuscript score of his Second Symphony,
inscribing it "To Piotr Tchaikovsky in memory of Prague. Anton
Dvořák. February 18, 1888."

The February 19 concert at the Rudolfinum consisted of *Romeo
and Juliet*, the B-flat minor Piano Concerto (with Siloti again as
soloist), the elegy from the Third Suite, the Violin Concerto (with
Karl Halíř as soloist), and *1812*. "I never even suspected how devoted the Czechs are to Russia," Piotr Ilyich wrote Nadezhda
Filaretovna, "or how much they hate the Germans." Detailing this
first concert in his diary, he wrote: "In general, this is, of course,
one of the most memorable days of my life. I have become very
fond of these good Czechs. And with reason!! Heavens! How much
enthusiasm! And not for me, really, but for dear Russia."

Piotr Ilyich's second Prague concert took place at the National
Theatre on February 21. The purely musical part was made up of
the Serenade for Strings, the last movement of the Third Suite, a
piano solo played by Siloti, and *1812*. Then there was a "splendidly
staged" second act of *Swan Lake*. "Tremendous success . . ." says
the composer's diary. "*A moment of absolute happiness*. But only a
moment. Supper. Speeches." The man who could with confidence
and poise conduct two concerts of his own music in two days in
a strange city, receive without painful confusion delegates sent to
honour him, and even memorize and deliver speeches in a foreign
language had progressed far indeed from the confused neurotic
who had once been forced to hold onto his beard while conducting.
As he left Prague in a railway carriage banked with flowers, the
Russian must have felt, mingled with sadness over parting from
new friends, assurance that he had been a goodwill ambassador.
He was to feel extremely bitter that not one newspaper in Russia
carried a single line about his extraordinary successes in Prague.

Political considerations again took an important part in the
public's attitude toward Piotr Ilyich and his music. France had
instituted its policy of close collaboration with Russia, and all
things Russian were *de rigueur* in Paris. The local musicians there
paid him every sort of compliment, many volunteering to partici-
pate either in his public concerts or in private musicales in celebration of his visit. From his arrival on February 24 to his departure for London on March 19, he was the centre of attention
for a mixed group of musicians, social figures, politically minded

amateurs, and newborn Russophiles. A wealthy Russian began the festivities by hiring Colonne's orchestra for Piotr Ilyich to conduct during a soirée at his fashionable home. The program included the Serenade for Strings, songs, and the inevitable orchestrated *Andante Cantabile*. The leading tenor, baritone, and bass of the day — Jean de Reszke, Jean Lassalle, and Édouard de Reszke — sang. Piotr Ilyich's comment was: "A notable evening. . . . Many mistakes while accompanying Lassalle. However, all went well." During the ensuing weeks honour was paid the visiting composer by Gounod, Fauré, Viardot-García, Paladilhe, Massenet, Godard, and Thomé among the musicians. He met the twenty-eight-year-old prodigy Ignace Jan Paderewski, whom he described as "a magnificent pianist."

Encountering Ernest Guiraud again after many years, Piotr Ilyich again described the French-American as "very charming." At the Church of St. Sulpice he heard the "excellent organist," Charles-Marie Widor. At an audition in the Salle Érard, Diémer and his pupils lavished honour on Piotr Ilyich by performing for him some forty of his compositions, after which he understandably felt "touched, but very tired." The Russian Embassy held a fête. The Baronne Tresderne threw open for a time her home, in which *Der Ring des Nibelungen* had first been heard in Paris. He conducted at two Concerts Châtelet. At the first, on March 4, he was applauded noisily — Gounod ostentatiously led the ovation — and the Waltz from the Serenade had to be repeated. At the second the Paris audience proved itself incapable of distinguishing among his works by lavishing its approval on minor bits and neglecting *Francesca da Rimini*.

The attitude of the Paris press set the mould for much of the future's critical attitude toward Tchaikovsky the composer. Modest surmised that its writers had studied César Cui's tendentious book, well known in France as *La Musique en Russie*. They found Piotr Ilyich's music lacking the impress of such a brilliantly defined personality as gave individual force to the music of the true Russians — among whom, curiously, they included not only Rimsky-Korsakov and Borodin, but such ghostly and indeterminate figures as Cui himself and Anatoly Lyadov. He was accused by Frenchmen of being too German, just as the Germans had accused him of being too French, too like Bizet and Delibes. He was taken to task for not having Saint-Saëns's impeccable command of form and Gounod's probity of harmonic enchainment. His works, the critics pontificated, were too long.

Before this visit to Paris came to a close, Piotr Ilyich was a very tired and discouraged man. At one point he considered the plan of returning straight to Russia, but disliked the prospect of doing so with empty pockets. He had promised to go to London to conduct the Philharmonic Society's orchestra, and he kept his promise. Just before embarking for England, he wrote Jürgenson that the tour had not been a financial success, but that he had not undertaken it for money. His idea had been to increase his reputation internationally. "I have won some celebrity," he admitted, "but every hour I ask myself — Why? Is this worth while? And I answer that it is much better to live quietly without fame." He lived scarcely long enough to know that he had not even won enduring fame in France, which within a few years was to begin that neglect of him that until this day has differentiated the French capital musically from the other metropolitan centres of the Western world.

The journey from Paris to London in midwinter was hard, and at moments terrifying. The Channel was so tempestuous that the steamer's passengers lived several hours in fear of catastrophe. Piotr Ilyich's train (whether in France or England is not clear) was stalled by a snowstorm. Nobody welcomed him on his arrival in London. He remained four days mostly alone, for the English reversed the emphasis of his Paris visit: they neglected him personally, but took his music to their hearts and kept it there. At a nerve-racking, boring rehearsal, he found the acoustics of the St. James Hall even worse than those of the Châtelet. At the concert of March 22 he conducted the Serenade for Strings and the Theme and Variations from the Third Suite. "Conducted well," he recorded. "The Serenade was a great success, the suite not so great." He wrote Nadezhda Filaretovna that the audience had recalled him three times, "a good deal from the reserved London public."

The critical press was unanimously well disposed toward Piotr Ilyich as both composer and conductor. The *Musical Times* wondered logically at his not having selected more serious music as the vehicle of his introduction to London. It is clear, more than half a century after the fact, that he would have established himself higher and more quickly had he put the Fourth Symphony on his tour programs. Questions of insufficient rehearsal time and conductorial reticence may have led him to place so much emphasis on the Serenade for Strings, and to schedule the Violin Concerto and *Francesca da Rimini* seldom, the symphonies almost not at all. From London, on March 24, a very weary and antisocial man set out on the long journey home. "Thus came to an end the torments, worries, flurries, and — to be truthful — the joys of my first concert tour abroad." On March 26 he was in Vienna, where he went to a performance of *The Mikado* — "Could scarcely stand two thirds of one act." The next day he wrote Modest that Vienna was as dull and disgusting as ever, and the day after that he left by train for Russia.

Stopping in Taganrog for three days to visit his brother Ippolit, whom he had not seen for two years, Piotr Ilyich arrived in Tiflis on April 7. From there he wrote Modest a letter showing that Pushkin's *The Queen of Spades* had been up for consideration in his mind as a possible opera subject. "I am not at all sorry not to compose The Queen of Spades," he wrote on April 9. "After the failure of The Enchantress I wanted revenge, and was ready to throw myself at any subject. I was then envious that I wasn't composing this.[3] Now that is all over. First of all, during the coming summer I shall *positively compose a symphony*. Secondly, I shall write an opera only when I come upon a subject that really stirs me deeply. The Queen of Spades does not move me, and I could write only a fair to middling opera on this subject." The Fifth Symphony was to materialize as foreseen, but his attitude toward Pushkin's story was to change sufficiently to make it the subject of, after *Yevgeny Onyegin,* the finest and most successful of his operas.

From Tiflis, Piotr Ilyich went to Moscow, remaining there ten days. On May 6 he went to Frolovskoye. There, on a tree-covered hill, he found the house that Alexey Sofronov had been preparing for his occupancy. The house was in itself not so comfortable or well furnished as the one at Maidanovo. But it was remote from the routes of travellers, and was set in thickly wooded country. Beyond the woods, furthermore, opened a wide, unending vista of the flat central Russian plains Piotr Ilyich loved. He became strongly attached to Frolovskoye, though he retained the house there only three years. His ostensible reason for leaving it at the

---

[3] Modest had been vainly trying to turn *The Queen of Spades* into a libretto for a composer named Nikolay Semyenovich Klenovsky.

end of that period was that the gradual thinning-out of the near-by forest had spoiled the place's special charm. On the day he first saw it, he wrote Mme Shpazhinskaya that he was tremendously enthusiastic "over the house, the scenery, the garden, and everything else." He did not settle down to composing for some time, writing Nadezhda Filaretovna that all the news in the papers about his plans was false. He was firmly determined to compose another symphony.

Piotr Ilyich's second official presentation to Alexander III took place in St. Petersburg on May 14, 1888. His impression was that the Tsar's former personal warmth toward him had disappeared, resulting in a rather frigid, protocol-filled meeting. Returning to Frolovskoye, he wrote Modest that the urge to work still eluded him. "What does it mean?" he continued, echoing himself. "Is it possible that I have utterly written myself out? I have neither ideas nor inclinations! Nevertheless I am hoping that little by little I shall accumulate materials for a symphony." He re-examined the Fourth Symphony in detail from the orchestral parts just published by Jürgenson, and wrote Nadezhda Filaretovna that he was certain that it was his best work. By the date of that letter — May 30 — he was actually launched on the Fifth Symphony. As he put it, "I am at last starting to squeeze out, with difficulty, a symphony from my bedulled brains." [4]

The truth was that Piotr Ilyich was composing simultaneously — or perhaps alternately — two large orchestral pieces. In addition to the symphony he was fulfilling a promise made to Lucien Guitry. The French actor had promised him to play the role of Hamlet if Piotr Ilyich would compose incidental music for the production. Beginning with a half-formulated plan to compose something minuscule for a small orchestra, he went on, under the combined inspiration of Shakespeare and his own facility, to complete

---

[4] The following incomplete notes for the Fifth Symphony were discovered in a notebook in the Tchaikovsky Museum at Klin:

"Program of the First Movement of the Symphony: Introduction. Complete resignation before Fate, or, which is the same, before the inscrutable predestination of Providence.

"Allegro I) Murmurs, doubts, plaints, reproaches against XXX [three crosses in the original]

"II) Shall I throw myself into the embraces of Faith???"

In the corner of the notebook leaf is written: "A wonderful program, if I could only carry it out."

a long, full-dress Overture that was to be his Opus 67. Both *Hamlet* and the Fifth Symphony were complete in sketch by July 4. Piotr Ilyich began orchestrating the latter some time before August 6, completing it in about three weeks. He turned to that of *Hamlet* before September 27, and wrote finis to the Overture on October 19.

Piotr Ilyich wrote Nadezhda Filaretovna on June 22 that he intended to work hard, being terribly eager to prove to the world that he was not dead. Less than two weeks later, having completed the sketch of his Fifth Symphony, he told her that he found comparison of it with "our" Fourth and the other symphonies extremely difficult. It seemed, however, to lack the ease that had formerly characterized his output. On August 19 he wrote her: "Now that the symphony is nearly completed . . . I can say that it is, thank God, no worse than the others. This knowledge is very sweet to me!" He permitted himself to be more positive about it when it was wholly finished, writing her on August 26: "My symphony is ready, and it seems to me that I have not failed, that it is good." No long work was ever so consistently satisfactory to him as the Fourth Symphony; the Fifth was to waver widely in his esteem. He had no means of realizing that it would challenge the popularity of Beethoven's Fifth and would eventually become the most beloved and popular of his own large compositions for orchestra alone.

Laroche had composed in sketch an Overture that Piotr Ilyich liked. With the Fifth Symphony out of the way, he therefore turned to the task of orchestrating his friend's work. Within a day or two, also, he wrote Modest that Vsevolozhsky had sent him the libretto for a ballet, to be called *Sleeping Beauty*. "It is excellent," he pronounced. He put it aside and went to Kamenka for a ten-day visit. Labouring on Laroche's Overture and the first proofs of the Fifth Symphony, he was very happy to learn that the latter was creating a furor among his Moscow friends. "S. I. Taneyev," he wrote Modest on September 19, "(and this is most precious to me) is completely enraptured. And I thought it good for nothing." When the Laroche Overture stood completely orchestrated, Piotr Ilyich varied work on proofs of the Fifth Symphony with orchestration of *Hamlet*. He had to go into Moscow twice shortly after September 28, called first by news that his old friend Hubert was hopelessly ill, and then — after he had returned to Frolovskoye —

by a telegram from Hubert himself: "My hours are numbered." On October 12 he attended Hubert's funeral. In a letter to Mme Shpazhinskaya he referred to the dead man as "one of my closest, oldest, and dearest friends."

"I have finished all my tasks, and am now preparing to conduct," Piotr Ilyich wrote Parasha on October 28. He had completed *Hamlet,* was so well advanced on the proofs of the Fifth Symphony that further corrections could be entrusted to Siloti, and had completed his Opus 65, Six French Songs, which he dedicated to Désirée Artôt. He had agreed to the most strenuous conductorial effort of his career. In addition to other compositions, he was to conduct the Second Piano Concerto and the world *première* of the Fifth Symphony in St. Petersburg on November 17, *Hamlet* and a repetition of the Fifth Symphony on the 24th, and then — in Prague — the Second Piano Concerto and the Fifth Symphony before December 6, and the Prague *première* of *Yevgeny Onyegin* on that date.

At the St. Petersburg Philharmonic Society's November 17 concert Sapelnikov played the solo part in the Second Piano Concerto. One review that appeared between the November 17 and November 28 concerts praised the concerto as "no less interesting than the first," and found it intensely Russian, "though in order to achieve this, Tchaikovsky has not resorted to folksong themes. The concerto should be as popular among pianists as the first." Continuing, the reviewer (one Ivanov) found the Fifth Symphony less good than the Second and the Fourth, and reminiscent of *Francesca da Rimini.* He called the orchestration brilliant, but criticized excessive use of the wind choir. "But where the brass and percussion instruments reach an orgy is in Laroche's Overture, orchestrated by Tchaikovsky. One can go no farther — for any additional effect . . . nothing would do but the demolition of the auditorium. It would be impossible to achieve greater noise. The audience seemed completely stunned."

On November 22 Glazunov called on the tired, happy, and busy Piotr Ilyich, presenting him with the manuscript of his *Stenka Razin,* on which he had written: "To the deeply respected Piotr Ilyich Tchaikovsky, from an admirer of his talent and mastery. A. Glazunov. November 22, 1888." Two days later Piotr Ilyich conducted the second half of a Russian Musical Society concert. In addition to one song, he led the world *première* of *Hamlet* and the second performance of the Fifth Symphony. The next day he left for Prague. The November 27 issue of *Novoye Vremya* carried a review of *Hamlet*. This pointed out that Shakespeare's philosophical tragedy "does not lend itself to music" — a judgment no composer has successfully disproved.

In Prague, meanwhile, Piotr Ilyich was rehearsing both *Yevgeny Onyegin* and the compositions for the concert. During the previous season he had conducted two Prague concerts gratis. This time the managers of the Prague Theatre, at which *Yevgeny Onyegin* was to be sung, had organized the concert so that he was to receive half the profit. Because of a poorly chosen day, and because of what he considered mismanagement, the concert was thinly attended. A relative handful heard the Fifth Symphony and the Second Piano Concerto, again with Sapelnikov. The gate was meagre. In something of a dudgeon Piotr Ilyich declined the 300 florins representing his portion, instructing that they be paid to a local pension fund for musicians. This action was noised about, the newspapers took it up, and the merely inept management was loudly blamed. Partly because of this imbroglio, but more because the opera truly appealed to them, those present at the performance of *Yevgeny Onyegin* raised their collective voice in ovation after ovation. The opera established itself in Prague and was repeated there time after time for many years.

Stopping off in Vienna, Piotr Ilyich learned with sorrow that his niece, Vera Davidova, who had married a Rimsky-Korsakov, had died. Retailing this news to Nadezhda Filaretovna, whose son had married the dead girl's sister, he described Vera as "an unusually sympathetic person, mild and charming." The sting of two deaths, Hubert's and his niece's, remained in Piotr Ilyich's always death-haunted mind as he went via St. Petersburg to Frolovskoye. He sank into myopic gloom. To Nadezhda Filaretovna, on December 14, he wrote: "Having played my new symphony twice in Petersburg and once in Prague, I have come to the conclusion that it is not successful. It contains something repellent, an excess of colour and insincerity, something laboured that audiences recognize instinctively. It was clear to me that the applause I received was for my earlier labour, and that the symphony itself did not really please the public. This awareness brings me a sharp pain of dissatisfaction. Am I really worked out, as they say? Can I merely repeat myself and ring the changes on my earlier idiom? Last night

I went through *our* symphony. What a difference! How imm
urably better it is! This is very, very sad!" Later, after the
Moscow performance of the Fifth Symphony, he added to this
harsh critique.

Finding refuge from an access of pessimism in a fury of work,
Piotr Ilyich took up Vsevolozhsky's libretto for *Sleeping Beauty*
and the outline of needed music supplied by Petipa. In little more
than five weeks he completed the ballet. In the midst of this fruitful period he again visited St. Petersburg. At a concert in which
Rimsky-Korsakov, as both composer and conductor, was the central attraction, Piotr Ilyich conducted *The Tempest* with unusual
success. "I am very glad," he wrote on December 31, "to have had
this chance to demonstrate publicly that I am outside all parties,
and that I consider it flattering to be where Rimsky-Korsakov is
the principal actor." Having further heard his Third String Quartet played, Piotr Ilyich returned to Frolovskoye in a contented
state of mind and resumed work on *Sleeping Beauty*. Jürgenson,
using Alexey Sofronov as his proxy, surprised him with two Christmas presents. One was a diminutive Christmas tree, the other as
complete a collection of Mozart as could be obtained in Russia.

On January 14, 1889, in Prague, Antonin Dvořák sat down and
wrote Piotr Ilyich:

Dear Friend, — When you were recently in Prague with us I promised to write you about your opera *Onyegin*. I am moved to do so now,
not only because you asked me to, but also because I am impelled to
express all I felt on hearing your work. I confess with joy that your opera
made a profound impression on me, the sort of impression I expect to
receive from a true work of art. I have no hesitation in telling you
that none of your other compositions has given me so much pleasure
as *Onyegin*.

This is a wonderful creation, full of warm emotion and poetry, and
finely made in all details; in short, this music is captivating, and enters
our hearts so deeply that we can never forget it. Whenever I go to hear
it, I feel transported into another world.

I congratulate both you and ourselves on this work. May God grant
that you give us many another like it.

I embrace you, and remain your sincerely devoted

Anton Dvořák

During the morning hours when he did not work at *Sleeping
Beauty*, Piotr Ilyich read Jahn's *Mozart*, at the same time examin-

ing the compositions of which Jahn spoke. "Thanks to Jürgenson for his present," he wrote in his diary. The ballet grew swiftly on some days, with difficulty on others. At a meeting of the directorate of the Russian Musical Society on January 19 Piotr Ilyich saw his old friend I. A. Klimenko for the first time in seventeen years. From time to time visitors sought him out at Frolovskoye — Jürgenson, Klimenko, Siloti, and Taneyev among them. There were arguments about Tolstoy, discussions of Mozart and of Piotr Ilyich's Fifth Symphony, which his guests often liked better than he did. He read Chekhov and Dostoyevsky, writing Mme Shpazhinskaya: "Have you read anything by Chekhov? In my opinion, this young writer promises to be a great literary force." By January 29 he had completed the first four scenes of *Sleeping Beauty*. Two days later, he took them to St. Petersburg. On February 2 a preliminary rehearsal of excerpts from the score took place at the Bolshoi. The following day the composer conferred about problems of ballet with Vsevolozhsky and Petipa. He was about to embark on his second international tour, and left for Germany on February 5.

XVI

HAVING tarried briefly in Berlin, Piotr Ilyich was in Cologne on February 10. The following day he twice rehearsed his Third Suite, and attended a supper given for him by the Musicians' Society. Once during that day, he wrote Modest, he had been seized by homesickness "and a wild yearning for April 20" — the day he was scheduled to return to Russia. The concert of February 12 was an unquestionable success, and when the audience recalled Piotr Ilyich, the members of the orchestra honoured him with a fanfare. Two days later the critic of the *Kölnische Zeitung* had high praise for the Third Suite, though — evidently under the influence of Liszt or Berlioz — he wondered "whether Tchaikovsky would not have done well further to elucidate the titles of the separate sections . . . by the addition of a program."

On February 13 Piotr Ilyich went to Frankfurt am Main. During a rehearsal there the managers of the orchestra, alarmed by the thunderous finale of *1812*, timidly asked him to drop it from the program and confine himself to the Third Suite. To this he agreed, but with "an unpleasant consciousness of failure." The following day's rehearsal went unexpectedly well. Writing to Jürgenson about the concert, Piotr Ilyich described the reception of the Third Suite as "a genuine ovation, all the more remarkable in that the audience there is cold, and is fond only of the classics and of Brahms." The *Frankfurter General-Anzeiger* of February 16 described the ovation as "so hearty and prolonged that nothing like it has been accorded any novelty in recent years except perhaps when Richard Strauss conducted his First Symphony."

Dresden was not so encouraging to Piotr Ilyich as Cologne and Frankfurt am Main had been. The orchestra proved much less than first-class; and he was to conduct, not the moderately difficult Third Suite, but the Fourth Symphony and the B-flat minor Piano Concerto, which overtaxed the instrumentalists' capabilities. Piotr Ilyich began his Dresden visit badly by attending a performance

of Goldmark's *Die Königin von Saba,* which struck him as false
and conventional. The rehearsals of February 18 and 19 distracted
him: his own diary phrase for his state after the second is "fussed
to exhaustion." On the morning of the concert day a visit to Raphael's *Sistine Madonna* refreshed him considerably. The pianist in
the concerto was Emil Sauer, a pupil of both Liszt and Nikolay
Rubinstein, and an artist for whom Piotr Ilyich held the highest
regard. In his diary, Piotr Ilyich admitted that "the musicians tried
hard." He added: "Very nervous, and conducted poorly. The audience did not like the first movement of the Fourth Symphony very
much. They liked the Andante better, and the Scherzo still more.
After the Finale, a real success. The musicians played a fanfare."
In a letter to Modest, however, he described that success as smaller
than he had enjoyed in Cologne and Frankfurt. After the concert
there was the traditional supper in his honour, this time tendered
by Sauer.

On the night of February 23 Piotr Ilyich was attending a party
at the Berlin home of Désirée Artôt de Padilla. During five days
in the city he saw her every day, and none of the spell she had
always cast on him was lost. Wherever he went, she was invited
with him, and — he wrote Modest — he loved her very much. At
the rehearsal on February 25 he found the orchestra marvellous.
His part of the concert the next day was made up of the Serenade
for Strings and *Francesca da Rimini.* Although he entered in his
diary: "Not so good; full house," Piotr Ilyich wrote Nadezhda
Filaretovna that the audience rose enthusiastically to the Serenade,
while *Francesca,* drawing hisses from a minority, won loud applause from a majority. On the eve of his departure from Berlin,
Piotr Ilyich attended a party given in his honour by his old con-
frere Karl Klindworth, now one of the city's leading musicians.
Klindworth was one of those Piotr Ilyich invited to be a guest conductor of the Moscow Russian Musical Society's concerts during
the forthcoming season, the others being Massenet, Dvořák, and
Brahms. "That would be grand!" was his comment on the idea of
inviting Brahms. His admiration for the man remained uncoloured
by his very real dislike of the composer.

Before departing from Berlin, Piotr Ilyich received news of the
death, in Moscow, of Karl U. Davidov. He enjoyed spending time
with Adolf Brodsky, at whose home he met Brodsky's young
pupil Ottokar Nováček and the Norwegian composer Christian

Sinding. During the evening there was a performance of "my Third Quartet in a phenomenal rendition."

Arrived at his hotel in Hamburg on March 11, Piotr Ilyich was pleased to discover that the next room was occupied by Brahms. His pleasure turned to delight when he was told that the German composer had remained in Hamburg an additional day solely in order to attend the first rehearsal of the Fifth Symphony. That rehearsal occurred on March 12. Piotr Ilyich received an entirely cordial reception from the members of the orchestra. The reading of the symphony went fairly well, but Piotr Ilyich could sense that neither the musicians nor Brahms liked the final movement. "What is most important," he added in reporting this to Modest in a letter written immediately after the rehearsal, "I myself find it odious."

Piotr Ilyich and Brahms lunched together. As before, they found nothing to dislike in each other's personality, the Russian describing Brahms as "very sympathetic," and speaking appreciatively of "his frankness and simplicity." Brahms said flatly that he liked the Fifth Symphony except for the Finale, and Piotr Ilyich, though not in any tone of *quid pro quo*, confessed to not caring greatly for those of Brahms's compositions that he knew. He invited Brahms to conduct in Moscow and was genuinely disappointed when met with refusal. After this meeting Piotr Ilyich was at first inclined to be offended at Brahms's judgment of the Finale of the symphony, but gradually he forgot the sting of the German's admirable forthrightness and found himself again full of admiration for the innate nobility of Brahms's character. Nothing except a basic change in Brahms's music could have altered his opinions about that.

After the March 14 rehearsal Piotr Ilyich felt that the men in the orchestra had begun to like the Fifth Symphony. That night he went to a gathering at the Society of Musicians. "German humour. However, nice people," he noted succinctly in his diary. Looking back on the March 15 Philharmonic concert from Hanover two days later, Piotr Ilyich was in a mood to tell Nadezhda Filaretovna that the Fifth Symphony had won a great success, and that everybody in Hamburg had received him like an old and beloved friend. To Modest he added: "Most pleasant of all is the fact that I no longer find the symphony bad, and love it once again."

In Paris, on March 22, Piotr Ilyich attended a rehearsal of a

Trio by Cécile Chaminade. It is impossible to say whether his diary entry refers to the lady or indirectly to the music: it reads simply: "I don't like her." He was better pleased by an Opéra-Comique performance of Lalo's *Le Roi d'Ys*. He had three meetings with Massenet, who appeared flattered by the invitation to conduct in Moscow and who temporarily accepted it. Piotr Ilyich also "engaged Paderewski, who has had a colossal success in Paris. He is not inferior to D'Albert, and one of the leading pianists of the day."

At the Opéra Piotr Ilyich heard Gounod's *Roméo et Juliette*, with Jean de Reszke and Emma Eames. He found Eames, who had made her Opéra debut in the same role two weeks earlier, "most attractive." He went to a rehearsal by Colonne of the Theme and Variations from his Third Suite, and was hurt by the audience's indifference. The next day, however, after a visit from Paderewski — "a charming man" — he went to the concert itself and found the same music a great success. "Massenet enthusiastic," he noted to Nadezhda Filaretovna. He attended a Jeune France rehearsal, devoted to younger French composers, and talked with Vincent d'Indy. On April 7 he heard "with the greatest of pleasure Berlioz's best work, La Damnation de Faust. How I love this composition." This was in a letter from London to Bobyk Davidov, in which he also told of his last evening in Paris, spent at Viardot-García's. "I heard an opera that she composed twenty years ago to a libretto by Turgenyev [*Le Dernier Sorcier*]. The singers were her two daughters and her pupils, among whom was a Russian who performed a national dance to the delight of all the spectators. I have seen the famous Tour Eiffel quite near. It is very fine."

Piotr Ilyich had arrived in London on April 10 and had immediately rehearsed his First Suite and First Piano Concerto with the London Philharmonic, with Sapelnikov as soloist. He found the members of the orchestra cold and indifferent. The following day, after writing Bobyk Davidov that he had decided to compose a French opera to be called *La Courtisane* (to a libretto by Galée and Detroyat), he went to another rehearsal in the St. James Hall. There a young American composer named Reginald De Koven took up so much time that Piotr Ilyich wrote in his diary: "I was furious." The orchestra men continued aloof, but the concert that night was received by the London public with vociferous indications of pleasure.

Early on April 12, the morning after the concert, Piotr Ilyich left London for Marseille. There he boarded a Messageries Maritimes steamer for Batum. En route through the Mediterranean, he worked on the Polonaise for the third act of *Sleeping Beauty,* alternating that labour with reading Théophile Gautier's *Capitaine Fracasse.* On April 17 he went ashore at Syra, the following day at Smyrna. On shipboard he made friends of a Moscow University student and a fourteen-year-old boy who were travelling together. The three of them spent the 20th ashore in Constantinople, where they went sightseeing. "Savage singing — the cries of some fanatic," his diary records. "Sancta Sofia is the most grandiose of the ancient relics, but there are many additional things of interest in Constantinople." After an evening ashore they returned to the ship. "I shall miss them very much," Piotr Ilyich wrote Modest of the two boys, and Modest adds that he went to his cabin and cried bitterly, "as if he knew in advance that he would never again meet this lovable and highly gifted boy on earth. Volodya Sklifasovsky died in January 1890."

The following day Piotr Ilyich noted that the Bosporus, "with its palaces, villas, and gardens, is marvellously beautiful and picturesque." Having finished *Capitaine Fracasse,* he was reading Sainte-Beuve's *Nouveaux Lundis.* But on April 23 the ship docked at Batum, and two days later, with a visit to Ippolitov-Ivanov in Tiflis, he was back in the world of musical Russia. He remained in Tiflis until May 14, attended several concerts, continued on the third act of *Sleeping Beauty.* A dinner was given on May 7 in celebration of his forty-ninth birthday. "It was gay," he said. A morning musicale of his compositions was put on by the Tiflis Artists' Circle, and he had a thoroughly good time.

En route to Moscow, and stopping at Mleti, Piotr Ilyich was again "allowed to spend the night in the imperial chambers." He had been sorry to leave Tiflis and the Caucasus behind. "In Tiflis . . . it is wonderful just now; all the fruit trees are in bloom," he had told Nadezhda Filaretovna. "The atmosphere is so clear that all the far-away snow-peaks are visible, and the air is rich with the sensation of spring, fragrant and life-giving. After the London fog it seems so beautiful that I cannot find phrases for it." In Moscow he was at once thrown headlong into musical politics. Taneyev had resigned the directorship of the Conservatory, and Safonov, to whom the position had been offered, had made Al-

brecht's resignation a condition of his acceptance. Piotr Ilyich
supported Albrecht's cause to the point of threatening to resign
from the board if the cellist were not decorated for his faithful
services. He waited long enough to attend the examinations in
counterpoint and free composition and then, on May 27, went to
St. Petersburg.

July 1889 would round out half a century in Anton Rubinstein's
career as a pianist, and Piotr Ilyich was a member of the committee to arrange the celebration of that anniversary. On May 29 he
found the great man "very cordial." That evening, forcing himself to stop in at a restaurant for supper, he met, among others,
Rimsky-Korsakov, Lyadov, and Glazunov. "They threw us out
at two o'clock." That sort of strenuous metropolitan life no longer
had the charm that it had held for him more than twenty years
earlier, and it was with relief that he left for Frolovskoye the next
morning. He was to remain there almost constantly until late
September. For a week he worked away at Act III of *Sleeping
Beauty*. As part of this task he read the score of Adolphe Adam's
Giselle "diligently." He composed the Mazurka on June 6 and completed *Sleeping Beauty* the next day. On this first draft of the
ballet he wrote: "Finished draft June 7, 1889, 8 o'clock in the evening. Thank God! All together, I worked ten days in October,
three weeks in January, and now another week; all together some
forty days." The orchestration was begun, after a brief official
visit to Moscow, on June 12. One day he would describe himself as
working "hard," another "desperately," another "like a madman."
On June 21 it was: "Worked and worked and worked" on the
orchestration of *Sleeping Beauty*. On the 25th, "with pleasure,"
he orchestrated the Waltz, but did not forget to note in his diary:
"Anniversary of Mother's death, thirty-five years ago." Shortly
later he wrote Nadezhda Filaretovna that the ballet was progressing, that he considered it one of his best compositions, and that he
was finding orchestration more difficult than formerly. He had,
he told her, created several entirely new orchestral effects, which
he hoped would prove both interesting and beautiful. On August
28, with a feeling that "a whole mountain has fallen off my shoulders," he completed the "huge" score.

Yevgeny Onyegin was to be restaged in Moscow, and Piotr
Ilyich had agreed to conduct the first performance. The rehearsals
lasted about six days. Piotr Ilyich thought the revival exceedingly

luxurious. He was satisfied with the performance on September 30, and described it to Nadezhda Filaretovna in the terms he reserved for successes that pleased him.

During ten days in St. Petersburg, Piotr Ilyich composed his contributions to the Rubinstein jubilee. One was a chorus to words by Polonsky: *Greetings to Anton Rubinstein,* the other an Impromptu for piano. The latter was included in an album presented to the pianist by his former students of the St. Petersburg Conservatory. Piotr Ilyich also attended survey rehearsals of *Sleeping Beauty* at the Marinsky. Returning to Moscow on October 13, he moved into an apartment on Troitskaya Street that he had rented for the winter some time before and that Alexey Sofronov had arranged for him. He had decided to live temporarily in Moscow because his official duties would require his constant presence there and because he sometimes found the long evenings at Frolovskoye lonely. He missed Laroche, who was staying in St. Petersburg.

Piotr Ilyich had been reading Chekhov with increasing admiration and had freely recommended the young man's work to various friends. Now he learned that Chekhov was planning to dedicate a book to him. On October 26 he called on the author to thank him. The collection of short stories — *Sombre People* — duly appeared with the following dedication: "To Piotr Ilyich Tchaikovsky from a future librettist. October 26, 1889. A. Chekhov." It is just as well that the implied opera never came into being: a less likely librettist than Chekhov would be impossible to name for any composer other than Debussy or Delius. The day after Piotr Ilyich's visit Chekhov, in a letter to Suvorin, wrote: "I had a visit from Tchaikovsky yesterday, which flattered me a great deal, in the first place because he's a big personality, and secondly because I love his music very much, particularly *Onyegin.* We want to write a libretto (on Lermontov's *Bela*)."

One of Piotr Ilyich's turns as conductor of the Moscow Russian Musical Society came up on November 9, when he led a program that included his Violin Concerto. Two weeks later he wrote Mme Shpazhinskaya: "I have my holiday moments when I succeed in accomplishing something — for example, my Moscow concert of November 9." On the day after this letter he again conducted, and this time Siloti took the solo in the B-flat minor Piano Concerto. Then Piotr Ilyich had to go to St. Petersburg for the Rubinstein jubilee. At a rehearsal there, he told Nadezhda Filaretovna, he felt "like a real martyr." His *Greetings to Anton Rubinstein* was sung at the Society of Nobles on November 30, and on the same occasion the album of tributes from his former pupils was formally presented to the great pianist. Members of the imperial family were present. Georg, Duke of Mecklenburg-Strelitz — grandson of Rubinstein's first patroness, Yelena Pavlovna — made a speech. There were delegations from foreign countries. Taneyev and Safonov were there. Of the mighty who might have been expected to attend, only Alexander III, his anti-Semitism aroused and his now impenetrable gloom unpierced, was not there. Balakirev, once again retiring into mystic inertia, was absent too. His reply to an invitation had been: "Rubinstein has done nothing but harm to Russian music."

On December 1 Piotr Ilyich conducted a Rubinstein jubilee concert of the St. Petersburg Russian Musical Society — an all-Rubinstein program that included the G minor ("Russian") Symphony, a *Conzertstück* composed especially for the occasion — with Rubinstein playing the solo as only he could — and the symphonic poem *Russia.* Again there were cheers and speeches, again the honoured man sat impassive and dark-browed, showing only fitful signs of either appreciation or emotion of any sort. This was only the first or second time Piotr Ilyich had, in public, led any compositions but his own. The following day, however, at the Society of Nobles, he conducted an even more taxing program — again all-Rubinstein. This included dances from the opera *Feramors,* as well as a complete performance of the Biblical opera-oratorio *The Tower of Babel,* the latter with a chorus of seven hundred. "From November 13 to December 1," Piotr Ilyich confided to Nadezhda Filaretovna, "I went through a martyrdom, and I still wonder how I endured it."

Activity had become perpetual with Piotr Ilyich. Returning to Moscow, he plunged into rehearsals again, this time of a Musical Society special concert for the benefit of musicians' widows and orphans. At that concert, on December 7, the *Pezzo Capriccioso* for cello and orchestra had its first Russian performance, and Piotr Ilyich spread his wings with a reading of Beethoven's Ninth Symphony. Then it was back to St. Petersburg for more preliminary rehearsals of *Sleeping Beauty.* He conducted again on December 22 — *Hamlet* and the Concert Fantasy. He attended a meeting of the imperial theatres directorate at which there was talk of his composing an opera to Pushkin's *The Queen of Spades,* and even discussion of the staging of this work, "not a single note of which is composed," he wrote Nadezhda Filaretovna in amazement on January 7, 1890. He was forced to remain in St. Petersburg because the sets for *Sleeping Beauty* were being delayed. He decided that, once the ballet had been performed, he would go to Italy and rest — which meant begin the new opera.

On January 14, 1890, at the Marinsky, in the presence of Alexander III and a crowd of nobles and high officials, the dress rehearsal of *Sleeping Beauty* was held. Piotr Ilyich's diary is ironic regarding the Tsar's comment. " 'Very charming'!!!" is his quotation of it. "His Majesty treated me in a most offhand manner. God be with him." The public *première,* with Carlotta Brianza dancing Princess Aurora, Marie M. Petipa as the Lilac Fairy, Paul A. Gerdt as Prince Désiré (now called Prince Charming), and Enrico Ceccheti as the male Bluebird, and with Riccardo Drigo conducting, took place on January 15. The production was said to have cost 80,000 rubles (about $40,000), and was of unprecedented splendour. Marius Petipa had lavished his unrivalled mastery of choreographic technique on it. Piotr Ilyich, labouring with earnestness and love, had composed for it one of the richest scores ever designed for dancing. The Perrault story on which it was based fitted flawlessly into a ballet book. But the public that first night, though politely attentive, showed little more enthusiasm than had the Tsar. The full symphonic character of the music bewildered them.

In that they have remained almost alone; for *Sleeping Beauty* persisted, becoming one of Russia's most enduring popular theatrical entertainments, as it is to this day. It became known throughout the world — though mostly in excerpts — and its music, or at least several sections of it, belongs among the universally familiar. In 1921, at the Alhambra Theatre, London, Sergey Diaghilev, with the assistance of a remarkable group including Bronislava Nijinska, Leon Bakst, Sir Oswald Stoll, and several dancers and other artists who could recall the 1890 St. Petersburg production of *Sleeping Beauty,* revived the ballet entire as *The Sleeping Princess.* When Diaghilev chose to include some numbers that existed only in piano score, having been dropped before the St. Petersburg *première,* Stravinsky, a confirmed Tchaikovskyan, orchestrated them. Carlotta Brianza, teaching in Paris, agreed to dance the role of the evil fairy Carabosse. With a richness of staging that challenged the 1890 production, and with a cast that included the greatest active classic dancers of the period — Vera Trefilova, Lubov Egorova, and Olga Spessivtseva alternating as Aurora, Vladimirov as Prince Charming, and Lydia Lopokova as the Lilac Fairy [1] — *The Sleeping Princess* was a dazzling artistic event, but a dire financial failure.

Out of the ruins of *The Sleeping Princess* have grown at least two smaller ballets, still clinging to shreds of Piotr Ilyich's wonderful score. *Aurora's Wedding* and *Princess Aurora* are familiar to balletomanes in France, England, Australia, and the United States. Who could forget Baronova or Markova as Aurora? Or Ian Gibson, to name the most brilliant of recent male dancers, as the Bluebird? More than half a century after its *première*, *Sleeping Beauty*, though maimed — only the music would be recognizable to Piotr Ilyich, and not all of that as it is performed by a ballet orchestra of today — is entirely alive. American and English ballet audiences, at least, are wise and trained enough today so that a brilliant revival of *Sleeping Beauty* entire would have a better than fair prospect of success. What we lack is a Diaghilev.

In *Sleeping Beauty* Piotr Ilyich showed himself the supreme master of the specialized technical art of composing music for ballet. His music is not only beautiful — it survives concert performance admirably — but danceable, and of service to the peculiar problems of choreography. The "Bluebird Variations" are the supreme test of virtuosity in the dance, and the music accompanying them exhilarates and sets off that virtuosity. The story and the choreography are mated to the music superbly, but that is because Piotr Ilyich knew better than anyone else has ever known how to mate them so. The score is glittering and gala, as a balletic fairy-story score should be. Piotr Ilyich need not have compared himself unfavourably with Delibes: he had as far surpassed the Frenchman in this branch of musical art as the Frenchman had surpassed nearly all of his predecessors.

On January 26 Piotr Ilyich departed for western Europe with no definite destination in mind. Alexey Sofronov had to remain behind: his wife lay on her deathbed. Piotr Ilyich therefore took Modest's manservant with him instead. In Berlin he hit upon the

[1] The ensemble included young Anton Dolin.

idea of going to Florence, where he arrived on January 30. The very next day he began to compose *The Queen of Spades*. He had not begun with enthusiasm for the idea, but the libretto Modest had made for Klenovsky from Pushkin's tale had been approved by the theatrical authorities. He completed the first scene in nine days. On January 31, just having begun work, he wrote in his diary: "Not bad. (The beginning is stolen from Napravnik.)" With few interruptions, he worked at the first sketch until March 15, writing Modest on that date that he had completed the opera three hours before. He set to work the following day on the piano score, finishing that on April 5. The orchestration was begun within about four days, and was finished at Frolovskoye on June 5, the entire task having occupied one hundred and twenty-six days.

From Florence, on February 4, Piotr Ilyich wrote Modest that he found the libretto of *The Queen of Spades* very good, but somewhat wordy. In completing and revising it, he suggested, Modest should be as brief and succinct as possible. He added that he was omitting a few details. All was going with reasonable smoothness when, on February 11, Piotr Ilyich received a letter from Jürgenson. It contained news of Antonina Ivanovna that, he wrote in his diary, "upset me terribly. . . . Was like a maniac the whole day long. . . . Could not work." No further reference to this news, no clue to its import can be found. Possibly Piotr Ilyich's wife was showing clear signs of the insanity that was to land her in an asylum six years later. Possibly she had been gossiping about her husband, or merely threatening to gossip. He raged over this for one day — and then turned back to *The Queen of Spades*. This was almost the last reference he made, at least in writings that survive, to poor, nymphomaniac, self-deluded Antonina Ivanovna.

In the fourth scene of *The Queen of Spades* the hero, Hermann, appears before the old Countess in her bedroom. As she falls asleep, he begs her to tell him the secret of the three mysterious cards that enabled her always to win. When she refuses — she has been warned that to reveal the secret again will cause her death — Hermann points a pistol at her. She dies of fright, having failed to name the cards. This scene deeply impressed Piotr Ilyich, and he wrote Anna Merkling that while composing it he was terrified. Days after, he added: "I am still under the impress of this terror." In his diary he wrote: "Have been very nervous from working. . . . Curious that I should be both so madly inspired and yet find the work so full of difficulties." On February 23, having completed this fourth scene, Piotr Ilyich turned back to the third. Composing the pastiche intermezzo that accompanied an eighteenth-century ballet-divertissement at a ball, he noted in his diary: "At times it seemed to me as though I were living in the eighteenth century, and that after Mozart there was nothing."

The most renowned single number in *The Queen of Spades*, Liza's ever popular third-act arioso: "It is near to midnight," was written, both words and music, on March 7. Piotr Ilyich remarked that he agonized while writing the words. "Definitely, I am no poet." The following day he received word from Alexey Sofronov, who had just carried out his wish by renting the Frolovskoye house so that he might be free to lease a place more to his liking. Alexey's wife had died. "Wept," says Piotr Ilyich's diary. He wept again a few days later while composing Hermann's final aria. "Caused by weariness," he guessed, "but maybe because it is really good." Time had done nothing to toughen the light skin that overlay his emotions. Individual suffering, whether real or fictional, could always draw out his easy, sincere, and unashamed tears.

On March 13, having considered his relation to the Moscow Russian Musical Society from all sides, and having discussed the matter by letter, he wrote officially to the Society resigning from its directorate and declining to conduct six concerts during its coming season. He had decided to free himself from all outside duties except those involved in foreign tours, and to use his time as he pleased — which meant in composition. He had learned that his musical friends in Russia were planning to make a jubilee celebration of the twenty-fifth anniversary of his debut — at the Moscow Conservatory, in 1865 — as a professional musician. "Of course," he wrote Anatoly, "I shall decline all celebrations."

With the piano score of Act II of *The Queen of Spades* all but complete, Piotr Ilyich on March 31 gave his opinion of the opera as a whole in a letter to Modest. "Either I am terribly and inexcusably mistaken, or The Queen of Spades is really my chef-d'œuvre. Some of the passages in the fourth scene, for example, on the arrangement of which I was working today, fill me with so much fear, terror, and emotion that *it is impossible* that listeners should not feel at least part of this. . . . I wrote the opera with complete forgetfulness of self and with delight; the orchestration will undoubtedly give me pleasure." On April 8, having completed the piano score, he added: "It seems to me now that the history of the world is divided into two periods: the first consists of everything that has happened since the creation of the world up to the composition of The Queen of Spades. The second began a month ago."

Before leaving Florence on April 7, Piotr Ilyich paid a duty call on the Uffizi Gallery. "I must confess," he wrote Modest, "that painting, particularly the old masters, is in general beyond my comprehension and leaves me cold." Some days later, in Rome, he turned to orchestration — an art that left him far from cold — and began to clothe his sketch of *The Queen of Spades*. "I find this work easy . . . and very pleasant," he wrote Anatoly. He had orchestrated the entire first act by April 19. That morning he was guest of honour at a musical held in Sgambati's home. He wrote Nadezhda Filaretovna about it the same day: "Sgambati, the first musician of Rome, learned that I was in Rome, and therefore added my first quartet to his program, and asked me to be present at his morning musicale . . . and so I was forced to spend my working hours in a stuffy hall, to listen to a mediocre performance of my quartet, and to be the subject of the audience's attention and curiosity." He wrote Anatoly that the quartet had been a signal success, and that the newspapers had praised him most warmly. That his mind, as always, turned to Russia was proved by his remarking to Nadezhda Filaretovna that times were bad: "The spirit of reaction has reached such limits that Tolstoy's works are hounded as if they were revolutionary proclamations." He was himself no revolutionary, either political or artistic, but there cannot be doubt that his works, too, would have been hounded were the ideational processes behind music as plain to the average and official mind as are those of literature.

By May 4 Piotr Ilyich was in St. Petersburg. While there, he went to Pavlovsk, where the Waltz from *Sleeping Beauty* was played. He stopped in Moscow for a brief business conference with Jürgenson, after which he continued on to Frolovskoye. Three days later, writing to Anatoly, he said: "I am now going through a period of special love for life. I am full of the awareness of a successfully accomplished tremendous task . . . it seems to me

. . . that The Queen of Spades is a successful opera . . . for the time being, I am certain of its brilliant future. In Rome I succeeded in orchestrating the first half of the score, and I have begun the second here. Then I want to draft a sextet for stringed instruments." This last was his first mention of what became the *Souvenir of Florence*, opus 70, scored for two violins, two violas, cello, and double bass.

Writing to Grand Duke Konstantin Nikolayevich on May 30, Piotr Ilyich expressed ideas that would undoubtedly have put him in disfavour with Alexander III, but which he must have known the enlightened Grand Duke would find palatable. "Mozart, Beethoven, Schubert, Mendelssohn, Schumann composed their immortal compositions exactly as a shoemaker fashions boots — that is, from day to day and chiefly to order. The result was colossal. Had Glinka been a shoemaker instead of a squire, he would have composed — instead of two (truly excellent, I must admit) operas — some fifteen, and ten marvellous symphonies besides. I could cry from irritation at the thought of what Glinka would have given us had he not been born in a landowner's family of the pre-emancipation era." Piotr Ilyich's facts were shaky — it would be difficult to prove that Schumann's "immortal compositions" were written to order, and impossible to prove that Schubert's were — but his premise was sound. That he was willing to state it so forcefully to an imperial dilettante is a tribute not to his courage, but to his belief in his own judgment of men, even of grand dukes. What may have been in his mind was that he was about to compose a string sextet because he had promised such a piece to the St. Petersburg Quartet Society.

Piotr Ilyich wrote "End of opera" on the manuscript orchestra score of *The Queen of Spades* at Frolovskoye on June 5. He looked into *A Dream on the Volga*, Arensky's opera to a libretto by Modest, and wrote Ippolitov-Ivanov that he found in it a great deal to like. On June 25 he set to work on the sextet. "Am writing under unusual strain," he told Modest. "Am embarrassed not by any lack of ideas, but by the novelty of the form. I need six independent and at the same time similar voices. This is incredibly difficult. Haydn could never conquer this difficulty, and never composed any but quartet chamber music." Two remarks are necessary here: Piotr Ilyich himself notably failed to conquer the six difficult voices in *Souvenir of Florence*, and he was misinformed about Haydn, who wrote several quintets and at least one sextet.

At the end of June there were guests in Piotr Ilyich's house at Frolovskoye: Jürgenson and Kashkin were there, eager to hear him play over the score of *The Queen of Spades*. "Complete approval," he reported to Modest by letter on July 3. "Do you know, it must really be good, for there are several passages I am completely unable to play; I want to cry each time I come to them, so filled am I with emotion." Soon after that, he was writing Nadezhda Filaretovna that he was becoming more and more interested in raising flowers, and that he was pleased with his sextet. On July 16, four days after writing Modest that he had completed the rough draft of the sextet, he added: "What a sextet — and what a fugue at the end — it's a pleasure! Awful, how pleased I am with myself. . . . I am becoming more and more fascinated by it, and have cooled off considerably toward The Queen of Spades." New love was always best love with Piotr Ilyich, and he was, in all faith, momentarily unable to discern that *The Queen of Spades* was an exceedingly good opera, *Souvenir of Florence* an exceedingly bad sextet.

In response to an invitation from Piotr Ilyich, Arensky visited Frolovskoye on July 13 to discuss *A Dream on the Volga*. His host wrote Nadezhda Filaretovna that he found this opera greatly to his liking, and described Arensky as a strange, sickly, and nervous man for whose future he had the gravest fear. After Arensky's visit Piotr Ilyich went to Moscow, where Kashkin joined him for a trip to Lobinskoye, the estate of Nikolay N. Figner, for whom he had designed the role of Hermann in *The Queen of Spades*. On July 19 the three of them read the score, and Piotr Ilyich wrote Modest that the singer was ecstatic about it. "He speaks of it with tears in his eyes — a good sign! . . . All his intentions correspond wholly to my wishes. I am worried about one thing: he asks for a transposition of the brindisi a whole tone down, telling me with good reason that he cannot, for fear of croaking like a frog, sing these really difficult high notes at the end of the opera." He learned, too, that Figner's wife, Medea, was enthusiastic about the role of Liza. This was important, for while there is reason to believe that Vsevolozhsky had asked for *The Queen of Spades* with the Figners in mind, they were sufficiently popular and well established to have refused to appear in it had they not liked their roles. Their presence in the cast would guarantee a measure of temporary popularity for any opera.

On August 19 Piotr Ilyich left Moscow for southern Russia. For six days he visited at Grankino, the estate of the family of Modest's charge, Kolya Konradi. Then, on August 27, he began a two-week visit to Kamenka. But Kamenka and the Davidovs had altered, and he sadly confessed to Nadezhda Filaretovna that everything there seemed to him to have aged and grown melancholy. Look as he did, he could detect no signs of the gaiety that once had brightened Kamenka for him. Travelling with Kolya, he visited Kiev and Kopilovo, the estate of A. L. and N. K. von Meck. In Kiev he attended the opera, finding performances there superior to those in Moscow. When the director to whose intelligent care he attributed this superiority asked to be allowed to stage *The Queen of Spades,* Piotr Ilyich enthusiastically agreed. From Kiev he and Kolya went on to Kharkhov, and from there to Tiflis, where they arrived and met Anatoly on September 19.

Piotr Ilyich settled down happily. Tiflis soothed and attracted him. He enjoyed seeing Anatoly again. Then an almost wholly unprepared-for catastrophe occurred. On October 4 he received from Nadezhda Filaretovna a cold and tightly written letter announcing her financial ruin and the consequent discontinuance of his pension, and insinuating that now he would lose all interest in her. The letter had the awful sound of a door slammed to for ever. He answered it the same day:

My loved, dear friend —

I just received your last letter. What you said in it makes me intensely sad, not on my account, but on yours. This is said in purest sincerity. It would be false were I to pretend that so radical an alteration in my budget will not affect my financial state at all. But it will affect me much less than you probably think. My earnings have grown markedly during recent years, and there is no cause for suspicion that they will not go on growing rapidly. So if in the midst of your many worries you are also a little worried about me, I beg you, for God's sake, to rest assured that I have not felt the slightest bitterness over this material loss. Believe me, this is the simple truth; I am no master of the dissembling phrase. The real crux of the matter, therefore, is not that for a short time I shall have to cut my expenditures, but that you, so used to a handsome scale of living, will have to become acquainted with privation. This is terribly bitter and vexatious.

I should like to lay the blame for all this on someone (it is clear that you are blameless), but I have no way of knowing who the actual culprit is. Besides, my indignation is pointless, and I have no right to poke into your purely family affairs. Rather than press you, I think it preferable that I request Vladislav Albertovich [Pakhulsky] to tell me when he can write what you mean to do, where you will live, and to what degree you must undergo privation. I have no words with which to tell you how sorry I am for you and how terrified. I cannot imagine you without wealth.

The final words of your letter ["Do not forget, and think of me sometimes"] wounded me a little, but I cannot believe that you meant them seriously. Do you really think me able to recall you only when making use of your money! How could I even momentarily forget everything you have done for me, everything I owe you? Without exaggeration, I can say that you saved me, that I should certainly have lost my sanity and perished had it not been for your friendship and sympathy. With the funds you gave me as an assurance of safety, you helped me rally my failing forces, and gave me back my will to continue on my musical road. No, dear friend, be sure that I shall remember and bless you until I have no more breath. I am happy that, precisely when you can no longer share your wealth with me, I can be free to express the full measure of my boundless and passionate gratitude. You yourself probably fail to comprehend the extent of all you have done for me. If you did, you could never have written what you did — that now, being poor, you hope I shall think of you "sometimes." In all truth I have never for a single moment forgotten you, nor ever will, for every thought that relates to me relates also to you.

With all the warmth in my heart I kiss your hands, imploring you to realize, once and for ever, that nobody has greater sympathy for you, or considers himself more truly part of your troubles, than I do.

Another time I shall write about myself and all that I am doing.

Forgive this hastily scribbled note. I am too badly upset to write clearly.

Some critics have written that Piotr Ilyich took too seriously the purely formal phrase: "Do not forget, and think of me sometimes." But in view of Nadezhda Filaretovna's succeeding actions — she never communicated with him directly again, and refused to answer his letters — it is at least likely that she had intended it as a farewell. Her reason, or reasons, for thus abruptly terminating an intense friendship of fourteen years have been the subject of multiple speculation. It is very unlikely that she divulged her exact reasons to anyone, and it is possible that she had none, but acted out of a mélange of half-reasons.

Nadezhda Filaretovna had not been reduced to even comparative penury. Her reason for stopping Piotr Ilyich's pension could not have been that she could no longer afford it. Perhaps she believed that she could not — to a wealthy eccentric, an unimportant diminution in fortune may appear as ruin. When Piotr Ilyich learned that she had not lost her fortune, he did not think to be relieved for her sake; he flew to the extreme of retroactively blackening the entire relationship from its inception to its close. Had he been the deceived plaything of a heartless woman? Had he been induced into repeated protestations of love and affection to a woman who, all the while, was merely enjoying her power over him? His faith in human integrity and human good qualities, never firm, was profoundly shaken. The loss of the pension was unimportant. His royalties and performance fees had by 1890 made him independent. But the loss of faith was one from which he did not recover. Those nearest him sensed the change. He became old at fifty. All his tendencies toward misanthropy, self-doubt, and pessimism of the rankest growth were intensified. Nadezhda Filaretovna had treated him cruelly. He bore the scars of her cruelty the three remaining years of his life.

Many have suggested that someone who stood to gain by having Piotr Ilyich's pension stopped — Nadezhda Filaretovna's son Vladimir, her daughter Julia, or Julia's husband, Pakhulsky — told Nadezhda Filaretovna that her composer-friend was homosexual. This is possible, but there is no tiny item to prove it. Nothing in her letter suggests that she was reacting from a shock of surprise. Another surmise is that she was decided by a strong sense of guilt. Her eldest, and favourite, son, Vladimir, was mentally and physically disintegrating, and it is not without the bounds of possible reasoning for her to have believed this a punishment. In one sense it is true that she squandered on a remote artist the affection and some of the wealth Vladimir may well have believed his right.

One fact and one half-fact appear to suggest an explanation more appropriate to Nadezhda Filaretovna's character. She was herself ill — she spent the time from just before sending that final letter until 1894 in various stages of slow death. Phrases in her daughter Julia's correspondence indicate that her illness at times, or eventually, affected her mind. She was extremely nervous, and suffered from acute pains that seem to have had a psychic origin.

When Pakhulsky at a later date wrote Piotr Ilyich that he could not risk showing her a letter from her former friend, and that she was unable to write, he may have been telling the exact truth. Fear of death, fear of insanity, a permeating sense of insecurity brought to a climax by otherwise negligible financial setbacks — all these factors, combined with Vladimir's horrible, wasting sickness may easily have led her into herself ever more completely, may have persuaded her to cut her only living link with the world outside her family and her domain. She had always been a ruthless and imperious woman. There can be no doubt that if, in truth, she had decided that she could die in more comfort cut off from Piotr Ilyich, she would have cut him off with a penstroke. Her cruelty was innate and unintentional, and has the marks of inner compulsion. So the best interpretation of her action seems to be that her relationship with Piotr Ilyich had, from her unquestioningly selfish point of view, outlived its usefulness. She ended it exactly as she might have dismissed a servant.

Piotr Ilyich's first reaction was hysterical. He would be poor, he would have to remake his life. To Jürgenson he wrote: "I must rebegin my life on an entirely new financial scale. In all probability I shall have to look for some work in Petersburg that will bring me a good salary. All this is most humiliating — yes, humiliating is the word!" A few days later, writing to Modest, he was more tempered: "The decrease in my income worries me little. . . ." He soon forgot the financial side of it altogether. His genuine affection for Nadezhda Filaretovna, his gratitude to her, at last weathered the later information that she was not financially embarrassed at all. He tried to get in touch with her. He wrote to Pakhulsky. Pakhulsky answered, formally polite with regard to his mother-in-law, chatty about other matters. At last, on June 18, 1891, Piotr Ilyich addressed him at length. He repeated his detestation of the fact that all connection between himself and Nadezhda Filaretovna had ceased as soon as he ceased to receive the pension. "This situation lowers me in my own sight, makes the memory of the money I accepted from her almost unbearable, worries and weighs on me more than I can say." Pakhulsky returned this letter, stating that he could not show it to his mother-in-law because of her serious nervous illness. In Nadezhda Filaretovna's inmost heart, he said, her affection for her old friend burned as always. This was thin fare. Piotr Ilyich never attempted after that to re-establish contact with his "well-beloved friend." Their unlikely and astonishing friendship ended in as unlikely and astonishing a way as it had begun.

Piotr Ilyich left Tiflis on November 3, stopping at Vladikavkaz and also at Taganrog to visit Ippolit. He stayed in Moscow only one day — "I was met by all my friends, who gave me a dinner at the Hermitage" — and was back in Frolovskoye on the 13th. There he took up the problem of revising his songs for Jürgenson's projected complete edition. "Only if you publish a complete collection of the *original* songs (and no transpositions) do I consent to your stating that it is an *edition newly revised by the composer*." It was not that Piotr Ilyich was a purist in the matter of key changes, but that he could not face the tiring task of performing, or even of supervising, the transpositions. He had his way. He had arrived at a position from which he could dictate the manner of the performance and publication of his works. Jürgenson, for example, transmitted to him a request for permission to perform isolated choruses from *The Queen of Spades*. Piotr Ilyich refused it. "They are either incomplete in themselves, and so cannot be played separately, or (like that in the third scene) they are essentially a slavish re-creation of the style of the last century, and are therefore not creative works, but rather borrowings."

On December 6 Piotr Ilyich attended a concert of the St. Petersburg Russian Musical Society. Leopold Auer conducted the rarely played *Manfred*. Reporting on this occasion, *Moskovskiye Vyedomosty* noted that "The symphony's composer, so beloved of the public, was called to the platform thrice." In his own St. Petersburg quarters Piotr Ilyich had *Souvenir of Florence* played for a group of friends including Laroche, Glazunov, and Lyadov. He could not entirely escape his twenty-fifth anniversary as a professional musician: the St. Petersburg Conservatory held a celebration of that event on December 15, and he was forced to attend. He was in St. Petersburg for the final rehearsals of *The Queen of Spades*. The dress rehearsal occurred in the presence of Alexander III and Marya Fyodorovna on December 17,[2] the first public performance on the 19th. Napravnik conducted. The singers, some of them artists of the first rank, were at their best. "Throughout the whole evening," Modest says, "artists and audience alike experienced a sense of complete satisfaction rarely felt during any oper-

[2] Not December 18, as often stated.

atic performance." The audience was cumulatively enthusiastic. *The Queen of Spades* was an established, an immediately and permanently established, success.

On December 22 Piotr Ilyich left Moscow for Kiev. There he heard a performance of Meyerbeer's *Robert le diable* and one of Anton Rubinstein's *The Demon*. On the 31st the Kiev *première* of *The Queen of Spades* occurred. Piotr Ilyich, not conducting, had the opportunity to listen carefully. "In regard to the enthusiasm with which it was received, it would be ridiculous even to compare Kiev with St. Petersburg," he wrote Modest. "This was something incredible. The performance was in general good, but after Petersburg everything seems a little pale, of course." He attended the second performance the following day, and then went to Kamenka. The New Year's Eve celebration there was very gay. This was the last time he was ever to see his sister.

While in Kamenka, Piotr Ilyich thought hard about subjects for a new opera and a new ballet. "Give a thought to King René's Daughter," [3] he suggested to Modest. "I shall probably go to Italy to compose, and I need a subject by the end of January. And what ballet?" Having planted that seed, he returned to Frolovskoye. On January 22, however, he was in Moscow, to hear Arensky's *A Dream on the Volga* at the Bolshoi. He was moved to tears, and found it an excellent opera, taking time to expound its virtues at length in a letter to Vsevolozhsky. Returning to Frolovskoye, he worked on incidental music he had promised Lucien Guitry for a performance of *Hamlet*. When Rimsky-Korsakov asked him to conduct his new symphonic ballad, *The Voivode*, at a St. Petersburg concert on February 8, he answered: "I haven't written one single note of the Voivode score. Circumstances have prevented me from doing it. Let's leave this for next year. Besides, a bad arm interferes with my conducting." At almost fifty-one, Piotr Ilyich intended to do very little that he did not want to do. He was learning to say no. He completed the pieces for *Hamlet* — which included a contracted version of the Fantasy Overture he had composed in 1888.

Modest, whom Piotr Ilyich described to Parasha as "becoming a fashionable Petersburg playwright," was doing a new play. His

[3] The vastly popular lyric play by the Danish-Jewish poet Henrik Hertz had been translated into Russian by Zvantsev. From this, Modest fashioned the libretto of Tchaikovsky's last opera, *Yolanta*.

fame no longer depended on his being Piotr Ilyich's brother. Both brothers were in constant demand. In St. Petersburg, on February 15, Piotr Ilyich conducted his Third Suite at a concert that included Édouard de Reszke's singing of his *Don Juan's Serenade*. Six days later, at the Mikhailovsky Theatre, he attended Lucien Guitry's farewell benefit. It was the performance of *Hamlet* with Piotr Ilyich's incidental music.[4] The composer wrote Anatoly that Guitry was superb, and that everybody liked the music. He was in error: a critic for *Peterburgsky Listok* described it as "very melodic and pretty, but not always appropriate to the text," while *Novosti* declared that it was marvellously poetic in places, but had passed unnoticed by the public.

Once again at home in Frolovskoye, he worked on a new ballet, *The Nutcracker*.[5] "I am labouring with all my might, and am beginning to be reconciled to the subject of the ballet," he told Modest. "I think I shall finish a good deal of it before my departure." An inscription on the manuscript states that he began the *Waltz of the Snowflakes* on March 9. Two days later he left for Moscow, tarrying there scarcely longer than it took him to dine with Siloti and Arensky, and then continued on to St. Petersburg. There he conferred with Petipa [6] and the directors of the imperial theatres

[4] This consists of the reduced Overture, three melodramas, fanfares, four entr'actes, two scenes for Ophelia (vocal), a song for the gravedigger, and a final march. One of the melodramas is repeated, as is the last entr'acte, a funeral march. The repeated melodrama (No. 4 in the printed score) repeats — key, melody, and all — part of the second, Alla Tedesca, movement of the Third Symphony.

[5] The libretto was taken from Alexandre Dumas's *Casse-Noisette*, which had been based on E. T. A. Hoffmann's *The Nutcracker and the Mouse King*.

[6] Having read the scenario of *The Nutcracker*, Petipa handed the following outline of music needed to Tchaikovsky:

1. Soft music. 64 bars.
2. The tree is lighted. Sparkling music. 8 bars.
3. The children enter. Animated and joyous music. 24 bars.
4. Moment of surprise and admiration. A few bars tremolo.
5. A march. 64 bars.
6. Entry of the *incroyables*. 16 bars, rococo (minuet tempo).
7. Galop.
8. Drosselmeyer enters. Awe-inspiring but comic music. A broad movement, 16 to 24 bars.

The music slowly changes character. 24 bars. It becomes less serious, lighter, and, at last, gay in tone.

Grave music for 8 bars. Pause.

about the new ballet, and with the latter also about the new opera. On the 18th he left for western Europe and for the United States, where he had promised to conduct at the ceremonies connected with the opening of Music (now Carnegie) Hall, in New York.

Repeat the 8 bars. Pause.
Four bars expressing astonishment.
9. Eight bars of mazurka rhythm. 8 more. 16 still in mazurka rhythm.
10. A piquant, spicy waltz, strong in rhythm. 48 bars.

XVII

EN ROUTE to Berlin, Piotr Ilyich worked on *The Nutcracker*. "The principal thing is to get the ballet out of the way," he told Anatoly. "I am so interested in the opera, and like its subject so much, that I shall certainly complete it on time if given only two peaceful weeks." Arriving in the German capital on March 20, he attended a concert incognito and heard both *1812* and the *Andante Cantabile*. "It is fun to be listening to one's own works played among strangers and be unknown to anyone," he wrote Bobyk. He left for Paris the next day. The first rehearsal of the Colonne concert he was to conduct took place on March 31. The musicians greeted him cordially, and he was pleased by the rehearsals. The program, presented on April 5, was made up of the Third Suite, the Second Piano Concerto (Sapelnikov), the *Melancholy Serenade*, songs, the *Andante Cantabile, The Tempest*, and the *Slavic March*. "The concert was very successful, and I was the centre of the Paris public's attention for several days. The rehearsals, the concert — all that, of course, excited and fatigued me," he wrote Parasha. "But this type of fatigue is rather pleasant." For diversion, while waiting for the moment to take the boat-train to Le Havre, Piotr Ilyich visited Rouen.

Modest, Sapelnikov, and Piotr Ilyich's friend the renowned pianist Sophie Menter, who were all in Paris, had planned to meet him in Rouen on April 16 and to see him sail from Le Havre late the following night. But on April 10 Modest received a telegram containing word that Alexandra Davidova had died the preceding day. He at once felt that he must break this news to his brother *viva voce*, and set out for Rouen. Face to face with Piotr Ilyich, whom he found in a happy mood and in possession of his ticket to New York, Modest faltered and at last chose not to break the news of their sister's death. It would be better, he thought, for Piotr Ilyich to learn of it amid the distractions of the United States. In Paris, Piotr Ilyich had become irritated because Modest did not long as he did for Russia. In Rouen, Modest therefore led him to believe that he had come to Rouen simply because he felt homesick and was leaving for Russia the next day. This pleased Piotr Ilyich, and the brothers parted with what Modest calls "a touching farewell." All would have been well had not Piotr Ilyich's mood turned black. He decided to return to Paris for two days before proceeding to Le Havre.

Visiting a reading-room in the Passage de l'Opéra, Piotr Ilyich picked up a copy of *Novoye Vremya*. On its last page he read a notice of the death of Alexandra Davidova. "I ran out as though stung by a serpent. Later I went to Sophie Menter's and Sapelnikov's," he wrote Modest. "What a fortunate thing, their presence! I spent the night with them. Today I leave for Rouen and Le Havre. At first I thought it my duty to abandon America and to go to St. Petersburg, but later I realized this would be useless. I should have had to give back the 5,000 francs I received, to give up the balance, and lose my ticket. No, I must go to America. Mentally I am suffering a great deal. I am very anxious about Bobyk, though I know from my own experience that at his age we get over such blows easily. . . . For God's sake, send me all details to New York. Today even more than yesterday I feel the absolute impossibility of portraying the 'sugar-plum fairy' in music."

Piotr Ilyich had accepted young Walter Damrosch's invitation to New York partly because it had arrived during the period when he was feeling that the cessation of his pension from Nadezhda Filaretovna meant that he must take every way of enlarging his income. He had never really wanted to go so far from home, and by the time the S.S. *Bretagne* was ready to sail from Le Havre — 5 a.m. on April 18, 1891 — he wanted to go nowhere but back to Russia. He was in a desperately agitated and gloomy state. Hardly had the ship begun to move when there was a commotion on deck. He learned that a young man in second class had jumped overboard, committing suicide. Piotr Ilyich sat down to write Modest: "During the voyage I shall keep a diary, which I shall send you when I get to New York." He found the ship luxurious, "truly a floating palace." There were about eighty first-class passengers, but he had dined with an American family and found that experience both uncomfortable and boring. As he closed that day's instalment of the diary-letter, the *Bretagne* was moving so quietly through a calm sea that he found it difficult to believe himself on the water. "We have just seen the lighthouse at Lizard – the last glimpse of land before we reach New York."

The next day, however, the *Bretagne* began to toss frighteningly, increasing Piotr Ilyich's nervousness. Some of the passengers were afraid, he said, not of being drowned, but of becoming seasick. He himself enjoyed a little timorously the grand spectacle of a disturbed ocean. He read. He admired the huge gulls. He could not compose. Falling into conversation with a travelling salesman in the second class, he admitted his personal depression, which was intensified when the man remarked: "Well, at your age it is natural." In the saloon a young lady sang Italian songs throughout the evening, "and her performance was so abominable, such an effrontery, that I was astounded nobody said anything rude to her." When most of the passengers retired for the night, Piotr Ilyich walked the decks, noting a diminution in the wind. By the time he too retired, the sea again was calm.

The first-class passengers Piotr Ilyich found too correct and respectable, the only exception being a Canadian bishop returning from Rome, where he had been sent to receive a blessing from Leo XIII. He celebrated Mass privately in his cabin, and Piotr Ilyich attended. But he preferred visiting the second class, finding the travelling salesman and his companions less formal and stiff. As April 20 drew to a close in mid-Atlantic, the swells began to increase again. That night the pitching of the *Bretagne* awakened Piotr Ilyich, who instantly had an attack of what he called "palpitations and nervous fear." A glass of brandy and a turn on the decks in bright moonlight reassured him. By morning the warm air told him that they had entered the Gulf Stream. A few sailing vessels passed along the horizon. A huge whale spouted high into the air.

So the days alternated between calm and storm. On the 24th a dense fog came off the Newfoundland banks. The *Bretagne*'s reduced speed, the intermittent sound of its siren, the possibility of collision – all struck up Piotr Ilyich's worrisome nerves again. Passengers had begun to detect his identity, and he was being pressed to oblige at the piano. He began by refusing, but realized that the begging would last until he complied. At last, that same day, he became violently seasick. "Since yesterday evening I have been a martyr." That night, unable to face the thought of going to bed, waiting tensely for the sickening shocks that ran through the ship whenever its screw was lifted out of the water, Piotr Ilyich sat on the sofa in his cabin. Propped between the wall and his trunk, he finally fell asleep. At two o'clock the next afternoon, April 25, the New York pilot was taken aboard. "I am very glad the trip is nearly over; I simply couldn't bear to stay on shipboard any longer. I have decided to leave New York on a German liner on May 12. By May 22 or a little later, *D. V.*, I shall be in Petersburg again."

It was five o'clock in the afternoon before Piotr Ilyich was rid of immigration and customs officials. He found himself in the hands of a welcoming delegation of one woman and four men. They took him directly to one of New York's leading hotels, the Normandie, located on the southeast corner of Broadway and Thirty-Eighth Street, one block below the Metropolitan Opera House. There he quickly learned that he would not be able to depart for Europe on May 12. Morris Reno, president of the Music Hall Company, greeted him with news that he was to conduct concerts out of town as well as in New York. This information tipped the balance between self-control and despair. Ridding himself as suddenly as possible of the well-intentioned greeters, Piotr Ilyich gave way to the bitterest of tears. At last he dined alone and then went for a brief constitutional down Broadway. True European that he was, he did not allow the density of his mood to prevent him from experiencing amazement at the sight of buildings nine stories high, and at the presence of Negroes on the street. Returning to his room at the Normandie, he retired for the night and cried himself to sleep.

Ferdinand Mayer, of the Knabe piano firm, called the next morning to take Piotr Ilyich to breakfast and then on a brief tour of the city. As a welcome offering, he presented the visitor with a box of one hundred fine cigarettes. Before they could leave Piotr Ilyich's room, a reporter appeared. Mayer — who spoke German — assisted by interpreting during the interview. Then Reno dropped in to inform Piotr Ilyich that he was expected immediately at a rehearsal taking place in Music Hall. Postponing breakfast, they walked to Seventh Avenue and Fifty-seventh Street, where the new glories of Andrew Carnegie's auditorium impressed the Russian favourably. They found Damrosch completing a rehearsal of Beethoven's Fifth Symphony. The members of the orchestra greeted Piotr Ilyich noisily, and Damrosch delivered an impromptu address of welcome. Rehearsing only the first and third movements of his First Suite, the composer found the Symphony Society Orchestra excellent. Again under the guiding ægis of Ferdinand Mayer, he then proceeded to buy a hat and have breakfast. That accomplished, Mayer swept him into the bar of the Hoffman House, which Piotr Ilyich described as "decorated with the most beautiful pictures,[1] statues, and tapestries."

That afternoon Reno proved adamant to Piotr Ilyich's request that his unwanted engagements in Philadelphia and Baltimore be cancelled. He took the composer to his home and introduced him to Mrs. Reno and his daughters. Then the two men went to Damrosch's, where Piotr Ilyich was to be a dinner guest. After this agreeable meal Damrosch took the celebrity to the home of Andrew Carnegie at 5 West Fifty-first Street. Piotr Ilyich rather wildly described the steel magnate as "the possessor of thirty million dollars," adding that in appearance he was "very like our dramatist Ostrovsky." Carnegie stated that he admired Moscow — he had visited there in 1889 — and Scottish folksongs, some of which latter Damrosch obligingly played on a "magnificent Steinway grand." The rest of Piotr Ilyich's description of April 27 deserves quotation in full: "After these visits I went with Hyde [Francis Hyde, president of the New York Philharmonic Society] and Damrosch to see the Athletic Club and another, more serious in tone, which I might perhaps compare with our English Club. The Athletic Club amazed me, especially its swimming pool, in which the members bathe, and its upper gallery, where they skate in winter. We ordered drinks in the serious club. I reached home at about eleven o'clock. Needless to say, I was exhausted."

New York was to continue to mean exhaustion to Piotr Ilyich. Tuesday, April 29, included a visit to Napoleon Sarony, a photographer who looked like a caricature of Napoleon III, a drive with the Mayers through Central Park, dinner with them at Delmonico's, attendance with them at a performance of "a boring oratorio"[2] at the Metropolitan Opera House — and a Delmonico supper of oysters "with a sauce of small turtles," cheese, champagne, and peppermint liqueur. It seems likely that the restlessness that pursued Piotr Ilyich through the night was as much digestive as

[1] One of these pictures was the recently rediscovered Bouguereau *Nymphs and Satyr.*
[2] *The Captivity,* by Max Vogrich.

TCHAIKOVSKY ON APRIL 29, 1891
From a photograph by Napoleon Sarony (New York)

mental. Tuesday, however, was as nothing to Wednesday, which culminated in a formal dinner at Reno's.

The ladies — all in full evening dress. The table decorated with flowers. Beside each lady's place lay a bunch of flowers, while the men had lilies of the valley, which we put in our buttonholes as soon as we sat down. Each lady also had a small picture of myself in a pretty frame. The dinner started at seven thirty and lasted until eleven. I am not exaggerating when I say this, for this is the custom here. To describe all the courses is impossible. Midway in the dinner, ices were served in small boxes to which, with pencils and erasers, were attached small slates on which quotations from my works were beautifully written. The conversation was very lively. I sat between Mrs. Reno and Mrs. Damrosch, the latter a most charming and graceful woman. Opposite me sat Carnegie, the admirer of Moscow and possessor of forty [sic!] million dollars. His likeness to Ostrovsky is astonishing. Tortured by the desire to smoke, and almost sick from overeating, I made up my mind at about eleven o'clock to ask Mrs. Reno's permission to leave the table. Half an hour later we all departed.

Better than the fleshpots of Manhattan were letters from Russia, received on the 30th. However, even the strenuous round of American hospitality had its compensations. To Bobyk that day he wrote: "I am certain that I am ten times as famous here as in Europe. At first, when other people told me this, I thought it only their exaggerated kindliness. But now I see that it is really so. Several of my works that are unknown even in Moscow are played here often. I am a far more important person here than in Russia. Isn't that strange?" Later that day he was taken to look at Brooklyn Bridge and to meet Gustav Schirmer. He received Ivy Ross of the *Journal* and agreed to write an article on Wagner for her. He did manage, in the midst of all this activity, to get to Music Hall for another rehearsal, this time with the group that was to sing his a cappella choruses.

On May Day, Piotr Ilyich went off on another tour with Reno. Looking down on Broadway from the roof of a thirteen-story building, he felt giddy and could not understand how anyone could live so high. They went to the Mint, where fussy officials were persuaded to allow their distinguished visitor to hold ten million dollars in bills in his hands. Thence they went to see Francis Hyde in his financial sanctum, visited the Stock Exchange, and dropped in at a café for lemonade. Back at the Normandie, Piotr

Ilyich completed his piece on Wagner. Walking along Broadway that evening, he happened on a Socialist May Day parade. He later read that the marchers had carried banners reading: "Comrades! We are slaves in free America. We will no longer work more than eight hours." But on sight the demonstration struck him as farcical. "I think the natives also look at it that way, for very few people had the curiosity to stand and watch — the others walked about as usual."

May 2 saw another rehearsal at Music Hall, this time of the First Suite, the March composed in 1883 for the coronation of Alexander III, and the orchestral part of the first movement of the B-flat minor Piano Concerto. The next day was again mostly social — a visit to Schirmer's home, where guests were conveyed to the fourth floor by elevator, attendance at a Music Hall rehearsal of Leopold Damrosch's oratorio *The Shulamite* and a "wearisome cantata," [3] supper at Schirmer's. At ten thirty the guests were presented with bunches of splendid roses, "conveyed downstairs in the lift, and sent home in Schirmer's carriage. One must do justice to American hospitality: there is nothing like it — save, perhaps, in our own country."

After breakfast with Hyde at the Down Town Club the morning of May 4, Piotr Ilyich was taken to a song recital by Sir Charles Santley, "an elderly man who sang arias and songs in a fairly rhythmic manner, but with no tone, and with truly English stiffness." The critics swarmed about Piotr Ilyich. He met Henry T. Finck, who had expressed approval of the *Hamlet* Overture by letter the previous year. In his diary Piotr Ilyich noted that Adele Aus der Ohe — who was to be the soloist in his concerto on May 9 — had come to America penniless four years earlier and had earned more than one hundred thousand dollars by concertizing across the continent. "Such is America!" After a quiet family dinner at the Renos' that night, he was shown to a tramway. Not everyone had a carriage. "It has suddenly turned very cold." Perhaps it had — but Piotr Ilyich may have been recalling with chilly abruptness that the next evening he was to conduct at the opening concert of Music Hall.

At seven thirty p.m. on May 5 Reno's brother-in-law called at the Normandie for Piotr Ilyich and drove him in a carriage to Music Hall. The coachman had some difficulty in getting up to the

[3] *The Seven Last Words,* by Heinrich Schütz.

entrance: a line of carriages moving toward the hall was creating a problem for the police. The crowd inside was estimated by the *Herald* to number fifty-five hundred. Four hundred members of the Oratorio Society and the one hundred musicians of the Symphony Society were on the stage. Piotr Ilyich described the auditorium, "lit up and crowded with people," as "very fine and effective." One box contained Walter Damrosch's father-in-law, Secretary of State James G. Blaine. Another, centrally located, was occupied by Andrew Carnegie and his party, still another by John D. Rockefeller and members of his family. The social and financial aristocracy was out in full force. Pointed out were Abram Hewitt, Seth Low, Henry Clay Frick, and — representing Boston — Colonel Henry Higginson. It was also noted that half the audience held in their hands scores of the Berlioz *Te Deum*, in which the soloist was to be Italo Campanini.

The ceremonies began with congregational singing of *Old Hundred*. Then Reno made a beneficently brief, nervous address of welcome. One chorus of *America* followed. "Then," Piotr Ilyich noted, "a clergyman made a very long and tiresome speech eulogizing the founders of the hall, Carnegie in particular." This was Bishop Henry C. Potter, whose words dealing with the "therapeutics of music" also bored the *Herald* reporter. At last Walter Damrosch, handsome, long-haired, and twenty-nine, took up the baton and launched into the "Leonore" Overture No. 3. There was enthusiastic applause, followed by an interval to allow Piotr Ilyich to get to the stage and walk to the podium. He conducted, not one of his five symphonies, but the *Coronation March* he had composed as part of the municipality of Moscow's celebration of the enthronement of Alexander III. This pleasant, undistinguished music, with its quotation of the Russian national anthem, was received well enough for the composer-conductor to be obliged to return to the stage twice to acknowledge the applause. Then came the chief musical event of the evening, the New York *première* of Berlioz's *Te Deum*, which Piotr Ilyich thought "somewhat boring; only toward its close did I begin to enjoy it thoroughly. Reno carried me away with him. An improvised supper. Slept like a log."

The New York newspapers of May 6 naturally devoted more space to Music Hall and its human contents than to the music played there. Piotr Ilyich read the *Herald*, for he quoted with three exclamation points its description of himself as "a tall, gray, well built, interesting man, well on to sixty." (He was two days short of fifty-one.) He likewise quoted what followed: "He seems a trifle embarrassed, and responds to the applause by a succession of brusque and jerky bows. He conducts with the authoritative strength of a master and the band obeys his lead as one man. His 'Marche Solennelle' is simple, strong and sober, but not surprisingly original. The leading theme recalls the 'Hallelujah' chorus, and the treatment of the first part is Handelian. The strings for some time have things to themselves. Then the orchestration grows more rich and varied, the cymbals, the brass as [sic!] the woodwinds join in. And at last we return to the original theme, working gradually up to a grand climax, in which all the instruments take part. Of the deep passion, the complexity and poetry which mark some other works of the composer's — his 'Romeo' overture, for instance — there is no sign in this march. It is a broad, a scholarly and worthy effort. But a dozen other men might have produced it." This is excellent criticism, though it is to be feared that the critic had confused solemnity and Handelianism.

"It irritates me," Piotr Ilyich put in his diary, "that, not satisfied with writing about my music, they must also write about my personal appearance. I cannot bear to think that my shyness is noticeable or that my 'brusque and jerky bows' fill them with surprise." Piotr Ilyich was not to conduct on the second day of the festival, but rehearsed the Third Suite, at the end of which the members of the orchestra shouted something that sounded to him like "Hoch!" That evening Mr. and Mrs. Hyde called for him about seven thirty and took him to Music Hall. "Mendelssohn's oratorio Elijah was given. A splendid work, but rather too long. During the intermission I was dragged the round of the boxes of various local magnates."

On his fifty-first birthday Piotr Ilyich wrote that he felt very excited. "The concert begins at two o'clock with the suite. . . . This odd fright from which I suffer is very curious. How often have I already conducted the suite and had it go splendidly? Why this anxiety? Nevertheless, I suffer horribly. I do not remember ever having felt so anxious. Perhaps this is because over here they look so closely at my outward appearance and consequently make my shyness more noticeable." Once on the podium, however, and having acknowledged a thunder of applause, he conducted the Third Suite to his own and the audience's entire satisfaction. When

THE AUDITORIUM.

reared us many fine buildings. In other countries and among other governments such a building as this would have been one of the State's subscriptions and man who can do so brilliant a thing in so modest a way.

"And now my task is done. But one more word remains and I am glad and thankful to pronounce it. To Man and women of New York, we bring this inaugural of the New York ... merry and use it for its highest ends.

"In the name and on behalf of the president and directors of the Music Hall of New York I proclaim this building open and henceforth dedicated and set apart to aid the purposes for which it has been reared."

MUSIC OF THE EVENING.

Then, with a sigh of relief, the audience rose and lifted up its thousand voices to the tune of "America." The trained choir on the platformed the anthem.

After that (as the Shah said in a passage of his diary which described some piano playing at Queen Isabella's) "we had some music." The building had been admirably planned. So far, at all events, as we could judge from the orchestra. The acoustics were perfect; there was no echo, no unduly reverberation. Each note was heard. The sound was more than usually grand. The overture seemed to direct the ...

Tschaikowsky is a tall, gray, well built, interesting man, well on to sixty. He seems a trifle embarrassed, and responds to the applause by a few jerky bows. But as soon as he begins his self-confidence returns. There is no sign of nervousness about him as he conducts with the authoritative strength of a master and the band obeys his lead.

ENTRANCE ON FIFTY-SEVENTH STREET.

and forever sacred to the art which men have said to be divine.

Science and letters, wealth and brains, musicians, Beauty beamed and culture fawned while the Bishop explained the end and purpose of the temple. And then at last he vouchsafed to forsake the floor and make way for the music.

Apart from this ovation, which was slightly overpowering, the celebration was a great and grand success.

A success for Mr. Carnegie, the conceiver of the

divine. Croker might idle ... some time, and in such an event there would be a scramble for the leadership. Just remember that there are several very big men in Tammany, each feeling qualified to assume the leadership. On the surface the Mayor seems to have the best end of it.

Mr. G. Welling, of No. 2 Wall street, said that he was thoroughly dissatisfied with the appointments in the house. The servant says the same secretary Harnaby's death around the Worrell household as ... speaking terms with Mrs. Harnaby ... of her death until they read of it in the papers.

NAME HILL FOR GOVERNOR

Two hundred members of the Seventeenth Assembly district Democracy of the Seventeenth Assembly district met last night in Wendel's Assembly Rooms, in West Forty-fourth street, to make arrangements looking toward the organization of a social club in connection with the political machine of the district.

A committee was named with power to secure suitable quarters and report the result of their labors at the next meeting.

Police Captain ... father of the district organization, made a lengthy speech regarding the present democratic outlook throughout the State and country. He praised Governor Hill in lively fashion, and intimated that the Senator-Governor would have to come to the front notwithstanding the fact that he is being pressed for such honors. This State, he said could not afford to let the Governor go to Washington and be buried. On the contrary he must lead the party to victory in New York next November.—And, continued one speaker, "when the ballots are counted next fall I believe that Governor Hill will be the next President of the United States."

INHARMONIOUS REPUBLICANS.

The harmonizing republican committee of five, who have been delving into the affairs of the Fifth Assembly district for some time, completed their scrutiny of the enrollment list of that district last night.

They met in the rooms of the Third district organization, at No. 135 Eighth street, with Charles H. Murray in the chair.

"Tig" Allen, the notorious dive keeper, looked after the interests of the Steve French faction, while Cornelius Donovan fought for the opposition.

Hard swearing, challenging and threats kept the committee amused. It seemed a card question to determine the political faith of the men on the enrollment list, and many had to go by the shadings of the doubts in the minds of the committeemen. As a late hour, however, man declared the scrutiny closed.

Other well known republicans will be put on the enrollment list, after which a new primary will be ordered. It is said that a leader will be named who must be acceptable to both factions.

The departure of Mr. and Mrs. ... the HERALD next Sunday ... pleted in six instalments of ... ... Jones, the twenty-year-old daughter ... ...

UNDERWENT TWENTY

[BY TELEGRAPH TO THE HERALD.]

ANDERSON, Ind., May 5, 1891.—... muscles and ligaments of the ... bone, so the arm was hung in ...

Since then some twenty similar operations have been performed, of late the ... to the lower limbs, and on Sun... died.

WOMEN PROFESSORS AT

[BY TELEGRAPH TO THE HERALD.]

LANSING, Mich., May 5, 1891.—A bill reported to the State Senate proposes a marked innovation in the world.

Ann Arbor was the first of the great universities to admit young woman students, known as "Co-Eds," to the full privileges it is now proposing that two lady professors be appointed to the chair.

The believers in the higher education ... idea conceived by Mrs. Lucinda... mance, the veteran teacher, ... for the admission of girl students

ITALO CAMPANINI.

gleamed than even when sitting together on the box seat of a coach in the Highlands of Scotland. While bowing again and again to the plaudits of the house we in the front rows thought that the noblest glance, the fondest smile, was directed to his great father-in-law, but to the foster father who had made such triumphs possible.

After this affairs proceeded more namely. There was time to look about, to see ... the charming proportions of the grand Damrosch the ... faith of ... men on and electric lights on the doubts in the ming of the auditorium, the comfort of the chairs.

The audience, too, was most interesting as a study of music lovers not under the pressure or medium of fashion. The men were nearly all in evening dress, and many were the same who

MUSIC CROWNED IN ITS NEW HOME.

Brilliant Inauguration of Music Hall by the First Festival Concert.

TSCHAIKOWSKY AND BERLIOZ

The Russian Composer and His "Marche Solennelle" Given a Splendid Greeting and the French Master's "Te Deum" Finely Rendered.

CAMPANINI AND DAMROSCH.

About the Programme, the Performance and the Huge Audience Assembled for the Great Event in New York's Musical History.

BISHOP POTTER'S ORATION.

SPLENDID is the new temple of music that was formally inaugurated last night with the first concert of a largely planned festival, and splendid was the audience assembled for an event which marks a new epoch in the musical history, in which one brilliant page now follows the other, of this metropolis.

The new Music Hall, for which New York is so largely indebted to the public and artistic spirit of Mr. Andrew Carnegie, is the first thoroughly adequate building to be erected here as the special home of orchestral and choral music.

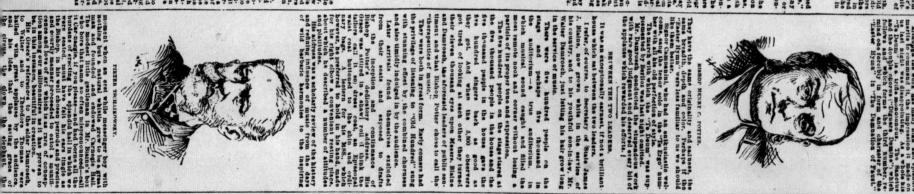

ANDREW CARNEGIE.

CONDUCTOR WALTER DAMROSCH.

PIETER TSCHAIKOWSKY.

BISHOP HENRY C. POTTER.

THE DEDICATION.

"The task which, according to the order placed in your hands this evening, has been set for me," began Bishop Potter, "is much less than any gift of mine would warrant, me in undertaking, or any most generous patience of yours would consent to endure.

"I have no oration to deliver"—[this was at the exhibition in the Palace of the Trocadéro. It at once established his reputation.

BETWEEN THE TWO LEADERS.

It was an exceptionally earnest, if not a brilliant house which sat between the two leaders.

SENDING EAST FOR THE...

District Attorney Stevens, Wants Mother and Son — Grand Jury Investigation Was Begun There yesterday.

MRS. BARNABY'S ... FILED AT ...

It Will be Contested by ... with Very Good Chance ... lieved, of Break...

NO FLOWERS FOR KEATING.

HE SURVEYS THE SCENE OF HIS FUTURE LABORS AND IS CONGRATULATED.

No flowers awaited the newly appointed clerk of the City Court, "Jimmy" Keating, when he strolled into his quarters in the City Hall yesterday.

ODD CONDUCT OF THE...

the concert and its aftermath were over, he politely refused all invitations. "Relieved — and in a measure happy — I went for a walk, ate my dinner, and tarried in a café, enjoying the silence and solitude." At his hotel he found a present from Ernest Knabe — a miniature replica of the Statue of Liberty. "Will I be permitted to take it into Russia?" he wondered bitterly.

Piles of letters containing requests for his autograph made hard work for Piotr Ilyich. Many came from distant sections of the United States, and he conscientiously answered each. Reporters bedevilled him, as did eager librettists and budding composers. On May 8, arriving at Music Hall for a rehearsal with Adele Aus der Ohe of the Piano Concerto, he found himself forced to wait overlong while Damrosch occupied the orchestra. The rehearsal passed off satisfactorily. Back at the Normandie, Piotr Ilyich found among his callers a Russian lady; the result must have astonished the onlookers. "Suddenly the tears came into my eyes, my voice trembled, and I could not suppress my sobbing. I fled into the next room and could not appear again for a long time. I blush from shame when I remember this unexpected episode." Of his conducting of one of his *Cherubim Songs* — *Our Father* — and an *a cappella* arrangement of *Legend*, opus 54, at the concert that evening, he stated that "they went well, but might have gone better had I not been so unstrung. Sat in a box with Reno and Hyde during the beautiful oratorio *The Shulamite*. Walked with Reno and Carnegie to sup with Damrosch." Although he himself confessed that "a good deal of champagne was drunk," he berated himself severely for talking to Gustav Dannreuther, his neighbour at table, about Edward Dannreuther, when the man he was describing was actually Frits Hartvigson. "My absentmindedness is becoming almost unbearable, and is a sign of advancing age," he complained to Modest. "However, everyone was surprised to learn that I was only fifty-one yesterday — Carnegie in particular was much amazed. They all, except those who knew something about my life, thought me much older. Probably I have aged a great deal during recent years. I feel that I have lost vitality. I returned in Carnegie's carriage. This conversation about my age resulted in awful dreams: I thought that I slipped down a tremendously steep wall into the ocean and then climbed up onto a small rocky projection.

"My concerto went beautifully, thanks to Aus der Ohe's brilliant performance. The enthusiasm was much greater than anything I have encountered, even in Russia. I was called back over and over again. Handkerchiefs were waved, the audience shouted 'Upwards' — in fact, it was obvious that the Americans really took me to heart. But what I most valued was the enthusiasm of the orchestra. Owing to the heat and my efforts, I was bathed in sweat and unfortunately could not listen to the scenes from Parsifal." Such was Piotr Ilyich's own reaction to his part in the last afternoon concert of the festival. Some who noticed his absence from the hall during the playing of the *Parsifal* excerpts must have laid it to his anti-Wagnerism. His *Journal* article, appearing on May 3, and stating reasonably that Wagner was greater as a symphonic-orchestral than as a strictly operatic composer, had raised storms of protest. Anton Seidl, doyen of New York Wagnerians, had felt called upon to answer it in another *Journal* article (May 10), reaffirming the Wagnerian creed *in toto*.

During the final evening concert of the festival Piotr Ilyich sat for a time in the Carnegie, Hyde, and Reno boxes and heard what he called, without further comment, "the whole of Handel's oratorio Israel in Egypt." Sunday morning was full of visitors and visits. "All the cafés are shut on Sundays," Piotr Ilyich informed Modest. "This English Puritanism irritates me intensely. It is said that the men who put this law into effect in the State of New York were themselves heavy drinkers." Then, in a hired carriage — "which had to be brought from some distance, and was very expensive" — he drove to Carnegie's for dinner. He ticked off the guests as "Mr. and Mrs. Reno, Mr. and Mrs. Damrosch, the architect of Music Hall and his wife, an unknown gentleman, and a stout friend of Mrs. Damrosch's." As always, Piotr Ilyich found Carnegie eager to be friendly and to honour him. "During the evening he pointedly expressed his liking for me. Grasping both my hands in his, he declared that, though uncrowned, I was a true king of music. He embraced me (without kissing — men do not kiss over here), stood on tiptoe and stretched his hand up to measure my greatness, and at last made the entire party laugh by imitating my conducting. He did this so solemnly, so well, and so like me that I was myself quite delighted." Despite these pleasantries, Piotr Ilyich confessed that he had been glad to return to the Normandie at eleven o'clock, having felt somewhat bored.

May 11 and 12 were taken up with a two-day trip, arranged by

Ferdinand Mayer, to Niagara Falls. Piotr Ilyich travelled alone, but Mayer had him met at Buffalo, put on the right train, and lodged at the Falls in an unpretentious hotel "after the style of the small Swiss inns, but very clean and convenient, as German is spoken. I went to bed early. The roar of the waterfalls is very audible in the stillness of the night." The following day he twice walked to the Falls, which he wisely did not attempt to describe. Speaking of his afternoon visit, he told Modest that he could not free himself of "a curious — probably wholly nervous — lassitude" that kept him from full enjoyment of the view. In his diary he added: "On the Canadian side I was forced, in order not to be tortured by the thought of cowardice, to put on a very ugly costume, to go down under the Falls in a lift, walk through the tunnel, and finally stand right under the Falls, which is very interesting, but somewhat frightening." At six fifteen that evening he left for New York in a Pullman. At five in the morning he started awake in his berth, "full of anxious thoughts about the coming week, which I dread so much."

Back at the Normandie, Piotr Ilyich learned of an attempt made on the life of the Tsarevich, the future Nicholas II, and was as much saddened by that news as by a complete dearth of letters from Russia. Hiring a carriage, he drove to say farewell to Damrosch, who — to his envy — was leaving for Europe. "He asked me to accept him as a pupil. Naturally I refused, but am afraid that I involuntarily showed far too clearly my horror at the idea of Damrosch arriving at my country place to study with me." From Damrosch's he drove to Reno's, not without having difficulty in making a drunken coachman understand the address and route. Then to Mayer's, and with his host to the East River steam ferry. They spent the night at Mayer's summer home on Long Island. "His family is good and kind, but all the same I was bored and longed to get away. In the afternoon we strolled along the beach; the sea was rather rough. The air here is so fresh and pure that my walk really gave me pleasure and braced me up. I spent the night at Mayer's, but slept badly."

Back in New York on May 14, Piotr Ilyich talked with Ivy Ross, who wanted him to answer Anton Seidl's answer to his article on Wagner; he spoke halting English with a Philadelphia reporter who admired him intensely, and strolled in Central Park. "Accord-

ing to my promise I went over to Z's to write a testimonial for the
* * * pianofortes." [4] This bit of advertising copy, when Piotr
Ilyich finally saw it, read: "I consider the * * * pianofortes
without doubt the best in America." He was scandalized. "Now as
I do *not* think so at all, but value some other makers' much more
highly, I refused to have my opinion expressed in this form. I told
Z that notwithstanding my sincere gratitude to him, I could not
tell a lie." Not all artists have been thus scrupulous.

Arriving at the Hydes' for dinner, Piotr Ilyich was greeted by
his host with two sentences of memorized Russian. "Mrs. Hyde
immediately invited me to smoke a cigarette in her drawing-room
— the climax of hospitality in America." To his astonishment, when
they sat down to dine, Hyde made a solemn face and murmured
the Lord's Prayer while the others sat looking fixedly down. "Then
began an endlessly long dinner." From the Normandie, later that
evening, a Knabe employee assisted Piotr Ilyich in crossing the
Hudson by ferry and in boarding another Pullman. The "friendly
Negro" porter awakened him one hour before the train reached
Baltimore.

The orchestra Piotr Ilyich found on the Lyceum Theatre stage
was both inadequate (it had only four first violins) and insufficiently rehearsed in his pieces. The Third Suite had to be dropped,
the Serenade for Strings substituted, and only the best efforts of
Piotr Ilyich and Aus der Ohe made the Piano Concerto possible.
During the overbrief rehearsal, Emil Mollenhauer, the concert-
master (it was Victor Herbert's orchestra) plagued Piotr Ilyich by
showing his hurried impatience. The concert went well. The *Sun*
described it as "one of the greatest treats that have been given to
music-loving people this season" — but the event aroused no enthusiasm in the honoured visitor himself. Ernest Knabe, whose hospitality Piotr Ilyich found "as colossal as his figure," took Aus der Ohe,
her sister, and the composer home for dinner, again an endless one.
"During the second half of the dinner I felt quite exhausted. A ter-
rific hatred of everything came over me, particularly of my two
neighbours." It was after midnight before Knabe took the Aus der
Ohe sisters and Piotr Ilyich to their hotels.

Impressions of Baltimore went into Piotr Ilyich's diary. He
found it "a very nice, clean city. The houses aren't large. All are

[4] There is every reason to believe that "Z" was Mayer, the piano in question
the Knabe.

red brick, with white stone steps at the entrance. First of all we went to the Knabe factory and carefully looked through the whole enormous piano plant. . . . From there we went to the central square, which has a beautiful view of the city and the harbour. From there to the Peabody Institute, an enormous building beautifully built with the money of the wealthy Peabody. It contains an enormous library, open to all, an art gallery of painting and sculpture (unusually poor and pitiful, which does not prevent the Baltimore inhabitants from being very proud of it), and a conservatory."

Piotr Ilyich went from Baltimore to Washington on May 16. There he was guest of honour at a dinner in the Metropolitan Club. "The dinner was very gay, and I was so happy to speak Russian again, though this happiness was dimmed a little by the sad fact that my s, shch, ch, are beginning to sound rather indistinct from age." A telegram, and then a telephone call, informed the diners that the Russian Ambassador had returned from New York especially to receive his distinguished countryman. At ten o'clock that evening, therefore, the entire group adjourned to the Embassy, where a company of about one hundred — diplomats and their families — had gathered. Again Piotr Ilyich could understand and make himself understood, for the common language was French. Innocently, the program of music had been arranged to include a Brahms quartet as well as Piotr Ilyich's Trio. A cold supper followed, and then everyone except ten of the men left. Until three a.m., they sat at a round table, drinking excellent wine.

On May 17, strolling about Washington, Piotr Ilyich found it "very charming, all drowned in luxuriant spring verdure." He visited the Washington Monument and the Capitol, and admired the views. Washington was not curious about one more visitor: the only reference to him in the local press was in the *Post,* under "At the Hotels," where he appeared as "P. Tschoikoisky, Russia." He lunched with the Russian Ambassador. Attracted by the society of Russians, he remained another night at the Arlington Hotel and did not reach Philadelphia until three o'clock the afternoon of his concert there. No rehearsal was required, for the orchestra was again Victor Herbert's, the program the one played in Baltimore. The Academy of Music was full to capacity, and the newspapers reported the concert a success. All that Piotr Ilyich cared for was getting back to New York as quickly as possible, which he did immediately after the concert. His last day in America would be May 20.

On the 19th Piotr Ilyich's letter-diary recounted little. He at last signed the testimonial to the Z piano, the offending phrase having been omitted. His day of farewells was far more strenuous. It began with his refusing to compose an opera to an aged writer's libretto. Then he accompanied Gustav Dannreuther to a rehearsal of the chamber music to be played that evening during a party in his honour. "The quartet was played indifferently, the Trio badly, for the pianist — a bashful, nervous man — was bad. He could not even count." Then Piotr Ilyich called at the Renos', where he was piled high with gifts, including cologne water, a cigar case, and a selection of cakes for his sea journey. At the Hydes', too, he was bidden farewell with effusive kindness. At the Normandie, he worked up a backache by packing his trunk. Mayer was his dinner guest at Martelli's. At eight o'clock the two men went to the Metropolitan Opera House, where the Composers' Club gathered in Piotr Ilyich's honour. Besides a quartet and the Trio, some of his songs were on the program, which he called too long. An address of praise was read, and Piotr Ilyich stirred up a furor of enthusiasm by replying in French. After that, he was introduced to crowds of people, including the Russian consul-general, and had to autograph about one hundred programs. In a real frenzy of admiration, a lady threw a bouquet of roses full in his face. "I reached home half dead of weariness."

The S.S. *Fürst Bismarck* was to weigh anchor at five a.m., so there was still no rest for the tired lion. He let Reno and Mayer wait in the lobby while he changed his clothes, and then joined them in disposing of two bottles of champagne. They drove to the pier, where he found his cabin — which he had rented directly from one of the ship's officers at three hundred dollars for the crossing — quite as luxurious as the one he had enjoyed west-bound on the *Bretagne*. "I bade farewell to my dear American friends, and retired straight off. I slept poorly, and heard all the noise when the ship started at five o'clock. I came out of my cabin as we passed the Statue of Liberty." Three days after the ship had sailed for Cuxhaven, the *New York Herald* editorially disapproved of the scant public attention the United States had paid to Piotr Ilyich Tchaikovsky, and closed its remarks with its selection of the living geniuses: "Bismarck, to head the list, of course, Edison,

Tolstoy, Sarah Bernhardt, Ibsen, Herbert Spencer, Dvorák, and Tchaikovsky."

On shipboard Piotr Ilyich heard with relief that the voyage was likely to be brief: on its westbound maiden voyage the previous week the *Fürst Bismarck* had crossed the Atlantic in six days and fourteen hours. He tried to work on sketches for a new symphony, but found concentration difficult. Two days out, despite the season, the weather became bad, and on the 24th Piotr Ilyich could eat nothing but an orange. Two nights at least he passed sitting up on the sofa in his cabin. On the 27th the ship entered Southampton. He enjoyed the sight of Folkestone and Dover and seemed to regret passing Helgoland by night. On the morning of the 29th he disembarked at Cuxhaven and was in Hamburg by midday. On June 1 he was again among friends and was enjoying the St. Petersburg spring.

XVIII

IOTR ILYICH's spirits rose in St. Petersburg. The city pleased him so much that he commissioned Modest to search for a suitable country retreat in its neighbourhood. Frolovskoye without its forests had long since lost its charm for Piotr Ilyich, and during his absence in America, Alexey Sofronov had moved the household back to the former house in Maidanovo. This failed to please his master, who found it on the road to decay and disliked the prospect of too many summer visitors. Nevertheless, he resumed work on *The Nutcracker* there on June 14, and wrote Parasha that it was progressing well. In connection with the new ballet, he asked Jürgenson to buy him a celesta from its inventor, Victor Mustel of Paris, for the equivalent of $240. The instrument was then unknown in Russia. "I don't want you to show it to anybody," he warned, "for I'm afraid that Rimsky-Korsakov or Glazunov will smell it out and take advantage of its unusual effects before me." Here was the origin of the charming orchestral colour of the *Dance of the Sugar-Plum Fairy*.

Modest, Bobyk, and Count A. N. Litke, a son of one of their cousins, visited Piotr Ilyich at Maidanovo. On June 16, the four of them went into Moscow to visit the Franco-Russian Exposition. Prejudiced against it in advance, Piotr Ilyich found it fascinating. He remained six days, and later thought of revisiting Moscow especially to see the exposition again. At home he did "convict labour" in correcting several early compositions about to be republished, and then completed the rough draft of *The Nutcracker*. On July 7 he wrote Bobyk: "The ballet is definitely inferior to Sleeping Be[auty] — of that I'm positive. We'll see what happens with the opera." In the same letter he returned, though jocularly, to a favourite theme: "Yes, the old man is getting worn out. Not only is his hair turning white as snow and beginning to fall out, not only is he losing his teeth, not only are his eyes growing weaker and tiring more quickly, not only do his feet begin to drag — but he is growing less capable of accomplishing anything."

Before taking up work again on *King René's Daughter*, Piotr Ilyich passed a week in St. Petersburg. While there, he visited the zoological garden almost daily, and told Bobyk that in general he was acting "like a merchant who has just come into a fortune and has gone on a spree." When he was at last deep in sketching the opera, he found that Modest's libretto pleased him more and more. He was going through a wave of interest in Spinoza, reading him, buying books about him, absorbing everything that came to hand that was remotely connected with him. To Modest, however, he complained that the opera was not going well and in places too closely resembled *The Enchantress.* "Strange that when I was composing the ballet I kept on thinking that it wasn't very good, but that I would show them what I can do when I began the opera. And now it seems to me that the ballet is good and the opera not so good." At last, however, he seemed to have begun examining his own vacillations of opinion: "Yet you know from experience that authors are often wrong in evaluating their works while in the throes of creation, and that exactly what seems to them terrible sometimes turns out to be good." On August 13 he for the first time referred to the new opera by the name of its heroine, the name which he finally gave it — *Yolanta.*

Yolanta was completed at Maidanovo on September 16. Piotr Ilyich immediately began to orchestrate *The Voivode,* the symphonic poem he had composed in Tiflis in 1890. His health was good, and he was generally in unwonted high spirits. Two events only troubled him. Around August 1 a thief entered his house and stole a present Nadezhda Filaretovna had given him in 1888, the clock decorated with a Joan of Arc, an Apollo, and muses. Not only was its sentimental value high, but it had cost the equivalent of $2,000. Suddenly, after months of inaction, the police turned up with the thief. "Today," Piotr Ilyich wrote Modest, "he was brought to me in the hope that I could persuade him to tell the truth. . . . He promised to confess if they would leave him alone with me. We went into the adjoining room. There he threw himself at my feet and begged me to forgive him. Of course I forgave him and only asked that he tell where the clock was. Thereupon he became very silent, and later asserted that he had never taken it at all!" In addition to the trying quality of the scene itself, Piotr Ilyich worried over the supposition that telling about it might set the natives of Maidanovo against him.

The other irruption into his peaceful days was a letter from

New York. Morris Reno held out a three months' American tour of twenty concerts for a fee of $4,000. Piotr Ilyich was insulted: he had previously been paid $2,400 for four concerts. He replied: "Non. Tchaikovsky." Later, Modest asserts, he came to understand that this offer was in no way insulting. But it did not tempt him. Only fees of Barnumesque proportions could have lured him across the Atlantic again to travel in Pullmans and eat dinners for whole evenings at a time. Laroche was his house guest, and they were enjoying four-hand bouts at the piano. Or Laroche read aloud. Life was sweet, after all, and had its gratifications. By October 4, the orchestration of *The Voivode* was complete and that of *Yolanta* begun. "It is a one-act opera," he explained to Bobyk on the 24th, "but actually very long, and demands a good deal of attention."

On November 18, at a Siloti concert in Moscow, *The Voivode* was heard for the first time, on a program that included Grieg's Piano Concerto and works by Bach, Glazunov, and Napravnik, as well as dances from the operatic *Voivode*. "Passionate ovations. My new work, The Voivode, turned out to be very unsuccessful, and I shall destroy it." This he proceeded to do the next day, tearing the score into pieces. Siloti, however, had kept the orchestral parts. After Piotr Ilyich's death the score was reconstructed and published. One of its comparatively rare performances occurred in New York in 1897 under the baton of Walter Damrosch. Curiously, the critics of the Moscow press were laudatory about this work that was unloved by its first audience and loved insufficiently by its creator.

"Do not regret The Voivode," Piotr Ilyich wrote Jürgenson from Maidanovo. "It was good only for that. I am not in the least sorry, for I am profoundly convinced that this composition could only have compromised me. Had I been an inexperienced youth, it would have been another matter, but an old man with white hair should either progress (even that is possible, for Verdi, as an example, continues to develop, and he's almost eighty) or remain on the heights he has already reached. Should something like this happen in the future, I shall again tear it into shreds — or stop composing completely. Not for anything in the world will I go on scribbling up paper when everything has given up the ghost." He still had confidence in *Cherevichki*, for on December 2 he wrote to Jürgenson: "Wait, some day it will awaken from its sleep."

In December, Piotr Ilyich journeyed to Reval to visit Anatoly, who had been appointed vice-governor of Estonia. He remained only a few days, and by the 21st was in Maidanovo revising *Souvenir of Florence*. On the 28th he reported to Modest that *Yolanta* was finished, and on that day he left for Kiev. There he conducted two identical Russian Musical Society concerts of his own works, reviving selections from the operatic *Voivode* between the Third Suite and *1812*. Thence he went to Kamenka and Warsaw. From the latter city, having heard a performance of *Cavalleria Rusticana*, he wrote Kolya Konradi: "This opera is truly remarkable, particularly in its fortunate choice of subject. Let Modya smell out a subject of this type." Then rehearsals began for his first Warsaw concert. This occurred on January 14, 1892. "Both the public and the musicians received me with passionate warmth," he wrote Anna Merkling. "The concert was a brilliant success." *Varshavsky Dnievnik* obliged with a review in the same spirit, and Piotr Ilyich found that "the Polish countesses were enchantingly cordial." Warsaw, however, was tiring in its exuberance, and he found it necessary, en route to Hamburg, to stop off a full day in Berlin to rest.

In Hamburg, Piotr Ilyich was able to rehearse *Yevgeny Onyegin* only once before his announced appearance to conduct it in public. It had been well learned, and he judged the staging not bad. But the changes in the recitatives, inescapable in translating from Russian into German, mixed him up, and he at last flatly refused to conduct the performance. Of the man forced to take his place he wrote Bobyk: "The local conductor, by the way, is not some mediocrity, but a man of genius who is dying to conduct the first performance." This was Gustav Mahler, and Piotr Ilyich's high opinion of him was chiefly derived from a "most marvellous performance of Tannhäuser" on January 18. On the next day, conducting *Yevgeny Onyegin*, Mahler lived up to this standard. "The performance was positively superb."

In Paris, searching for concrete artistic signs of France's touted Russophilism, the best Piotr Ilyich could find was a Russian clown at the Folies-Bergère. This man presented an act of two hundred and thirty trained rats — "at the same time that we are playing [Massenet's] Esclarmonde," he commented bitterly. "Not a single concert, not one dramatic or operatic theatre houses anything Russian." He tried once more to read Zola, this time selecting *La Bête humaine*. He found it false: "It is simply a crime story *à la Gabo-*

riau overburdened with obscenity." After ten days in Paris he returned to St. Petersburg. By February 9 he was at Maidanovo orchestrating the sections of *The Nutcracker* that he was making into a suite, a task he completed in twelve days. He conducted the first performance of the *Nutcracker Suite* at a concert of the St. Petersburg Russian Musical Society on March 19, when it scored a clear success. During that visit to the northern capital, too, Piotr Ilyich visited the scene of his legal studies, conducting the School of Jurisprudence orchestra in *Song without Words* and the Waltz from *Sleeping Beauty*. Then at Maidanovo between March 21 and April 6 he polished up all details of *The Nutcracker*. He had agreed to conduct *Faust* and *The Demon* (he would have preferred *Carmen*) at Pryanishnikov's Operatic Society in Moscow, though he had never before led a stage performance of another composer's opera. Before beginning the rehearsals, however, he went once more to St. Petersburg, ostensibly to attend Mass on the first anniversary of Alexandra Davidova's death, but really to spend some time with Modest, who had just completed a new play and was about to leave for Paris.

Back in Moscow, Piotr Ilyich rehearsed *Faust* on April 19 and conducted it thirteen days later. In 1901, answering a query by Modest, Pryanishnikov had this to say about the conducting: "It is hard to point out exactly what was new in Piotr Ilyich's interpretation of Faust, but it is quite true that in his hands some passages, particularly in the third act (in Marguerite's garden), received new and very pretty shadings. It would be more correct to say that he put something fresh and original into them. At his first appearance as an operatic conductor, Piotr Ilyich was met with thunderous applause and a flourish from the orchestra and the whole cast as the curtain rose. He could not start the opera for a long time because of the prolonged ovation." Two days later he led *The Demon*, a performance which he described briefly to Anatoly as "quite satisfactory." On May 8 what he called "my Moscow tortures" came to an end when he conducted *Yevgeny Onyegin*, "at which, of course, there were ovations." Pryanishnikov would have liked him to remain to conduct more operas, but dared not ask him. When Piotr Ilyich left for St. Petersburg, the troupe accompanied him to the Nikolayevsky Station.

Piotr Ilyich, on May 17, moved into his last residence, the house at Klin that eventually became the Tchaikovsky Museum,

Tchaikovsky's home at Klin. The first photograph was taken before the Nazi invasion. The second shows some of the wreckage found by the Russians after recapturing Klin. The third shows one room as reopened to the public.

and that achieved worldwide fame when the Nazi armies wrecked it in 1941.[1] There, after several pieces of editing and amending, he began to compose a symphony. The old doubts crowded back: it went poorly, and he feared the onset of his end as a composer. He never completed this symphony, eventually using material from its sketches as the basis of his Third Piano Concerto. No sooner had he begun it, in fact, than he went abroad with Bobyk, visiting Berlin, Paris, and Vichy. Back in Russia, for several months he did not compose, but spent all his time correcting proofs of new editions, supervising other composers' transcriptions of his works — "hellish convict labour," he called it — and doing a large stint of reading. In Moscow, meanwhile, the many symphonic concerts given in connection with an electrical exposition looked like a Tchaikovsky festival, including as they did performances of the Second Symphony, *Romeo and Juliet, Manfred,* the *Nutcracker Suite* (twice), the *Melancholy Serenade,* Waltz-Scherzo, *Italian Caprice,* the Elegy from the Serenade for Strings, dances from *The Voivode* and *Vakula the Smith,* the Violin Concerto, and *1812* (twice). Piotr Ilyich kept up his travelling to St. Petersburg and Moscow, complained bitterly that his time was being wasted on practical details — and continued attending to them minutely. It was September 10 before he completed overseeing work on the scores and piano scores of *Yolanta* and *The Nutcracker.*

On September 18 Piotr Ilyich arrived in Vienna.[2] He intended to conduct a concert related to a large theatrical-musical exhibition then being held there. The exhibition itself interested him, but he found the orchestra he was placed before during a rehearsal feeble to the point of laughter. After rehearsing all morning and part of the afternoon, he refused to conduct the scheduled concert and left with Sapelnikov and the pianist Sophie Menter for the latter's castle in the Tyrol. There, in Itter, he spent more than two weeks before journeying to Prague to attend the *première* there of

[1] When the Soviet armies recaptured Klin, the authorities at once set about restoring the Tchaikovsky Museum. The building, one room of which was left showing the full results of Nazi anticultural fury, was reopened to the public on March 15, 1942.

[2] During this visit to Vienna, Piotr Ilyich discovered that Pietro Mascagni was occupying the next room in a hotel. Wishing to make the acquaintance of the composer of *Cavalleria Rusticana,* he attempted to call on him. Finding a line of like-minded admirers queued up outside the Italian's door, he abandoned the idea, however, and never met Mascagni.

The Queen of Spades. This performance took place on October 12. A week later Piotr Ilyich wrote Anatoly that "it went off very well, enthusiastic ovations."

On his first day back at Klin, Piotr Ilyich wrote to refuse an invitation to conduct *The Queen of Spades* in Odessa. In explanation he said that operatic conducting wore him out, "and, to confess, I have no ability in this direction." He was again at work on what he intended to be his sixth symphony. On October 24 he wrote Modest that he was labouring diligently and expected to complete the first draft shortly.

In St. Petersburg, on November 8, Napravnik conducted the one-hundredth Marinsky performance of *Yevgeny Onyegin.* The Figners graced the roles of Tatyana and Lensky, and — to quote *Moskovskiye Vyedomosti* — "the beloved composer was greeted with stormy ovations and presented with a wreath." During this visit to the northern capital Piotr Ilyich heard a performance of Rimsky-Korsakov's *Mlada.* In his *Memories of N. A. Rimsky-Korsakov* V. V. Yastrebtsev quotes Piotr Ilyich as saying: "The public is too stupid and musically undeveloped, and consequently has no business with this composition. But for us musicians here is something to hear, something to learn!" He was also attending the preliminary rehearsals of *Yolanta* and *The Nutcracker,* which were to be presented on a double bill. While these were being held, Piotr Ilyich was being honoured in Paris. On November 27 at a meeting of the Académie française Ambroise Thomas rose and nominated Piotr Ilyich Tchaikovsky to be a corresponding member. When the vote was tallied, thirty-two out of thirty-five votes were affirmative.

The Tchaikovsky brothers still played an important part in the musical-theatrical life of St. Petersburg. On December 5 Modest's new play, *A Day in St. Petersburg,* had its *première* (a failure) at the Alexandrinsky Theatre. The following day the program of the Russian Musical Society chamber-music concert included the first St. Petersburg reading of *Souvenir of Florence.* The same sextet was repeated by the St. Petersburg Chamber Music Society the day after that. (Its Moscow *première* took place on December 15, when the performers included, in addition to Piotr Ilyich's old friend Grzhimali, the future conductor of New York's Russian Symphony Orchestra, Modest Altshuler.) The dress rehearsal of both *The Nutcracker* and *Yolanta* was held in the presence of

Alexander III on December 17. The Tsar was visibly pleased, "called me to his box, and was full of compliments." The success of both works, and of the opera in particular, seemed assured. "The staging of both is superb," Piotr Ilyich wrote Anatoly, "and in the ballet even too magnificent — the eyes weary of so much gorgeousness." Rimsky-Korsakov, present at this or one of the other late rehearsals, quickly found *Yolanta* one of Piotr Ilyich's feeblest efforts, and called everything in it a failure. He was more nearly right in his appraisal than either Alexander III or the infatuated composer.

The result of the first public performance of *Yolanta* and *The Nutcracker* was summed up by a letter Piotr Ilyich wrote to the young composer George Edwardovich Conus on February 17, 1893: "The opera was evidently very well liked, the ballet not. And truth to tell, it was a little boring despite the magnificence of the setting. The papers, as always, reviled me cruelly." Not even the Figners could save *Yolanta*, while the knowing conductorial hand of Drigo could do little with the unwieldy length of *The Nutcracker*. *Yolanta* would seem to be completely dead outside the Soviet Union, while the ballet survives principally because of the undiminishing popularity of the suite Piotr Ilyich fashioned out of it, and only secondarily through sporadic stage mountings of some of its sections.

While the critics were tearing apart his latest works, Piotr Ilyich went off to western Europe. In Berlin, on December 28, he sat down and wrote Bobyk a long letter. The proposed sixth symphony did not please him. "Have decided to throw it out and forget about it. This decision is irrevocable." And again: "It may still be possible for a subject to inspire me, but I ought no longer to attempt pure — that is, symphonic or chamber — music. At the same time, to live without work that engulfs one's time, thoughts, and powers is very dull. What then remains for me to do? Shrug my shoulders and forget composition? It is very hard to decide. . . ." After a few days in Basel he went to Montbeillard to visit his beloved governess of almost half a century before, Fanny Dürbach. In advance he dreaded the visit — in his depressed state over the supposed withering of his creative powers, he had been giving way to fits of weeping, and felt that this visit might be like "entering the kingdom of the dead."

It was three o'clock the afternoon of January 1, 1893 when Piotr

Ilyich reached Montbeillard. He went straight to the six-room, three-story house belonging to Mlle Fanny and her sister. "Mlle Fanny came to the door, and I knew her at once," he wrote his brother Nikolay. "She does not look her seventy years. . . . I had dreaded tears and an affecting scene, but there was nothing of the sort. She greeted me as though it were a year since we had met — joyfully and tenderly, but quite simply. . . . The past rose up so clearly before me that I seemed to be inhaling Votkinsk air and hearing my mother's voice distinctly. . . . When she asked me which of my brothers I loved most, I replied evasively that I was equally fond of all of them. At this she became a trifle indignant and said that, as you were my childhood playmate, I ought to care most for you. And truly, at that moment I felt intense love for you because you had shared all my young joys." The following evening, having bade affectionate farewell to this lively relic of another day, Piotr Ilyich left for Paris, promising to return.

In Paris, Piotr Ilyich saw Réjane and Lucien Guitry in *Lysistrata*. The play he described to Modest as "very talented, witty, and of boundless obscenity, but dullish in places. Guitry seemed to me a vulgarian, and all together I don't like him. But Réjane is incomparable." He had to be in Brussels on January 11 for a rehearsal of the concert he was to conduct there on the 14th. His trip from France to Belgium was warmed by a telegram announcing that *Yolanta* had won appreciable success in Hamburg. At the all-Tchaikovsky Brussels concert Franz Rummel played the solo in the B-flat minor Piano Concerto, and also several solo pieces. The balance of the program was made up of the Third Suite, the *Nutcracker Suite*, the Waltz and Elegy from the Serenade for Strings, and *1812*. Although Piotr Ilyich was miserable with nervous agitation and nostalgia, he delighted the musicians by refusing to accept his fee, having learned that the concert was for charity. The Brussels public received him well, and he was honoured in a speech by the eminent pundit Gevaert.

No less peripatetic than when younger, Piotr Ilyich went from Brussels via Paris to Odessa. There he supervised rehearsals of *The Queen of Spades*, and himself rehearsed the Odessa Russian Musical Society's orchestra for an all-Tchaikovsky concert, which he conducted on the 28th. This concert and the *première* of the opera were succeeded by many festive days, including three on each of which banquets were given in his honour by local Odessa groups. Then, on February 4, he conducted a second concert consisting, with one exception — *1812* — of other composers' works.[3] Again the following afternoon he conducted, this time another program entirely of his own works: *The Tempest*, the *Andante Cantabile*, the *Nutcracker Suite*, and songs. During the days between January 24 and February 6 Piotr Ilyich posed for a painter named N. D. Kuznetsov. The resulting portrait pleased all onlookers, including its subject, who described it as "in its expressiveness, vividness, and reality, if I am not mistaken, really wonderful."

The Kuznetsov portrait shows Piotr Ilyich in a frock coat, under which he wears a shirt with rolled collar and a cravat with a pearl tie-pin. He stands with his left hand on some opened music. His sparse hair is pure white, as are his close-cropped beard and most of his wide moustache. His expression is sombre, and he is frowning slightly. It is a face showing some ravages of pain and inner tempest, but not without the quicksilver possibility of humour. The firm-gazing eyes are most attractive and full of mental activity. While in general this appears to be the portrait of a well-preserved man of many more than Piotr Ilyich's actual fifty-two years, it is not the portrait of a man decrepit, approaching senility, or likely to be burned out. The personal charm that affected all who came into contact with Piotr Ilyich his life long is quite believable in the engagingly straightforward-looking, handsome man who gazes thoughtfully from Kuznetsov's portrait.

From Kamenka, on February 9, Piotr Ilyich wrote Modest at length about his thirteen-day stay in Odessa: "Never have I been so worn out by conducting as in Odessa, for I had to conduct five concerts. Nowhere, on the other hand, have I been so extolled or so fêted. Too bad you don't have the Odessa papers, for from them you could learn the extent to which Odessa honoured my accomplishments. There were many unendurably difficult hours (the gala supper at the English Club, for example), but many delightful ones as well. If some day I could only receive in our two capitals one tenth of the honours showered on me in Odessa! But that

[3] These were Borodin's First Symphony, Heinrich Wilhelm Ernst's F-sharp minor Violin Concerto, a Scherzo for orchestra by P. Molchanov, and Sophie Menter's *Viennese Fantasy* for piano, with the composer herself performing the solo.

is impossible, and besides I don't really need it. What I need is to believe in myself again, for my faith in myself is terribly shattered, and it seems to me that my role has ended."

Piotr Ilyich's role had not ended. In a way it was approaching its climax. At Klin, on February 16 — exactly one week after that letter to Modest — he began to compose the symphony known wherever music is known as the *Pathetic*. One week after beginning the symphony, he had its entire design in mind. "As you know," he wrote to Bobyk, "I destroyed a symphony that I had partially finished and orchestrated in the autumn. I acted wisely, for it contained little that was really good — a vacant pattern of sound, without inspiration. Just as I was starting on my trip,[4] the idea for a new symphony came to me. This time with a program, but a program of a sort that remains enigmatic to everyone — let them guess it who can. The work will be called A *Program Symphony* (*No. 6*). The program is full of subjective emotion. While I was composing it during my trip, I frequently cried. Now that I am again at home, I have settled down with such ardour to sketch out the work that in less than four days I finished the first movement, while the rest of the symphony is clearly outlined in my head. There will be much in the work that is novel as regards form. For example, the Finale will be, not a great allegro, but an Adagio of considerable dimensions. You cannot imagine what happiness I experience at the conviction that my time is not yet over and that I may still accomplish a lot. Perhaps I am mistaken, but this doesn't seem likely. Don't speak of this to anyone but Modest."

For three years Piotr Ilyich had not conducted a concert of the Moscow Russian Musical Society. Now he interrupted work on his new symphony to go into the city, and on February 26 conducted a benefit program consisting of the Moscow *première* of *Hamlet,* the *Fantasy* for piano and orchestra (Taneyev), and the *Nutcracker Suite.* Eleven days later, at a concert conducted by Safonov, he heard Conus's suite for chorus and orchestra, *From Child Life.* This so delighted him that he suggested to the young composer that it be shortened and brought to a different conclusion. Piotr Ilyich later gladly accepted an invitation to conduct this composition. While he was in Moscow, a nineteen-year-old composer presented him with an opus 3 — five pieces for piano. It was Sergei Rachmaninoff.

[4] He had left on December 24, 1892.

On March 23 Piotr Ilyich was attending a performance of *Rigoletto* in Kharkov. Again he was to conduct an all-Tchaikovsky concert. There were the usual speeches, the now customary honours. He was happy to return to Klin on the 30th and begin work on the symphony again. He completed it in sketch on April 5. On that same day he fulfilled a promise made to his cousin Andrey Petrovich Tchaikovsky by composing a *Military March* for the 98th infantry regiment, of which Andrey was colonel. "The orchestration will have to be done by your conductor," he wrote in the note that accompanied the score, "as I do not know the make-up of the orchestra he conducts. Am sending you only the bare piano sketch." He then turned to other work and does not seem to have begun orchestrating the new symphony until August 1.

Several of the Eighteen Piano Pieces, Opus 72, which Piotr Ilyich began to compose on April 19, sound like discarded fragments from the symphony. One of them, *Meditation,* is perhaps the best of all his compositions for solo piano. It is not long, but it is wide and deep, and exploits more types of pianistic and interpretative resource than any other of his piano pieces. While at work on Opus 72, he spoke of its pieces slightingly to Bobyk. One day it was: "These children are very precocious and mediocre. I haven't the smallest wish to compose them, and am doing so only for money. I am trying only not to make them too bad." Another it was: "Am continuing to bake my musical blini." He rested by reading a Hindu-legend libretto, *Nal and Damayanti,* that Modest had submitted to him. "Too far removed from life," was his comment. "I need a subject on the order of *Cavalleria Rusticana.*" It was 1899 before an opera on *Nal and Damayanti* appeared, and then it was by Arensky. Piotr Ilyich also, for the last time, rejected the prospect of composing an opera to a libretto based on Zhukovsky's *Undine.* Again he told Modest that he wanted something resembling *Carmen* or *Cavalleria Rusticana.*

Completing the eighteenth piece of Opus 72 on May 4, Piotr Ilyich began to compose his Opus 73 the next day. This consists of six songs dedicated to Nikolay Figner. He worked at them on and off until May 17. On the 9th he was in Moscow, at the Bolshoi, for the *première* of young Rachmaninoff's opera *Aleko,* which he described as a charming work that pleased him very much. His old friend Albrecht was dying, and he wrote Jürgenson that, if it became necessary, the publisher should help Albrecht's family out of "my present, or future, funds." He had intended to depart for St. Petersburg and western Europe on May 16, but remained at Klin one extra day in order to complete Opus 73 and to transcribe Mozart's Piano Fantasy No. 4 for vocal quartet with piano. This *Night* has words of Piotr Ilyich's own writing. He rounded off that day by complying with his cousin Andrey's request that he add a trio to the *Military March of the 98th Regiment*. Then, and only then, he left for St. Petersburg.

At a party given by Rimsky-Korsakov, and attended by, among others, Belyayev, Lyadov, and Glazunov (who by this time was making a habit of presenting his manuscripts to Piotr Ilyich), the visitor learned that he was to be invited to conduct the coming season's concerts of the St. Petersburg Russian Musical Society. He neither accepted nor rejected this implied invitation, but seems to have told Taneyev that he would lead at least four or five of the concerts. After one week in the northern capital he left for Germany and England. He had, together with Max Bruch, Arrigo Boïto, Saint-Saëns, and Grieg, been bidden to Cambridge, there to receive the honorary degree of *Musicæ Doctor*.

Arriving in London ("one of the worst cities" and "this ugly city") on May 29, Piotr Ilyich met a long-time acquaintance, the French pianist Diémer, on the steps of his hotel. "To my great astonishment, I found myself delighted to see him. . . . In consequence of our meeting, I had to go to his recital." Three days later, at a concert of the London Philharmonic Orchestra, Piotr Ilyich conducted his Fourth Symphony to triumphant success. "The unanimous opinion is," he wrote Modest, "that I had a triumph, so that Saint-Saëns, who conducted after me, suffered a little as the result of my extraordinary success." London was proving faithful to its admiration for the music of Tchaikovsky.

The directors of the Philharmonic honoured Piotr Ilyich and Saint-Saëns with a Westminster Club dinner the day after the concert. "Incredible chic and sumptuousness," Modest learned. Walter Damrosch, who was present at this dinner, sat next to Piotr Ilyich and there first learned of the composition of his Sixth Symphony. The composer expressed a wish that Damrosch be the first to conduct it in America and promised to send him score and parts as soon as possible. Back in New York that autumn, Damrosch heard of Piotr Ilyich's death and supposed the matter closed. Shortly later, however, he received a package containing the promised score and parts. Rushing the *Pathetic* into rehearsal, he presented it to a New York audience on March 16, 1894. It was so well received that he repeated it soon after.

As the Cambridge ceremony was not to occur until June 13, Piotr Ilyich had many crowded days in London. "All the future doctors except the ailing Grieg are here," he wrote Modest. "Besides Saint-Saëns, only Boïto attracts me. Bruch is a nastily over-inflated person." Had Piotr Ilyich met Boïto earlier and been able to persuade him to supply a libretto, his last opera might have been something more viable than *Yolanta:* the man who had supplied Ponchielli with that for *La Gioconda* might have given him something as good as the libretto of *Cavalleria Rusticana,* while the man who had made Verdi's *Otello* and *Falstaff* was even capable of fulfilling his wish for "something like *Carmen.*" Piotr Ilyich also visited Sarasate, finding the fantastically renowned violinist "wonderfully kind." He also looked more carefully at London. "It is hard to give you an impression of the mad traffic of London's streets," he told Modest. "Paris is positively a village compared with London. There is such sumptuousness and beauty of harness and so many carriages during the riding hours on Regent Street and in Hyde Park that the eyes cannot encompass it all."

At Cambridge, as his part of the concert devoted to works by the composers about to be honoured,[5] Piotr Ilyich conducted *Francesca da Rimini,* driving Saint-Saëns into a rash of superlatives. On June 13 the doctorates were solemnly awarded, Grieg's *in absentia.* Piotr Ilyich must have cut a commanding figure in his red and white robe. He was completely outshone, however, by one of the nonmusical recipients of an honorary degree, the Maharajah of Bhaunagar, who wore a diamond necklace and a cloth of gold turban set with gems. There was a breakfast, closing with the passing round of a traditional loving-cup. Then the vice-chan-

[5] It also contained a composition by the future Sir Charles Villiers Stanford, president of the Cambridge University Musical Society. It was the Society's fiftieth anniversary that explained the splendour of the quintet of composers selected for doctorates. The entire program was: excerpt from *Odysseus,* for soloists, chorus, and orchestra (Bruch); *Africa,* fantasia for piano and orchestra (Saint-Saëns, who played the solo); prologue from *Mefistofele,* for soloist, chorus, and orchestra (Boïto); *Francesca da Rimini; Peer Gynt Suite No. 1* (Grieg); and *The East to the West,* for chorus and orchestra (Stanford). The soloists of greatest importance were the future Sir George Henschel and Marie Brema.

cellor of the university gave a garden party. By that evening Piotr Ilyich was back in London, and the next day he went to Paris. "Cambridge, with its colleges resembling monasteries, its special traditions retaining a good deal of the Middle Ages, its buildings reminding one of the long-gone past, creates a very favourable impression," he wrote Jürgenson.

After a few days in Itter as Sophie Menter's guest, Piotr Ilyich returned to Russia, meeting Bobyk at Grankino. During his absence abroad, Albrecht had died. Piotr Ilyich did not know it, but Apukhtin was dying too, in St. Petersburg. Now he received word that Vladimir Shilovsky, formerly one of his closest friends, had also died. Modest comments, however, that this piling-up of news of death failed to shake Piotr Ilyich's composure. "A few years before," he writes, "one such grief would have affected Tchaikovsky more sharply than all of them occurring together now did. Death now seemed to him less enigmatic and frightening. Whether his feelings were less acute, or whether the mental anguish of mature years had showed him that death is often a deliverance, I cannot say. I merely emphasize the fact that, despite the unsettling news that met him from all directions, from the time of his return from England until the end of his life Tchaikovsky was as serene and cheerful as at any time in his existence."

Opera still haunted Piotr Ilyich's waking thoughts. From Grankino, on July 5, he besought Modest to think of a libretto for him. "I should like to compose an opera this winter." He was revising the original draft of the Third Piano Concerto. A note on the manuscript reads: "The end, God be thanked! Began the revision on July 5 and completed on July 13, the day of Boba's departure. Grankino, July 13, '93." Three days later he came to the end of some retouchings he was applying to the Sixth Symphony, which he had agreed to conduct in Moscow at a benefit concert for a fund devoted to the widows and orphans of artists. To Safonov, nevertheless, he expressed doubts about the Moscow public's interest in the new work. Before returning to Klin to initiate the major project of orchestrating it, he spent ten days with his brother Nikolay at Ukolovo.

Writing to Modest from Klin on August 3, Piotr Ilyich commented on the task of orchestrating the Sixth Symphony, begun the previous day. "The farther I get, the more difficult I find orchestration. Twenty years ago I dug on all spades, without stopping, and it came out well. But now I have become cowardly and am unsure of myself. Today I spent the whole day on two pages without getting what I want. Still, the work is getting on." He probably did not know that on that same day, in far-off Chicago, a Czech conductor named Woizech Ivanovich Hlawach was delighting a Columbian Exposition audience with the *Nutcracker Suite*. He went ahead with his orchestration. On August 9, feeling pleased with himself, he wrote Anna Merkling: "I think that the symphony I am now orchestrating will turn out, if not the best, then one of the best of my compositions." By the 13th he had nearly done with the third movement and informed Taneyev that he expected to complete the Finale in not more than three days. However, he could not inform Jürgenson that it was done until August 24, and on the 30th and 31st he was still putting in order small details.[6]

During the last days of work on the Sixth Symphony Piotr Ilyich reread Nadezhda Filaretovna's letters. It was Jürgenson who heard from him of his reaction to this journey into the past: "I have recently reread N. F. von Meck's letters and wondered at the fickleness of women's passions. One would think, on reading these letters, that it would be more possible for fire to turn into water than for her subsidy to cease. One would wonder, rather, that I should be content with so paltry a sum when she is ready to give me practically all she has. And suddenly — farewell. What is more important is that I actually believed that she had lost all her money. But nothing of the kind. Simply woman's fickleness. It's irritating — the devil take it. However, I don't give a damn!" His nonchalance was solidly based on satisfaction with the new symphony. Details in its orchestral dress were not exactly what he had wanted to produce, but he told Bobyk that he considered it the very best, and particularly the most sincere, of all his works. "I love it as I have never loved a single one of my offspring." He reiterated this to Jürgenson: "On my honour, never in my life have I been so pleased with myself, so proud, so happy in the knowledge that I have really created something good." Not even the comparative slowness with which he had rounded out the sym-

---

[6] It is noteworthy that Tchaikovsky spent parts of only twelve days in sketching the rough draft of the Sixth Symphony. Its complete orchestration — and the simultaneous preparation of a piano-duet version — took less than thirty days.

phony could quash his high spirits, for he wrote Anatoly that it was caused, not by deterioration of his powers, but by greater severity in his demands on himself.

One of Piotr Ilyich's oldest friends, Apukhtin, died in St. Petersburg on August 29. Piotr Ilyich did not go to the funeral, as he had to clear up all work on the symphony before leaving for a revival of *Yolanta* in Hamburg. On the day of the ceremony, however, he noted to Bobyk: "While I write this, funeral services are being held for Lelya Apukhtin!! Although his death was not unexpected, it is nevertheless fearful and painful. He was at one time my closest friend!" Shortly later Grand Duke Konstantin Konstantinovich suggested that Piotr Ilyich compose a setting of Apukhtin's *The Requiem.* He refused. "For the music to be worthy of the poem you like, that poem would have to warm my creative feelings, to touch and agitate my heart, to awaken my imagination. The general mood of this piece does, of course, call for musical reproduction, and my last symphony (particularly the Finale) is permeated with a similar mood. But if one turns to the details, there is a great deal in this poem of Apukhtin's that, though expressed in excellent verse, does not call for music — is, in fact, even antimusical." He added, in a remark that casts light on his conception of the *Pathetic* Symphony, that he was afraid of repeating himself if he took up so quickly a composition akin in spirit and character to the one he had just completed. By the time he had made this decision — the letter was written October 8 — he had made brief visits to Hamburg and Moscow and had stopped at Mikhailovskoye to see Anatoly. Then he had settled down at Klin to orchestrate the Third Piano Concerto, which he finished on October 15.

Except for private readings of the piano transcription, the first performance of the Sixth Symphony occurred on October 20 and 21, when students of the orchestra class of the Moscow Conservatory, assisted by various of the professors (including Grzhimali), and conducted by Safonov, read through it. A day later Piotr Ilyich arrived in St. Petersburg, staying with Modest, to rehearse the orchestra of the Russian Musical Society for the public *première* of the symphony. The program of that concert of October 28 — all conducted by Piotr Ilyich — was the Sixth Symphony, Laroche's *Karomzina* Overture, Piotr Ilyich's First Piano Concerto, with the solo played by Adele Aus der Ohe, dances from Mozart's *Idomeneo,* and Liszt's *Spanish Rhapsody.* "I recall," wrote Rimsky-Korsakov in *My Musical Life,* "having asked him, during the intermission, after the performance of the symphony, whether he had a program for this composition. He replied that there was one, of course, but that he did not wish to announce it."

The following morning Modest entered his brother's room, to find him seated before the manuscript of the symphony, which he wanted to send to Jürgenson in Moscow that day. He was puzzling over what to call it. He had abandoned *A Program Symphony,* and was on the point of designating it simply *No. 6.* Modest had no suggestion except *Tragic Symphony* — which Piotr Ilyich immediately disliked — until he had left the room again. Then, according to Modest's own statement, "the word 'pathetic' occurred to me, and I returned to suggest it. I remember, as though it were yesterday, how my brother exclaimed: 'Bravo, Modest, splendid! Pathetic!' Then and there, in my presence, he added to the score the title by which the symphony has always been known." As though some doubt might be cast on this story, Modest added the following footnote: "There was no witness of this incident other than myself. But it is clear from the program of the concert of October 28 that this title had not then been given to the work. Moreover, anyone can see at a glance at the title page that this name was written later than the rest."

Piotr Ilyich had been somewhat depressed during rehearsals by the musicians' obvious indifference to his new symphony. The public at the October 28 concert had expressed polite approval, but nothing approaching enthusiasm. Rimsky-Korsakov disliked the explanation that Piotr Ilyich had not conducted it well, and that its improved reception later on resulted from superior conducting by others. "The public simply had not fathomed it the first time, had not paid enough attention to it; precisely as several years earlier it had failed to give due attention to Tchaikovsky's Fifth Symphony." Not that anyone's reaction deflected Piotr Ilyich's confidence in the composition. Informing Jürgenson on October 30 that it was to be dedicated to Bobyk, he added: "Something strange is happening to this symphony! Not that it is disliked, but that it seems to puzzle people. As for me, I am prouder of it than of any of my other compositions."

The subsequent career of the *Pathetic* Symphony has, of course, fully justified Piotr Ilyich's confidence and pride. A good case can be made for calling it the most beautifully achieved symphony

since Beethoven. Of its last movement, so unlikely a Tchaikovskyan as Sir Donald Tovey wrote: "The slow finale, with its complete sincerity of despair, is a stroke of genius which solves all the
artistic problems that have proved most baffling to symphonic
writers since Beethoven." Played as Piotr Ilyich intended — not
dragged out, that is, or rushed, or melodramatized — that passionate "adagio lamentoso" is something new and unexcelled as the
rounding-out of the formal structure in a tragic symphony. The
Pathetic is unique among Piotr Ilyich's symphonies in that a very
large part of its power derives from the satisfactory form in which
it is cast.

On October 30 Piotr Ilyich wrote Jürgenson that he would be in
Moscow in a few days to discuss details of the new symphony's
publication with him. On November 2 he felt unwell. When he
did not appear at the breakfast table, Modest went to his room.
Piotr Ilyich had passed a sleepless night, suffering from indiges-
tion. During the morning, however, he went out for half an hour
to call on Napravnik. Returning to Modest's still uncomfortable,
he refused all suggestions that he send for a doctor. He sat down
to lunch with Modest and Bobyk. Feeling thirsty, he poured out
a tumbler of water, brushed aside his companions' warnings that
it was unboiled — cholera was epidemic in St. Petersburg at the
time — and drank it off. During the afternoon his discomfort became aggravated, but when Modest renewed urging that he send
for Dr. Lyov Bertenson, Piotr Ilyich attributed his increasing discomfort to a large dose of Hunyadi water he had taken during
the morning. By evening his condition was so bad that Modest
himself sent for Dr. Bertenson.

During the afternoon Glazunov had called. He found Piotr
Ilyich very sick and willing to admit that cholera might be the
cause. When Dr. Bertenson at last arrived, he at once saw that
the patient's case was grave and sent for his brother, also a physician, to consult with him.[7] Piotr Ilyich had begun to suffer from
a terrible feeling of chest congestion. Modest states that he several times repeated: "I believe that this is death." The Doctors
Bertenson pronounced his sickness to be cholera. During the night
of November 2–3 nursing had to assist him through attack after
attack of the sharp cramps that characterize the disease. When not
in acute pain, Piotr Ilyich spoke jestingly to those near by, urging

[7] A third physician was eventually called in.

them to retire for the night. On Friday, November 3, he felt so much better that he spoke of having been snatched from the jaws of death. On Saturday, however, his spirits sank as the pains returned increased, and he asked the Bertensons to leave, telling them that they could do him no good. "I shall never recover," he said.

Soon he passed into the stage of cholera in which the kidneys fail to act. Sleeping fitfully, he became delirious. From time to time he spoke Nadezhda Filaretovna's name in what Modest calls "an indignant or reproachful tone." Alexey Sofronov arrived from Klin, but his master was unable to recognize him. Nor does he seem to have known his brother Nikolay. At last, as was then customary, the dangerous final remedy was attempted: he was placed in a hot bath. This was in vain: his pulse began to weaken. At Nikolay's request, a priest was fetched for the purpose of administering extreme unction. This he was unable to do for the reason that by the evening of November 5 Piotr Ilyich was totally unconscious; instead he prayed aloud "in clear and distinct tones, which, however, did not seem to reach the ears of the dying man."

Early on the morning of November 6 a gloomy, apprehensive group gathered about Piotr Ilyich's bed. There were his brothers Modest and Nikolay. There were Bobyk and his cousin Count A. N. Litke, a friend of Bobyk's named Buxhövden, the Doctors Bertenson and one of their colleagues, and Alexey Sofronov. Some time between three o'clock and five o'clock an expression that Modest describes as "clear recognition" passed over the patient's face. It remained only a moment. When it had gone, they knew that he was dead. He had lived fifty-three years and six months. Four days later he was buried in the cemetery of the Alexandro-Nevskaya Church.

XIX

TCHAIKOVSKY's death struck people with slow wonder and amazement. Memorial concerts began the day after his funeral: the Moscow Philharmonic Society performed the Serenade for Strings, the *Italian Caprice*, and *Romeo and Juliet*, and Emilia de Macchi sang one of his songs. There were three Moscow memorial concerts, three in St. Petersburg, two in Kharkhov, and two in Kiev. Most important of them, as the occasion that truly launched the *Pathetic* Symphony on its career of world conquest, was that of the St. Petersburg Russian Musical Society on November 18. Then Napravnik conducted, besides the symphony, the Violin Concerto (with Auer as soloist — Auer who had once disdained the concerto), and *Romeo and Juliet*, as well as several songs and Onyegin's arioso. Rumour had begun to insinuate, on no basis whatever, that Tchaikovsky had committed suicide [1] and that the program of the *Pathetic* Symphony involved some occult statement of his morbid intention. The audience was taut and nervous. Napravnik con-

---

[1] Nicolas Slonimsky, to whom I am indebted for this information, found the following letter in the Tchaikovsky archives at Klin. The translation is Mr. Slonimsky's.

St. Petersburg, November 6, 1893

My very dear Modest Ilyich:

I would like to embrace you and to tell you how deeply I am shocked by our common horrible misfortune, but I can hardly stay on my feet and cannot go out.

The dread disease which carried off your cherished brother made me feel at one with him, with you, and with all those to whom he was dear. I cannot recover after this horrible tragedy which I was destined to witness, and cannot tell you all the agonies I am going through now. I can tell you only one thing: that I feel what you feel.

Your faithfully and deeply devoted

Lyov Bertenson

As Mr. Slonimsky has pointed out, "It is inconceivable that such a letter, written at such a moment to Tchaikovsky's own brother by a physician and friend, would contain an attempt at concealment of true circumstances of Tchaikovsky's death."

ducted with tact and loving care. The success was stupendous. One of the two or three most popular symphonies ever composed came into its own exactly twelve days after its composer's death.

Havelock Ellis may very probably have been making the most brilliant of guesses when he called the *Pathetic* the "Homosexual Tragedy." It is certain, however, that this symphony no more needs a literary prop than does Beethoven's Fifth or Seventh, or Piotr Ilyich's own Fifth, its only rivals in continuing popularity. It was his last work, for he did not complete the Third Piano Concerto, leaving that thankless job, by his death, to Taneyev. As has often been said, the *Pathetic* was a miraculously appropriate capstone to his career, for it is a microcosm of his unique virtues and inescapable faults, with the former by much predominant. No other successor of Beethoven, not even Brahms, ever composed a large symphony at once so rich in melodic invention and so annealed into unity by the blazing of deeply compressed emotion. It is possible to prefer, among Piotr Ilyich's seven symphonies, and for personal reasons, the Fourth or the Fifth. What is impossible is not to sense beyond all questioning that the *Pathetic* is his greatest work.

In England and America, as in Russia, Tchaikovsky's reputation began at once to expand unpredictably. Germany, too, by early in the twentieth century, was in his domain. The Latin countries responded to him, as they do to all far northern composers, less certainly and warmly. By the time Modest died — at Klin, of cancer, in 1916 — he had seen his brother's reputation established, his popularity eclipsing that of any other Russian musician of the present or past. Nikolay had died in 1911, Anatoly in 1915. Bobyk had committed suicide at Klin in 1906. But Ippolit Ilyich Tchaikovsky, surviving to eighty-three, and dying in 1927, saw all but the final apotheosis of the strangest conquest of all.

Alexey Sofronov purchased the house at Klin, left there the furniture his master had bequeathed to him, and set out to collect and install in the house every memento, every bit of Tchaikovskyana he could discover. Four years later Modest and Bobyk bought the house from him. Ippolit, surviving them both, became unofficial curator of the Tchaikovsky Museum there when old age forced him to give up active use of his rank of admiral in the imperial navy. The revolution that shook the world could not dislodge him, and the Soviet government confirmed his right as assistant curator. In 1899 the Museum had welcomed only two visitors, in 1900 four. In 1913, the twentieth anniversary of Piotr Ilyich's death, the number soared to two hundred and seventeen. But a regime and a self-conscious people that might have been expected logically to despise the bourgeois and intensely personal music of Piotr Ilyich Tchaikovsky had learned, instead, to value him above all other Russian composers. His music could move great masses of people, and that — rather than innovation and experiment — had been stated officially to be the prime characteristic of revolutionary art. Josef Stalin was believed to prefer Tchaikovsky's to all other music, and was quoted as having stated that *Yevgeny Onyegin* and *The Queen of Spades* were his favourite operas. By 1926, the year before Ippolit Ilyich Tchaikovsky's death, more than one thousand visitors walked through the old house at Klin annually. For 1938, though the building was closed for repairs and for preparations toward building an extension museum on the grounds, the registered visitors totalled 7,674. Branches of the Museum were opened in Votkinsk and on the former Davidov estate at Kamenka.

Finally, in 1940, the centennial year of Piotr Ilyich's birth, he became, in the Soviet Union, what can only be called an industry. Celebrations of mammoth scope were planned and carried out in the larger cities. Travelling troupes presented his operas and ballets. Complete cycles of his songs, piano and chamber pieces, and choral works were presented and broadcast. The government published more and more of his correspondence — with Nadezhda Filaretovna, with Jürgenson, with friends and the members of his family. Biographies and musicological books dealt with him. In sober fact, hundreds of people throughout the Soviet Union must have spent most of their energy for the better part of a year on the glorification of Piotr Ilyich and his music. No nation anywhere, at any time, has ever so supported the performance of music. Not the slightest of Tchaikovsky's works was passed over. In the country he loved, a regime he might have had difficulty in understanding had demonstrated the whole justice of a decision he had made seventy-five years before, the decision to give up being a civil servant and enter upon the career of a musician.

Time, which has lifted three of Tchaikovsky's symphonies, two of his concertos, and two of his other orchestral compositions to a place with Beethoven's in frequency of performance, may undoubtedly alter its judgments, the steadiness of time's judgments being an illusion caused by human brevity. Time may, for example, as it already shows signs of doing, increase the popularity of the Second and Third symphonies. It may enact artistic justice by bringing out of inexplicable obscurity *The Tempest, Manfred,* and the Second Piano Concerto. It may find, outside the Soviet Union, reasonable methods of performing adequately *Yevgeny Onyegin, The Queen of Spades, The Maid of Orleans,* and *Cherevichki.* It may demote the Fifth and the *Pathetic* from their present sovereignty. What it will probably not do, however, is learn to neglect Tchaikovsky altogether. Something of his passionate and undeviating sincerity will always burn through. Something of the pervasive musicality that drenched all his actions and his life, that shaped all his best compositions — even when intellect and taste wavered — will endure. Dargomizhsky's fate, Cui's fate, Anton Rubinstein's fate — deserved or undeserved from other points of view — is not likely to become Tchaikovsky's. So long as orchestral music is played, so long as human thought and emotions respond to other human thought and emotions transformed into sound — for that long we shall hear in the concert hall, in recorded form, and on the air lanes, the alternately sombre and ebullient, but always intensely musical voice of Piotr Ilyich Tchaikovsky.

CATALOGUE OF WORKS

I. PIANO WORKS (SOLO)

OPUS 1. *Russian Scherzo; Impromptu.* Dedicated to Nikolay Rubinstein. (*Russian Scherzo* was based on the first theme of the Andante of the String Quartet in B major. *Impromptu* was published by mistake.)

OPUS 2. *Souvenir of Hapsal:* 1. *Ruins of a Château;* 2. Scherzo; 3. *Song without Words.* Dedicated to Vera Vasilyevna Davidova. (Scherzo was a student-period composition.)

OPUS 4. Waltz-Caprice. Dedicated to Anton K. Door.

OPUS 5. Romance. Dedicated to Désirée Artôt.

OPUS 7. Waltz-Scherzo in A major. Dedicated to Alexandra Ilyinishna Davidova.

OPUS 8. Capriccio in G flat major. Dedicated to Karl Klindworth.

OPUS 9. 1. *Reverie.* Dedicated to Mlle N. A. Muromtseva.

        2. *Salon Polka.* Dedicated to A. V. Zograf.

        3. *Salon Mazurka.* Dedicated to Alexander I. Dubuque.

OPUS 10. 1. *Nocturne;* 2. *Humoresque.* Dedicated to My friend Vladimir Shilovsky.

OPUS 19. 1. *Evening Reverie.* Dedicated to Nikolay D. Kondratyev.

        2. *Humorous Scherzo.* Dedicated to Vera V. Timanova.

        3. *Album Leaf.* Dedicated to Anna K. Avramova.

        4. *Nocturne* in C sharp minor. Dedicated to M. V. Terminskaya.

        5. Capriccioso. Dedicated to Eduard L. Langer.

        6. Theme and Variations in F major. Dedicated to Herman Laroche.

OPUS 21. Six Pieces on One Theme: 1. Prelude in G sharp minor; 2. Fugue (4 voices) in G sharp minor; 3. *Impromptu* in C sharp minor; 4. *Funeral March* in A flat minor; 5. Mazurka in A flat minor; 6. Scherzo in A flat major. Dedicated to Anton Rubinstein.

OPUS 37. Sonata in G major. Dedicated to Karl Klindworth.

OPUS 37 bis. *The Seasons: January — At the Fireside; February —*

Carnival; March — Song of the Lark; April — Snowdrop; May — May Night; June — Barcarolle; July — Reaper's Song; August — Harvest; September — Hunting; October — Autumn Song; November — Troika; December — Christmas.

OPUS 39. *Children's Album:* 1. *Morning Prayer;* 2. *Winter Morning;* 3. *Little Horseman;* 4. *Mama;* 5. *The Toy Soldiers' March;* 6. *The Sick Doll;* 7. *The Doll's Funeral March;* 8. Waltz in E flat major; 9. *The New Doll;* 10. Mazurka; 11. *Russian Song;* 12. *Song of the Rustic;* 13. *Kamarinskaya;* 14. Polka in B flat major; 15. *Italian Song;* 16. *Ancient French Song;* 17. *German Song;* 18. *Neapolitan Song;* 19. *The Old Woman's Story;* 20. *The Witch;* 21. *Sweet Reverie;* 22. *The Song of the Lark;* 23. *Organ Grinder's Song;* 24. *In the Church.* Dedicated to Vladimir Lvovich Davidov.

OPUS 40. Twelve Pieces of Moderate Difficulty: 1. Study in G major; 2. *Sad Little Song;* 3. *Funeral March* in C minor; 4. Mazurka in C major; 5. Mazurka in D major; 6. *Song without Words* in A minor; 7. *In the Village;* 8. Waltz in A flat major; 9. Waltz in F sharp minor; 10. *Russian Dance;* 11. Scherzo in D minor-D major; 12. *Interrupted Reveries.* Dedicated to Modest Ilyich Tchaikovsky.

OPUS 51. 1. *Salon Waltz* in A flat major. Dedicated to Marya S. Kondratyeva.

    2. *Polka peu dansante* in B minor. Dedicated to Anna Lvovna Davidova.

    3. Menuetto scherzoso. Dedicated to Anna Petrovna Merkling.

    4. *Natha Waltz* in A major. Dedicated to Natha A. Pleskaya.

    5. *Romance* in F major. Dedicated to Vera Rimskaya-Korsakova.

    6. *Sentimental Waltz* in F minor. Dedicated to Emma I. Zhenton.

OPUS 59. *Dumka (Rustic Russian Scene).* Dedicated to Antoine-François Marmontel.

OPUS 72. 1. *Impromptu* in F minor. Dedicated to V. I. Maslova.

    2. *Lullaby.* Dedicated to Piotr Moskalev of Odessa.

    3. *Tender Reproaches.* Dedicated to August A. Gerke.

    4. *Characteristic Dance.* Dedicated to A. I. Galli.

    5. *Meditation.* Dedicated to V. I. Safonov.

6. Mazurka for Dancing in B major. Dedicated to Mlle E. P. Jürgenson.
7. Concert Polonaise in E flat major. Dedicated to Paul A. Pabst.
8. *Dialogue*. Dedicated to Yekaterina I. Laroche.
9. *A Little of Schumann*. Dedicated to A. I. Maslova.
10. Scherzo Fantasy in E flat minor. Dedicated to Alexander Siloti.
11. *Valse bluette* in E flat major. Dedicated to N. D. Kondratyeva.
12. *L'Espiègle*. Dedicated to Mlle A. P. Jürgenson.
13. *Rustic Echo*. Dedicated to A. I. Brullova.
14. *Elegiac Song*. Dedicated to the Memory of V. Sklifasovsky.
15. *A Little of Chopin*. Dedicated to Sergey M. Remezov.
16. Waltz in Five-Eight Time. Dedicated to N. K. Lenz.
17. *Distant Past*. Dedicated to Nikolay S. Zverev.
18. *Dancing Scene (Invitation to the Trepak)*. Dedicated to Vasily Sapelnikov.

Opus 80. Sonata in C sharp minor (posthumous).

Allegro in C minor. (Student work; manuscript lost.)

Impromptu in A flat major. (Written for album presented to Anton Rubinstein.)

Impromptu Caprice in G major. (Composed for and originally published in *Gaulois*.) Dedicated to Mme Sophie I. Jürgenson.

Lyric Moment (Impromptu) in A flat major. (Left incomplete; completed by Taneyev.)

Piece on "Near the River, Near the Bridge." Dedicated to Herman Laroche. (Manuscript lost.)

Theme and Variations in A minor. (Manuscript lost.)

Waltz. Dedicated to Anastasya Petrovna Petrova. (Juvenile work; manuscript lost.)

Waltz-Scherzo in A major.

II. PIANO WORKS (DUET)

Fifty Russian Folksongs.
Funeral March on motives from *The Oprichnik*.

III. ORCHESTRA WORKS

OPUS 13. Symphony No. 1 in G minor (*Winter Reveries*). Dedicated to Nikolay Rubinstein.

OPUS 15. Festival Overture on the Danish National Hymn.

OPUS 17. Symphony No. 2 in C minor ("Little Russian"). Dedicated to the Moscow Russian Musical Society.

OPUS 18. *The Tempest* (fantasy overture). Dedicated to Vladimir Vasilyevich Stasov.

OPUS 29. Symphony No. 3 in D major ("Polish").

OPUS 31. *Slavic March.*

OPUS 32. *Francesca da Rimini* (fantasy). Dedicated to Sergey Ivanovich Taneyev.

OPUS 36. Symphony No. 4 in F minor. Dedicated to My Best Friend.

OPUS 43. Suite No. 1 in D major: 1. Introduction and fugue; 2. Divertimento; 3. Intermezzo; 4. Miniature March; 5. Scherzo; 6. Gavotte.

OPUS 45. *Italian Caprice.* Dedicated to Karl U. Davidov.

OPUS 48. Serenade for String Orchestra in C major. Dedicated to Konstantin Karlovich Albrecht.

OPUS 49. *1812* (a Solemn Overture).

OPUS 53. Suite No. 2 in C major: 1. *Play of Sounds;* 2. Waltz; 3. *Burlesque Scherzo;* 4. *Dreams of a Child;* 5. *Savage Dance in the Style of Dargomizhsky.* Dedicated to Parasha V. Tchaikovskaya.

OPUS 55. Suite No. 3 in G major: 1. *Elegy;* 2. *Melancholy Waltz;* 3. Scherzo; 4. Theme and Variations. Dedicated to Max von Erdmannsdörfer.

OPUS 58. *Manfred* Symphony. Dedicated to Mili Alexeyevich Balakirev.

OPUS 61. *Mozartiana* (Suite No. 4): 1. Gigue; 2. Minuet; 3. *Preghiera* (after a Liszt transcription); 4. Theme and Ten Variations.

OPUS 64. Symphony No. 5 in E minor. Dedicated to Theodor Ave-Lallemant of Hamburg.

OPUS 67. *Hamlet* (fantasy overture). Dedicated to Edvard Grieg.

OPUS 71 bis. The *Nutcracker Suite:* 1. Miniature Overture; 2. Characteristic Dances — a. March, b. *Dance of the Sugar-Plum*

Fairy, c. Trepak, d. *Arabian Dance,* e. *Chinese Dance,* f. *Shepherd's Dance;* 3. *Waltz of the Flowers.*

OPUS 74. Symphony No. 6 in B minor (*Pathetic*). Dedicated to Vladimir Lvovich Davidov.

OPUS 76. *The Storm* (overture). (Posthumous.)

OPUS 77. *Fate* (symphonic poem). Dedicated to Mili Alexeyevich Balakirev. (Posthumous.)

OPUS 78. *The Voivode* (ballad). (Posthumous.)

Agitato in E minor. (For small orchestra; student work.)

Allegro vivo. (For classic orchestra; student work.)

Andante ma non troppo in A major. (For small orchestra; student work.)

Concert Overture in C minor. (Student work.)

Coronation March.

Elegy in Memory of I. V. Samarin. (For string orchestra.)

Jurisprudence March.

Military March for the 98th Regiment of Infantry. (Not orchestrated by Tchaikovsky.)

Overture in F major.

Romans in the Colosseum. (Student work? Sketched for orchestra?)

Romeo and Juliet (fantasy overture). Dedicated to Mili Alexeyevich Balakirev.

Serenade on Nikolay Rubinstein's Saint's Day, 1872. (For small orchestra.)

Skobelyev March. (Signed P. Sinopov.)

Symphony. (Intended as No. 6, but not completed. Materials used in Concerto No. 3 for piano and orchestra, opus 75 and opus 79.)

IV. CONCERTOS AND CONCERTED PIECES WITH ORCHESTRA

OPUS 23. Concerto No. 1 in B flat minor for piano and orchestra. Dedicated to Hans von Bülow.

OPUS 26. *Melancholy Serenade* in B minor for violin and orchestra. Dedicated to Leopold Auer.

OPUS 33. *Variations on a Rococo Theme* in A major for cello and orchestra. Dedicated to Wilhelm Karl Friedrich Fitzenhagen.

OPUS 34. Waltz-Scherzo in C major for violin and orchestra. Dedicated to Yosif Yosifovich Kotek.

Opus 35. Concerto in D major for violin and orchestra. Dedicated to Adolf Brodsky.

Opus 44. Concerto No. 2 in G major for piano and orchestra. Dedicated to My Friend Nikolay Rubinstein.

Opus 56. Concert fantasy for piano and orchestra. Dedicated to Sophie Menter.

Opus 62. *Pezzo capriccioso* in B minor for cello and orchestra. Dedicated to Anatoly A. Brandukov.

Opus 75. Concerto No. 3 in E flat major for piano and orchestra, Allegro brillante only. Dedicated to Louis Diémer. (Posthumous.)

Opus 79. Concerto No. 3 in E flat major for piano and orchestra, Andante and Finale only. (Adapted from discarded symphony by Taneyev.)

V. CHAMBER WORKS

Opus 11. String Quartet No. 1 in D major. Dedicated to Sergey A. Rachinsky.

Opus 22. String Quartet No. 2 in F major. Dedicated to Grand Duke Konstantin Nikolayevich.

Opus 30. String Quartet No. 3 in E flat minor. Dedicated to the Memory of Ferdinand Laub.

Opus 42. *Souvenir of a Loved Place* (violin and piano): 1. *Meditation* (original Andante of the Concerto for violin and orchestra); 2. Scherzo in C minor; 3. Melody in E flat major. Dedicated to Braïlov.

Opus 50. Trio (piano, violin, and cello). Dedicated to the Memory of a Great Artist.

Opus 70. *Souvenir of Florence* (2 violins, 2 violas, and 2 cellos). Dedicated to the St. Petersburg Chamber Music Society.

Adagio in C major for wind quartet. (Student work.)

Adagio in F major for wind octet. (Student work.)

Adagio molto in E flat minor (2 violins, viola, cello, and harp). (Student work.)

Allegretto in D major (violin, viola, and cello). (Student work.)

Allegretto in E major (2 violins, viola, and cello). (Student work.)

Allegro in C minor (2 violins, viola, cello, contrabass, and piano). (Student work.)

Allegro in A major (2 violins, viola, cello, contrabass, and 2 flutes). (Student work.)

Allegro ma non tanto in G major (2 violins, viola, cello, and contra-
  bass). (Student work.)
Allegro vivace (2 violins, viola, and cello). (Student work.)
Andante molto in G major (2 violins, viola, and cello). (Student
  work.)
Ensemble for wind octet. (Student work.)
Prelude in E minor (2 violins, viola, cello, and contrabass). (Stu-
  dent work.)
String Quartet in B major. (Student work.)

VI. VOCAL MUSIC (SOLO SONGS)

Opus 6. 1. "Believe Not, Friend of Mine" (Alexey Tolstoy). Dedi-
  cated to Mme A. G. Menshikova; 2. "A Summer Love Tale" (M.
  Hartman and A. N. Pleshcheyev). Dedicated to Nikolay Kash-
  kin; 3. "Both Painful and Sweet" (Countess Rastopchina).
  Dedicated to Mme A. D. Kochetova; 4. "A Tear Trem-
  bles" (Alexey Tolstoy). Dedicated to Piotr Ivanovich
  Jürgenson; 5. "Why?" (Heine, translated by L. A. Mey). Dedi-
  cated to I. A. Klimenko; 6. "None but the Lonely Heart"
  (Goethe, translated by L. A. Mey). Dedicated to Mme A. A.
  Khvostova.
Opus 16. 1. "Lullaby" (A. N. Maikov). Dedicated to Mme Na-
  dezhda Nikolayevna Rimskaya-Korsakova; 2. "Wait!" (N. P.
  Grekov). Dedicated to Nikolay Andreyevich Rimsky-Korsakov;
  3. "Understand but Once" (A. A. Fet). Dedicated to Herman
  Laroche; 4. "The Song That You Sang Long Ago" (F. Gimens
  and A. N. Pleshcheyev). Dedicated to Nikolay Albertovich
  Hubert; 5. "What Does It Matter?" ("N. N."). Dedicated to
  Nikolay Rubinstein; 6. "Greek Song" (on Dies Iræ) (A. N.
  Maikov). Dedicated to Konstantin Karlovich Albrecht.
Opus 25. 1. "Reconciliation" (N. F. Shcherbina). Dedicated to
  A. P. Krutikova; 2. "As Though on Hot Ashes" (F. I. Tyutchev).
  Dedicated to Dmitri A. Orlov; 3. "Mignon's Song" (Goethe,
  translated by Tyutchev); 4. "Canary" (Mey). Dedicated to
  W. I. Raab; 5. "I Have Never Spoken to Her" (Mey). Dedicated
  to I. A. Melnikov; 6. "The Tsar's Drinking House" (Mey).
Opus 27. 1. "Invocation to Sleep" (N. P. Ogarev); 2. "The Cloud"
  (Grekov); 3. "Do Not Leave Me" (A. A. Fet); 4. "Evening"
  (Mey, after Shevchenko); 5. "From the Day That I Was

Born" (Mey, after A. Mickiewicz); 6. "My Favorite" (Mey, after A. Mickiewicz). Dedicated to Princess Yelizaveta Tserteleva, *née* Lavrovskaya.

Opus 28. 1. "No, Whom I Love I Will Not Name" (Grekov, after Musset). Dedicated to Anton N. Nikolayev; 2. "The Corals" (Mey, after Sirokoml). Dedicated to Alexander M. Dodonov; 3. "Why?" (Mey). Dedicated to M. I. Dundakova-Korsakova; 4. "No, I Have Never Loved." Dedicated to E. Massini; 5. "No Tidings Came from Thee" (Apukhtin). Dedicated to B. B. Korsov; 6. "Terrible Moment" ("N. N."). Dedicated to E. P. Kadmina.

Opus 38. 1. "Don Juan's Serenade" (Alexey Tolstoy); 2. " It Was in the Early Spring" (Alexey Tolstoy); 3. "During the Ball" (Alexey Tolstoy); 4. "Oh, Could You But for One Short Hour" (Alexey Tolstoy); 5. "The Love of One Dead" (Lermontov); 6. "Pimpinella" (arranged by "N. N."). Dedicated to Anatoly Tchaikovsky.

Opus 47. 1. "If I Knew Him" (Alexey Tolstoy); 2. "The Soul Flew Heavenward" (Alexey Tolstoy); 3. "Evening and Morning" (N. V. Berg, after Mickiewicz); 4. "The Sounds of Day Are Still" (Alexey Tolstoy); 5. "To the Forests" (Alexey Tolstoy); 6. "Always for Thee" (Apukhtin); 7. "Was I Not a Blade of Grass?" (I. Z. Surikov). Dedicated to A. V. Panayeva.

Opus 54. *Sixteen Songs for Children:* 1. "Grandmother and Grandson" (Pleshcheyev); 2. "The Little Bird" (Pleshcheyev, from the Polish); 3. "Spring: the Grass Grows Green" (Pleshcheyev, from the Polish); 4. "My Little Garden" (Pleshcheyev); 5. "Legend: Christ Had a Garden" (Plescheyev, from the English); 6. "On the Banks" (Pleshcheyev); 7. "Winter Evening" (Pleshcheyev); 8. "The Cuckoo" (Gelert and Pleshcheyev); 9. "Spring: the Snow Is Melting" (Pleshcheyev); 10. "Lullaby during the Storm" (Pleshcheyev); 11. "The Little Flower" (L. Ratisbonn and Pleshcheyev); 12. "Winter" (Pleshcheyev); 13. "Spring Song" (Pleshcheyev); 14. "Autumn" (Pleshcheyev); 15. "The Swallow" (T. Lenartovich and I. Z. Surikov); 16. "Children's Song" (K. S. Aksakov).

Opus 57. 1. "Tell Me, What Are You Thinking?" (V. A. Sollogub). Dedicated to F. P. Komissarzhevsky; 2. "On the Yellow Field" (Alexey Tolstoy). Dedicated to B. B. Korsov; 3. "Do Not Question Me" (Goethe, translated by A. S. Strugovshchikov). Dedicated to Y. Pavlovskaya; 4. "I Should Like to Sleep For Ever" (Dmitri Merezhkovsky). Dedicated to Vera V. Butakova; 5. "Death" (Dmitri Merezhkovsky). Dedicated to D. A. Usatov; 6. "You Alone" (A. Kristen, translated by Pleshcheyev). Dedicated to A. P. Krutikova.

Opus 60. "Yesternight" (A. S. Khomyakov); 2. "I Shall Tell You Nothing" (A. A. Fet); 3. "Ah! If You Knew" (Pleshcheyev); 4. "The Nightingale" (V. Stefanovich and Pushkin); 5. "Simple Words" (P. I. Tchaikovsky); 6. "Mad Nights" (Apukhtin); 7. "Song of the Gypsy Girl" (Polonsky); 8. "Farewell" (N. A. Nekrasov); 9. "Night" (Polonsky); 10. "Beyond the Window" (Polonsky); 11. "Daring Exploit" (A. S. Khomyakov); 12. "Starry Night" (Pleshcheyev). Dedicated to Her Imperial Majesty the Tsarina of Russia (Marya Fyodorovna).

Opus 63. Six Songs ("K. R.," pseudonym of Grand Duke Konstantin Nikolayevich): 1. "I Did Not Love You at First"; 2. "I Opened the Window"; 3. "You Do Not Love Me"; 4. "The First Rendezvous"; 5. "The Lights Were Being Dimmed"; 6. "Serenade."

Opus 65. Six French Songs: 1. "Sérénade" (Turquety); 2. "Déception" (Collin); 3. "Sérénade" (Collin); 4. "Qu'importe que l'hiver" (Collin); 5. "Les Larmes" (Blanchecotte); 6. "Rondel" (Collin). Dedicated to Désirée Artôt de Padilla.

Opus 73. Six German Songs (D. M. Rathaus): 1. "An dem schlummernden Strom"; 2. "Nacht"; 3. "O, du mondhelle Nacht"; 4. "Sonne ging zur Ruhe"; 5. "In trüber Stund"; 6. "Weil' ich wie einstmals allein." Dedicated to Nikolay Figner.

"Blue Eyes of Spring" (Heine, translated by M. L. Mikhailov).

"The Forgotten One" (Apukhtin).

"I'd Like in a Single Word" (Heine, translated by Mey).

"Mezza notte" (A. A. Fet, from the Italian). (Juvenile work.)

"My Genius, My Angel, My Friend" (A. A. Fet). (Juvenile work.)

"O Not for Long Are We to Stroll" (N. P. Grekov).

"Our Mama in Petersburg" (with sister Alexandra). (Juvenile work.)

"So Soon Forgotten" (Apukhtin).

"Take Away My Heart" (A. A. Fet).

"Who Goes?" (Apukhtin). (Juvenile work.)

"Zemphira's Song" (Pushkin). (Juvenile work.)

VII. VOCAL MUSIC (TWO OR MORE VOICES)

Opus 46. Duets: 1. "Evening" (I. Z. Surikov); 2. "Scottish Ballad" (Alexey Tolstoy); 3. "Tears" (Tyutchev); 4. "In the Garden near the River" (I. Z. Surikov and T. G. Shevchenko); 5. "The End of Passion" (Alexey Tolstoy); 6. "Dawn" (I. Z. Surikov). Dedicated to Tatyana Lvovna Davidova.

"Blessed Is He Who Smiles," chorus for students of Moscow University, for 2 tenors and 2 baritones a cappella ("K. R.," pseudonym of Grand Duke Konstantin Nikolayevich.

Cantata for pupils of the Patriotic Institute, for 4 female voices (text by the pupils).

Cantata for opening of the Moscow Polytechnic Exposition, for tenor, mixed chorus, and orchestra (Y. P. Polonsky).

Chorus dedicated to choristers of the Imperial Opera, for mixed voices a cappella.

Chorus for fiftieth anniversary of the School of Jurisprudence (P. I. Tchaikovsky). Dedicated to the Founder of the School.

"Evening," for 3-part male chorus a cappella (P. I. Tchaikovsky?).

"The Golden Cloud Slept," for mixed chorus a cappella (Lermontov).

Greetings to Anton Rubinstein, for mixed chorus a cappella (Y. P. Polonsky).

"Lamenting Angel," for mixed chorus a cappella.

"Moscow," cantata composed on the occasion of the coronation of Alexander III, for mezzo-soprano, baritone, chorus, and orchestra (A. N. Maikov).

"Nature and Love," for 2 sopranos, contralto, chorus, and piano. Dedicated to Mme B. Valtsek.

"Night," for soprano, contralto, tenor, bass, and piano, after Mozart's Fantasia No. 4 (P. I. Tchaikovsky). Dedicated to Y. A. Lavrovskaya.

"The Nightingale," for mixed chorus a cappella (P. I. Tchaikovsky). Dedicated to the Mixed Chorus of the St. Petersburg Imperial Opera House.

"Not a Cuckoo in the Forest Damp," for mixed chorus a cappella (N. G. Tsiganov). Dedicated to the Free Choral Class of I. A. Melnikov.

"Ode to Joy" (Schiller, translated by K. S. Aksakov and others). (Student work.)

"On Coming Sleep" (N. P. Ogarev). (Student work.)

"Romeo and Juliet," for soprano and tenor (Shakespeare, arranged by A. L. Sokolovsky). (Voice parts only; accompaniment arranged from the orchestral *Romeo and Juliet* by Taneyev.)

"Spring," for female chorus a cappella.

"To Touch the Heart of Man," cantata for fiftieth jubilee of Ossip Afanasyevich Petrov, for mixed chorus and orchestra (Nekrasov).

"Why Silence the Voice of Joy?" for 4-part male chorus a cappella (Pushkin). Dedicated to the Free Choral Class of I. A. Melnikov.

"Without Time," for 4-part female chorus a cappella (N. G. Tsiganov). Dedicated to the Free Choral Class of I. A. Melnikov.

VIII. OPERAS

Opus 3. *The Voivode.* Libretto by Ostrovsky (Act I) and P. I. Tchaikovsky (Acts II and III), based on Ostrovsky's play *The Voivode, or A Dream on the Volga.* Three acts. (Surviving fragments: 1. Overture; 2. Entr'acte and *Dances of the Serving Maids;* 3. several unimportant solos in manuscript.)

Opus 14. *Vakula the Smith.* Libretto by Yakov Petrovich Polonsky, based on Gogol. Three acts. (Later revised as *Cherevichki,* also known as *Oksana's Caprices.* Four acts.) Dedicated to the Memory of Grand Duchess Yelena Pavlovna.

Opus 24. *Yevgeny Onyegin.* Libretto by P. I. Tchaikovsky and Konstantin S. Shilovsky, based on Pushkin. Three acts.

Opus 68. *The Queen of Spades.* Libretto by Modest Ilyich Tchaikovsky, based on Pushkin. Three acts.

Opus 69. *Yolanta.* Libretto by Modest Ilyich Tchaikovsky, based on K. I. Zvantsev's translation of Henrik Herz's play *King René's Daughter.* One act.

The Enchantress. Libretto by I. V. Shpazhinsky, based on his play of the same name. Four acts.

The Maid of Orleans. Libretto by P. I. Tchaikovsky, based on Zhukovsky's translation of Schiller's *Die Jungfrau von Orleans; Wallon;* a play by Jules Paul Barbier; and the libretto of Mermet's opera *Jeanne d'Arc.* Four acts. Dedicated to Eduard Franzevich Napravnik.

Mandragora. Libretto by Sergey A. Rachinsky. (Surviving frag-

ment: *Chorus of Insects,* for mixed chorus and orchestra, orchestrated by Glazunov.)

Mazepa. Libretto by V. P. Burenin and P. I. Tchaikovsky, based
on Pushkin's *Poltava.* Three acts.

The Oprichnik. Libretto by P. I. Tchaikovsky, based on Lazhechnikov's play of the same name. Four acts. Dedicated to Grand
Duke Konstantin Nikolayevich.

Undine. Libretto by Vladimir Sollogub, based on Zhukovsky's *Undine.* Three acts. (Surviving fragments: 1. Aria, "The Spring Is
My Brother"; became part of incidental music to *Snyegurochka;*
2. Wedding march from last act; became Andantino marziale
of Symphony No. 2; 3. Love duet between Gulbrand and Undine, became an adagio in *Swan Lake.*)

IX. BALLETS

OPUS 20. *Swan Lake.* Scenario by V. P. Begichev and V. F. Geltser.
Four acts.

OPUS 66. *Sleeping Beauty.* Scenario by Marius Petipa and I. A.
Vsevolozhsky, based on Perrault. Prologue and three acts. Dedicated to I. A. Vsevolozhsky.

OPUS 71. *The Nutcracker.* Scenario by Marius Petipa, based on
Alexandre Dumas fils's version of E. T. A. Hoffmann's story
"The Nutcracker and the Mouse King." Two acts.

X. THEATRICAL MUSIC OTHER THAN OPERAS AND BALLETS

OPUS 12. Incidental music (19 numbers) for Ostrovsky's play
Snyegurochka, a Legend of Springtide.

OPUS 67 bis. Incidental music (17 numbers) for Shakespeare's
Hamlet.

An Entanglement, couplets for a vaudeville by P. S. Fedorov.

Incidental music for Beaumarchais's *Le Barbier de Séville:* couplets for Count Almaviva.

Incidental music for O. Felye's *The Fairy:* Lullaby.

Incidental music for Ostrovsky's play *The False Dmitri and Vasily
Shuisky:* Introduction and Mazurka.

Incidental music for Ostrovsky's play *The Voivode, or A Dream
on the Volga:* scene of the domovoy.

Incidental music for Pushkin's *Boris Godunov:* the fountain scene.

Montenegro at the Moment of Receiving the News of War between

Russia and Turkey: A Village Elder Reading the Manifesto: music for a tableau vivant.

Recitatives and chorus for Auber's *Le Domino noir.*

Recitatives for Mozart's *Le Nozze di Figaro* (also translation of the libretto into Russian).

XI. RELIGIOUS MUSIC

Opus 41. Liturgy of St. John Chrysostom, for 4-part mixed chorus a cappella (15 numbers).

Opus 52. Vespers (Mass), essays at harmonizing religious canticles, for mixed chorus a cappella (17 numbers).

Hymn to St. Kyrilla and St. Mefodyi, an old Slavonic melody arranged for choir a cappella (P. I. Tchaikovsky).

Nine Liturgical Choruses, a cappella: 1. Cherubim I; 2. Cherubim II; 3. Cherubim III; 4. "We Sing to Thee"; 5. "It Is Worthy"; 6. "Our Father"; 7. "Bliss I Chose"; 8. "May My Prayer Be Granted"; 9. "Today the Heavenly Powers."

Oratorio, for soloists, mixed chorus, and orchestra. (Student work.)

XII. MUSICAL JESTS

"Low Cur," inscription in album for M. A. Golovina, for voice and piano (P. I. Tchaikovsky).

"No News from the Beloved One," sent to Vladimir Lvovich Davidov, for voice and piano.

"Waltz-Jest" in A major, for piano, composed for the periodical *Artist.*

XIII. TRANSCRIPTIONS AND ARRANGEMENTS

Beethoven

Orchestration of first movement of Sonata for piano and violin in A major, opus 47 ("Kreutzer"). (Student work.)

Orchestration of first movement of Sonata for piano in D minor, opus 31, no. 2 ("Tempest"). (Student work.)

Cimarosa

Arrangement for 3 voices and piano of trio from *Il Matrimonio segreto.*

Dargomizhsky

Arrangement for 3 voices and orchestra of "The Golden Cloud Slept."

Transcription for piano of *Kazachok* (orchestral fantasy).

Dubuque
  Orchestration of "Marya Dagmar."
Glinka
  Arrangement for orchestra and large chorus of Slavsya chorus
    from *A Life for the Tsar*.
Gung'l
  Orchestration of "The Return."
Haydn
  Orchestration of "Gott erhalte Franz den Kaiser."
Kral
  Orchestration of Solemn March.
Laroche
  Orchestration of *Karomzina* Overture.
Liszt
  Arrangement for voice and piano of "The King of Thule."
Mamontova
  Arrangement of Children's Songs on Russian and Little Rus-
    sian refrains.
Menter
  Orchestration of *Ungarische Zigeunerweisen*, a piano concerto.
Prokunin
  Arrangement for voice and piano of sixty-six Russian Songs.
Rubinstein, Anton
  Transcription for piano duet of Overture to *Ivan the Terrible*.
  Transcription for piano duet of *Don Quixote*.
Schumann
  Arrangement for voice and orchestra of "Eternal Sleep" (bal-
    lad).
  Orchestration of two of the Études symphoniques. (Student
    work.)
Stradella
  Arrangement for voice and orchestra of "O del mio dolce."
Tarnovskaya
  Transcription for piano duet of "I Remember All" (song).
Weber
  Orchestration of Scherzo from Sonata, opus 39, for piano. (Stu-
    dent work.)
  Transcription for piano, left hand alone, of Perpetuum mobile
    (finale) of Sonata, opus 39, for piano. Dedicated to A. U.
    Zograf.

folksong
> Arrangement of "Gaudeamus igitur" for male chorus and piano (text translated by N. V. Bugayev).

XIV. LITERARY AND EDITORIAL WORKS

Autobiography, written for Neitzel. Partially completed; lost.

Brief Textbook of Harmony Adapted to the Reading of Russian Church Music (1874).

Complete Edition of the Church Music of Dmitri Stepanovich Bortnyansky. 12 volumes.

Diaries: 1858–9 (accidentally burned in 1866); 1873; 1882 (lost); 1884; 1885 (lost); 1886; 1887; 1888 (Diary of My Tour); 1889; 1890; 1891.

Edition of a compilation of children's songs.

History of Literature in Our Class (juvenile work).

Reviews and critical articles, distributed as follows: 1868 – 1; 1869 – 1; 1871 – 4; 1872 – 10; 1873 – 11; 1874 – 15; 1875 – 15; 1876 – 1; 1891 – 1.

Textbook for the Practical Study of Harmony (1871).

Translations
> of Gevaert's *Traité général de l'instrumentation.*
>
> of texts of six Italian songs by Glinka.
>
> of text of a vocal quartet by Glinka.
>
> of Lobe's *Katechismus der Musik.*
>
> of the libretto (Da Ponte) of Mozart's *Le Nozze di Figaro*. Translation redone by Modest Tchaikovsky for a St. Petersburg production in 1901.
>
> of the texts of Anton Rubinstein's *Persian Songs* and 19 other Rubinstein songs.
>
> of Schumann's *Rules and Advice for Young Musicians.*
>
> of the text (Scribe) of the page's aria from Meyerbeer's *Les Huguenots.*

Poems (1847–8) – 18 (juvenile works). *Lilies of the Valley* (1878).

Miscellaneous
> Editing of musical terms in Volumes II and III of *Dictionary of the Russian Language*, published by the Russian Academy of Science.

BIBLIOGRAPHY

ONLY *after weighing the value of other plans did I settle upon the one adopted for the following bibliography. The list contains only books and other publications dealing wholly or in part with Tchaikovsky used, directly and indirectly, as sources of information in writing the present book. I cannot too strongly emphasize the statement that any writer or student desiring to explore the farthest attainable reaches of Tchaikovsky's life must have constantly at hand the third book on this list.*

"Beloved Friend": the Story of Tchaikowsky and Nadejda von Meck, by Catherine Drinker Bowen and Barbara von Meck. Random House, New York, 1937. 484 pp.

Catalogue of the Tchaikovsky Exhibition in Celebration of the 100th Anniversary of His Birth (*Vistavka posvyashchennaya 100-letiyu so dnya roshdeniya P. I. Tchaikovskovo; katalog*). Gosudarstvennaya Konservatoriya (Tipografiya Gazeti *Pravda* imeni Stalina), 1940. 178 pp.

Days and Years of P. I. Tchaikovsky: Annals of His Life and Work (*Dni i godi P. I. Tchaikovskovo: lyetopis zhizni i tvorchestva*), compiled by E. Zaidenshnur, V. Kyselev, A. Orlova, and N. Shemanin, edited by V. Yakovlev. Muzgiz, Moscow-Leningrad, 1940. 743 pp.

Free Artist: the Story of Anton and Nicholas Rubinstein, by Catherine Drinker Bowen. Random House, New York, 1939. 412 pp.

"From My Recollections of P. I. Tchaikovsky (Iz moikh vospominany o P. I. Tchaikovskom)," by H. A. Laroche, in *Syeverny vestnik,* Vol. II, pp. 175–86. St. Petersburg, 1894.

"Hanslick on Tchaikovsky (Hanslik o Tchaikovskom)," in *Muzikalnaya gazeta,* St. Petersburg, 1899, pp. 1189–97, 1259–63, 1296–7, 1329–35.

Introduction to the Practical Study of Harmony: a Textbook Prepared by P. Tchaikovsky, Professor, Moscow Conservatory (*Rukovodstvo k prakticheskomu izucheniyu harmonii*: uchebnik sostavlenny professorom moskovskoy konservatorii P. Tchaikovskym). P. Jürgenson, Moscow, 1871. 155 pp.

The Life and Letters of Peter Ilich Tchaikovsky [by Modest Tchaikovsky], edited from the Russian [and from Paul Juon's German translation] with an Introduction by Rosa Newmarch. John Lane, The

Bodley Head, London, and John Lane Company, New York, 1906. (Original: *Zhizn Petra Ilyicha Tchaikovskovo*, 1900, 1901, 1902. 3 vols.).

Musical Calendar-Almanac for 1890 (*Muzikalny kalendar-almanakh na 1890 goda*), by N. Lisovsky. St. Petersburg, 1889.

Musical Feuilletons and Articles of Piotr Ilyich Tchaikovsky, With a Portrait, Autobiographical Description of His Tour Abroad in 1888, and an Introduction by H. A. Laroche (Muzikalniye felietoni i zametki Petra Ilyicha Tchaikovskovo, s prilozheniyem portreta, avtobiograficheskavo opisaniya puteshestviya zagranitsu v 1888 godu i predisloviya H. A. Larocha). S. P. Yakovlev, Moscow, 1898. 429 pp.

My Musical Life, by Nikolay Andreyevich Rimsky-Korsakoff. Alfred A. Knopf, New York, 1923, 389 pp.; third edition, 1942, 480 pp. (Original: *Lyetopis moyei muzikalnoy zhizni.* 3rd edition, Moscow-Leningrad, 1928.)

My Recollections of 50 Years of Russian Music (*50 liet russkoy muziki v moikh vospominaniyakh*), by M. Ippolitov-Ivanov. Moscow, 1934.

My Recollections of P. I. Tchaikovsky (*Moyi vospominaniya o P. I. Tchaikovskom*), by I. Klimenko. Ryazan, 1908.

Ostrovsky and Russian Composers: Letters (*Ostrovsky i russkiye kompozytori: pisma*), edited by E. M. Kolosova and V. Filippov. Moscow-Leningrad, 1937.

"Recollections of P. I. Tchaikovsky (Moyi vospominaniya o P. I. Tchaikovskom)," by V. V. Bessel, in *Yezhegodnik imperatorskikh teatrov*, Vol. II, pp. 19–43. St. Petersburg, 1896–7.

Recollections of P. I. Tchaikovsky (*Vospominaniya o P. I. Tchaikovskom*), by N. Kashkin. Moscow, 1896. Also selections in *Russkoye obozreniye*, Moscow, 1894 – Vol. IX, pp. 249–58; Vol. V, pp. 392–407; 1895 – Vol. I, pp. 93–110; Vol. III, pp. 249–58; Vol. V, pp. 392–407; Vol. IX, pp. 155–68; Vol. X, pp. 679–890; Vol. XI, pp. 262–81; Vol. XII, pp. 772–82.

"Recollections of P. I. Tchaikovsky (Vospominaniya o P. I. Tchaikovskom)," by K. de-Lazari, *Rossiya*, 1900, Nos. 388, 393, 405, 441.

Recollections and Letters (*Vospominaniya i pisma*), edited by Igor Glebov. Leningrad, 1924.

Reports of the Russian Musical Society (*Otcheti russkovo muzikalnovo obshchestva*).

"P. I. Tchaikovsky," in *Proshloye russkoy muziky: materiali i izsledovaniya*, by Boris Vladimirovich Asafyev, Vol. I. Ogni, St. Petersburg, 1920. 184 pp.

Tchaikovsky: History of a Lonely Life (*Tchaikovsky: istoriya odinokoy zhizni*), by Nina Nikolayevna Berberova. Petropolis, Berlin, 1935. 300 pp.

Tchaikovsky, by Edwin Evans, Jr. J. M. Dent and Sons, London, 1906; revised, Dent and E. P. Dutton and Co., New York, 1935. 236 pp.

Peter Tschaikowsky, by Jwan Knorr. Berlin, 1900.

"P. I. Tchaikovsky," by A. S. Ogolevets, in *Novy mir*, Vol. VII, pp. 192–209. Moscow, 1940.

Tschaikowskij, by Richard H. Stein. Deutsche Verlags-Anstalt, Stuttgart Berlin und Leipzig, 1927. 508 pp.

P. I. Tchaikovsky (for secondary schools) (*P. I. Tchaikovsky, dlya shkolnikov starshevo vozrasta*), by Nina Vladikyna. Muzgiz, Moscow, 1940. 213 pp.

P. I. Tchaikovsky: His Symphonic Music (*P. I. Tchaikovsky: symfonicheskaya muzika*), by Andrey Yevgenyevich Budyakovsky. Leningradskaya Philarmoniya, Leningrad, 1935. 273 pp.

Tchaikovsky anniversary issue of *Sovietskaya muzika* (*Soviet Music*), Moscow, 1940, Nos. 5/6. 153 pp.

P. I. Tchaikovsky: a Sketch of His Work (*P. I. Tchaikovsky: ocherk yevo deyatelnosti*), by Vladimir Sergeyevich Baskin. A. F. Marks, St. Petersburg, 1895. 202 pp.

Tchaikovsky and the Theatre: Essays and Materials (*Tchaikovsky i teatr: stati i materiali*), edited by Alexander Isakovich Shaverdyan. Gosudarstvennoye izdatelstvo iskusstvo, 1940. 425 pp.

"P. I. Tchaikovsky as Conductor (P. I. Tchaikovsky kak dirizher), by I. Pryanishnikov," in *Russkaya muzikalnaya gazeta*, St. Petersburg, 1896, pp. 1001–8.

"P. I. Tchaikovsky as Music Critic (P. I. Tchaikovsky v roli muzikalnovo kritika)," by G. Timofeyev, in *Russkaya muzikalnaya gazeta*, St. Petersburg, 1899, pp. 704–14, 742–8, 769–74.

Tchaikovsky's Correspondence with M. A. Balakirev (*Perepiska M. A. Balakireva s P. I. Tchaikovskym*). St. Petersburg, 1912. Also selections in *Vestnik Yevropi*, No. V, St. Petersburg, 1912, pp. 139–58.

"Tchaikovsky's Correspondence with Bessel (Perepiska Tchaikovskovo s Besselem)" in *K novim beregam muzikalnovo iskusstva*, Moscow, 1923, No. I, p. 42, and No. II, p. 42.

Tchaikovsky: His Life and Works, with Extracts from His Writings, and the Diary of His Tour Abroad in 1888, by Rosa Newmarch. London, Grant Richards, 1900. 232 pp. Revised, with a Complete Classific Account of Works, Copious Analyses of Important Works, Analytical and Other Indices; also, Supplement Dealing with "The Relation of Tchaikovsky to Art-Questions of the Day," by Edwin Evans. London, William Reeves, 1908. 418 pp.

Tchaikovsky's Orchestral Works, by Eric Blom. Oxford University

Press, London, 1927. 51 pp. (Works analysed: *Romeo and Juliet;* Concerto No. 1 in B flat minor; Symphony No. 4; *Nutcracker Suite.*)

Tchaikovsky's Correspondence with P. I. Jürgenson (Perepiska s P. I. Jürgensonom), edited and annotated by V. A. Zhdanov and N. T. Zhegin, with preface by B. V. Asafyev. Muzgiz, Moscow.

Tchaikovsky's Correspondence with N. F. von Meck (Perepiska s N. F. von-Mekk), 3 vols. (Vol. I, 1876–8; Vol. II, 1879–81; Vol. III, 1882–90), edited and annotated by V. A. Zhdanov and N. T. Zhegin, with a preface by N. S. Pshibyshevsky. Akademiya, Moscow, 1934–6.

Tchaikovsky's Correspondence with E. F. Napravnik, 1872–93 (Perepiska P. I. Tchaikovskovo i E. F. Napravnika, 1872–93).

Tchaikovsky's Correspondence with S. I. Tanayev (Pisma P. I. Tchaikovskovo i S. I. Taneyeva), edited by Modest Ilyich Tchaikovsky. Petrograd, 1916.

"P. I. Tchaikovsky's Letters to Bessel (Pisma P. I. Tchaikovskovo k Besselyu)," in *Muzikalnaya nov.,* Moscow, 1923, Nos. I and III, pp. 51 and 43.

Tchaikovsky on the Stage of the Kirov [formerly Marinsky] *Theatre of Opera and Ballet, 1840–1940 (P. I. Tchaikovsky na stsenye Teatra i Baleta Imeni S. K. Kirova, 1840–1940),* edited by A. M. Brodsky, Gosudarstvenny akademichesky teatr operi i baleta; [Leningrad] Akademichesky teatr opera i baleta imeny S. K. Kirova, 1941. 448 pp.

Tchaikovsky's Diaries, 1873–91 (Dnyevniki P. I. Tchaikovskovo, 1873–91), edited by Ippolit Ilyich Tchaikovsky, annotated by N. T. Zhegin, with introduction by S. Chemodanov. Gosudarstvennoye izdatelstvo: muzikalny sektor, Moscow, 1923. 306 pp.

Index

i

Index of Works by Tchaikovsky
Referred to in the Text

IV. CONCERTOS AND CONCERTED PIECES WITH ORCHESTRA

A NOTE ON THE TYPE USED IN THIS BOOK

The text of this book is set in Caledonia, a Linotype face designed by W. A. Dwiggins. Caledonia belongs to the family of printing types called "modern face" by printers — a term used to mark the change in style of type-letters that occurred about 1800. Caledonia borders on the general design of Scotch Modern, but is more freely drawn than that letter.

Mr. Dwiggins planned the typographic scheme and designed the binding. The book was composed, printed, and bound by The Plimpton Press, Norwood, Massachusetts.